LANGUAGE AND RELATION

Language and Relation

...that there is language

CHRISTOPHER FYNSK

Stanford University Press
Stanford, California

Stanford University Press
Stanford, California
© 1996 by the Board of Trustees of the
Leland Stanford Junior University
Printed in the United States of America

CIP data appear at the end of the book

Stanford University Press publications are
distributed exclusively by Stanford
University Press within the United States,
Canada, Mexico, and Central America;
they are distributed exclusively by
Cambridge University Press throughout
the rest of the world.

Photos on p. 272 copyright © Dia Center
for the Arts. All reproduction rights
reserved. Photo Credit: John Cliett.

Acknowledgments

The work presented in this volume was initially undertaken in the context of seminars at the University of Strasbourg and Binghamton University. The project is inseparable from these teaching experiences, and I am grateful for the patience and generous response of more individuals than I could possibly mention here. Composition required time that was granted to me by Binghamton University and by the School of Social Science of the Institute for Advanced Study with the support of the Mellon Foundation; I am pleased to have this occasion to express my gratitude for the gracious hospitality of the School's faculty and the Institute's staff. A number of friends also provided crucial intellectual and moral support, among them Judith Butler, Jacques Derrida, Rodolphe Gasché, Susan Hanson, William Haver, Sandra Jamieson, Philippe Lacoue-Labarthe, Carol Less, Jean-François Lyotard, Avital Ronell, and Joan Scott. To Katherine Rudolph I owe special gratitude. Her unfailing support and her keen critical eye shaped this volume in many ways. I would also like to express my appreciation for the help provided to me by Niklaus Largier and Ingeborg Harms in matters of translation, and for the editorial wisdom of Helen Tartar and Nancy Young of Stanford University Press.

Three chapters have already appeared in print: "Noise at the Threshold" (*Research in Phenomenology*, 19 [1989]: 101–20), "The Realities at Stake in a Poem: Celan's Bremen and Darmstadt Addresses" (*Word Traces*, ed. Aris Fioretos, Johns Hopkins University Press, 1994), and "The Claim of History" (*Diacritics*, 22, nos. 3–4 [1992]: 115–26). I thank the publishers for permission to republish these essays in slightly revised form.

C.F.

Contents

Abbreviations

NOTE: Quotations in this book are cited from the following sources by the abbreviations shown below. Citations give the page numbers (or volume and page numbers) from the original editions, followed by a slash and the corresponding page numbers from the published translations identified below. I have silently modified these translations as I deemed necessary and in some instances have given my own translations, citing the page numbers from the published editions merely as a reference for the reader. Most frequently, I have tried to honor the decisions of the original translator. Translations cited only from an original source are always my own.

WALTER BENJAMIN

GS   *Gesammelte Schriften*, ed. Rolf Tiedemann and Hermann
        Schweppenhäuser, 7 vols. to date (Frankfurt am Main:
        Suhrkamp, 1972–). (GS citations give the volume, part, and page
        number, thus: GS 1.1 213.) Translations of works from this
        source are as follows: "The Task of the Translator" and "Theses
        on the Philosophy of History" appear in Benjamin's *Illuminations*
        (I), ed. Hannah Arendt, trans. Harry Zohn (New York:
        Schocken, 1968), 69–82 and 253–64 respectively; "On Language
        as Such and on the Language of Man" appears in Benjamin's
        Reflections (R), ed. Peter Demetz, trans. Edmund Jephcott (New
        York: Schocken, 1978), 314–32; "Konvolut N" of the *Passagen-
        Werk* appears in *Benjamin: Philosophy, Aesthetics, History* (B),
        ed. Gary Smith, trans. Leigh Hafrey and Richard Sieburth
        (Chicago: University of Chicago Press, 1989), 38–83; *The Origin
        of German Tragic Drama* (O) is translated by John Osborne
        (New York: NLB, 1977).

MAURICE BLANCHOT

A   *L'Arrêt de mort* (Paris: Gallimard, 1948); *Death Sentence*, trans.
       Lydia Davis (Barrytown: Station Hill Press, 1978).

ED   *L'Ecriture du désastre* (Paris: Gallimard, 1980); *The Writing of the Disaster*, trans. Ann Smock (Lincoln: Nebraska, 1986).

EI   *L'Entretien infini* (Paris: Gallimard, 1969); *The Infinite Conversation*, trans. Susan Hanson (Minneapolis: University of Minnesota Press, 1993).

EL   *L'Espace littéraire* (Paris: Gallimard, 1955); *The Space of Literature*, trans. Ann Smock (Lincoln: University of Nebraska Press, 1982).

PF   *La Part du feu* (Paris: Gallimard, 1949). Lydia Davis's translation of the chapter "Literature and the Right to Death" appears in Blanchot's *The Gaze of Orpheus*, ed. P. Adams Sitney (Barrytown, N.Y.: Station Hill Press, 1981), 21–62.

PAUL CELAN

GW   *Gesammelte Werke* (Frankfurt am Main: Suhrkamp, 1983). Translations by Rosemarie Waldrop appear in Celan's *Collected Prose* (Manchester: Carcanet, 1986).

MARTIN HEIDEGGER

G   *Gelassenheit* (Pfullingen: Günther Neske, 1959); *Discourse on Thinking*, trans. John M. Anderson and E. Hans Freund (New York: Harper and Row, 1966).

H   *Holzwege*, vol. 5 of *Gesamtausgabe* (Frankfurt am Main: Klostermann, 1977). Translations of chapters from this source are as follows: "The Origin of the Work of Art," trans. Albert Hofstadter, appears in Heidegger's *Poetry, Language, Thought* (P) (New York: Harper and Row, 1971), 15–87; "The Anaximander Fragment" appears in Heidegger's *Early Greek Thinking* (E), trans. David Farrell Krell and Frank A. Capuzzi (New York: Harper and Row, 1975), 13–58.

HH   *Hölderlins Hymnen "Germanien" und "Der Rhein,"* vol. 39 of *Gesamtausgabe* (Frankfurt am Main: Klostermann, 1980).

PM   *Parmenides*, vol. 54 of *Gesamtausgabe* (Frankfurt am Main: Klostermann, 1982); *Parmenides*, trans. André Schuwer and Richard Rojcewicz (Bloomington: Indiana University Press, 1992).

US   *Unterwegs zur Sprache*, vol. 12 of *Gesamtausgabe* (Frankfurt am Main: Klostermann, 1985); *On the Way to Language* (OW), trans. Peter D. Hertz (New York: Harper and Row, 1971). Albert

Hofstadter's translation of the chapter "Die Sprache" appears as "Language" in Heidegger's *Poetry, Language, Thought* (P), 187–210.

VA   *Vorträge und Aufsätze*, 4th ed. (Pfullingen: Neske, 1954). The chapter "The Question Concerning Technology" appears in Heidegger's *"The Question Concerning Technology" and Other Essays*, trans. William Lovitt (New York: Harper and Row, 1977), 3–35.

WHD   *Was Heisst Denken?*, 2nd ed. (Tübingen: Niemeyer, 1971); *What Is Called Thinking?*, trans. J. Glenn Gray (New York: Harper and Row, 1968).

LUCE IRIGARAY

S   *Speculum de l'autre femme* (Paris: Minuit, 1974); *Speculum of the Other Woman*, trans. Gillian G. Gill (Ithaca, N.Y.: Cornell University Press, 1985).

LANGUAGE AND RELATION

Introduction

THE linguistic turn in modern thought tends to sweep right by the most basic, but admittedly elusive, fact — the simple fact *that there is language*. Thus, the questioning that should proceed from this fact, the question, to start, of the "essence" of language, is left to the residual obscurities of a few guiding texts. The result is a general impoverishment of all the analyses that have been enabled by this linguistic turn and the notion of the linguistic construction of identity — analyses throughout the disciplines of the humanities and social sciences that have been of immeasurable importance for cultural and sociopolitical study. What has been lost? Almost everything of what Martin Heidegger tried to approach under the name of "ontology" until the word proved too laden by common misapprehension to be of use. Most immediately: everything of language that exceeds the order of signification, together with the human share in this "excess" that is the (non)ground of history and the material site of all relationality, beginning with that unthought that is widely termed "culture." However liberating structural linguistics and semiology have been in their various theoretical applications (not to speak of recent developments in pragmatism), they have not avoided the hold of Fredric Jameson's evocation of a "prison-house of language" whenever they have closed off the kind of "fundamental" reflection Jacques Derrida pursued in *Of Grammatology* and through all his meditations on the trace. The latter was an exploration not of the "prison's" labyrinth but of its limits: which is the only way of passage (for reflection) to a thought of freedom and the possibility of a materialist relation to history. There is a name available for this articulation of freedom and the material: it is "finite transcendence," and it begins, where reflection on language is concerned, when thought engages with the fact of language.

The present study follows a series of configurations of this latter experience, starting from Heidegger's elaboration of it in *On the Way to Language*. It pursues thereby the problematic of finitude, but it does so via the question of the relation between language and human being.[1] Language is the principle focus here, but I approach it from the assumption (as I work *toward* the assumption) that the question of the essence of language requires reflection on the manner in which language is offered to thought, and ultimately a thought of the difference — the event — that (dis)articulates this relation and sets it under way as the material relation of language and what is perhaps best designated at this point simply as "the human." The question of language can certainly be pursued apart from the question of existence in far-reaching ways, as Walter Benjamin shows us, or as Michel Foucault indicates in *The Archaeology of Knowledge* with his reflection on the being of the *énoncé*. But a thought of language opens only with access to the site of relation I have described (if only in an experience of the strange opacity that marks its essence). By returning in various ways to this "limit-experience" (as Maurice Blanchot terms it), I have sought to work at this opening and maintain the question.[2]

The theme of an "experience" with language thus persists throughout this study, as does a Heideggerian emphasis on the problem of existence. But I would also note that the volume is devoted to a kind of departure from Heidegger's text, a movement into a series of quite different contexts where the "same" questions are taken in significantly different directions: questions about language and materiality, language and history, language and the other, and language's relation to the "quasi-transcendental" that is the event of its opening. The reader may in fact start with any section; none of them presuppose earlier work. But as I have suggested, a long reading of Heidegger is at the origin of the current project, and I believe that I might best approach a summary of its concerns by underscoring what I consider most important in the reading it contains of Heidegger's *On the Way to Language*. Two facets of this reading bear emphasis: its attention to the *manner* of Heidegger's meditation on language and its gradual foregrounding of the limit of language from the basis of its "fact."

I stress the manner of this reading here because my approach to Heidegger's text, the mode of commentary I undertake, also characterizes, to some extent, my approach to all the other texts under consideration in this volume. The question of "method" is not, in fact, dissociable from the most fundamental matter at hand. For Heidegger is concerned with demonstrating (and the point, no less than the exigency of the demonstration, is assumed in some way by each of the authors I take up) that the way to language is initially the way *of* language. To read him, therefore, one must attend to an implication of approach and object that is no less intricate than (though fundamentally different from) the one proposed by Hegel. One must find one's way to his admonition to attend not to *what* he is saying but to the way he takes in saying it, and to what happens with the way itself as he goes along.* We are not yet reading, where Heidegger is concerned, if we have not engaged this statement, and for this statement the concept does not suffice. "Philosophy" (or "theory") reads Heidegger for a set of propositions or theses that it finds conveyed in what it takes either for concepts or for figures. It cannot do otherwise and remain philosophy in the accepted sense of the term (the sense guarded by the discipline that takes its name). And there is no denying that philosophy goes quite far in this mode of explication, that the work of philosophy is not only an obvious prerequisite for engaging the text but also a crucial "lever" for critical questioning. But there is a point where philosophy (the concept) loses its hold and cannot, as philosophy, read Heidegger. This is the point where Heidegger requires that we think from language, that we read *from the text*. Philosophers, as such, are in fact the best and the least prepared to make this step. The best, because it is indeed a matter of thought and its tradition (though I will have to emphasize this point against the lapse that seems almost inevitably to be induced in Heidegger's commentators by his passage by way of poetry). The least, because philosophy, as such, is utterly unconcerned with the "fact" of language and the way it presents itself in the grain of the text—a concern that requires a more than aesthetic engagement with literature or the text of philosophy itself. Of course, I am speaking generally and even a little facetiously; I know few philosophers *as such* (at least among those who are willing to read Heidegger). But still, a limit is marked here that philosophy has been wary, for essential reasons, of approaching.

What would it mean to engage the text, the *way* of Heidegger's meditations, in the manner it requires? Initially (and philosophy is perfectly capable here, though its drive to conceptualize almost inevitably makes it stop short), it means close reading that attends to the movement of the text, what we might call the text's syntax, at the level of both argument and phrase. Heidegger's works are highly *wrought*—any thoughtful approach to them requires meticulous attention to their form.† It is not just a matter of attending to detail here (and certainly not a matter of attending simply to wordplay in the average sense of this term)—it is a matter of moving past what we think we have understood at any point (the concep-

---

*I am referring here in particular to the second paragraph of "The Way to Language" (US 229/OW 111), but also to the second paragraph of Heidegger's *Identity and Difference* (trans. Joan Stambaugh [New York: Harper and Row, 1969], 1).

†A term I would use *also* in light of the discussion of form in "The Origin of the Work of Art" (H 51/P 64) and in reference to the description of the "way" of language as its *forma* or *Gestalt* in "The Way to Language" (US 250/OW 130).

tual "signified") and beyond the "scenes" of understanding that inevitably form: the "scene" to which Heidegger lends us in listening to "the poem," for example (I will have to insist that *On the Way to Language* approaches a *thinking* experience with language, not a grateful and fulfilled audition of poetry). A kind of ascesis is required here because the text is a *presentation of thought*; reading requires a relation to the text *as* presentation (a kind of *Darstellung*) and as a presentation of *thought* (for which conceptual expertise and empathy will simply not suffice, however "feeling"). It requires constant recollection of the fact that as long as we are interpreting, we are not yet reading.

The initial step must therefore be attention to every step — a full "construction" of the path of reflection engaged in the text. A strong reading proceeds from such constructions and normally casts them aside at some point, like a ladder. But the character of reception of Heidegger's work has prompted me to leave the ladder in place (and suffer the limitations that come with the mode of commentary). Moreover, I have felt that only a close and sustained reading will bring forth and demonstrate the point I want to make here concerning Heidegger's "performance" in the texts in question, a performance that requires emphasis in that Heidegger's thinking is so easily dismissed as "mystified" — which means for most commentators "in submission" (a submission ideologically determined or lending itself to such determination). Distinguished readers in philosophy and literary theory have understood Heidegger to be seeking something like an immediate transcription of the "voice of Being." But not only is such a proposition unthinkable in Heideggerian terms (the immediate is the problem here, not to speak of what is meant by "voice" or "Being"); it also passes right by an extraordinarily subtle and complex textual play that demonstrates constantly its own singularity.[3]

But reading Heidegger also requires attention to a second dimension of the "presentation" to which I have referred. For Heidegger clearly attempts at certain points to push his reader (or auditor) *beyond* representation — beyond the signified or concept — and *into language*, in such a way that thought begins to proceed *from* language itself. The rhetorical structure of the text to which I have referred contributes to this purpose, as I will demonstrate in my reading of "The Essence of Language." But beyond the "staging" Heidegger practices, beyond even the folding movements involved in Heidegger's own versions of the "speculative" sentence, there is a movement *into language*, principally via prefixes and etymons, that is unremitting and immeasurable. Once again, Heidegger thinks from language, and the task in reading him is to engage this movement. I have merely scratched the surface of his textual practice, but I hope I have done so enough to indicate why I say that as long as we are interpreting Heidegger (philosophically or critically), we are not yet reading.

The second facet of my study to which I have referred concerns what I might call its philosophical "results." My ambition has been to follow Heidegger's "step back" on the way to language in a mode of questioning explication, and to bring forth in this process as much as possible concerning language and difference, the form of this relation as it engages the essence of human being in its mortality, the historicity of language as it presents itself under what Heidegger understands as the reign of *Technik*, and the possibility and form of philosophical and poetic language that is no longer (merely) a language of representation. At the horizon as it is marked by my leitmotiv, the notion of *Brauch* ("usage"), lies a kind of crossroads for contemporary reflection where motifs like desire, praxis, and freedom conjoin. Any number of directions open here (which I will be following for some time to come in a project on practical philosophy), as does one philosophical point that seems of crucial significance: the fact that language does not offer anything like a ground for Heidegger. Heidegger is commonly listed among the "antifoundational" thinkers of this century; but the assertion is quite a bit easier than the demonstration if one carries the discussion to the level Heidegger himself would take it. For it is difficult not to turn language into "the first or the last" (US 255n), especially in the current philosophical climate to which I referred in my opening remarks, and for which a weak understanding of Derrida's phrase *il n'y a pas de hors texte* ("there is no outside of the text") marks a kind of extreme limit, despite all the attention lavished on the topics of materiality and the body. Reiner Schürmann himself—someone who knew about anarchy—argued that language remained something like a "transcendental illusion" for Heidegger. But my effort will be to demonstrate that Heidegger's thought of finitude, taken "back" to the relation of *Ereignis* (following Hofstadter: "the disclosure of appropriation" [P xxi]) and *Brauch*, makes such a conclusion untenable, as Heidegger himself saw clearly in his late essays. A thought of the "relationality" of language itself (which Heidegger still treats in "The Essence of Language" as "the relation of relations" [US 203/OW 107], even as he *interrupts* it implicitly with a reference to mortality) is the prerequisite for engaging the thought of *Ereignis* and anything that the latter might allow: a notion of singularity, for example, and the questions of freedom and materiality. The trajectory I have followed through *On the Way to Language* via the *fil conducteur* of "usage" (*Brauch*) leads to this thought of relationality.

Is it possible to think a relationality *beyond* language? The term "beyond" proves impossible here, because Heidegger will suggest that all relation opens with language; and for this thought of finitude, there is no "beyond."* Throughout the essays that follow, I will concentrate on this opening, which is the opening, once again, of relation (of all relation of self and other, and of relation in general). Drawing out this relation as it is given by language, always singularly, will be my principal concern in this volume. But I will not leave Heidegger (and I believe I am touching here on the condition of "leaving" Heidegger) before exploring how this opening must be thought from an event that is not *prior* to the advent of language — the opening of its "essence," Heidegger would say — but also not immanent to it. Language, for Heidegger, is not the subject, no more than it is the "object" (*die Sache*). At the limit marked here, Heidegger situates the relation of *Brauch* and *Ereignis* — a relation that is itself marked by a kind of interruption or "caesura," a "nonrelation" (or "relation without relation," as Blanchot would say) *from which* Heidegger thinks death, but also motifs like freedom and a "free use of the proper" (where the "proper" is thought from the body). The notion that relation is to be thought *from language* is still to be fought for philosophically, but I am also convinced that there is a further step, which I have tried to approach via the Heideggerian notion of "usage" (*Brauch*). Only here do we accede, I believe, to the true "groundlessness" of Heidegger's thought.†

Let me now sketch briefly my efforts in the remaining portions of this volume, starting with the very last section devoted to Blanchot. I invert the order of presentation here, for although the essays on Blanchot were written last (one of them directed to a "theoretical" essay, "Literature and the Right to Death," one addressed to a narrative, *Death Sentence*), their place in this volume and their scope do not fully reflect the role Blanchot's text has played in this project — its role as the constant presence of an experience with language that challenges deeply Heidegger's reflection on the gathering character of the way to language. I could well say that the question of literature as Blanchot phrases it (a question of unlimited reach and echoing always with Blanchot's own literary writings: "What is at stake in the fact that something like art or literature could exist?" [EI vi/xi]) has been my way of access to the question of language in Heidegger.

---

*A situation whose extremity Blanchot captures — somewhat more radically than would Heidegger — with a phrase expressing the knowledge that opens and closes with the event: "Nothing is what there is, and first of all nothing beyond" (*Rien est ce qu'il y a, et d'abord rien au-dela*). The phrase is from the brief "scene" Blanchot presents in *The Writing of the Disaster* (ED 117/72).

†"Finding me was easy. . ., Nietzsche observed." The condition of this freedom is access to the interruption to which I have alluded. Of course, "leaving" Heidegger means a free relation, not the kind of "overcoming" demanded by the marketplace of ideas, where the commodification of names and concepts renders them outmoded well before they are thought and can take on any historical *bite*.

In more direct terms, I could say simply that the resonance or density of Blanchot's language has forced me back constantly to the "fact" of language as it is engaged by contemporary literature, art, and even some philosophy. Recently I have recognized that at the heart of what Blanchot names "exigency" we find the relation Heidegger names *Brauch*. Thus I could add that a term I tried to translate many years ago in Blanchot also guided me to the question of relation as I have begun to approach it here.

The reading of "Literature and the Right to Death" I have presented is concerned principally with Blanchot's understanding of what is offered by the fact of language as it is given in literature. I have focused on one of the "slopes" of this essay and followed, in this manner, Blanchot's engagement with the *il y a*. But I have also attempted, in the same movement, an engagement with Derrida's own reflection on Blanchot in "Pas (préambule)," and have used the latter as a transition to the problematic of the other (in the sense of other human beings: *autrui*). The latter problematic provides my central focus for my reading of *Death Sentence*. The question of language and relation, I want to emphasize, is also the question of *autrui*.

What I tried to evoke above about the presence of Blanchot's language is fundamental for the current project. I have tended to turn in my research to philosophy rather than to literary theory and criticism because it has seemed imperative to rethink the latter's guiding presuppositions about language and interpretation in order to overcome what I perceive to be the abstractness of their relation to literary language. (Philosophy's relation to its own language tends to be no less abstract, and the same fundamental problem is at work; but the discrepancy between the language of commentary and the language of its object is not as consistently obtrusive as it is in literary study.) It has seemed imperative to define the necessity and possibility of answering to a text, or any work of art for that matter — imperative, in other words, to think the address of its language beyond all the extant categories of grammar and rhetoric (except where the latter reaches its uncertain limits in concepts like "tone" or "voice"). Literary interpretation as such (*as interpretation*, that is to say) inevitably passes by the language of a text inasmuch as interpretation is concerned with the text's "signified" (or turns the text's form into the "signified"). Philosophical commentary, of course, does exactly the same in its conceptual presentations. In literary criticism (and once again, I am speaking very generally — there are magnificent exceptions), the result is a kind of frivolousness or secondariness that the genre can never quite shake off; in philosophy, the result is an abstraction — translated in reader response by lassitude — that is compensated for all too frequently by pathos or sentimentality: profound feeling or an "ethical" good conscience is offered in lieu of thought.

Thoughtful commentary in literary study and philosophy, however, engages with the *matter* of its concern only in and by an engagement with language. This is not an "aesthetic" engagement with what I have called the presence of language but rather, ultimately, an engagement with what language "communicates" beyond the order of the signified — what it communicates of what I tried to evoke above with the term "ontology." In this respect, the initial astonishment or fascination provoked by a literary or philosophical text must be thought from the reader's *interest* (*inter-esse*: involving an essential implication) and thus from his or her relation to what the text itself gives of relation — an offering of its own relation to what has provoked its existence. This is not a simple matter of reference, to be sure, no more than the communication I am evoking is a simple structure of signification, but my evocation of ontology is meant to emphasize that nothing less — and even more — than the meaning of Being, as Heidegger once referred to it, is at stake in this singular (and thus historical) configuration. To this reference to ontology, I would add also the ethical, meaning first of all the possibility of relation to the other (human being),* and the political, since we are touching here on the an-archic grounds of sociality. One cannot simply leap into such a relation to the text, and I certainly would not want to suggest that we can or should discount in any way the import of a text's "signified." But I would argue that reading only begins in such engagement and consists, where it is strongest or "truest," in an exploration of the relations at stake there. Benjamin, as I want to show, ascribed to such a historically founded engagement with the text's "address" the very highest political import. For better or for worse, I have taken him seriously.

To the work on Heidegger and Blanchot that was programmed quite early on I have added chapters on Luce Irigaray, Paul Celan, and Benjamin. The chapter on Irigaray is addressed to her brief text "La Mystérique," which I read as a singular exploration of the "exquisite crisis" (what Irigaray terms an *ex-schize-crise de la différence ontico-ontologique*) that is provoked once philosophy touches the question of sexual difference. Irigaray's miming of a feminine mystic discourse stages a way to language that mirrors but also departs from the way evoked by Heidegger as it explores the limit that Heidegger himself named the "bodily." It has offered me here the possibility not only of developing the notion of mimesis that continues to play an important role in my reading of Heidegger but also of carrying the question of language back to the problem of

---

*This is a question, once again, that Blanchot keeps before us (in large part through his dialogue with Lévinas). Avital Ronell has answered this reminder in an exemplary way in her written work and has recalled me to it many times throughout the course of my work on this volume.

ex-sistence in ways Heidegger evokes only abstractly. Irigaray's evocation of that *ex-schize-crise* follows with perfect consequence the Heideggerian problematic of finitude and demonstrates profoundly how far it might be taken. It has also given me another glimpse of the reach of questioning and practice (or, I might say, usage) that is required by a true engagement with the question of culture as it presents itself today.[4]

The chapter on Celan is devoted to two of his prose statements that explore the problem of relation from the basis of an experience with language that is no less "concrete" than those evoked by Heidegger and Blanchot, and that leads in a comparable way to the question of the human in its ontological and ethical dimensions. My emphasis here falls upon the structure of "singularity" Celan explores in evoking the individuation of the poetic self, and the way in which the *passage* of this individuation, a passage toward the self and toward the other (an "other" quite a bit more unsettling than Heidegger would ever allow), is a reaching in and through time. The essay is therefore about language and historicity, about the possibility of engagement with the other *in time* that is offered by language. My aim is to convey Celan's understanding of the precariousness of this historial possibility as it is offered in the second half of this century, and something of the *need* in which it is given.

The remaining part of the work presented in this volume is devoted to three texts by Benjamin from different stages of his thinking on language: the essay on translation, the study of the German *Trauerspiel*, and the methodological reflections on the dialectical image that accompany the Arcades project. My overarching purpose in the three chapters is to explore the continuity, but also the gradual *historicization* of Benjamin's reflections on the philosophy of language. This continuity involves a notion of the self-presentation of language (what Benjamin terms a *Relationsbegriff*) that evokes powerfully the Heideggerian motif of language's speaking and involves a comparable complexity of intervention on the part of those "actors" (poets, philosophers, critics, translators, etc.) who are impelled to bring language to speech. But Benjamin's meditations on the "essence" of language are anchored in a political and historical engagement that is probably no more impassioned than Heidegger's, although certainly more concrete and reflected in its facticity. This is not to say that they are more safe or "trustworthy" in a contemporary political perspective, for the fact remains that they are speculative in character, sometimes outright messianic. But Benjamin's drive to historicize a thought of finite transcendence (while preserving difference) and his unwavering political engagement (an engagement that is always from and in language) offer an invaluable lead for reflection on the political import of philosophy of language.

Other authors could well have been taken up in this study to bring forth still more the reach of the questions involved.[5] But my ambition has not been a comprehensive treatment of the ways in which the question of the essence of language has been taken up in contemporary thought, nor anything like a full consideration of the questions that open once this problematic is addressed at the level indicated by Heidegger or Benjamin. For reasons that should now be clear, I have not tried to write a (contemporary) history of an idea in all its manifestations and conceptual ramifications. I have been attempting instead to engage this problematic via the texts of a group of writers who have played defining roles in contemporary philosophy and critical thought (several of whom may be situated in a post-Heideggerian legacy, but who challenge this legacy in fundamental ways). And because this problematic offers itself always singularly, I have avoided attempting to synthesize what I have termed the results of these analyses, practicing instead, and in response, a kind of philosophical ascesis. Once again, I am not seeking a concept; I have not sought to propose a philosophy of language and its history (though I do believe that a thought of language like the one I have pursued here lends Foucault, for example, the possibility of a history writing that is no longer representational). A formal or "general" account of the singularity to which I have referred is, of course, conceivable and even latent, but I have held in abeyance any temptation to summarize and thereby leave the sites (the texts) of the experience in question. Of course, the determination of this "site" as the "object" of this study — the site of an engagement with something I do not hesitate to name after Heidegger "the essence of language" (though I want to bring forth how strange this phrase is, even perverse) — implies a "fore-structure" of reading. But the passage in each case is singular because the "object" is always singular,* and I have preferred to respect that singularity in all its textual density rather than carry it into a general reflection. I could not deny, and certainly would not want to, that there is also something singular about each of these readings in another sense — that is, in the sense of a distinct signature defined by a whole set of determinations, and then perhaps something else. I am not the one to judge here. But I would like to say that I have allowed my commitment to the singularity of encounter to hold back any "philosophical" impetus in the sense of the term delimited by Heidegger when he speaks of the history of "theses" or "positings" (of Being) that have defined the tradition of metaphysical thinking. I have pursued, again, a kind of conceptual asce-

---

*This has been borne home to me by the differences in tone and approach required by each of these texts. Beyond all the contingencies that shaped this work, there have been the exigencies of the texts themselves, translated here in different modalities of writing (which may be more or less sensible to the reader, but which I have found quite imperative).

sis — striving always for understanding and engagement, but avoiding synthesis and conclusive statement, a "third" position that would offer the truth of these readings. I offer no theory of language in this volume and precious little in the way of a philosophical statement, in search precisely of the *limits* of theory and statement — limits that are offered in always singular configurations by the texts I have sought to read. To be sure, I come close to statements about those limits at various points — statements about the "fact" of language and the (im)possibility of relation. And I would be disingenuous if I were to pretend that I have not been drawn constantly by the question of relation as such (as given in language), a question, once again, of ontological, political, and ethical import. I am drawn to a thought of the an-archic relationality of Being, and the possibility of an affirmative assumption of that relationality — both for the extremity of play it involves and for what it promises of engagement: that quite *real* engagement Friedrich Hölderlin talks about when he speaks of being pushed back to the earth, or that Francis Bacon evokes when he speaks of "the brutality of fact." As I noted above, the question of relation is the question of freedom *and* the question of engagement with something like "materiality." But in this volume, I do not try to philosophize upon these issues; I try to engage them, and I do so via a series of authors for whom the question of relation opens *in their texts* with the question of language.

no language, Wittgenstein asserts in his "Lecture on Ethics," could express mean-
ingfully what is given in the experience from which he tries to think ethical value:
his experience of wonder at the existence of the world. A phrase such as Heidegger's, for example, Dass es Seiendes ist — und nicht Nichts ("that there are beings,
rather than nothing") exceeds the limits of signification as Wittgenstein describes
them and would be judged nonsensical: the "fact" that there is a world is not a de-
scribable fact among others. Nevertheless, the compelling force of this experience
("I at once see clearly, as it were in a flash of light") leads Wittgenstein to entertain a formulation that carries the question of an ethical language in the direction
"of what is generally called Aesthetics." He tries, in passing, the following:

> Now, I am tempted to say that the right expression in language for the miracle
> of the existence of the world, though it is not any proposition in language, is
> the existence of language itself. *

The fact that there is language would express the fact of being.

Upholding firmly the limits of signifiable meaning in this meditation on the
possibility of a language of ethics, Wittgenstein cannot but dismiss the formulation that has tempted him. A shift from expression by means of language to expression by the existence of language, as he puts it, does not make whatever we
say about the "absolute miraculous" any less nonsensical. But this reassertion of
the limits of sense also works to remark the limits of sense (as he has defined
them). Showing the restrictive sense of "nonsensical," it implicitly opens the question of an "expression" that exceeds the order of signification. A kind of hint or
feint, this advance and withdrawal of the formulation that has tempted him indicates.[1]

Wittgenstein may even be pointing in a precise direction. For it could well be
that he is commenting on the phrase from "What Is Metaphysics?," Dass es
Seiendes ist — und nicht Nichts, a phrase, Heidegger suggests, that folds with its
last words in such a way as to give the "is" it holds and to "say" thereby the possibility of significant language through the redoubling of a kind of echo. Die
Sprache spricht — Wittgenstein seems to have glimpsed something of the meaning

*Ludwig Wittgenstein, "Lecture on Ethics," *Philosophical Review*, 74 (1965): 11.

of this phrase of Heidegger's long before it was announced and restaged in phrases such as "The essence of language: the language of essence." And while he does not follow Heidegger so far as to envision in such a speaking the opening of a relation to what is (he continues to speak in terms of a "correct expression" — two terms that call for long commentary in themselves), he recognizes in it a presentation of language that will draw Heidegger in his own way toward what Wittgenstein termed "Aesthetics."

But it must be said that the question of Wittgenstein's precise relation to Heidegger here is of less importance than the questions that open at this limit marked by his lecture (and the question of the relation can only be entertained in the light of the fact that Wittgenstein is engaging a tradition of reflection on language that also makes possible the startling proximity of Heidegger and Benjamin). What is given to an always astonished thought with the "fact" of language — for ethics, for art, for politics, for all reflection on existence? What if we think and write (from the fact) that there is language?

PART I

Heidegger

in
memory
of
Reiner
Schürmann

1

Noise at the Threshold

"LANGUAGE," the first essay in the German edition of *On the Way to Language* (1959), offers perhaps an ideal starting point for this study. It is an *exemplary* essay in that it constructs a kind of allegory of poetic language from a reading of Georg Trakl's poem "A Winter Evening" (a poem, Heidegger says, that lends itself uniquely to such usage), and does so within the framework of the dialogue between thought and poetry Heidegger pursues throughout the volume. The essay's evident staging of this dialogue also engages what I take to be one of the fundamental problems of *On the Way to Language* — the relation between language and humankind — by pointing to a key difficulty in Heidegger's description of the relation between human speech and what Heidegger calls the speaking of language: namely that human speech introduces into this speaking what I will term "noise." By developing the meaning of this latter term in a rapid reading of the movements of "Language," I hope to sketch out the first step in Heidegger's articulation of the relation between language and humankind. I will also raise a question about Heidegger's fundamental claims for poetic language that will permit me to point toward the subsequent discussion of Blanchot.

Heidegger begins his essay by proposing to invert the traditional approach to language. He proposes to think it not in reference to humankind, as has been done throughout the tradition, but in itself, and to think the essence of the human from the place of its advent. This means abandoning the traditional armature of concepts about language which Heidegger summarizes in three basic notions: that language would be a means of expression of thought and feelings; that language would be a form of human activity by which humankind makes itself, or makes a world for itself; and that it would be a representation of what is (whether real or imagined).

But the inversion Heidegger proposes actually requires more than the abandonment of these concepts; it requires, to a certain extent, the abandonment of the concept itself, if we understand by this the representation of the essence of a thing, in this case, language. For as soon as we arrogate the right to represent to ourselves the essence of language, we posit a relation between it and human knowing, and refer language back to humankind; we posit language as an object for a subject capable of representing that object in its essence. Some combination of the three traditional notions of language is inescapable if we proceed within the structure of representation. So Heidegger finally invites us to avoid not only the traditional understanding of language as a means of representation but also the positing of language itself as the object of representation. We are to think language from out of itself — proceeding from language and not approaching language from our position as theoretical subjects.

To approach language in itself, he suggests, we must ask how language *is* as language or comes about as language. Heidegger's response to this question comes immediately. Language *is* language, he says, and he explicates this apparently tautological phrase by asserting that language *speaks*. So to follow language in thought, *die Sprache nachdenken*, to think *after* language (in the sense of the phrase "after the fashion of"), is to engage with the speaking of language. Thought must allow language to speak, and this means that the language of thought must *answer* to language. Only when thought reveals itself as answering to the essence of language will the inversion Heidegger is seeking be achieved.

But on what grounds can Heidegger affirm that his own answer to the question of how language *is* as language answers to the essence of language and is not merely another concept for language? How can he know that he is answering to language when he insists that language speaks? Heidegger himself raises the problem just as quickly as he gave his answer. He writes: "Is this, seriously, an answer? Presumably [*Vermutlich*]* it already is — that is, when it becomes clear what speaking is" (US 10/P 190). So Heidegger's proposition, that language speaks, will reveal itself as having answered to the essence of language once we know what it means to speak. The thesis will become meaningful, it will *speak*, once we know what speaking is. It will reveal itself then as a reply to language; for as Heidegger asserts near the end of his essay, a language that answers to the speaking of language *counters* language or works by rejoinder: it is *entgegnend* ("countering"). As such, it draws out a distance that makes it possible to think "after" language (or over against it) — but without turning language into an object, a *Gegenstand*. (I will return to the question of the nature of the countering reply.)

Heidegger's answer, *die Sprache spricht*, will reveal itself as answering

---

*I will try to demonstrate in my next chapter that the essential mode of thoughtful saying as it replies to language is one of "presumption," so this word is not falling here by accident.

to language, then, once we know what speaking is, and the question of course immediately follows: How do we recognize the speaking of language? Where do we find it? Heidegger again answers with a series of propositions or theses that are strongly marked as such by their clipped quality and by the way they follow one after another. The last is described as a naked assertion (*nackte Behauptung*) — and the epithet in fact applies to each of them. There are at least four (depending on how closely we consider them): (1) The speaking of language is found in what is spoken (*das Gesprochene*). (2) The speaking of language accomplishes itself in the spoken and is sheltered there; its speaking does not cease in the spoken but rather gathers there the manner in which it continues to unfold in its essence — that is to say, it gathers or orders the movement of its becoming-speech in the spoken. (3) The spoken is pure (and most suitable for our attention in meditating on language) when the speaking that accomplishes itself in it by composing itself there is originary or marks a beginning. One will recognize this theme from Heidegger's "The Origin of the Work of Art" (1935–36), and so the fourth point, the one Heidegger termed a "naked assertion," will come as no surprise. (4) The purely spoken is the poem (*das Gedicht*).

Now, we can let these assertions stand in their nakedness, Heidegger says, if we manage to hear the purely spoken in a poem. Once again, the proposition awaits its confirmation in a speaking. But to which poem are we to turn if we do not know what speaking is and how we are to listen for it? Heidegger responds that our *one* choice will not prove to be an arbitrary one (US 14/P 194) if we let ourselves be guided by what has been indicated to us (*zugedacht*) by the speaking of language when we follow it in thought. Heidegger's answer, *die Sprache spricht*, has already spoken and already bound our hearing.

We are of course moving in a circle. Heidegger turned to the poem in order to make his answer concerning how language *is* sound as an answer. Heidegger now tells us that we will hear what is happening in the poem if we have heard the answer as an answer. Listening to the poem, he says, we will make a few steps toward understanding what is binding in the bond already created by our following language in thought (*das Bündige jener Bindung*). In other words, we will discover what makes Heidegger's answer *conclusive*.

But Heidegger is doing more than punning here and doing more than turning in circles — and I would like to stress in this respect a point that has some bearing on his reading of Trakl's poem. If Heidegger is underscoring so ostentatiously the specifically philosophical character of his approach, or to put this perhaps in more appropriate terms, if he calls special attention to the character of his own language as the language of thought (focusing first on the guiding phrase, then highlighting the assertive character of his propositions about poetic language — the relation between philosophy and thought still a very indistinct one), it is because he thinks that our only access to the speaking of language that is the source of thought as well as of poetry (though for each in a singular manner) is through the difference between poetry and thought. As Heidegger asserts in "The Essence of Language," each mode is blind to its own origin — it is only by remarking the difference between them that each can have access to itself as a site where language speaks. Each comes to itself, as a unique mode of saying, by way of the other. Thus it is probably misleading to speak in terms of a logical circle. We have to do rather with a play of juxtaposition or contrast, and, once again, a kind of *countering*, since thought and poetry, as Heidegger says elsewhere in the volume, stand over against one another: *einander gegenüber* (US 176/OW 82). The crucial point is that language gives itself *as language*, that is, as speaking, only by way of a kind of contrast, or countering, that is, in and through the *difference* between modes of speaking. We will see a related idea made in every essay in which Heidegger takes up the topic of language: that is to say, each time he has recourse to the dialogue between thought and poetry, or recourse to the concept of dialogue itself, as in his conversation with the Japanese scholar. We will also see it in his reading of Trakl's poem, which works, he claims, by way of a differential structure.

Let me turn now to Heidegger's reading of "A Winter Evening." Heidegger claims that the three stanzas of Trakl's poem each enact a different mode of saying in that they draw out successively the difference to which the poem as a whole answers (what Heidegger calls here the difference between world and thing). I will be focusing essentially on the third stanza, but I would like to summarize Heidegger's reading of the movement of the first two in order to suggest what Heidegger means when he says that this third stanza draws out the difference between the modes of speaking of the first two stanzas and thereby allows the speaking of difference to occur. It will also be necessary to move quickly through the poem in order to set up the terms of the allegory Heidegger reads in it.[1]

> Window with falling snow is arrayed,
> Long tolls the vesper bell,
> The house is provided well,
> The table is for many laid.

> Wandering ones, more than a few,
> Come to the door on darksome courses.
> Golden blooms the tree of graces
> Drawing up the earth's cool dew.

Wanderer quietly steps within;
Pain has turned the threshold to stone.
There lie, in limpid brightness shown,
Upon the table bread and wine.
        (cited in US 14–15/P 194–95)

Heidegger initially approaches the poem by sketching a reading of it that would proceed from a notion of language as expressive and representational, and that would appeal to aesthetic categories in order to account for its particular beauty. But he then asserts that if, on the contrary, we listen to the poem with the phrase "Language speaks" in mind, we shall be aware of the inadequacy of this approach. In answering to this phrase, a *different measure* will bind us ("adequacy," as we see, shifts from representational rectitude to a kind of correspondence), a measure that manifests itself (*bekundet sich*) now in this same "demanding" phrase (US 17–18/P 197–98). Heidegger's "answer," once again, does not take the form of a conceptual proposition; it does not *posit* anything. Rather, it transcribes in such a way as to allow something of language itself to reveal itself.

We have seen allusions to this measure in the opening pages of Heidegger's essay. It is understood as a site *from which* we are to think our relation to language and from out of which language itself may be thought ("to discuss language, to place it [*erörtern*], means to bring to its place of being not so much language as ourselves: our own gathering into the appropriation" [US 10/P 190]).* Once again, the point, at least initially, is to take a distance from language *from language*. This distance is figured by Heidegger in these opening pages as an abyss (the abyss named by Johann Georg Hamann) spanned by a height and a depth ("The two span a realm in which we would like to become at home" [US 11/P 192]). When he turns to the poem, it figures as the *opening* of a spatiotemporal site that will ultimately be measured rhythmically. How precisely thought and poetry answer to this same measure is a question we will have to defer for now. Suffice it to say here that against the measure given in "Language speaks," a different *Erörterung* of the poem ("discussion" as attention to the site; cf. US 33/P 159) is possible. Heidegger's concern, when he returns to the poem, is the manner in which the poem opens a site in its speaking.

The first stanza speaks by *naming*, Heidegger says. It does not affix terms to familiar objects; rather, it brings things into what he describes as a presence sheltered by absence. This is a "nearness" and thus marked by a

---

*In this essay, "gathering into the appropriation" will be thought entirely from out of language. Later, as we will see, the event of *Ereignis* will be thought somewhat differently and will again allow us to speak of language itself *in relation*. The thought of *Ereignis* will be the "key" evoked by Hamann.

certain spatiality, but it is a nearness marked by temporality. What the stanza names, Heidegger emphasizes, is the time of the winter evening. The snowfall makes things last longer, he says, and thus the vesper bell, which tolls daily for a strictly delimited time (*streng begrenzte Zeit*), tolls longer. "Strict time" would seem to point to Hölderlin — specifically to the "Remarks on *Oedipus*" and the "Remarks on *Antigone*," in which Hölderlin defines the modern relation to the divine in terms of a most severe historicity.* Hölderlin will never be far off in this commentary. But my point in evoking Hölderlin at this point is to emphasize the temporal character of the measure (a presence sheltered in absence) to which the poem calls things, and to suggest one way in which the measure cast by the poem defines the relation of things to the four components of what Heidegger calls the world. The long tolling of the vesper bell brings mortals before the divine, Heidegger says; the snowfall brings mortals under the sky; the house and table join mortals to the earth. The naming of the first stanza, in other words, engages mortals with the other elements of what Heidegger calls the fourfold and thus implicitly evokes the world, which is the unity of the four elements in their play. Thus by naming things, the first stanza already implicitly calls upon the world and is already beginning to draw out the measure of the relation of relations that gathers the relation between world and thing.[2]

The second stanza will unfold and remark in its turn what remains implicit in the first stanza. It will call up the world by addressing itself to mortals (this is how Heidegger initially interprets the reference to those who wander on dark courses), to the earth and the sky, and to the divine. I will not dwell over Heidegger's discussion here; I note simply that like the naming of the first stanza, the calling of the second is double, though it reverses the movement of the first. The first stanza brought things to their presence in the world; the second entrusts world to things. So the second stanza draws out the relation of world and thing implicit in the first stanza and remarks it in its distinct fashion of speaking by inverting it. Heidegger's justification for this claim (or even its precise meaning) concerns me less here than his insistence upon the difference in modes of speaking between the two stanzas. They differ as modes of speaking, Heidegger asserts, because they answer to the difference that exists between world and thing in their respective movements. By tracing out this difference in their very speaking (though only implicitly), they remark what I have referred to as the relation of relations, and what Heidegger also speaks of

*Note that if "homecoming" is thought from the basis of the irreversible temporality described by Hölderlin, and if the wanderer may be compared to Oedipus, then it can never be anything more than a crossing of the threshold, never a "stay" (*Aufenthalt*, the word Heidegger uses in the opening pages of his essay) in the sense of a residence or sojourn.

as the ontological difference.* The third stanza will draw out explicitly this difference sketched out between the two stanzas.

Before describing the distinctive manner of speaking of this third stanza, Heidegger pauses to develop a series of terms with which to describe the difference between world and thing traced out in the first two. He refers to it as a scission between the two terms, an *Unter-schied* ("difference") that gathers them into a unity Heidegger describes with the Hölderlinian term *Innigkeit* ("intimacy"). (Heidegger used the term in "The Origin of the Work of Art" to describe the relation between world and earth [H 51/P 63], and indeed he is describing the same event as the one he described in that essay: the happening of truth in a work of art — the opening of the Open in which everything that is can come into presence.) Intimacy is defined in turn as the unity of what Heidegger calls the *diaphora*: a carrying apart of the terms it draws into a unity (again, world and thing) that does not mediate between these terms (*vermitteln*) in the sense that it would connect these already existent terms after the fact, but rather discovers them or dis-cerns them in an originary fashion (*ermitteln*). As such, the difference appropriates world and thing into their respective natures. The tracing out and unfolding of difference is *Ereignis*. And Heidegger finally adds that this difference cannot be thought as a relation or distinction (which would normally presuppose, again, already existent terms), but rather must be thought as a di-mension — a separation that measures out, *er-misst*. *Er-messen* implies decision or judgment, but we have to do here not with a judgment according to a previously established measure but with the original opening of a measure, an *Austragen* (a "carrying out") that gives the measure by which it decisively separates and joins into a unity.

Having defined in this manner the difference traced out by the modes of speaking of the first two stanzas, then, Heidegger turns to the third stanza and remarks that it speaks emphatically in its first verse, and then suddenly and strangely in its second. The second verse stands alone in the spoken in the poem, Heidegger says, because it is the only verse in the past tense. By evoking now his notion of the spoken, Heidegger calls us back to his initial propositions about the poem as the site of the purely spoken. In the spoken, he had said, the speaking of language does not cease but rather gathers in its essence. Likewise, he argues there that this past tense does not name something that no longer is but rather something that comes

---

*It is somewhat disappointing that Heidegger asserts but does not really clarify the difference between the modes of saying that characterize the two stanzas. He accounts for it by referring to the difference between "thinging" and "worlding" that is said by the two stanzas; but as he pursues the difference between these two movements, he leaves aside the question of the corresponding *modes* of speaking.

into its essence as already having been, that gathers or collects its essence in this way. It will turn out to be, as he said at the outset, the speaking of language, understood now as the tracing out of difference.

Heidegger moves quickly and allusively here, but the steps he makes are essentially the following. He proposes "pain" as another term for difference. Pain tears asunder, he says; it separates (the verb he uses here is *reissen*); but at the same time it draws together (*zieht auf sich*) what is rent, in the manner of an initial tracing out or sketch: *Vorriss* or *Aufriss* (US 24/P 204). These are again terms that appeared in "The Origin of the Work of Art" to describe the difference traced out by the work as it joins together world and earth (H 51/P 63). They are also the terms Heidegger uses to define the essence of language elsewhere in *On the Way to Language*. The tracing of the *Riss* ("rift"), Heidegger argues in "The Essence of Language," is the speaking of language. Language speaks by drawing out, tracing out the differential articulation that Heidegger is thinking here as the difference between world and thing. So "pain" names the difference as traced out in the speaking of language.

Why "pain"? To explicate this properly, we would have to pursue at length the difficult topic of the relation between language and death or suffering, which Heidegger has already evoked by defining the wanderers who travel on dark paths as mortals. Hölderlin, again, is an essential reference here.* But there is also a connection that proceeds more immediately by the relays of language, and that is through the word "pain" itself. Heidegger is drawing upon the etymology of the Greek word for pain, *algos*. It is related, as he suggests elsewhere, to the word *alego*, which comes from *lego* ("to speak"), and means, Heidegger says, "intimate gathering."† So the "pain" that hardens into stone in the threshold names the essence of language as a tracing out and gathering of the difference between world and thing.

One more step must be added now to explain the allegory Heidegger is setting into place. Heidegger had argued in "The Origin of the Work of Art" that difference must be set up in the work and fixed there. It must be composed in the work's *Gestalt*, set into the outline or boundary of the work (H 52/P 64). The threshold, as we can see, figures for Heidegger precisely this composing of the difference that is pain. It figures the work's form or boundary as that out of which the work comes to stand as the remarking of the event of the happening of truth. At another level, it is a

*Heidegger is surely recalling Hölderlin's third version of "Mnemosyne": "But evil are the paths" (Friedrich Hölderlin, *Poems and Fragments*, trans. Michael Hamburger [New York: Cambridge University Press, 1980], 499).

†See Martin Heidegger, *The Question of Being*, trans. Jean T. Wilde and William Kluback (New Haven, Conn.: Twayne, 1958), 71.

figure for the poem itself as a site where the speaking of language is gathered and set out — it is an instance of the setting into work of truth of which Heidegger speaks in "The Origin of the Work of Art" (there is also a pun at work here around the word *dicht* — "compact" or "dense"). And in a larger sense, it is a figure of the threshold that is language itself, inasmuch as language is defined as the articulation of difference by which difference comes about. Heidegger gives it this larger sense when he says that it defines a relation between the inside and the outside, which he will come to define in the essay as a movement into difference from out of difference by which world and thing are appropriated to their essences. World and thing *are* only in and by their difference; thus to call upon world and thing as the poem does is to call upon their difference. But the calling of the poem traces out this difference, articulates it in an originary fashion. It unfolds the difference in such a way as to enfold world and thing into its intimacy. In this sense, the poem calls difference to itself as the intimate union of world and thing. It brings difference to speech, and as Heidegger will add in the conclusion of his reading, it brings about the speaking of difference as a silent order or command, a *Geheiss*, that enjoins a disposition between word and thing to which all human speaking must answer and to which the poem itself will reveal itself as having answered. The logic of this argument can be dizzying, but it is really quite simple. What the poem does is call upon difference in the manner of a project (*Ent-wurf*, thought here as the tracing of an *Aufriss*, "rift-design") that anticipates what it answers to. It brings difference to speak and thus to unfold as difference. Heidegger thinks this unfolding, once again, as an *Austragen*, an *Ereignen*, an *Ermessen*, an *Eröffnen* ("opening up"), and, finally, as a *Sprechen* that sounds as a silent *Läuten* ("pealing"). The poem answers to difference, but retraces it in such a fashion as to make it come about as a difference that joins world and thing into a simple intimacy and brings about the sheltering that is figured with the image of the house and the splendor of bread and wine that stand in simple sufficiency by virtue of the way they are gathered in the fourfold.

The threshold, then, is language, as gathered in the poem, and thus as the measuring of the relation between world and thing; the poem would bring things into the intimacy of this simple measure and make possible a "homecoming." I have spoken of an allegory — we see now that this is an allegory formed around Heidegger's figure of language as the house of Being, and around Hölderlin's ambition of finding a measured and firm word (the "firm letter," he called it in "Patmos").[3] The wanderers of the second stanza of Trakl's poem are poets. The threshold of pain they would cross, quietly, is the threshold of language made firm in the poem. That to which they accede would be the intimacy of world and thing figured in the preeminent Hölderlinian symbols of bread and wine. Trakl's poem is an allegory of poetry as a founding word,[4] and in its own chiasmic structure of speaking, it traces and crosses the threshold it figures.

Now, one might expect Heidegger to stop at this point (since things are going so well) or shortly thereafter — that is to say, once he has developed the notion that the poem brings language to speak as the silent peal of difference that stills the movement of world and thing through the measured rhythm of its *melos*. But instead he adds a word on the need for poetry as a finite act of human speaking — a need that is as much *language's* need as a human need. He is following through the logic of finitude. The speaking of difference, though the condition of possibility of any signifying act, can only come about in singular articulations; it can only occur inasmuch as it is drawn out in distinct speech events (which are not necessarily linguistic in the restricted sense — poetry simply has the privilege of showing itself most demonstratively as such a performance). Heidegger pursues this point about language and finitude with reference to the event of appropriation as it concerns the human essence, thus returning to the question with which he began. Mortals are given to language, Heidegger said at the very outset of his essay (agreeing with the tradition) — this defines their essence. But, he added, they are given to language by language (and here he departs from the tradition). The point is implicit in what he has said about the event of appropriation that happens in the poem. Since mortals belong to the fourfold that is articulated in an originary fashion by the speaking that happens in poetry, their very essence is brought into play in poetry, defined there. Further, since it is of the essence of mortals to be given to language, the event of appropriation must also be thought as the giving of language; language must give itself in the poem, communicate itself in some way — it must give the possibility of significant speech. But language gives itself only inasmuch as it is brought to speak. This is why language *needs* poetry. Heidegger puts it this way: "Such an appropriating [the appropriation of the human essence and its 'appropriation' to the essence of language] takes place in that the *essence* of language *needs and uses* [*braucht*] the speaking of mortals in order to sound [*verlauten*] as the peal of stillness for the hearing [*hören*] of mortals. Only insofar as men belong [*gehören*] within the peal of stillness are mortals capable in *their* manner of a sounding speaking [*das verlautende Sprechen*]" (US 27–28/P 208). The appropriation of the human essence occurs inasmuch as language uses the speech of mortals to give itself to mortals, to make itself audible. For only insofar as mortals hear can they speak.

Heidegger makes this point again near the end of his essay, and again he points to the necessity of a speaking or a prior determining of the speaking of language. Mortals speak, he says, because they have heard, because they already belong or answer to the command of difference (the *Geheiss*). They speak, he says, because they listen, and when they speak they draw from language's command what they bring into the sounding word. In this sense, their speaking is always a response that corresponds, an *Ent-sprechen*. But while such correspondence presupposes what Heidegger describes as a kind of reserve (we must listen and hold back from speaking if our speaking is to answer in an authentic manner), this reserve must also be ready, Heidegger says, to anticipate upon the command of difference. It must go out ahead, *zuvorkommen*. This may seem like an overeager obedience, but it is what determines the manner of the mortal *Ent-sprechen*, which is an answering, a speaking, that *counters* or *rejoins* (*ent-gegnet*) precisely in order to draw from this encounter (*ent-nehmen*) its own possibility.*

We should attend to the echoing of the privative *-ent* in this concluding passage of "Language." The answering reply dis-appropriates or ex-propriates something of the speaking of language (which in itself is "singlefold" and so intimate it leaves difference "unspoken" [US 25/P 206]) precisely in order to make correspondence and appropriation possible. It deprives or alters in some fashion. And since language *needs* this reply *in order to speak* (to come about in its essence as a *Geheiss*: the essence of language is also at stake in the event wherein humankind is appropriated to it), we are undoubtedly justified in concluding that this originary disappropriation is related to the tearing (the *reissen*) that occurs with the drawing out of language—at least insofar as this tearing is indissociable from what Heidegger calls a "breaking" (as we will see momentarily). In this sense, the anticipatory speaking of mortals would constitute something like the "suffering" of language. Once again, the pain to which Heidegger refers has its source in language; as Heidegger cautions, it is not to be taken in anthropological terms. And though the related notion of intimacy is one that easily lends itself to a philosophical pathos (and perhaps cannot avoid its hold), Heidegger warns firmly against an "affective" appropriation: "Only we must not represent intimacy psychologically as the sort in which sentimentality makes a nest for itself" (US 25/P 205).[5]

But in what way does language suffer? There is what Heidegger himself describes as pain, of course (and we should not allow the motifs of stillness, peace, and gathered motion—or for that matter, the motif of a "simplefold difference"—to muffle completely the tearing that is named here: the structure is precisely homologous to the one Stéphane Mallarmé

---

*In a marginal note printed in the *Gesamtausgabe* (US 29), Heidegger adds *Ent-sagen*.

sets to work with the words "hymen" and "fold").⁶ But I would suggest that language also suffers from the introduction of what I want to call, provisionally, "noise." Shortly before the passage I have just been commenting on, Heidegger writes:

> At the proper time, it becomes unavoidable to think of how mortal speech and its utterance [*Verlautbarung*] take place in the speaking of language as the peal of the stillness of the dif-ference. Any uttering [*Verlauten*], *whether in speech or writing* [my emphasis], breaks the stillness. On what does the peal of stillness break? How does the broken stillness come to sound [*Lauten*] in words? How does the broken stillness shape [*prägt*] the mortal speech that sounds [*erklingt*] in verses and sentences? (US 28/P 208)

Heidegger would seem to be admitting here that there is no stillness except as broken. Only a broken stillness imprints mortal speech — breaking and imprinting are in fact indissociable. Now, Heidegger will immediately assert that we must not take *Verlautbarung* (and above all, not "expression" [*Ausdruck*]) as the element from which human speech takes its decisive measure. The structure of human speech can only derive from the mode, the *melos*, in which the speaking of language appropriates mortals. But Heidegger has also asserted that the speaking of language can only appropriate mortals to their (speaking) being by *using* the speaking of mortals (which as a *Verlauten* may be either speech or writing). And if all speaking of mortals breaks the silence, then the speaking of language can only sound for mortals through a certain noise. To put this very simply: we perceive only broken silence because we can only hear speech ("the essence of language *needs and uses* the speaking of mortals in order to sound as the peal of stillness"); we hear silence only through the contrasts of speech. To put this in terms drawn from Heidegger's essay: the structure (*Gefüge*) of human speech as appropriated by the speaking of language must in fact be thought as the *articulation* of the *melos* of saying (its mode or manner [*Weise*] of appropriating mortals in the "peal of stillness") out of the "double articulation" of human speaking: "Mortals speak insofar as they correspond to language in a doublefold manner [*zwiefältige Weise*], receiving and replying [or countering: *entnehmend-entgegnend*] (US 29/P 209).

The fact that there is no silence but broken silence would seem to unsettle in a fundamental way the claims Heidegger makes for poetic speech and the allegory he constructs on the basis of Trakl's "A Winter Evening." If the stillness of saying is broken, then it would seem that there can be no stilling of the relation between world and thing; the rhythmic articulation of the fourfold within which the thing is said to "repose" (US 26/P 206) would be disrupted, constantly disturbed. How could Heidegger not be aware of such a consequence? Or could he have thought that the rhetorical weight of his reading of Trakl's poem would still any questions raised by his concluding remarks? In which case, why raise them? It seems reasonable to suppose, on the contrary, that Heidegger was quite in control of the movement of his text, and that the questioning conclusion served to suspend what I have called the allegory of poetic saying. We have still to evaluate the status of such a rhetorical gesture in Heidegger's writing.*

But in "The Essence of Language," Heidegger proposes a solution to the difficulty he raises at the end of "Language." He argues near the conclusion of this essay that the "noise" of *Verlautbarung* is reabsorbed by the *melos* of poetic saying. "Noise" (in the sense of "sonority") plays a constitutive part in the sounding of the essence of language, he admits, but the occurrence of this sounding—the opening of a measure and a harmony—attunes the poetic saying in such a way as to carry it back into silence. Accordingly, Heidegger offers a very different notion of "breaking" in the final lines of "The Essence of Language" from the one we see in "Language." Human speech breaks the silent speaking of language, but breaks up as it is appropriated by the speaking it allows to occur: "To break up here means that the sounding word [*das verlautende Wort*] returns back into soundlessness [*ins Lautlose*], whence it was granted: into the ringing of stillness which, as Saying, moves the regions of the world's fourfold into their nearness. The breaking up of the word [*Zerbrechen*] is the true step back on the way of thinking" (US 204/OW 108).

The predominance of the imagery of sound (despite the fact that Heidegger refers consistently to both spoken and written language)† would lead us to suspect that the "noise" to which Heidegger alludes, in speaking of the breaking of silence, derives essentially from the material, sonorous character of human speech. Careful attention to the argument in "The Essence of Language" (to which I want to return) will bear out this point. But it should be noted that the words *Verlautbarung*, *Verlauten*, and even *Lauten* connote more than a simple "sounding." *Laut* does in fact mean "sound" or "tone" and is used in linguistics to designate the phoneme. As

---

*I should add that it is not uncommon for Heidegger to offer the means for an entirely different reading of his argument from the one his text seems to favor by its rhetorical movements. Not only does Heidegger's text deconstruct itself constantly; it also points to different paths of inquiry (as in the first volume of Martin Heidegger, *Nietzsche* [Pfullingen: Neske, 1961]). In this latter respect, Heidegger seems to be attempting to *prompt* thought on the part of readers.

†The reference to written language appears in the passage I quoted above concerning the "breaking" of silence. It appears also in the passage I am commenting on from "The Essence of Language" (US 193/OW 98). It goes without saying that if we were to pursue the question of written language, Heidegger's use of the term "speaking" would have to be brought into question.

an adjective, it means "loud," "noisy," or simply "distinct" or "audible." It can thus take on the figurative meaning of "public." The latter sense dominates in the term *verlautbaren*, which means "to report" or "to divulge," "to publish." *Verlauten*, in turn, is an intransitive verb meaning "to spread about" or "to give to understand"; *wie verlautet* means "according to what people say," "as it is rumored." Thus it is clear that these last terms connote something more than "making audible" — they have to do with the transmission of a signified content, what Heidegger refers to in his discussion of "idle talk" in *Being and Time* as "what is said-in-the-talk."* Indeed, *Verlautbarung* could designate precisely what Heidegger means by "idle talk" in that volume. In this respect, we might surmise that the "noise" in question derives from the repeatable character of the linguistic sign (understood as a relation between signifier and signified) that makes it possible for any speech to bear signification outside a fixed context, and thus to "empty out" as it is spread about and repeated without the "primordial understanding" deriving from a "primary relationship of being" toward the reality talked about. The noise in human speech would have its source in the conditions of what Heidegger calls "average intelligibility," conditions that make it possible for the sign to function as a sign: precisely the source of what Heidegger described in "Hölderlin and the Essence of Poetry" as the "permanent danger" attending all authentic use of language.[7] Those conditions are material, but they have to do with the significant character of language. We should not forget that the problem Heidegger is dealing with in discussing the articulation of human speech and the essence of language is also the problem of signification.

But when Heidegger takes up the question of *Verlautbarung* in "The Essence of Language," he emphasizes only the sensuous (referring to it as *das Sinnliche, das Leibhafte*) and primarily sonorous dimension of language. His aim is to account for its materiality with the concept of earth and to circumscribe the sign structure (a unity of sense and sound — Heidegger takes Aristotle's famous definition of the sign in *On Interpretation* for his example) with his notion of the relation between earth and world. In the economy of his essay, this move allows him to locate the saying of language in the broader context of the "countering" relations of the fourfold ("the over against one another [*Gegen-einander-über*] of the world's regions" [US 203/OW 107]) after he has described how its saying opens the neighborhood (the countering relation) of poetry and thought. The citations from Hölderlin (US 194–95/OW 99–100) work essentially to

---

*The citations from Heidegger's *Being and Time* in this paragraph are all from the translation by John Macquarrie and Edward Robinson (New York: Harper and Row, 1962), 212. I will return to Heidegger's use of the term *Lauten* in my next chapter.

this purpose. Having suggested indirectly that the concepts of melody and rhythm, and thus the kinship between song and speech, might shed light on the proper nature of the sounds and tones of speech (provided that these concepts are removed from any "metaphysical-technical" determination), and having suggested that we have yet to grasp what is conveyed in the German term for dialect, *Mundarten* (namely that dialects flow from the earth, always differently in accordance with the "landscape"), Heidegger turns to Hölderlin's figure of language as "the flower of the mouth." Each of the four citations merits consideration, given the critical attention that has been devoted to this figure (and we should remember that Heidegger would challenge this very term). But for my purposes here, I would stress merely Heidegger's claim that Hölderlin's figure names (and is) the advent of language as song in which the relation of world and earth is composed (*gefügt*) in the manner described in "The Origin of the Work of Art" when Heidegger defines how the work of art sets out the *Riss*-design (the difference between world and earth as it is traced out in the event of truth) by setting forth the earth in the Open of truth. This "composing" of language makes any "physiological-physical" explanation of its "earthly" character (based on "phonetic data") wholly inadequate (US 193/OW 98). "The sounding, earthly dimension of language," Heidegger writes, "is held within the harmony that attunes the regions of the world's structure [*die Gegenden des Weltgefüges*] to one another by playing them together" (US 196/OW 101). The material quality of poetic language is thus strictly equivalent to what Heidegger described as the "thingly" character of the work of art, and it is grounded in the same fashion. Heidegger has simply developed his notion of the differential relation of world and earth with his notion of the countering structure of the fourfold.

"When the word is called the mouth's flower and its blossom," Heidegger writes, "we hear the sound of language rising like the earth" (US 196/OW 101). That is to say, the poetic word is brought into and brings forth the articulation of world and earth as the speaking of language and is thus carried back into the silent peal of stillness, the source of its being. *Brot* ("bread") and *Wein* ("wine") in Trakl's poem presumably embody such a saying; following the allegory of poetic saying Heidegger constructs, they necessarily come forth in the same manner as Hölderlin's words when he names language "the flower of the mouth." For they are the accomplished naming, out of the difference of world and thing (and out of the speaking of difference), of these "fruits of heaven and earth." And Heidegger may well be assuming that as a citation of Hölderlin (for in modern German poetic language, these are also unavoidably Hölderlin's words) they work as a saying of language (like Hölderlin's figure), or a

saying of poetic saying.* Over the threshold of "A Winter Evening" unfolds the poetic language for which Hölderlin called in "Bread and Wine,"
if not, in some sense, the poem itself.

One might argue that this citation of Hölderlin (let us supply the quotation marks: *Da erglänzt in reiner Helle/Auf dem Tische "Brot und
Wein"* ["There lie, in limpid brightness shown, /Upon the table 'bread and
wine' "]) would constitute a kind of noise.† For wouldn't this residue of
textuality (the irreducible fact of the possibility of this citation and the
resultant ambiguity of the verse: the fact that "A Winter Evening" also
allows us to see a poem by Hölderlin on the table in the house, immediately rendering all "seeing" and "hearing" problematic as the language
of the poem foregrounds itself as language) dampen the clarity of the
poetic saying that gives bread and wine as earthly gifts from the divine? Or
wouldn't simply the echo of another poet's words (if we read somewhat
less "literally") interfere with the poem's silence? Heidegger would suggest, I believe, that such textual and intertextual play is subsumed in the
reflexive or allegorical structure of a poem that says the essence of poetry
and that what is said in "Brot und Wein" would in some manner be
repeated and re-collected in Trakl's poem. Or he would suggest (another
version of the same point) that one threshold opens upon another, that the
silent ringing of one word brings forth the ringing of another to produce a
manifold but harmonious silence.

If we link the questions raised by this instance of citation to the earlier
question of iterability (the "permanent danger" attending poetic language), these answers grow problematic. But even more fundamentally,
the entire notion of a "purely spoken," the notion from which Heidegger
begins in turning to the poem, becomes questionable, be it even as a regulative idea (the "regulative" idea, in fact, of a measure). "Purely spoken"
would imply a complete subsumption of the human *Verlautbarung* in the
melos of poetic saying; no element of the poem could remain outside the
melodic articulation it effects, no residue could be left, nothing of the
"petrified" letter could arrest movement. Such an ideal may represent a
philosophical necessity. But if we start from it, taking it as a telos, rather
than inscribe it in its conditions of (im)possibility as a thoroughgoing
notion of iterability would require, then there is no leaving "philosophy."

But rather than pursue the kind of deconstruction to which I have
alluded here (which should be predictable in its general lines, though it is
no less essential for being familiar), I would like to take a cue from Höl-

---

*In fact, the line concerning words that originate like flowers comes from Hölderlin's
"Bread and Wine" and is the "one word" about the word Heidegger wants us to retain from
his citations of Hölderlin.
†I thank Andrzej Warminski for this suggestion.

derlin and point to a different (though related) path of questioning to which I will return several times in the course of this volume. My *fil conducteur* is the motif that Heidegger identified in "The Origin of the Work of Art" under the name of dissemblance.

It is not easy to account for Heidegger's statement that Trakl's "A Winter Evening" represents the *one* choice for the questioning he wants to undertake in "Language" (and oddly enough, he tells us twice that he will not be able to explain himself). Certainly, the peculiarly "reflexive" character of the poem could be linked with Heidegger's notion of the "createdness" of the work of art (as Heidegger develops this notion in "The Origin of the Work of Art"). The poem, in Heidegger's reading, performs the movement it thematizes; as I have noted, it traces and crosses the threshold it names in its "allegorical" presentation — it gathers appropriatively its own language. But surely Heidegger could have found other poems of such an exemplary character. Why does this poem evince a singular fitness (US 17/P 198) for the task of reaching the saying of language? The key would seem to lie in the words *Brot* and *Wein*. If Heidegger's claim for the poetic saying of this poem holds, then the *language* that lies over the poem's threshold (i.e., at the point where it unfolds the speaking of language as the *Geläut der Stille* ["peal of stillness"], or where this speaking, as the *Geheiss* of language, issues, as "spoken," in and by way of the poem's gathering of what it has marked in its chiasmic movement) will have the character of the language for which Hölderlin called in the very poem named "Bread and Wine." In "The Essence of Language," Heidegger would have us retain *one* word from this poem. It lies in the lines *Tragen muss er, zuvor; nun aber nennt er sein Liebstes,/Nun, nun müssen dafür Worte, wie Blumen, entstehn* ("First he must suffer; but now he names his most beloved,/Now, now words for it must emerge like flowers" [cited in US 195/OW 99–100]). The *words Brot und Wein* in Trakl's poem must, if we follow Heidegger's reading, have such a character in that they are gathered into a relation of world and thing that the poem's multifold saying has articulated. They must themselves rise like the earth as gathered in the harmony of the fourfold. In other words, Trakl's last words in "A Winter Evening" not only cite Hölderlin's poem but also realize the saying for which it calls (or so Heidegger is implicitly claiming). This poem is binding or compelling above any other because it repeats Hölderlin in an originary manner, fulfilling Hölderlin's futural claim on German poetry. "Today" (I leave this to its ambiguity: Heidegger was writing in 1959) we have only one choice: an instance of saying that answers our destiny.

But whether or not this hypothesis holds (it is at least sufficiently outlandish to meet Heidegger's extraordinary claim that only one poem will serve our needs on this occasion), it is clear that the words "bread and wine" are implicitly being used to caution the claims Heidegger is making for the saying that occurs in "A Winter Evening." Yet Hölderlin himself, as I have tried to show, consistently questioned in his later poetry the possibility of achieving a measured poetic saying like the one Heidegger ascribes to him and to Trakl. Hölderlin indicated clearly that the "suffering" of language (his own, in any case) is irremediable — by which I mean not measurable or gatherable, not "compactible" in the way Heidegger suggests with his interpretation of Trakl's figure of the threshold that has turned to stone. The human suffering Hölderlin describes in his late poetry (I think first of "In lovely blueness . . .") is indissociable from this knowledge and in large measure proceeds from it; it is a suffering that proceeds from the *poetic* experience of the impossibility of mourning — that is to say, from an experience with language.

"Mourning" would designate here the capacity to assume mortality and the finitude that is revealed (Heidegger argues) in and by this preeminent human possibility. "In death," Heidegger writes in his commentary on the figure of the wanderers in "A Winter Evening," "the supreme concealedness of Being crystallizes [*versammelt sich*]. Death has already overtaken every dying" (US 20/P 200). "Death" names here the truth of all being-toward-death. For mortals, it is the impossible; that upon which Dasein opens in its assumption of its mortality (as it stands at the threshold, its opening to the Being of what is), but which it can never have in its grasp. Its meaning is defined (or a relation to it is established) in the poetic acts of language that trace the threshold, but this definition of meaning is not an appropriation. For Dasein cannot appropriate its own finitude; which is to say, it cannot mourn itself in such a way as to interiorize its exposure to alterity (its opening to what is). It may measure itself against this alterity, and may measure it *as difference* (difference opens only in such a measuring, Heidegger asserts: this is the gathering of the concealedness of Being, what Heidegger describes elsewhere as the drawing out of a nearness). But difference can never be Dasein's own. The logic of finitude strictly forbids any such possibility — and all of Hölderlin's later poetry and thought is devoted to thinking and obeying this injunction. For Hölderlin, a proper mourning would be nothing other than obedience to this injunction: purity and firmness before absence or (as in Hölderlin's "Remarks on *Oedipus*") irremediable loss.

But Hölderlin found no such measure — he could establish no such measure in a "firm letter." As he suggests in "Mnemosyne," mourning "fails" in his poetry.[8] In "In lovely blueness . . . ," this failure ("like brooks, the end of something sweeps me away") is figured in a flow of metaphoricity and in a series of figures expressing a lack of measure (the "third eye," the plaint of the poor man, etc.).* But I would like to call attention to one figure in particular in this last poem because it appears to touch upon the question of the materiality of poetic speech and may point to another dimension of the "noise" (though this term grows increasingly problematic — for we must go beyond the limitations implied by a metaphorics of sonority) that disrupts the harmonious articulation of the speaking of language and human speech, and thus disrupts the possibility of mourning as Heidegger describes it in his reading of Trakl.

I refer here to a figure that appears at the opening of the third and last section of "In lovely blueness . . .": "If someone looks into the mirror, a man, and in it sees his image, as though it were a painted likeness; it resembles the man." (*Wenn einer in den Spiegel siehet, ein Mann, und siehet darinn sein Bild, es gleicht dem Manne.*)

This unsettling line is intelligible only in the context of the concerns that occupy the first section of the poem. Hölderlin had opened the poem by implicitly asserting that a human being might appear, in its purity, as an image of divinity. Starting from the image of a man framed against the windows of a church steeple "blossoming" in lovely blueness, he had suggested that a *poetic* relation might be found between the beauty of nature and the beauty of human purity. Poetry would form the bridge between these forms of beauty and make possible a dwelling on earth by establishing humankind's capacity to be an image of divinity. It would ground this capacity like (and as) the *Bildsamkeit* that initially appears to the poet against the beauty of nature: "If now someone comes down beneath the bell, comes down those steps, a still life it is [*ein stilles Leben ist es*] because, when the figure is so detached, the man's plasticity [*Bildsamkeit*] is brought out."

The first stanza of the poem, then, asserts the possibility of establishing human *Bildsamkeit* as the condition of an appearance commensurate with the manifestation of the divine (which is said to appear, as Heidegger argues in his interpretation of the poem, *as* unknown, and like the manifestness of the sky). But in the second stanza, the poet begins to speak in the first person (for convenience, let us refer to this "I" as Hölderlin) and expresses both his desire to achieve the *Gestalt* of a pure soul and his difficulty in doing so. The third stanza then evokes his failure. When he looks in the mirror of his poetry (the constant references to conditions of representation and to the poet's own suffering make this equation almost unavoidable), he sees a kind of "still life." But the stillness of this image is of a very different form from the image that appeared in the window of the

*I will be citing Michael Hamburger's translation of this poem as it appears in Hölderlin, *Poems and Fragments*, 600–605.

church steeple as it was gathered in a play of light, color, and sound. It is of an uncanny, deathly stillness. And what the poet sees with his "third eye" is *resemblance*; not simply his reflection or image but the *likeness* of a painted representation.

What the man sees in the mirror, in other words, is his capacity to resemble something (himself) — he sees his *Bildsamkeit*. But this capacity for resemblance is surely not the condition of the appearance of a correspondence with the divine (the man does not see the *Gestalt* of the "pure soul" of which Hölderlin speaks in the poem's second section: *die Wesenheit, die Gestalt ist's*). The man does indeed see resemblance (not a resemblance, rather resemblance itself); but, as Blanchot would remind us, this is the very "impure" resemblance of the cadaver. "Man is made in his image," Blanchot remarks, "but this formula should first of all be understood in this way: *man is unmade according to his image*" (EL 354/260). Blanchot illustrates this statement with a long and extraordinary meditation on the ambiguous nature of the cadaver (neither fully a person nor fully a thing) as it slips from the world of significant relations and begins to resemble itself (not the human being it was but an anonymous being brought forth by this resemblance). The strange resemblance of the cadaver — that is to say, the appearance of what is properly unrepresentable: mimesis "itself," the possibility of appearing *like something* — brings to the surface a dimension of the image that art takes as its proper domain (a domain that undoes all "property," all essentiality). It is the domain of what Heidegger refers to in "The Origin of the Work of Art" as *Verstellung*, "dissemblance" (one of the two forms of concealment Heidegger recognizes in the play of concealment and unconcealment [H 41/P 54]).* Blanchot refers to it as "dissimulation." Prior to all negation of being, Blanchot argues, and thus prior to any constitution of meaning or ideality, there is dissimulation. It belongs to the very possibility of the appearance of what is, but is revealed only when objects withdraw in some way from the world as a realm of significant relations. Such withdrawal occurs for Dasein in various forms of "limit-experience" that all communicate in some way with the experience of death (not the death of negation but the death that is a slipping away from the capacity for negation), but it is the event that is proper to art. Literature, Blanchot argues, enters into this domain of appearance that is prior to the world — and only then does it become literature — when its language becomes image (EL 28/34). This is not to say that literary language is characterized by its use of images but rather to say that it becomes the image of language (in the same way the image seizes the cadaver) and allows language itself to show dissemblance.

*I will return to this topic in my next chapter.

Language that becomes the image of language, Blanchot says, takes on a spectral quality, and, as Blanchot argues in "Literature and the Right to Death," a strange opacity. It is like a thing, but a thing that does not achieve the muteness or silence of the thing (even if it actively pursues the destruction of signification, as in some poetic experimentation) because it will always appear *as language* and show the empty possibility of signification, a strange residue of meaning beyond meaning or before meaning (as achieved in any semantic configuration) that is neither "material" nor "ideal" and that belongs to the very possibility of meaning but cannot be subsumed or eliminated.

Further development of this dimension of poetic language will have to await my discussion of Blanchot at the end of this volume (though I will be returning frequently to the question of mimesis). I point to it here because I suspect that *such* an experience with language (and death) contributes to Hölderlin's experience of what I have called the impossibility of mourning. Heidegger himself, as I have suggested, is not insensitive to it, but a full exploration of its nature (as something resisting any *essential* determination) will unsettle Heidegger's most fundamental claims for poetry.

For Heidegger, the compact threshold of poetic language (the "firm letter") is a tombstone, the house is a sepulchre (the image is made explicit in "Language in the Poem" [US 49, 66/OW 173, 188] but is already suggested strongly by the images of "stilling" in "Language" — however much Heidegger insists that such stillness is not the absence but the highest form of movement in measure). The accomplished mourning of poetic remembrance would be an assumption of mortality. But it would hold in it the possibility of a kind of rebirth (again, a major figure in "Language in the Poem") and access to what we might call the life of the spirit. Heidegger looks to poetry, in other words, for what Blanchot would describe as "the possibility of dying."[9] But Hölderlin experiences precisely the impossibility of such an assumption of mortality through poetic *Stiftung* ("founding"). "Life is death," he writes at the end of "In lovely blueness . . . ," "and death is a kind of life." This line is not about redemption; it describes existence beyond the borders of a life circumscribed (and rendered meaningful) by death. An errancy ("poor stranger in Greece," Hölderlin writes of Oedipus) destined to no Colonus and no homecoming: a death that is not yet life and that is the impossibility of dying.

Other modern writers have described such errancy and such an experience with language: Kafka, Beckett,[10] Blanchot, Celan. They demonstrate that another articulation of the terms "life" and "death" is required — and one that is not necessarily tragic or even morose — once we assume the impossibility of dying (or to return to the figure from which I started, the impossibility of putting an end to the noise). In Heidegger, the way to language seems to lead inevitably to death in the sense of stillness (at least one powerful strain of his thinking takes that path, or takes its orientation from that possibility). But if we attend more to the noise in language than does Heidegger, very different paths will open.

2

In the Name of Language

IN the "experience" with language defined in the opening paragraphs of Heidegger's "The Essence of Language" (as in the subsequent description of the poetic experience presented by Stefan George in his poem "The Word"), we will recognize elements of the structure of relation between humankind and language sketched out in the concluding pages of Heidegger's "Language." When we speak of undergoing an experience, Heidegger says, we designate not an occurrence of which we are and remain the subject but rather an event by which something comes over us, overwhelms and transforms us: "To undergo here means to endure, to suffer, to receive perceptively what strikes us and to accede to it insofar as we conform to it" (US 149/OW 57). An experience with language is not of our making (as might be suggested by the phrase *eine Erfahrung zu machen*); rather, it is something that comes about (*es macht sich etwas*) — of such an experience, we might say, "it happened that . . ." (*es fügte sich, dass* . . .).

The notion of experience, as we will see, actually adds quite a bit to what we have recognized thus far regarding the relation between language and humankind. But the structure of the relation, once again, remains essentially the same. To undergo an experience with language is to mark and traverse a threshold by way of a receptive joining with a countering address (an address in which there speaks the binding *law* of language, its *Ge-heiss*). The term "experience" stresses the way of this passage (*Erfahrung*), and indeed the problem of relation will be thought in this essay via a notion of way-making. But in "The Essence of Language," Heidegger continues to move *within* and *from out of* the relation between language and humankind sketched out in "Language." The latter relation constitutes the point of departure for his effort to think the "relation of all relations."

The relation of countering reception sketched in "Language," in other words, structures an important part of Heidegger's very *manner* of proceeding in "The Essence of Language." Not only is it recalled in the notion of receptive joining announced in the discussions of experience and the poet's *Gelassenheit*, then elaborated in the long developments on the structure of countering (*gegen*, as we will see, is the principal word used here for thinking relation) — it is also *enacted* in Heidegger's text. The three long lectures that constitute "The Essence of Language" *stage* a countering reception of language that would bring it to speech. I will return in the course of my reading to the modes and significance of this very ostentatious performance, the *exemplary* character of this attempt at bringing language to speech. But here I would stress the fundamental point that Heidegger's effort in "The Essence of Language" is to engage the counterplay he describes in "Language" *in such a way* — that is to say, in a *thinking* experience with language — as to open the question of relation in general. Or such is the conjecture, the *Vermutung*, that will guide this reading.

To bring forth the way and the manner of Heidegger's progress, and thus to heed Heidegger's admonitions concerning the way his text is to be read (the admonitions to which I referred in my introductory remarks),[1] it is necessary to follow the *weave* of Heidegger's text quite closely. But the sheer size of "The Essence of Language," its range of linguistic play and its complex articulation of long periods of reflection, makes it necessary to sketch things out in advance. Once we have caught its form and movement, its *schema*, the text gains a measure that effectively transforms its almost oppressive length. But entering this movement (which means recalling it at every step) is no easy matter. Thus I would like to begin with a summary statement of its unfolding before moving to a closer examination.

The text moves generally by way of a counterplay of three modes of advance, two of which belong to thinking, one to poetry. The last is evoked in the first lecture and then described at greater length in the second lecture when Heidegger sketches George's path toward song and defines the tonality of poetic song in terms of wonder; the citations of Hölderlin in the third lecture will recall these developments and are meant to allow the saying of poetry to resonate as such. But the larger portion of the long analysis of George's poem has properly the character of a thinking — a thinking that moves in the neighborhood of poetry. Poetry, too, thinks, Heidegger insists, and he suggests strongly that his explication of the poem involves an unfolding of the thought that occurs in the poem. But poetry's relation to its source in saying is different from that of thought (just as obscure to it as thought's to this same source), and the way it pursues is unique. The entire meditation on the relation between word and thing, word and "is" in relation to George's poem, is properly a thinking encounter with poetry.

Heidegger accompanies this meditation, however, with a second, more overtly "philosophical" or "thinking" reflection on the "guideword" *Das Wesen der Sprache*—: *Die Sprache des Wesens* ("The essence of language—: The language of essence" [US 166/OW 72]). The analysis will point beyond what philosophy can think in these words—the colon, in fact, marks the point where the concept begins to lose its grasp and where *Wesen* and *Sprache* begin to undergo a radical transformation of meaning. But the speaking of the phrase in its full unfolding and "hinting" can only be characterized as that of thought. And here I would underscore an essential point about *On the Way to Language*. Heidegger is as concerned with characterizing the language of thought as he is with characterizing that of poetry. In fact he *must* be so concerned according to the essay we are reading: each mode of saying is said to need the other in order to be capable of the turn by which they think their source (US 163/OW 70). The language of poetry is constantly taken as the privileged point of focus (or audition) in readings of *On the Way to Language*, but Heidegger is no less concerned with the character of his own language (as a language of thinking) than he is with the language of poetry. The guidewords *Die Sprache ist: Sprache* and *Das Wesen der Sprache*—: *Die Sprache des Wesens* and words or phrases like *es gibt* and *Aufriss* all belong to the language of *thought*, in contrast (or counterpoint) to the language of poetry or that of any other mode of speaking.

Thus Heidegger's way of proceeding in the first two essays of "The Essence of Language" is to counterpose the speaking of poetry and thought, to draw out their *Gegeneinanderüber* and thereby render audible (and thinkable) the countering word (*das entgegnende Wort*) of the country (*Gegend*) that defines the region of the differential articulation of every mode of speech, and with this latter (insofar as the possibility of a world is articulated in language), the countering relations of the fourfold. The structure of relation—within the fourfold and from out of language—is a countering, one to which we have privileged access through the relation of poetry and thought. There is nothing quaint about this juxtaposition, despite the pastoral tones that might be evoked by motifs such as "song" and "country." Plato began philosophy, as Heidegger understands it, by thinking *over against* poetry; one way in which Heidegger seeks to leave philosophy is by rethinking the "against" as a possible point of access for rethinking the question of relation in general.

But we have not quite summarized the movement of "The Essence of Language" by observing the counterplay Heidegger sets up between poetry and thought. Or rather, we must appreciate the full scope of this counterplay. Because, once again, there are *two* interweaving paths of reflection in this text: the one accompanying the poet's and the one that guides this accompaniment. When Heidegger ventures a name (*Riss*) out of the sounding of the counterplay of thought and poetry at the end of the second lecture, this naming engages a demand made upon thought (by language) in the guideword *Das Wesen der Sprache* —: *Die Sprache des Wesens.* "The Essence of Language" presents a *thinking* experience with language because its *conjecture* (or presumption: *Vermutung*) that the difference between poetry and thought gives access to the saying of language answers to a *Zumutung*, an exigent demand issuing from what calls thought in the relation of essence and language. *Was heisst Denken?* This is also the problem, perhaps the fundamental problem of *On the Way to Language* (as a text of thought, concerned with language). The tracing of the counterplay, then, *answers*, in a daring *Vermutung*, the *Zumutung* of language that speaks in the guideword. And I would suggest that the tracing of the difference between poetry and thought is precisely the defining, anticipatory speaking (that movement of "stealing a march") that brings language to sound, according to the schema offered in "Language." The entire counterplay of poetry and thought set up in this text functions within the structure of usage (*Brauch*) described in "Language" while also moving to think its possibility. It can be described, I believe, as a *provocation* of the law. Near the end of this chapter, I will have to address the question to what extent the counterplay is (necessarily) a transgression or an "overreaching." But to approach this question, it will be necessary to follow closely Heidegger's staging of this provocation.

I draw the motif of the law from Heidegger's initial remarks on the everyday experience of language's *failing* us and from his first approach to George's poem. An experience we undergo *with* language, Heidegger notes in these first steps of his presentation, is one in which language itself is brought to language. Such an event does not occur in the everyday use of language inasmuch as our linguistic dealings presuppose that language does *not* bring itself to language. But language comes to the word, he says (US 151/OW 59), at moments when the "right word" for something escapes us. Language sounds in the word when the word is missing — a paradoxical construction that rests upon the distinction Heidegger will develop between "word" (*Wort*) and "words" (*Wörter*). This is a schema with which readers of Heidegger will be familiar: one might recall the broken hammer in *Being and Time*. Here, the absence of the correct name gives fleeting access to the *possibility* of naming. In the moment when we leave the thing we intend unspoken (a thing, Heidegger emphasizes, that concerns us and draws us to it [*was uns angeht, uns an sich reisst*]: terms with which Heidegger will define essence itself), we are grazed by the essence of language. We experience a speaking at this moment when we entertain a relation with the thing in its essence yet do not find the word that would bespeak this relation. At this moment, language furtively comes to the word: simultaneously giving and withholding itself. This "word" is what Heidegger will later call "the word by which words come to the word" (US 181/OW 87) — the word by which words come to name.

Heidegger will move quickly to this notion of the word in proceeding to George's poem "The Word." The poem, he says, brings into language the poet's own experience with the withholding of language.[2] Recalling the everyday experience he has just described, he goes straight to the poem's last couplet: "So I renounced and sadly see:/Where word breaks off no thing may be." The last line of this couplet, he asserts, "brings the word of language itself to language" (US 153/OW 60) and says something about the relation between word and thing. No thing is where the word that names is lacking, Heidegger concludes in an initial interpretation of the line. But what is a name?

Taking into consideration the mysterious character of what the poem itself says about naming, Heidegger suggests that a name must not be understood as a designation but is perhaps rather to be grasped through expressions such as "In the name of the king" or "In the name of God," where "in the name of" means "at the call, by the command" (*Unter dem Geheiss, nach dem Geheiss* [US 154/OW 61]). The forms of authority evoked here by example might give us pause — if only to consider that it is perhaps from the name, according to this argument, that we must think authority. But Heidegger's immediate point is that the naming word should be thought in relation to an injunction, a command, or an order that authorizes. No thing *is* where the word is lacking, George's poem says — from which Heidegger concludes that the word alone gives being to the thing. Understood as a command, the word would be what empowers or enables: what gives the capacity to be. A thing *is* in the name of its name.

This is obviously a scandalous or simply incomprehensible proposition for the instrumental conception of language active in modern technology (and assumed by the better part of Heidegger's audience, which comes, he suggests, not from philosophy but from the various sciences). But to illustrate his point, Heidegger takes his example precisely from the technological domain to illustrate the nature of the relation between word and thing he is attempting to define. His example is Sputnik. Cautioning against hasty thinking (such haste has its source in precisely what he will describe), Heidegger asks:

Is not even this "thing," what it is and the way it is, in the name of its name? Certainly. If that hurry, in the sense of the technical maximization of all velocities, in whose time-space modern machines and apparatus can alone be what they are—if that hurry had not bespoken man and ordered him at its call [*Geheiss*], if that call to such hurry had not challenged him and put him at bay, if the word framing that order and challenge had not spoken: then there would be no Sputnik. No thing is where the word is lacking. (US 155/OW 62)

It would probably be worthwhile to ponder over and play a bit with this curious example. What exactly is the status of this bizarre, even comical proper noun whose translation into English would yield something like "accompanying on a path"? Heidegger tells us simply that in the name "Sputnik" there speaks the enjoining and empowering word that lets this thing, Sputnik, *be* in the time-space of *Technik*, a disposition reigning over the relation between humankind and thing: in the name "Sputnik," there speaks the injunction of *Technik*. The name is a name only inasmuch as there speaks in it what Heidegger calls (in the sentences immediately following the ones I have quoted), "the word of language," or the word by which the word (here "Sputnik") comes to the word: inasmuch, in other words, as the name comes to speak out of the relation, defined by the word itself, between word and thing.

The word of language is a command, an order. We came across Heidegger's notion of the *Geheiss* in his essay "Language," where the term designates a "speaking" that governs and empowers all acts of bidding or calling. The third strophe of Trakl's poem, as we saw, gathers the respective modes of bidding (*Heissen*) of the first two strophes from out of the "intimate bidding" (*aus der Einfalt des innigen Heissens* [US 25]) that calls the difference between word and thing and is itself the call of difference in and by which difference unfolds in its "simplicity." The poem's own *Heissen* thus proceeds from and brings about, as we have seen, this speaking of difference, this *Heissen* that Heidegger designates as the essence of speaking, the speaking of language itself (US 26/P 206). Since it is the "authentic" bidding that gathers all bidding, Heidegger names it the *Geheiss* (the *ge-* expressing precisely this gathering or assembling).

Thing and world, Heidegger says, are bidden by language to come into the between of their difference. The command or injunction is thought here as a *Befehlen*, though the term is meant in the old sense of "commit," as in the phrase, "Commit thy way unto the Lord" (again, a markedly "speaking" example). Thus the bidding of language, Heidegger writes, commits things and world to the bidding (the *Geheiss*) of difference—it enjoins them to join in and to the articulation of their difference that sounds in the silent speaking/bidding of the essence of language. This speaking, again, is the gathering of all speaking, all bidding, and the source of their possibility: "The difference is the command [*Geheiss*] out of which every bidding [*Heissen*] itself is first called, so that each may follow the command. The command of the dif-ference has ever already gathered all bidding within itself (US 27/P 207). Hofstadter's translation is certainly correct here, but another reading of Heidegger's first sentence might be possible in that the sentence appears to formulate the command itself: "The difference is the command . . . that each should belong to the command" (*Der Unterschied ist das Geheiss, aus dem jedes Heissen erst gerufen wird, dass jedes dem Geheiss gehöre*). The command is that all should belong to the command: all speaking should answer to the command by first answering to its call. But the command is properly empty of any content in that it says nothing more than that all should answer to it — all should belong to it. The command itself runs: "that all should belong to the command." The law of language, the binding origin of any linguistic community, folds upon itself. Only where it is brought to speak in histor-ical conjunctures (unfolded in the manner we have seen in "Language" — that is, via a kind of intervention that involves the tracing of the *Riss*) does it have any content.

If the law (of language) were not formally empty at some point, it is difficult to see how historical change would be possible, or how the *Geheiss* could sound in two ways in the same epoch, as Heidegger implicitly tells us it does in reminding us of the historial stakes of this meditation on poetry. By evoking the law of *Technik* with his example of Sputnik, Hei-degger recalls to us that the passage he is trying to think in this essay is the passage to another disposition of the relation between humankind, word, and thing (perhaps not even a "disposition" but an entirely different *Stellen*: the one toward which he is working with *Stillen*) — to another order, and thus to another *Geheiss*. This other *Geheiss*, Heidegger tells us, is already audible in George's poem "The Word." The quasi-transcenden-tal character of the law — and it is a law: it is what binds in the relation of language and humankind inasmuch as every act of appellation, every *Heissen*, must heed the command to be such a call, to *speak* out of the relation between word and thing that the word (of the law) holds in it — makes it possible to conceive of a multiple speaking in a given epoch and transition between epochs.[3] It also allows us to conceive of the law in a post-epochal manner as a singular event that must be provoked. In a different context, the context of cultural politics, for example, we would speak of an intervention in the symbolic: *political* intervention that is an intervention *in language*. The post-epochal moment (at this time of the closure of the history of Being, when the word for Being is withheld and the relation of language and Being comes to the fore) opens the possibility of an an-archic conception of the ground of linguistic community.

Having developed his initial explication of the proposition "No thing is where the word is lacking," Heidegger pauses to ward off any hasty and triumphant assumption that we have actually heard George's poem by transcribing it in this way and can confidently sum up the experience presented in it with a phrase such as "Language is the house of Being." Such an assumption, which reduces poetry to a servant of the concept (its traditional role in most philosophical or theoretical appeals to literature) would simply stop short of the aim of these lectures, or *pass right by* their goal, which is to lead us to undergo an experience with language. The path of thought is not a railroad: "We must be careful not to force the vibration of the poetic saying onto the rigid rails of a univocal statement and so destroy it" (US 157/OW 64). Thus Heidegger will attempt to bring forth the *Schwingung* (vibration and oscillation) of the concluding lines of George's poem by attending to an ambiguity or a movement in the word *sei* of the last line ("no thing *may be*"). He hears in the injunction of the last line the call or command (*Geheiss*) to enter into the realm that opens with the poet's renunciation, namely a different relation between word and thing from the one he had formerly recognized. Previously, the poet thought that his art consisted in finding (or letting come to him) the right word for what he had imaginatively fashioned or held before his eyes. Poetic naming was the grasping or making firm (*dicht machen*) of a marvel or dream that existed in some manner independently of language: properly an expression of a thing that would bestow upon it density and thus a certain beauty. But the experience recounted in "The Word," Heidegger asserts, recalls to George's mind Hölderlin's line "But what endures is founded by poets" — where what is to be founded is a relation to the word as that which holds in it a relation between word and thing. With Hölderlin's line in his ears — *that is to say, via another poetic saying** — the poet gives voice to a renunciation in which echoes the word of language itself, the imperative "may be" that Heidegger defines as an imperative or a command. The last line of the poem expresses *both* the claim made upon the poet and the poet's submission (more literally, a conforming or joining to, a *sich fügen* in the *Geheiss* which Heidegger qualifies in his marginal notes as a form of *Gelassenheit* [US 158]). His resignation, Heidegger says, is an *Entsagen*,† an abdication or desistance; an *Absagen*, a withdrawal or declining; and a *Verzicht*, an abandonment or resignation (whose root, *ziehen*, is "the same word," Heidegger says, as the Latin *dicere* and the Greek *deiknumi*). With each of these words, Heidegger underscores that the poet's renuncia-

---

*As though poetry knows its own need to turn to its tradition in order to engage its source. Heidegger would appear to be suggesting here that a poetic saying is the medium for access to the source of the poet's vocation.

†The word appeared in Heidegger's marginal notes to "Language" to define the *Ent-sprechen* of human correspondence (US 29). The "desistance" we are observing must be thought within that structure.

tion is a saying in which the poet allows the word to say itself as that which "holds and sustains a thing in its being" (*Das Wort sagt sich dem Dichter als das zu, was ein Ding in dessen Sein hält und erhält* [US 158]). *Zusagen* means "to promise," "to engage oneself" (in the sense of accepting an invitation) or "to say openly to someone." The word thus promises itself to the poet, entrusts itself to him, and offers to him his calling.

But if the word says itself openly in its promise (and as the "already promised" [US 159/OW 66]), it says itself indeed as the "long hidden" and withdrawn. This is why the poet's renunciation is "sad," Heidegger says; its tonality is one of mourning. We should retain this reference to mourning for the later discussion of language and death. Authentic mourning, however, is not a despondency, Heidegger says, drawing on another verse from Hölderlin: it takes its tonality from "the most joyful," but does so as this most joyful withdraws (*entzieht: der Verzicht* answers to an *Entziehen*).[4] The poet thus experiences the "lofty sway" of the word in its reserve and draws thereby the primal knowledge (*Ur-kunde*) of that with which his saying is charged (*aufgegeben ist*: the poet's *Aufgebung* opens to the *Aufgegebene* — this is the source of his *Aufgabe*, that which is "highest and remaining" and which is both promised and withheld for a future advent, *eine anfängliche Ankunft* [US 159]).[5]

I am stressing the German here in order to suggest how Heidegger attempts to elicit the ambiguity he wants to hear in the last lines of George's poem. But I am also doing so in order to bring forth the manner in which Heidegger describes the poet's indirect (oscillating, ambiguous) manner of saying that which says itself only in a withholding. Only an abdication says the promise of the withheld word, which itself only communicates an injunction. There is no saying of the word of language in the sense of any full speech (*parole pleine*). What occurs essentially in the saying of the injunction is an *opening* upon a promise.

The thinking encounter with George's poem has noted two things: the communication (in a *Zusprechen*) of the promise (*Zusage*) of language, and the withholding that belongs to this communication. In its "primal tidings," language both conveys to and withholds from poetic saying what is assigned to it. Once again, the word of language — which is in itself what holds the thing in such a manner that it is — is understood to speak in a withholding. But with these observations, we still remain in the order of results, Heidegger says — we have merely summed up the poet's experience and have not entered into it. We are still *interpreting*, even if we have entered into the ambiguity of the *sei* and have touched the limit of meaning, the point of its very opening. In other words, we have not moved beyond an exposition of what we hear in the poem. What we have heard is not yet speaking, or not yet marking our language.

At this point, Heidegger will do no more than review the poet's experience with the word, noting the countering structure of the two triads of the poem and inviting us to reconsider the place to which the poet proceeds in seeking the name for the treasure that lies in his hand. He notes but does not activate the allegorical potential of the reference to the goddess of fate dwelling at the edge of the poetic landscape that is itself a boundary or a march (the motif of the "destinings" of Being). Much of what he notes has been implicit in his exposition thus far. He merely adds now a suggestion about the treasure that does not find a name, *presuming* that it is the "fullness of the simple" that comes to the poet as what is to be said in his later years. And since the poem succeeds in becoming a song of language, Heidegger asserts, it bears witness to the fact that the poet has achieved the renunciation that opens to what the poet must say.

Can we follow the poet here? Heidegger himself asks the question, but only, it would seem, after having provisionally closed the door to the poem with these remarks on "simplicity" and song, remarks that remain largely obscure at this point in his analysis—mystifying, and, to the impatient reader, undoubtedly, mystified. But I would suggest that Heidegger's move here is quite concerted, quite *staged*: that he is effectively pulling thought up before its difference with poetry, ostentatiously marking the difference in this manner in order to broach the theme of the neighborhood. For now, he will merely touch the theme before moving to reflect, from the basis of this arrest of thought, on the conditions of something like a thinking experience with language. He tells us simply that when it comes to extremes (the limits he will evoke later with his image of parallels intersecting in infinity), thought and poetry need each other (*brauchen einander*) in their neighborhood, each in its own manner.* Each has a singular relation to its origin in saying, but in their turn to this origin, they will always find themselves in the domain of their neighborhood with the other—moreover, they need each other in their neighborliness to make this turn. The turn by which they "think" their relation to their source passes *by way* of their difference from the other. This turn discovers the relation to the other and is made by way of this relation.

But we are not yet prepared to think such a notion of relation, or even (or consequently) to think the nature of thought itself, which Heidegger now announces, abruptly, with another mystifying phrase: "Thinking cuts furrows into the soil of Being"—an assertion he aligns with Nietzsche's statement that thought should have the fragrance of a wheatfield on a summer's night (US 163/OW 70). So he leaves the question of poetry's

---

*From which we may presume that the relation of *Brauch* I will develop in the next chapter marks all relation.

path to ask about the path of thought and *its* relation to language via a meditation on his title. He effectively starts over; having introduced the motifs of language's promise and address, and, perhaps more importantly, having marked the difference between poetry and thought, he states: "By now the two opening sentences of our lecture can be repeated with greater clarity [*Jetzt lassen sich die beiden Sätze deutlicher wiederholen*]. The three lectures bearing the title 'The Essence of Language' are to lead into the possibility of a thinking experience with language" (US 163/OW 70). (Note that Heidegger has added to his lecture's opening sentences a reference to thinking.) We are only in the preliminaries of such an attempt, he says, and therefore the title must be stripped of its presumptuous suggestion — conveyed in a distinctively philosophical rhetoric — that this essay will convey information about the essence of language. He thus suspends it with question marks: "The Essence? — of Language?" All inquiry into essence requires such a pause, but this inquiry into the essence of language entails the further complication that essence and language are essentially bound together. To ask about the essence of something, for something to come into question, that thing must have already offered an approach to us: it must have engaged our attention, addressed us in some manner (this is the necessity that prompts Heidegger to speak of a *Vorhaben*, a "fore-having," in the meditation on the hermeneutic circle in *Being and Time*). The same holds true of essence itself. It must have spoken. Thus, in treating of the essence of language, we find ourselves before the following situation:

If we put questions to language, questions about its essence, then clearly language itself must already have been granted to us [*schon zugesprochen sein*]. Similarly, if we want to inquire [*nachfragen*] about essence, namely the essence of language, then that which is called essence must also be already granted to us [*so muss uns auch, was Wesen heisst, schon zugesprochen sein*]. Putting questions and inquiring after require, here and everywhere [*Anfrage und Nachfrage brauchen hier und überall*], the prior grant [*Zuspruch*] of whatever it is they approach and pursue [*nachgehen*] in questioning. Every posing of every question already stands within the grant [*Zusage*] of what is put into question. (US 164–65/OW 71)[6]

On the basis of these considerations, Heidegger offers the suggestion that the "gesture" proper to thought is not one of questioning, as much of his prior work had suggested, but rather one of listening.* It is not a questioning because questioning has always implied the search for a ground. To ask what a thing is and to ask about the fact that such a thing should be is traditionally to seek the ground for a thing, where ground is

---

*Derrida has paused at length over the significance of this moment in *De l'esprit* (Paris: Galilée, 1987).

understood as something that *is*.* But no more than the word is essence something that is. So to avoid, or rather, to displace the structure of question and answer, Heidegger reinscribes this structure in language's speaking and the give and take of thought and language. Thought questions, but it questions out of a listening (a listening to language's *Zusage*), and that for which it questions is *language's* answer. Listening is thus prior to questioning; it is "the essential gesture needed now" (US 169/OW 75). And even if this listening unfolds necessarily as a questioning after the answer of language, its *Antwort* (US 169/OW 75) — questioning, it appears, is still unavoidable for thought — the answer it seeks does not conclude the movement of thought but rather sets it in motion, as an *entgegnendes Wort*, a countering word. The prefix *ant-* virtually translates *entgegnen*. Heidegger thus situates the structure of question and answer within the manifold structure of reply. And, of course, if the prior grant of essence comes in a countering reply, listening must have been a kind of pro-voking speaking (*entnehmend-entgegnend*), or must have determined in some way what it is listening for — and thus we are back within the problematic of usage (*Brauch*) developed in the essay "Language." Questioning moves in a kind of rejoining echoing.[7]

Since questioning is not the gesture proper to thought, Heidegger proceeds to strike the question marks from the title — revealing, in this manner, an incompleteness inaudible before they were added and raising the problem of how to *hear* it. The title, he says, now requires a supplement answering to the fact that we have access to the essence of language only if it has spoken, "promised" itself to us. Our thought of the essence of language must unfold out of a listening to what it has granted of itself: the title should be, or become, the echo of that granting. And the more our thinking enters into the grant of language's essence, the more that essence will speak in the title as the speech of essence. Heidegger thus "completes" the title in such a way as to turn it into an indication of the path we are to follow — into a guideword, words that point out ahead: *Das Wesen der Sprache — : Die Sprache des Wesens* (US 166).

It is now no longer a title, Heidegger asserts. It says "the echo of a thinking experience" before whose futural possibility Heidegger is seeking to bring us. I will not pause long over the difficult temporality implied here; I will merely suggest that if the enabling event (which may or may not happen)† toward which this meditation is proceeding is already echo-

---

*Later in the essay, Heidegger will refer to the inability of instrumental thinking to entertain the idea that the word gives being to the thing without conceiving of the word, in turn, as a thing.

†Heidegger is pushing possibility, *Möglichkeit*, in the direction of *er-möglichen* ("to enable"), while retaining a thought of possibility that escapes the notions of both chance and necessity.

ing, it is because we could not be under way at all if it had not already happened in some manner (or *will* not have already happened), and that if it has happened, it is because the relation of poetry and thought has already sounded (cf. "Language," where Heidegger asserts that our listening is already bound). In the proximity of poetic saying, thought has heard, indistinctly as yet, the saying toward which it is moving, the saying, as we will see shortly, that occurs *in* and *as* the demarcating of the neighborhood of poetry and thought. Unable as yet to perceive this saying *as such* (in fact, it will never hear it *as such*; it will never receive it except through contrast, reflection, and what Heidegger defines as "indication"), it is nevertheless exposed to it in the proximity of the speaking that occurs in the poem. Heidegger would be transcribing the experience for a philosophical ear that has necessarily already begun to perceive (all the more so as the reflective encounter with the poem has been *priming* the possibility of a thinking experience with its thematic introduction of the motifs of *Zusage* and *Zusprechen*) but is not yet fully capable of a "clear" hearing; he would be drawing out its echo in such a manner as to first open it to such a hearing, and thus to conception.

The echoing of the title, then, reflects language's reply to thought's entry into the speaking by which language gives itself to be thought. It reflects the *Zusage* of language as it is brought to speak in the initial (and initiating) steps of a thinking experience with language. The transformed title is the reflected saying of language itself. Heidegger makes this point discreetly but explicitly at the beginning of his second lecture when he reiterates the hermeneutic experience he described at the end of his first lecture:

If we are to think through the essence of language, language must first promise itself to us, or must have already done so. Language must, in its own way, avow to us [*zusprechen*] itself — its essence. Language essences as this avowal [*Zuspruch*]. We hear it constantly, of course, but do not give it thought. If we did not hear it everywhere, we could not use one single word of language. Language essences as this avowal. The essence of language makes itself known to us [*bekundet sich*: *bekunden* is to declare, betray, manifest, or evince] as the saying [*Spruch*: a dictum, a sentence, or simply a passage or text], as the language of its essence. But we cannot quite hear this originary writ [*Ur-kunde*], let alone "read" it. It runs [*sie lautet*]: The essence of language: The language of essence. (US 170/OW 76)

I pause over these words because Heidegger is making a most extraordinary claim. He is telling us (and though it is perfectly evident in the passage, it has proven unassimilable for most readers, including the translator) that his title, now transformed into a guideword, transcribes the speaking of language. The guideword is, quite *literally*, the saying of language. Language *occurs* in an exhortation (*Zuspruch*) that makes itself known or declares itself in this sentence in such a way as to be audible or legible. We have seen Heidegger work with the words *laut, verlauten, verlautbaren,* and *läuten.* Here, he adds *lauten,* which is a verb used in phrases such as *wie lautet* . . . — "What does the letter say?," "What were his words?," "How does the passage read?" — a verb used, in other words, when we seek the exact terms in order to seize meaning precisely.* The guideword gives the precise terms of language's primal "writ," its *dictum* that we do not yet know how to "read."

What is the status of this "dict"? Is it something on the order of an originary *text,* as the term *Ur-kunde* might suggest? Does language come to language in something like a writing? Heidegger's reference to reading might reinforce this hypothesis. And what would be the relation between the words of this *Spruch* and the words spoken by Heidegger in his lecture course and printed on the page of the book before us (the German, to begin with, but what about our various translations)? Heidegger asserts quite clearly that language speaks in the words that follow the phrase *sie lautet.* For in the immediately succeeding lines, he tells us that "what has just been said" (not "what we have just said," as Peter Hertz translates) is a *Zumutung,* an unreasonable expectation or demand, a "tall order" for thought that is not made by Professor Heidegger in the form of an assertion that might eventually be proven correct or false but that issues "from another source" (US 170/OW 77) — language itself.

But he also asserts that we can neither hear nor "read" correctly this *Ur-kunde* (presumably, not yet). The words are before us (or more precisely: *the word of language* — the status of "word" still to be defined here), but we cannot yet make them out. For as long as we are still attempting to grasp their meaning, we block our access to the speaking that occurs in them. The words do not signify in the sense that they would be vehicles of some signified, for language has given itself in these words im-mediately. As Heidegger repeats twice in the passage we have been reading, "Language essences as this avowal [*Zuspruch*]" (US 170/OW 76; the repetition of the phrase is obscured in the translation). Its "avowal" or exhortation† is the event in which language first comes about in its essence. Language's very occurrence is what declares itself, manifests itself (*bekundet sich*) in the *Spruch* that is the guideword. Whatever "translation," "transcription," or "transmitting" is occurring in language's passage into or from the *Spruch,* this movement cannot be thought as signification in any tra-

---

*We find it also in a phrase such as *das Urteil lautet auf Tod:* "The sentence is death"; we might be reminded here of the *Geheiss* of language's *Spruch.*

†We will see shortly that this exhortation must be thought in relation to language's *Zumutung,* its "unreasonable demand."

ditional sense of the term. Indeed, all the words I have adduced with "trans-" are misleading in that they inevitably suggest that "something," a signified, is being carried over into the words, when in fact that speaking that occurs in the guideword is originary for language (even if the guideword, as we will see, does no more than "hint" at what is occurring there: we are in the same "allegorical" structure as the one defined in "The Origin of the Work of Art").[8] Language is *saying* itself in the guideword, or *being said* — phrases that should be heard *almost* transitively, which is to say, in something close to the middle voice. Language is *saying* itself in the guideword; it "says" its coming about.

But if this transcription or transmission of language is not to be understood as a mode of signification or communication (unless we understand communication in a more immediate sense: as when we speak of the communication of a disease or a passion — or perhaps the communication of aesthetic pleasure; we will see Benjamin develop such a notion of immediacy), it nevertheless involves a form of articulation. For our listening to the words im-mediately before us (or our reading) must derive its "clarity," Heidegger suggests, from the saying of language itself. Two paragraphs before the passage I have been commenting upon, Heidegger writes, "This is what constitutes the peculiar property of listening: it receives its definiteness [*Bestimmtheit*] and clarity [*Deutlichkeit*] from what indications the grant gives to it [*was ihm durch die Zusage bedeutet wird*]" (US 169/OW 76). *Deutlichkeit* suggests distinctness, clarity. The hearing is distinct because the speaking articulates itself in such a manner as to be audible or legible. What it intimates, conveys, or signifies (*bedeutet*) lends to hearing the capacity to construe (*deuten*) in a precise manner. There must be an articulation of some kind in the *opening* (which is the very opening of meaning) by which language approaches and gives itself to be heard. But does the "listening" merely receive what is distinctly audible or legible? Our reading of "Language" and the thematics of reply in this same essay would suggest that listening or reading must itself articulate that to which it "corresponds" and which it brings to speech. Hearing does not merely interpret a meaning that is latent. Its interpretation, which must be understood along the lines of a *hermeneia*, as Jean-Luc Nancy has defined this term,* plays an essential role in making *deutlich* that to which it attends. Thus we may presume that however *Das Wesen der Sprache —: Die Sprache des Wesens* will eventually speak to us, its speaking will involve our (and Heidegger's) intervention. Indeed, I would venture, once

---

*See Jean-Luc Nancy, *Le Partage des voix* (Paris: Galilée, 1982); an English translation of this text, under the title "Sharing Voices," appears in *Transforming the Hermeneutic Context: From Nietzsche to Nancy*, ed. Gayle L. Ormiston and Alan D. Schrift (Albany: SUNY Press, 1989).

again, that the entire structure of this essay involves such an intervention: it is directed to making *sound* what calls thinking.

We cannot quite read or hear the words before us, but what they echo has nevertheless begun to sound, for the title, in its opacity, has "disappeared" (US 170/OW 77). It stood originally over the lectures as the name or designation of their object. But we must now think it from out of the "object" and as its address. With this shift in the title's topos, our stance has shifted from one of meditation on or about to one of advance from within (compare on this point the discussion at US 179/OW 85). The first movement of Heidegger's lectures is now complete as we prepare to take a "step" in the country that has opened before us. To summarize: the passage *by way of poetry* has allowed an initial, though still unclear, sounding of language's *Zuspruch* and *Zusage*. With these, a *Zumutung* has occurred that can be indicated (obscurely) as such. Thought now finds its country *before* it: "What follows, then, is not a dissertation on language under a different heading. What follows is the attempt to take our first step into the country which holds possibilities of a thinking experience with language in readiness for us. In that country, thinking encounters its neighborhood with poetry" (US 171/OW 77). Thinking is now properly on the way to language.

The question now is how to proceed in this "country," a term Heidegger has offered *in lieu* of "method" and after recalling the hold (in the mode of a *Stellen*, an enframing) that method has over the modern sciences. "In thinking," he writes, "there is neither method nor theme, but rather the country, so called because it releases, in countering, what there is for thinking to think" (US 168/OW 74).* Scientific or logical investigation cannot conceive this situation of thought where language is concerned, cannot even begin to conceive the "tangle" by which it is caught up in this "object" before it sets out to define it. Its analysis always lags behind the possibility of its own speaking, behind the event by which it is given to speak about language. No metalanguage can overcome this distance.

But the tangle drops away, Heidegger says, when we consider what is proper to the way of thinking—that it moves in the country, proceeding *from within* language (US 179/OW 85). When we look about in the country, the entanglement will fade away. How is thought to make this turn? What distance can it take from its situation in order to think it and move

---

*The German indicates that Heidegger is conjoining *geben* and *gegen*, the thought of countering and *es gibt*; it also indicates a "transitive" sense of countering—something that communicates with his later developments on reaching: *Hier gibt es weder die Methode noch das Thema, sondern die Gegend, die so heisst weil sie das gegnet, freigibt, was es für das Denken zu denken gibt.*

back upon its origin? The distance, or the leverage, to change figures, is given by thought's neighborhood with poetry. Thinking, as we have seen, is now in the country and before the poem ("In that country, thinking encounters its neighborhood with poetry"). And Heidegger adds: "This country is everywhere open in the neighborhood of poetry" (US 169/OW 75). It is via the neighborhood of poetry and thought — another threshold of sorts — that we go the way peculiar to thought. We come to where we are (and have been all along: the thinking experience has already echoed) by thinking the neighborhood as such.

The point is announced near the beginning of the second lecture but will take a full ten pages to develop — as though the step to which I have pointed remains as yet unthinkable (or is too easily thinkable: too easily represented and thus lost), and as though Heidegger wants us to understand to what extent it is a *leap*. Heidegger will begin essentially by repeating the gesture he made in pulling thought up short before George's poem. He will evoke George's, Hölderlin's, and even Nietzsche's path into song, arguing that this way (for George at least, who comes before an abyss like the one encountered by Hamann: "Wherein you hang, you do not know") "leads into darkness" and remains veiled there (US 173/OW 79).[9] Again he closes the door to the poem, but this time in such a way as to mark the relation. Thinking must leave poetry to its darkness, he says; it will not — could not — lift the veil. But in considering the poetic experience in this manner, thought implicitly observes its relation to the other. And he continues:

What thinking can do here depends on whether and in what way it hears the promise [*Zusage*] in which the essence of language speaks as the language of essence. However, it is not merely an expedient that our attempt to prepare for the possibility of a thinking experience with language seeks out the neighborhood of poetry; for the attempt rests upon the supposition [*Vermutung*] that poetry and thinking belong within one neighborhood. Perhaps this supposition corresponds [*entspricht*] to the imposition [*Zumutung*] which we hear only vaguely [*undeutlich*] so far: The essence of language: The language of essence. (US 173–74/OW 79–80)

The indirection of Heidegger's argument seems almost to declare itself here: something is left noticeably unspoken in this rhetorical alignment of statements ("However... for... Perhaps"). It is almost as though Heidegger is pointing to what he will not say as yet: that thought has access to the promise of language *in* the neighborhood of poetry and thought, and where this neighborhood is marked as such; that thinking the neighborhood *as such* will bring language to sound, and that thought must think the neighborhood in *such a way* (in and as a provoking response to the guideword) that the *Zusage* of language will uniquely concern thought. *Thought's* way of hearing and answering the *Zusage* of language, which only gives itself by such particular ways, is an answering to the demand to think the relation of essence and language. The answer, once again, *corresponds* (*ent-spricht*): the supposition regarding a countering relation of poetry and thought will release the countering word as such.

The path involves a multiple folding. Heidegger's aim is to lead us gradually from what thought can conclude from attending to the poetic experience with language toward a perception of thought's specific difference from poetry and a reflection on what is given to thought in and by such an experience of its "neighborhood" with poetry. He will move from *and by way of* what the poem indicates about the relation between word and thing (what we might call cautiously its "content" for thought — what it allows thought to thematize) toward a hearing of thought's language itself as thought begins to answer (already in this reflection on the poem) to what is demanded of it by its guideword. Already sensible to poetry's difference from thought, thought must now think the relation by becoming sensible to the manner in which poetry's relation to language, and hence its saying, differs from its own. Its manner of accompanying the other must mark the difference in such a way that accompaniment becomes divergence. In the "folding" of this divergence that opens as thought folds upon itself the possibility opens of hearing this divergence as it addresses or concerns thought — hearing the divergence *for thought* — and as the address of its own possibility. What thinking *can do* before the poem that veils itself, Heidegger says, depends on how and whether it hears the grant in which the essence of language speaks as the language of essence — how and whether it engages its own origin via the speaking that occurs in and as the demarcation of the relation between thought and poetry. It must come to hear the divergence *for itself*, edging gradually from what it can glean from the poem to what it can glean of itself in its difference from the poem. In bringing this differential relation to speech, thought can begin to entertain the question of what calls thinking.

Two paths, then: a path in the neighborhood of the poem that develops the terms of thought's *Zusage* (gathering the resonance of these terms as it gradually articulates their meaning in a reflection on what the poem has to say about language and thing — but this gathering will require its *determination*) and the path by which the resonance developed along the first path is played off against the specific resonance (in song) of poetic expression to make sound the neighborhood as such — *out* of which sounding, the *Gegend* may be drawn out for thought in the *Zusage* of a countering word. Thought is to go in the neighborhood of poetry in such a way as to bring forth the neighborhood as such and "for itself." The way and the manner of the way, as Heidegger reiterates in this passage, rest upon *conjecture (Vermutung)*.

In the pages that follow, Heidegger will underscore repeatedly that he is moving not by any logical deduction but rather by supposition, or "presumption," if I may push the hypothetical character of "presuming" in the direction of a certain audacity or daring. The risking of a hypothesis is here presumptuous: it is meant, in its very enormity (in a moment Heidegger will tell us that we must "conjecture" something that all of Western thought has failed to notice) to *provoke*. To provoke the auditor to thought, of course — which means, as we have seen, hearing something that has never been heard as such — but also to pro-voke what the auditor is to hear. Here is thought's *ent-sprechende* movement vis-à-vis what it is to answer to, its *anticipatory* move in relation to that to which it is to listen. It goes out ahead with a conjecture or supposition. But the supposition is in no way arbitrary, for it has been *prompted*. The *Vermutung* answers to the *Zumutung*, the "unreasonable demand" made upon thought in the guideword (the proposing of which, on Heidegger's part, is already one of the most presumptuous moves one can imagine in a work of philosophy — for once again, Heidegger declares that he is not the one who has written it). Moreover, the courage (*Mut*) for this *Vermutung* derives from the *Zuspruch* of language itself: the exhortation or encouragement that accompanies the granting of language's promise. Thought is letting itself be prompted; in this sense, it too shows the *Gelassenheit* of the poet. But its *presumption* is also peculiar to it. I have suggested that Heidegger is trying in *On the Way to Language* to indicate as much about the mode proper to the saying of thought as he is about the mode of poetic saying. Here we see Heidegger hinting strongly (though only hinting: by linking *Zumutung* and *Vermutung* and by repeatedly using the latter word) that the specific *Stimmung* of thought that determines its mode of proceeding is presumption.[10] Thought is called to no less audacity than it was in the 1930s.

Heidegger starts along the paths I have laboriously unfolded by returning to George's poem. We are not proceeding "blindly" toward the neighborhood, Heidegger tells us, because we are already attending to a poetic experience with language. From this return and those that follow, it is clear that there is no direct approach to the neighborhood as such, and that it is not a matter of getting past (in the sense of leaving behind) what is said in the particular saying whose difference from itself thought is seeking to apprehend. Rather, it is by appropriating more profoundly the "said" ("calling it over into thinking," Heidegger says [US 174/OW 80]) that thought will approach the saying. He recalls here that the last line concerns the relation between language and any being as such, a concern that is hardly foreign for thought in that it is one of the earliest matters to come into language in Western thinking, reaching it in the form of the relation between Being and Saying. It comes over thought in so astounding and bewildering a manner, Heidegger says, that it announces itself in a single word, "logos" ("Es lautet: λόγος" [US 174/OW 80]).

Was thought unable to *articulate* what spoke to it in so overpowering a manner? What is even more bewildering for us, today, Heidegger says, is the muteness of this saying (what is most thought-provoking, Heidegger said in *What Is Called Thinking?* [1954], is that we are not yet thinking): the saying of logos is not a thinking experience *with* language "in the sense that language itself should come to the word as properly itself and in the measure of this relation" (US 174–75/OW 80). Language comes to the word in logos and holds thought in its grip, but does not *speak* its essence in that word. The essence of language has not spoken in the word for the word as the language of essence, no more than it has spoken in poetic experience (presumably even in Hölderlin's thinking poetry, and even though Hölderlin himself is constantly working the "neighborhood" of thought and poetry).

Heidegger's evocation of his guideword in this passage indicates clearly that reflection on what the poem offers to thought has begun to respond to the demand of that guideword. The paths of reflection have begun to interweave in the manner I described above, and the "conjecture" Heidegger now offers is partially an answer to a meditation on language and essence. We can only conjecture, Heidegger says (and indeed, quite a bit is being presumed), why it is that from the earliest time of Western thought through the latest period of George's poetizing, the essence of language nowhere brings itself to language as the language of essence:

Much suggests [*Manches spricht dafür*] that the essence of language refuses to come to language, namely that language in which we make statements about language. If language everywhere withholds [*verweigert*] its essence in this sense, then such withholding belongs to the very essence of language . . . in which case we may no longer say that the essence of language is the language of essence, unless it should be that the word "language" in the second phrase bespeaks something different, in fact something in which the withholding of the essence of language — speaks. Accordingly, the essence of language does then bring itself to language in its own manner. (US 175/OW 81)

Heidegger then pushes further: "We must keep on conjecturing [*weiter vermuten*] why the peculiar 'speech' of language's essence passes all too easily unnoticed. Presumably [*Vermutlich*], it rests upon the fact that the two most distinguished modes of saying [*ausgezeichneten Weisen*], poetry and thinking, have not been sought out properly, and that means in their neighborhood."

There have been two conjectures here of at least equal importance:* a conjecture about the manner in which the *Sprachwesen* speaks, and a further assumption about why the *Verweigerung* (a powerful verb connoting "struggle," etymologically) has gone unperceived. The essence of language speaks as the language of essence in refusal, and such refusal is only audible (or is first and most easily so, for poetry and thought are the modes that are the most *distinguished* in their proper traits, whose traits are the most marked) via the neighborhood. To think the refusal, we must think the neighborhood.

But Heidegger is still reticent. He cautions against any figurative understanding of the term, and while he reminds us that we are already moving in the neighborhood as we consider what the poem says of the relation between word and thing (namely that the word brings the thing into the "is" by which it may be a thing and maintains [*verhalten*] it in its being, thus holding in itself the relation between word and thing: the word "is" the relation [*das Verhältnis selber*]), he insists that we are not yet in a position to think the neighborhood as such. A *thinking* experience with language presupposes we think the neighborhood, but we are in no position to do so, Heidegger tells us, and for fundamental reasons. Our difficulty is only a particularly distinctive case of a perplexity that attends all thinking and saying. We can think the terms of a relation, but we are rarely able to think the relation itself; how and from where it comes about, and how it is as a relation. *What is at stake in the question of the neighborhood is the question of relation as such.*

But in the description of this "perplexity," Heidegger adds (as happens so frequently in his lamentations about our incapacities) that if we cannot determine how the relation between poetry and thought comes about, we nevertheless know that the common element of poetry and thought is saying. Here again, he makes a step by presumption. Presumably, thought and poetry do not create their neighborhood by approaching each other; they already belong to each other by virtue of saying before they can draw together into a *Gegen-einander-über*. "Saying" would be the source of the possibility of neighborhood. Yet as soon as this step is made (which includes both the determination of neighborhood as a *Gegen-einander-über* and a determination of its source in saying), Heidegger draws back, telling us, in anticipation of remarks in this third lecture, that calculative think-

*One will note that Heidegger is following quite precisely here his earlier statement: "What thought can do . . ." (US 173–74/OW 79).

ing is hardly in a position to think the neighborhood, even if it "pervades everywhere our stay on this earth and our journeying in it" (US 179/OW 84). And once more he returns to the point he has been making now for over five pages: we are already in the neighborhood of poetry and thought, but we are not yet thinking the neighborhood as such. We must find a way to turn back to where we already are: that is, in the *Gegend*, before poetry. We are already *within* language, Heidegger says, letting language address us in its essence. Therefore — and this is the *third* time that Heidegger will return to the poem — we must not break off the dialogue with poetry. We must dare (*wagen*) to move back and forth in the neighborhood of the poem and hear anew what is said poetically. To which Heidegger adds, however, "we presume what may be demanded of thought, and with that we begin" (US 180/OW 85). Thought has progressed far enough to receive thoughtfully the demand that will occur in and with the marking of the neighborhood. We should now be open to the *Zumutung* issuing from the essence of language when it speaks as the language of essence, even as we attend to what is said specifically in George's words.

Heidegger had noted in his reading of the poem that its last line pointed to a difference between word and thing. Now he develops the notion by suggesting that if the word allows the thing to be, if no thing can be where the word breaks off, then the word perhaps *is* not as a thing is. George's line is furtive: as soon as we have an intimation of the difference between word and thing, the line slips from our grasp. But this is precisely the experience recounted by George's poem. Thus we are led to surmise that the treasure held by the poet was in fact the word itself: no word is available for the word because the word — "the word by which words come to the word" is no thing that is. The very elusive character of the last line has thus provided a hint about the word itself.

But what about the "is" granted by the word? This too, Heidegger adds, is not to be found among beings, like something added to them or placed on them: "Neither the 'is' nor the word attain to the essence of a thing [*Dingwesen*], to Being, nor does the relation between the is and the word" (US 182/OW 87). Nor are they nothing: they are there, given (translating somewhat severely and reductively, we read: the word is "given each time to give an 'is'" [*aufgegeben, jeweils ein "ist" zu vergeben*]). The poetic experience with the word, Heidegger says, has pointed to "something worthy of thought [*jenes Denkwürdige*] with which thinking has been charged [*zugemutet ist*], though in a veiled manner, from the beginning" (US 182/OW 87). We have come once again before the experience embodied in the word "logos," which proved to indicate something about the speaking that is of the essence of language: namely that it speaks as the speech of essence in a withholding. And once again, we are confronted with the "imposition" involved in thinking the guideword that says the withdrawal. The demand, we see now, is to think essence and its relation to the essence of language in terms other than those applicable to the being of what is (or to think without reference to beings, as Heidegger says in a later text*), and to think it from the basis of language's manner of giving itself and giving the "is." With its meditation on the word, the poem has indicated "what is there [*was es gibt*], and yet 'is' not" [US 182/OW 87]; read in the counter-light of the conjecture about what the experience with logos tells us regarding the speech of essence, it speaks to the guideword of thought.

Es gibt, then, names the manner in which language essences [*west*] as it gives a relation to what is — which is also to say that it names the mode of being of the relation between the word and the thing the word holds in being by granting the is, for the word itself is the relation. We must not say of the word, "it is," declares Heidegger; we must say, *Es gibt*, hearing in this locution, *Es, das Wort, gibt* — for the word is what gives: it gives to be. At the start of the paragraph we are reading here (US 182/OW 87), Heidegger introduced the motif of giving by remarking, "the word is charged each time with giving an 'is.'" The passive construction conveys appropriately that the "destining" referred to here is of the manner of an event (*Ereignis*) that is inseparable from the advent of language itself. Language is in no way a subject here, no more, in fact than the *Ereignis* in which it comes about. When we say, *Es, das Wort, gibt*, we are not hypostatizing the word as an agency or cause (again, it is no thing that is). The *Es* is nothing more, in a sense, than the reserve of the word that appears in and with the word's giving. We have seen that the word, when it gives itself to our hearing, gives itself in an originary fashion: its essence resides in its being given. So the *Es* happens with the giving: it first traces itself out with the giving, or rather marks therein its reserve or withdrawal, which derives, as Derrida has suggested, from the traction or contraction of the traits of the *Aufriss* Heidegger will shortly describe. *Es* does not subsist somewhere apart from what it gives; it comes about in its giving, and comes about as reserve. Put more abruptly: the word does not reserve itself in giving itself, in the sense that "it" would hold back: its reserve, "it," comes about with the giving.

There are no standards, Heidegger says (US 183/OW 88); there is no measure for determining what is said in the phrase *Es, das Wort, gibt*. The poet's own saying of the word's withholding indicates a kind of measure by evoking the way language brings near its withheld essence.[11] But the mode of this saying is wholly different from the saying of "*Es, das Wort,*

---

*See Martin Heidegger, *Zur Sache des Denkens* (Tübingen: Niemeyer, 1976), 25.

gibt" which is "scarcely determinable," and certainly, Heidegger says, not a singing.*

But the "measure" provided by the difference between the thoughtful saying as exemplified by *Es, das Wort, gibt* and poetic song will allow us to say something about the grant and the withholding that occurs in language's speaking. The nearness of the word opens to thought in and through the neighborhood of poetry and saying that is concealed (or so Heidegger would have us presume: *wir möchten uns mit der Vermutung befreunden*, "we should become familiar with the supposition" [US 184/OW 90]) in the very divergence [*Auseinander*] of their modes of saying: "This divergence is their real over-against-one-another" (*ihr eigentliches Gegen-einander-über*).

Nothing has prepared us for the description of this *Auseinander* that Heidegger now offers. Having produced words that say for thought the thoughtworthy (*Es, das Wort, gibt*) and that finally make it possible to hear the difference between poetry and thought, Heidegger passes to a description of the origin of neighborhood itself. We may say that he *names* the origin of neighborhood here — but it is important to recognize the extent to which what is named resists any representation. I cite the passage in its entirety, even though it is by now quite well known.

We must discard the view that the neighborhood of poetry and thinking is nothing more than a garrulous cloudy mixture of two modes of saying in which each makes clumsy borrowings from the other. Here and there it may seem that way, but in truth, poetry and thinking are in virtue of their essence held apart by a delicate yet luminous difference, each held in its own darkness: two parallels, in Greek, *para allelo*, by one another, against one another, eclipsing one another each in its own way. Poetry and thinking are not separated if separation is to mean cut off into a relational void. The parallels intersect [*schneiden sich*] in the in-finite. There they intersect with an incision [*Schnitt*] that they themselves do not make. By this incision, they are first marked, inscribed in the design [*Aufriss*] of their neighborly essence. This delineating diagram [*Zeichnung*] is the rift [*Riss*]. It draws poetry and thinking open [*aufreisst*: a tearing is also indicated here] to one another in nearness. The neighborhood of poetry and thinking is not the result of a process by which poetry and thinking — no one knows from where — draw one another into nearness, which first comes about thereby. The nearness, which draws near, is itself the event of appropriation [*Ereignis*] by which poetry and thinking are directed into what is proper to their essence. (US 184–85/OW 90)

A number of points must be made about this passage. We should note, for example, Heidegger's emphasis on the *distinct* character of the difference between poetry and thought, a distinctness defined by a play of light

---

*This is quite possibly a Heideggerian joke.

and darkness. We should note, too, the "quasi-transcendental" character of this difference. The parallels (and what is the status of *this* simile?) are not without relation, but rather cut into one another in the infinite (non-finite: not finite or defined); moreover, the cut they make is not of their own doing. *Schneiden*, I might add, has the precise technical meaning of intersection (of lines or planes) in mathematics. But Heidegger is using the term perversely to describe something other than a crossing. Inter-section here means incision-between; an incision by which the separation between the two is traced out. It would appear that Heidegger is playing with mathematical language precisely in order to subvert any representation of what he is describing.

But I would like to focus on the naming that occurs here. The incision traces what Heidegger calls the *Aufriss*, the "design" of the neighboring essence of thought and poetry. In discussions of the *Riss* and the *Aufriss*, Heidegger draws together and draws out three verbs: *reissen*, indicating a violent movement such as pulling, wresting, tearing away, or rending (its etymology crosses the English term "writing"); *ziehen*, meaning, as a transitive verb, "to draw" or "to pull," and as intransitive, "to move" or "to advance" (*Zug* comes from this term and can evoke among its many senses a drawing or traction, a movement or a passage, but also a stroke, feature, or characteristic); and *zeichnen*, "to draw," "to sketch," "to delineate," or "to sign." In "The Way to Language," Heidegger will also draw into this network *zeigen* ("to show" or "to indicate").

The motif of incision has prompted Derrida to translate *Aufriss* into French as *entame* (*entamer* meaning "to cut into" in both the sense of making an incision and the sense of starting into something). The term has the virtue of emphasizing the originary character of the incision for that which is breached through the tracing of this dia-gram and opened (*aufgerissen*) into its proximity with the other. The opening first brings a thing into its essence, starts it moving toward its proper being (but always in and by this relation to the other). The *entame*, Derrida notes, cuts a path, it is *frayante* — and we should recall in this respect that the differential relation opened here is in fact the path followed (and sought) by these lectures: the path that leads to the *Gegend* in the neighborhood of poetry and thought (and, as we will see, the path given by the *Gegend* which "counters" by giving ways and setting under way).

The *Aufriss* is thus the drawing of an incision that draws into movement: it "expropriates" the terms it both sets apart and exposes ("breaching" them, opening them to one another — though in an originary fashion, for this "breach" comes first) and sets them into the movement of appropriation. But the drawing also draws itself as it demarcates the distinctive traits of the elements it draws into relation (this is the "folding" of difference we saw in "Language"). It remarks itself in fact *only* in the delineated traits it draws forth — and not as a pattern or constellation, but in the difference of these traits or characteristics. Yet in so doing, it "contracts" with itself and "signs" in the manner of a "lay-out" (the translation has the benefit of alluding to *legein*) that joins into a unity the saying that is the essence of language. It signs invisibly in so contracting, thus giving itself in withdrawal, but it nonetheless *gathers* in this self-contraction. Heidegger stresses this gathering character of the *Aufriss* when he names it in "The Way to Language" (more demonstratively, but no less abruptly than in "The Essence of Language") the "unity" of the essence of language. It is what draws together as it draws out with its design the various traits of this essence:

May the sought-for unity of the essence of language be called the *Aufriss*. The name calls upon us [language is speaking in this term: we are called by it even as we call with it] to discern with greater clarity what is proper to the essence of language. *Riss* is the same word as *ritzen*. We know *Riss* only in its debased meaning, as for example: a fissure or crack in the wall [*Riss in der Wand*]. But in dialect, cutting furrows is still called today breaking open and clearing a field. The furrows open up the field so that it may shelter seed and growth. The de-sign is the whole of the traits of that delineating drawing that joins together and prevails throughout the open, unlocked freedom of language. The design is the delineating drawing of the essence of language. (US 240/OW 121)

The *Aufriss* is thus an incision, a drawing (apart, out, forth, toward, together) that is essentially a de-marcating or delineation, and a *self-demarcating* by which language gathers its essence and gives itself in the nearness of withdrawal. Language would not give itself — and it *must* give itself to humankind in order to come about — if it did not re-trace itself, contract with humankind. But this contracting, once again, is also a withdrawing or a re-traction, for language must also re-cede if we are to speak. We should remember that the demarcating we are dealing with in this essay is initially the de-marcating of the modes of speech. Language *articulates* itself in the difference between thought and poetry (perhaps principally, but certainly most distinctly), and then in all modes of discursive engagement with the essence of language — perhaps *all* modes of discourse, and certainly all those Heidegger designated as *technē* in the 1930s. These articulations join in defining the unity of language's unfolding, as we will see in "The Way to Language" (the relations between the spoken, the unspoken, speakers, and what is spoken about: i.e., the entire structure of the relation [*Ver-hältnis*] between humankind, word, and thing that makes it possible for humankind to say "is" of something). Thus they articulate what Heidegger once called the meaning of Being and which he now thinks from the *Gegen-einander-über* of the fourfold. The *Gegen-einander-über* of the modes of saying, as we will see, articulates the *Gegen-einander-über* of humankind, earth, sky, and the divine.

Can one represent to oneself this differentiating movement? If we do not attempt to do so, it is hard to see how we might even *begin* to understand what Heidegger is proposing, let alone make a step beyond "understanding." Representation or a certain thematization is unavoidable. And Heidegger himself has been encouraging a kind of sensible representation, calling up spatial, visual, auditory, and even olfactory imagery to give this incision of *difference* to our understanding. But even if it were possible to make sense of all these sensible images (which would not be easy: the parodic description of the geometry of the "origin" of poetry and thought, juxtaposed with the image of the farming of Being, makes it rather difficult to see, let alone hear, the silent tracing that is the speaking of language) we would stop short of the linguistic movement Heidegger is engaging. Bringing us before the possibility of an experience with language is not a matter of making things more concrete or more sensible, not a matter of providing an illustration or any kind of *aisthesis* in the traditional sense. The superabundance of images is designed not to make the difference more sensible to us (via a kind of synaesthesia) but to bring us before the limit of the sensible imagination in leading us back to the word. This limit does not point to a realm *beyond* sensibility, at least as Heidegger would try to think the term; it is rather that limit of thought that Heidegger attempts to define from the basis of his definition of the *Gemüt* ("disposition") and the heart, and thus a certain "sensing" where thought encounters what is to be thought.[12] Thus while an experience with language cannot be an *aesthetic* experience, it will nevertheless involve a kind of engagement that may well communicate with the "contact" that Blanchot attempts to think with his own meditation on the image. I will be returning to this site of experience in my next chapter and to the motif of a "touch" in subsequent discussions. Here I would note simply that the images Heidegger mobilizes approach it only in their complexity and not through what they might suggest in a quasi-literary or figurative manner. In his work with *Aufriss*, Heidegger is attempting to lead us *in and through language* to an experience with language. It is not that difference evokes a rift that cuts apart (painfully), like furrows, and so on — or again, it is not simply this. These thematic or figural connections are generated as much by relays of language as by a stock of thematic associations from peasant life, for example, or from mathematics. The essential relays are the *words*: *ritzen, reissen, Riss, Umriss, Aufriss, ziehen, Zug, zeichnen, Zeichnung, Zeichen, zeigen.* Heidegger's foregrounding of his wordplay (phonically, and through the *strain* of the images involved) suggests that he is in fact trying to turn us away from any image or chain of images prompted by these terms and back into the language by which they are generated—to the point that we begin to think *from and through* the terms, and in such a manner that we first come to learn what "cutting furrows" means from the basis of the word *Aufriss*, and not the other way around, as would be the case if we were dealing with a figure. We must think *from the word "Aufriss"* and through its inscription in a verbal chain. *Aufriss* cuts the path (or furrow) for thought.[13]

This is not to say that thought simply receives its direction, or takes dictation, from language. *Aufriss* is as much *wrested* from the German language as it is received from it. There is perhaps a kind of pattern latent in the words *ritzen, reissen, ziehen, zeichnen*, and so on (or even "wrest" itself, whose etymology passes by way of the Old Norse *reista*, "to wring" or "to bend"). But an initiative has been required to draw these terms together on the topic of language and to draw out the term *Aufriss*.[14] How else but by a leap of some kind could a thinking, even with the notion of transcendental schematism in mind, or Hölderlin's notion of judgment, come up with as odd a term as *Aufriss* for the essence of language? "Thinking cuts furrows into the soil of Being," Heidegger noted near the beginning of his lectures. It is clear that when he declares, "May the sought-for unity be called the *Aufriss*," and when he recalls the image of cutting furrows, he is himself cutting furrows. *Aufriss* is itself a furrow that will let us think furrows (and paths, boundaries, etc.). With *Aufriss*, Heidegger is laying out the boundary between poetry and thought, delineating their neighborhood—wresting from language the design latent in the "country" in which thought moves. But he is doing so in an *initiatory* fashion, so that language can first speak in terms such as *Gegend* or *Sage* ("fable," "myth," or "legend")—though one must probably say that the use of a term like *Gegend* itself is no less initiatory or provocative. Delineating the country (*Gegend*) with the word describing the neighborhood of poetry and thought first allows language to speak in its countering word (*entgegnendes Wort*) and to give itself in its nearness. There *is* no country as such; or better, no country is *given* before this naming. (Language is speaking all the time of course, whether this speaking is re-marked or not—we would not speak otherwise. But language does not speak explicitly in its countering word without such an initiating, provoking gesture; further, this gesture helps define the *way* language speaks.) And this is why Heidegger will be prepared to pass to the topic of "country" in the following paragraphs, which open the third lecture. The country has "opened," announced itself, in the neighborhood of poetry and thought, in *Aufriss*. *Aufriss* allows us to hear *Gegend*.

The status of *Aufriss* will come up again shortly, that is, as Heidegger begins to unfold the step he now makes as he draws together the weave of his reflections in a final "presumption." The contraction of the *Riss*, he says, is the source of the nearness that defines neighborhood (the nearness that *nears* in neighborhood). As such, it is the event of appropriation (*Ereignis*) that refers (*verweist*) poetry and thinking to their proper essence (US 185/OW 90). It is the *saying of the event*, the saying in which the event occurs and holds sway, and *thus* (here is the final *Vermutung*) the speech of essence in which language addresses to us its essence. Addresses *us*, Heidegger emphasizes, for *Ereignis* singularly claims humankind in and for the saying of essence (US 185/OW 90). The silent tracing that Heidegger now names the *Sage* (a term introduced in the poem by George cited on the previous page) is the event in which language grants its essence *in order* that it may be heard by humankind and thus come about in its essence.[15] Has thought moved perhaps *beyond Entsprechung* (a countering of language) when it thinks the contract between humankind and language from out of *Ereignis*, that "locality" of the human essence* to which the step back undertaken here and throughout *On the Way to Language* is to accede and to which Heidegger referred in defining the way proper to thought? In thinking in itself what calls thinking, does thought reach the limit of language? Heidegger will not make such a move in this essay, though he emphasizes that we are now moving beyond the presumptuous step that brought forth the countering word with a further presumption. Presumption, it would seem, goes beyond "correspondence" to think correspondence as such, in the contract of humankind and *Ereignis*.

But we are anticipating the very last moves of the essay and the next one, which Heidegger now approaches by attempting to think the essence of language as such, or more precisely, what essences in language, and which is the way-making that belongs to the opening of a world. What yields the ways (of language) is the *Gegend*. As that which counters, Heidegger writes, the country is the clearing (*Lichtung*) that gives free reign, where all that is cleared, together with all that conceals itself, attains the free (*das Freie*). The releasing-sheltering of the country is that way-making (*Be-wëgung*) in which the ways are yielded that belong to the country (US 186/OW 91).[16] Any number of references might help to clarify what Heidegger is saying here, but I would point back as far as "The Origin of the Work of Art," and precisely to what Heidegger termed an origin in that text: the opening of a relation between clearing and concealing that is the ground of the relation between world and earth. Heidegger does not, in fact, significantly modify the earlier discussion; indeed, "The

---

* *(Brauch — Eignis)*, Heidegger notes in his margin (US 179).

Origin of the Work of Art" already thought the essence of language with the notion of the *Riss*, naming this essence, as in the present text, *die Sage*. But he adds at least two fundamental notions in thinking the opening of the Open. The countering of the *Gegend* is a proferring of world, a *reaching* of world (if this can be heard in an almost transitive sense); it is a way-making. Reaching (which picks up the earlier *Ver-halten*) and way-making are thought via the term *langen*, with which Heidegger approaches "way."

For reasons that are unfathomable (i.e., abyssal), Peter Hertz saw fit to leave Heidegger's developments on *belangen* and *bewëgen* in his definition of "way" untranslated, assenting by omission (by what mechanism? — despite themselves, these moves are apparently *in response*) to the condemnation Heidegger anticipates when he says, "it would seem that by thinking in this fashion of what summons us [*das Be-langen*], we manipulate language willfully" (US 186/OW 91). The passage seems to have been too excessive for him, even though he translates elsewhere, and often successfully, passages of at least equal difficulty. He catches the basic lines of meaning in this passage (which is to say, *not the essential*, as we should recognize now) but downplays the importance of the two verbs *langen* and *wëgen*, and, perhaps most importantly, the prefix *be-*, which evokes the setting into movement and the "coming upon" that Heidegger describes in his definition of experience, as well as, very possibly, the coming up over against of *gegnen*. He loses, in other words, the whole possibility of *thinking through language*, and thus the possibility of an experience with language and all this entails. "Thought with sufficient reach [*hinreichend gedacht*: *reichen* is the key term in this particular section],"[17] Heidegger says, "the way is what lets us reach [*uns gelangen lässt*]: what lets us reach what reaches out after us [*nach uns langt*], by being our concern [*es uns belangt*]" (US 186/OW 91). *Belangen* is understood normally, Heidegger says, as "bringing before a hearing," or "summoning," and it can be translated, perhaps not inappropriately for Heidegger's purposes, as "suing." But we are to think it in a higher sense, he says: in the sense of *be-rufen* ("to call to," "appoint," "assign," "convene," or "assemble"; as an adjective, "to feel authorized," "called to"), *be-hüten* ("to keep or preserve from": *to ward*), *be-halten* ("to keep," "retain," "hold"). We hear in these words something of a preserving (the preserving Heidegger elsewhere assigns to *bewahren*, a term curiously absent here, as is a term that would make the connection to language: *verwahren*), which works by a holding (the holding of the *Ver-hältnis* Heidegger is describing) that comes over and upon (conveyed by the *be-*).[18] Of course, the separation of the prefix transforms each of these terms in ways that rapid definitions cannot begin to capture (which does not excuse Hertz's omission because such transformations are at work throughout Heidegger's text). And of course there is the reference to a calling. *Der Be-lang* is another name for the *Geheiss.**

Heidegger's reply to the suspicion that his play with a term like *belangen* is willful or arbitrary is that customary usage cannot be the standard for the reflective use of language. What is decisive, what provides the measure (*massgebend*), he says, is what the hidden riches (*Reichtum*) of language hold ready "in order to summon us [*be-langen*] therefrom for the saying of language" (US 186/OW 91).[19] The reflective use of language (*Sprachgebrauch*) must let itself be reached and used (the *Be-lang*, Heidegger notes in his margin, is *die Eignis (der Brauch)* [US 186]), called upon (the *Be-lang* is also a *Verlangen*: a demand or request that connotes a certain need) by the wealth — the reach — of words. *Belangen*, thought or heard in its full reach, itself *be-langt*. The way to the saying of language, once again, is by words. As is the case with the passage we are reading, Heidegger's way along this path is extravagant, perhaps even errant — he is *reaching*, frequently it seems, in order to call attention to this path and to provoke a general unsettling of our relation to all of his usage. But he is not straying or erring with respect to the saying of language — the "errand," we might say, drawing on an ancient meaning again — which gathers thoughtful or poetic speech. There is always a contract. Heidegger *indulges* in wordplay ("indulge" derives from the Greek *dolichos* and the Sanskrit *dīrghas*, meaning "long": it is the reaching that answers to the *Be-lang* of language), but the reach of this movement is always held and measured by the speaking of language. Or so Heidegger would have it. Every time he wrests from language some new path, he suggests, language contracts and reasserts its law. There is no *Gegend*, and it yields no ways (*be-wëgt*) — that is, the word *Gegend* does not *speak* or *name* — before *Aufriss* demarcates its boundaries and cuts its furrows. The ways, in turn, only begin to be traced as Heidegger moves through *langen*, *wëgen*, and *be-*. In a manner that verges on the unthinkable (and hence uncontrollable, unmonitorable), the words and the wordplay come first. But this opening of ways or paths always moves in the circle of language's speaking (or, more precisely, the contraction of the *Brauch* that occurs *with* language and via its *Belangen*): it is the *Gegend* that gives ways, Heidegger asserts. Language has always already spoken; it has already struck (*sie hat schon getroffen* [US 185/OW 90]) — or *will have* already struck in every

*Indeed, following its etymology, it says the same thing: we are called to *belong* — the pun is awful, but it is in all probability Heidegger's. I note also that *der Belang* (undivided by a hyphen) signifies "importance," "consequence," or "relevance." *Die Belange* are "concerns" or "interests." We are close here to Heidegger's meditation on "thing" and "res" in "The Thing" (VA 167–69/P174–76).

initiative (this is part of its promise). Of course, there is no way of demonstrating this assertion;* we are at best in the realm of the possible and the "presumable," and Heidegger's words are doing all the talking. Only our experience, perhaps, of a certain pressure (a contracting and a kind of surge—the same pressure we feel when we cannot find the right word) can give us an indication that we are still on the right path. The way is always somewhere between *wagen* ("to dare" or "to risk"), *wiegen* ("to sway"), and *wogen* ("to surge" or "to swell"): words, Heidegger says, that are in the same stream as *Weg*, whose etymology reaches back to the Indo-European word *uegh* and which the *Grosse Duden Herkunftswörterbuch* defines as meaning *sich bewegen* ("to move"), *schwingen* ("to swing, sway, vibrate"), *fahren* ("to travel"), *ziehen* (here, "to go").

Clearly, there is no way of settling the issue whether Heidegger's own way is or is not errant, or whether his very demonstrative reaching with terms like *Aufriss* or *Be-lang* is an overreaching. But there is perhaps a way of posing the question that is not explored by Heidegger in *On the Way to Language* and that I would like at least to sketch before following Heidegger in the last movement of this meditation on what calls thinking.

We have seen that Heidegger names the tracing of the *Riss-* design, a tracing in which speaks the essence of language, the *Sage*—a word that connotes legend, myth, or fable (I prefer "legend") and thus some kind of fictioning or mimesis. Later, in *On the Way to Language*, Heidegger will suggest that the *Gegend* is not to be understood in relation to myth, but in "The Essence of Language," he clearly draws it from this context of meaning via the poem cited by George, and once again it was in a meditation on art that the word first appeared (to my knowledge) in Heidegger's work. As in "The Origin of the Work of Art," saying in "The Essence of Language" is thought in "aletheic" terms, and as such is thought as both a clearing and a concealing. It necessarily conceals itself even as it yields the clearing in which beings themselves may stand forth or withdraw. In "The Origin of the Work of Art," Heidegger described this concealment (*die Verbergung*) as double in character, and he described the work's "createdness" accordingly. Concealment, he wrote, is both a *Verbergung* (a term he defines in relation to the *Versagung*, the "refusal" in virtue of which things withhold themselves to the point that we can say no more of them that they are) and a *Verstellung*, a dissemblance, of which Heidegger writes:

*Though any time spent in an etymological dictionary will impress upon the reader the density of the connections Heidegger is making: the pull of etymological links is astounding—has Heidegger answered to it or discovered it? Undoubtedly, the term "invention" is most appropriate here.

Here, concealment is not simple refusal. Rather, a being appears, but it presents itself as other than it is. This concealment is dissembling. If one being did not simulate another, we would not make mistakes or act mistakenly in regard to beings; we could not go astray and transgress, and especially *could never over-reach ourselves* [my emphasis]. That a being should be able to deceive as sem-blance is the condition for our being able to be deceived, not conversely.

Concealment can be a refusal or merely a dissembling. We are never fully certain whether it is the one or the other. Concealment conceals and dissembles itself. This means: the open place in the midst of being, the clearing, is never a rigid stage with a permanently raised curtain on which the play of beings runs its course. Rather, the clearing happens only as this double concealment. (H 40–41/P 54)

Concealment conceals and dissembles itself. Thus there is an irreduc-ible mimesis in *alētheia*, or at least the possibility of a mimesis that we can never discount or ignore ("we are never fully certain whether it is the one or the other") — all errancy must be thought from here. The inscription of dissemblance in the play of *alētheia* (even the strange evocation here of a stage: granted, it is not a rigid stage, so what kind of stage is it?) has enormous implications for the nature of art and for truth itself, implica-tions Heidegger approaches here with extreme caution and even some resistance. Carried into the present discussion, it might also have implica-tions for the particular form of presentation (is it *Darstellung*?) that is involved in *staging* this process of bringing language to language, and in offering, so ostentatiously, a word like *Aufriss*. In art, it means that there is something like an irreducible figurality about the work. The work, as I have put it before, is *the figure of nothing . . . other than itself*,* and in this "allegorical" mode it offers the presentation of truth as a play of clearing and concealment. It offers truth in its concealment. Concealment "con-ceals and dissembles itself." But if concealment simply concealed itself (or in regard to language, if withdrawal did not mark itself somehow), the event of truth would not appear. In art, how would concealment appear *except* by dissembling itself, by dissembling itself in semblance, in the *Schein* of art? Heidegger would assert that this play is *double*, that there is both *Verbergung* and *Verstellung* (and if there were not, difference would dissolve in a dissemination so fluid that any talk of truth would be beside the point, or the play); but how could one determine where the dissem-blance ends? Once he inscribes *Verstellung* in truth, Heidegger's claims for the gathering and defining character of truth in art (and all *Darstellung*, I would suggest) are subject to a constant unsettling.

There is an irreducible "figurality" about art, it would seem, that neces-

---

***Heidegger: Thought and Historicity*, expanded edition (Ithaca, N.Y.: Cornell University Press, 1993), 150.

sarily marks the saying that is its source and that Heidegger describes as "poetry." But if this is the case, how does the meditation that passes *by way of poetry* maintain the distinction between thought and poetry (at least as Heidegger describes it: as a delicate yet luminous difference)? If the borders of art are fluid or unstable, how could the distinction be drawn with any sharpness or clarity, and how could the borders be kept intact? Further, when it comes to naming the event of saying with a term like *Aufriss* (guided as we might be by the "hidden riches of language" — but don't these have something of a shimmering quality? aren't puns, as Gerald Bruns reminds us, notoriously unstable?), how are we to tell the difference between a proper use of a term and a "debased" use: between *Aufriss* as "furrow," for example, and *Aufriss* as "crack in the wall"?[20] The point is to move beyond figural or thematic meaning and toward the event that gives such meaning, but the figure or the theme, the signified, let us say, is ultimately irreducible. Thematic meaning attends every step as that *from which we move* in proceeding toward *Ereignis* and in choosing the path of language even as we let it speak (*Gelassenheit*). Heidegger is clearly concerned with controlling the difference between proper and improper even as he moves toward a notion of linguistic correspondence and indication (by hint, etc.) for which this distinction lacks pertinence. But how is Heidegger to preserve *Aufriss* from contamination by a term like *Aufreissen* in its crude connotation of a violent sexual appropriation? (Particularly since he cannot help recalling, consciously or otherwise, Creon's words to Haemon after he pronounced Antigone's death sentence: "There will be other fields . . .") How can we be certain this discussion of the *Riss* is not governed by the pull of a sexual metaphor? And would this be a generalized detour on the way to language, or something that goes directly to the matter? In general, how do we tell the proper from the improper when we answer the *Be-lang* of language and move to the extreme or the threshold that Heidegger seeks to occupy when he offers a name for the essence of language? Granted, Heidegger is pointing clearly to the singular and even contingent character of the name *Aufriss*. We cannot even exclude the possibility that he is offering it with a certain humor.[21] Of course, Heidegger is quite serious in proferring this word (this *is* Heidegger, after all), and the word works in astounding ways. But it is not clear that he is "seriously" offering it as a name, and it is certainly clear that anyone who comes away from the lecture with the notion that they have learned the essence of language with this name will cut a ludicrous figure when they propose it in "serious" discussion. Heidegger has set it up so that any "Heideggerianism" will sound absurd: one simply cannot follow Heidegger in the manner of a disciple without sounding ridiculous (I am watching my words). And if one denounces the jargon of authenticity without some awareness of the wholly *tentative* character of this language, one will have missed the point entirely. Heideggerianism and anti-Heideggerianism (in the form of denunciations of mystification) are simply mirror images of each other, proceeding from equally flawed conceptions of language.

Yet we must still ask: has Heidegger himself escaped the trap? How could he presume to govern the play of language, as we have seen him do? In general, how could anyone pretend to *legislate* when they speak in the name of language?

We started on this line of questioning by asking whether Heidegger's own way is possibly errant or marked by an overreaching, and we have determined that it is impossible to exclude the possibility. Once the question of mimesis opens in the course of this meditation on language, the distinctions and "counterings" we have considered thus far grow problematic. Which may simply mean *denkwürdig* ("thoughtworthy") and uncertain — something that is only a problem for a thinking seeking certainty. Or is the latter remark too generous? Heidegger's concern in distinguishing the proper from the improper has as its most fundamental motive the possibility of thinking a "way" that does not lead back finally to "method" and that will allow him to think the way defined by Laotse (to which he will turn shortly) as more originary than the latter — indeed, of thinking this latter way of method as a mere runoff of the more originary stream (US 187/OW 92) — and to think the former treatment of the earth from a more authentic "furrowing." He wants to control the relation between *Aufriss* and *Aufriss*, once again, and to be certain that the one is not a *Verstellung* of the other, each of them answering to the call of *Technik*. So the stakes are high.

But there is also another perspective on this danger of trespass, errancy, or transgression. For Heidegger has made it clear that the danger is unavoidable and, as such, to be assumed. The speech that would bring language to the word is unavoidably guilty, "wanting" vis-à-vis a law whose dictates are only issued when the law is provoked. (Which, of course, makes "guilt" a very problematic concept — for guilt here precedes the law and fashions it.) It is drawn out, Heidegger tells us, only in reply. Thought will always involve overreaching if it is to *be* thought.* The character of the errancy will be decided with time: perhaps *Aufriss* is another turn in the tropic economies of phallogocentrism, or turns, in its violence, back into them after marking a difference in its catachresis. But as soon as the transgression occurs, the possibility of errancy opens, and in thought there is no innocent or "correct" speech. Hence the necessity of recognizing and

---

*So are we in the tragic mode of Heidegger's earlier work? I rather suspect that the *play* I am trying to describe in this text points to something very different.

assuming the always *singular* character of the language of thought: both its evenemential nature and its strangeness, its *wanting*. The task for thought is to maintain a *free usage* of its language (a motif to which I will return in the next chapter): to presume to think (or answer to) the difference, while recognizing that there is no "authorized" speaking in the name of the difference. This is, I would say, an essential aspect of the "ethics" of deconstruction as a practice of language.[22]

We have seen that by the time Heidegger begins to think "way" after the completion of the second lecture, he has implicitly done two things. First, he has defined and *enacted* the structure of correspondence out of which the countering word of language is brought to sound for mortals: presuming that language speaks as the speech of essence, presuming that speaking occurs in and by the neighborhood, and presuming the *relation* between these assumptions. Second, he has thought this structure in such a way that the promise of language may sound for thought and present its "demand" — which is to think essence from *es gibt*. He has opened the possibility of *thinking* the relation between humankind and language *from* that relation and, as we see in the third lecture, as the way of access to thinking relation as such. Again, two points: Heidegger is concerned with thinking the way the human essence (as the essence of mortals) is engaged by the essence of language, and with thinking this engagement as the way of *thought*.

The concerns are marked discreetly but persistently as Heidegger works through the notion of "way" (in relation to *belangen* and *be-wëgen*). The second appears as Heidegger remarks that *Weg* holds in it, as an *Urwort*, "the mystery of all mysteries of thinking saying." In this, it translates the word *Tao*. Much might be made of this moment of exoticism, culminating in the declaration "All is way" (and what is a scientific audience to do with *this*?) near the beginning of the third lecture. But at least two things beyond the exoticism should be retained. If way and *Tao* say the same, if they issue from the same source, this latter is not the stream of etymology. With all of Heidegger's emphasis on word origins, he is not *grounding* his reflection in etymology (and certainly not in the concrete experience or entity evoked by word roots, as Nietzsche might have been tempted to do at a certain point in thinking spirit from "breath"). If *Weg* can translate *Tao*, it is because *both* "translate" in some originary fashion the "origin" of reason* (at least for an ear capable of letting them translate back into what Heidegger calls here their "unspoken," capable of a certain *Gelassenheit*).

*Which Heidegger names with both *Vernunft* and *Raison* — again, we are touching the possibility of translation.

Each "translates" in an originary fashion the originary opening of difference that Heidegger has now named a *Be-wëgung*, the country's providing
and opening of ways.[23] As such, they speak to "what first enables us to
think what Reason, Spirit, Sense, and Logos, properly, that is to say, from
out of their proper essence, mean to say" (US 187/OW 92). Out of the
opening of language that occurs with the tracing of the ways of the country, we gain the possibility of thinking what is *said* in words such as
"reason" or "logos"—once again, the possibility of a *thinking* experience
with language and a knowledge of what calls for thinking. Here, once
again, is the latter of the two concerns I noted above.

The first concern (regarding language and humankind) is marked as
Heidegger develops his notion of "way" in relation to that of the *Be-lang*.
The way, he suggests, leads to what concerns "us"—we mortals (the word
will appear noticeably when Heidegger returns to the poem)—in the saying of essence. It lets us reach what summons our essence in the mode of a
Brauchen; "*Der Be-lang*: what in reaching after our essence, *requires* it [*es
verlangt*—my emphasis], and thus allows access into that wherein it belongs" (US 186/OW 91). The movement of essencing (*wesen*), as we will
see shortly, *engages* the human essence: "*Es west* means: it presences to:
lasting, it concerns us, moves and sues us" (US 190/OW 95). But to think
the summons of the *Be-lang* in relation to the saying of essence,* we must
move back to think the way-making of essence. For this, Heidegger argues, we need the "lead" offered by the guideword.

We are in the country that "makes itself known" (*bekundet sich*) in the
neighborhood of poetry and thought; we have heard a name for the source
of this neighborhood—*Sage*, "legend"—and the assumption has been
made that in this word we have the speaking wherein the essence of language engages the human essence with its *Zusage*. But to think this latter
engagement in such a way that we undergo a thinking experience with
language (which Heidegger emphasizes three times here in the opening of
his third lecture as his aim), in such a way, that is, that our relation
to language is transformed, we need the supplemental movement of the
guideword.[24] What thought can do, Heidegger said, depends on how and
whether we hear the *Zusage* in which the essence of language speaks as the
language of essence. Answering the guideword, we have brought the essence of language to speech; we must now think this (via the guideword)
as the speech of essence in a way we have only just glimpsed, which is to
say, out of the *Nähe* ("nearness") that defines or determines neighborhood. We must think saying out of the way-making of the country (what

---

*In fact Heidegger will not do this explicitly in this essay, though the problematic named
as *Brauch* clearly opens here; he will only address the relation of language, *Ereignis*, and
humankind in "The Way to Language."

essences in saying, Heidegger says; *Das Wesende im Sagen*), and we must think this way-making as the movement of nearness.

This trajectory will only be completed in the full course of the third lecture. It is prepared (described and to some extent engaged, though to a certain extent we are also in the realm of *Vorstellung*) through a transcription of the guideword that incorporates what Heidegger has offered about the way-making of the *Gegend* and what he adds to this notion through a new definition of essence. After recalling rapidly its metaphysical determination from Plato through Hegel, Heidegger abruptly offers the following to explicate the meaning of essence in the second phrase of the guideword, underscoring that one cannot get from the first half of the guideword to the second from the basis of the traditional concept:

The word "essence" no longer means now what something is. We hear "essence" as a verb, "essencing" [*wesend*] as in being present [*anwesend*] or "being absent" [*abwesend*]. "Essence" implies "lasting" [*währen*] or "staying" [*weilen*]. But the phrase *Es west* says more than only: it lasts and continues. *Es west* [Heidegger is echoing the *es gibt*] means: it presences to, lasting it concerns us, moves and summons us [*Es west an, während geht es uns an, be-wëgt und be-langt uns*: the *an* evokes a movement toward — it translates to some extent the *be-* prefixes here]. Thought in this way, essence names the persisting, what concerns us in all things [*in allem Angehende*] because it moves and makes a way for all things. Therefore, the second phrase in the guideword, "the language of essence," says this: language belongs to this essencing, is proper to what moves all things as what is most proper to it. The all-moving moves in that it speaks. (US 190/OW 95)

Essence, as we see, names the movement of the country, a movement of way-making that occurs properly in the speaking of language. But to underscore the almost *vorstellende* character of this substitution of one definition of essence for another, Heidegger observes that it is still not clear how we are to think essence, and that the meaning of "speaking" here is even more obscure. To *think* these terms, he suggests, we must recall that we are following the guideword from the place we have reached in our meditation on neighborhood. To the extent that the guideword hints, Heidegger says, it can only offer a hint about the nearness that determines the neighborhood demarcated by saying. Nearness and saying have already appeared furtively together (and already in answer to the demand of the guideword inasmuch as the meditation on neighborhood answered its *Zumutung*), but now we are to think them as the same — which is to say, as we will see, *in relation*. The relation of essence and language is to be thought out of the relation of nearness and *Sage*, the one articulating the other as the source of the relations drawn out as language reaches between the elements of the fourfold in such a way as to let each reach its own. A mean demand, Heidegger says.[25] But he adds that if we were to reach where the newly transcribed guideword hints, we would reach what would enable us to undergo an experience with language, namely, the relation of essence and language as it involves the *human* engagement in the speaking of essence. The transcribed guideword runs as follows: "That which concerns us as language receives its determination from out of the saying as the all-moving that moves in opening ways" (*Das, was uns als die Sprache angeht, empfängt seine Bestimmung aus die Sage als dem alles Bewëgenden*) (US 191/OW 95).

Could we perhaps have here a hint about language in its *Dass-sein* in this reference to the determination that gives language to us in its being? This determination (a term marked presumably in the original guideword by the colon) is to be thought as something like the speaking of essence, in a most active sense, and where the genitive is both subjective and objective; a speaking of essence that is the drawing out of and the drawing into relation whereby essence comes about as what engages us. What determines in the *Sage*, Heidegger has told us, is the *Nähe* (US 190/OW 95); thus in the reaching of the country's way-making by which everything reaches its own (and to which language belongs "most properly"), language "nears" as what concerns us. The guideword bespeaks something like the nearing of language (the genitive again subjective and objective) in the mode of *es gibt*. If we can approach that nearing, we will be able to undergo an experience with language.

But the hint is limited in its reach — and perhaps precisely by its definitional (and in this, *vorstellende*) character; it is as though we have once again hit the limit marked by the problem of thinking neighborhood as such. A hint, Heidegger says, can point simply and in such a manner that we release ourselves univocally in the direction it indicates (in short, it can sweep us away). But it can also work doubly so as to caution us *away* from something while *against* this pointing to something we can only begin to surmise (*vermuten*) as being thoughtworthy. Heidegger has begun to move us away from the received definition of essence; he begins now to engage in a transformation of the received concept of speech in such a way as to restage the relation of nearness and saying.

Language has been conceived, he says, from the basis of what presents itself most immediately — the phenomenon of speaking as it occurs in humankind: "the activation of the organs of speech, mouth, lips and tongue" (US 191/OW 96). The very name for language in the Western languages attests to this experience of language: *Glossa, lingua, langue*. But these elements of the phonetic phenomenon of speech are also understood essentially in relation to their conveying of a meaning or a signified of some kind: the tongue conveys the holy spirit. For the articulation of signifier and signified, Heidegger cites the famous passage from *On Interpretation* in which Aristotle describes the sign-structure linking letters, sounds, the passions of the soul, and the matters of which the latter give representations. Heidegger's claim that this is the "standard for all later considerations of language" has been demonstrated powerfully by Derrida in *Of Grammatology*.

Thus Heidegger's target in his deconstruction of the traditional concept of language is the sign structure, conceived as the articulation of a phonic (or even written) substance and the meaning it would convey. And as I have noted, he will proceed to displace this structure by focusing upon the "physical" character of language and by attempting to think it in relation to the opening of the fourfold (or the granting of world, as Heidegger has spoken of it thus far in his essay). The "physical" offers itself as a starting point because it is the closest to hand: what most immediately presents itself of a phenomenon that is taken to be the determining property of humankind. Since it is what is most immediate, most available to study, we might easily be tempted to think of it as the most familiar; yet when we consider the evacuation of the physical character of language through its subsumption in meaning, it begins to emerge as the least familiar. In this regard, we might well think of Celan's reference to Lucile's words in Georg Büchner's *Danton's Death*. She sees the other speaking, and Celan's own effort in reading Büchner will be to achieve such a relation to the language of the text. Or we might recall Blanchot's meditation on the material character of the letter in "Literature and the Right to Death" and his approach thereby to a kind of uncanny presence in language. I will be returning to these cases; but with these texts in mind, as well as Heidegger's meditation on the earth, we will recognize that Heidegger is now approaching this most familiar aspect of language, its "physical" character, as what is most difficult of access.

But he is also proceeding again by *counterpoint*, restaging the problem of saying and nearness, as I have suggested, through a renewed juxtaposition of poetry and thought. A simplistic way of understanding what happens here would go as follows: If thinking together nearness and saying is such a mean demand, it is in part because it is so exceedingly difficult to make what Heidegger has presumed *sensible*. No passage of this essay has been more "abstract" than the last reflection on the guideword, in part because it is so caught up by the language of philosophy. And from the beginning, Heidegger has aimed to bring his auditors before an *experience* with language. Thus we might be tempted to wonder once more whether he is circling back to re-mark the possibility of a certain *aisthesis*. But even apart from the considerations I noted earlier, it would be simplistic — in fact, it would be a regression to the metaphysical notions Heidegger has just denounced in evoking the traditional structure of the sign — to conclude here that the juxtaposition of poetry and thought has been serving all along merely to render an abstract thought more concrete (a classic configuration of the relation of poetry and thought, the one *exemplifying* the other). For the point is to offer the possibility of experiencing the "thingliness" or "physicality" of language in its *Dass-sein* and to offer access thereby to a thought of the finitude of language in its character as the *threshold* of relation (recalling here the central motif of my reading of "Language"). The "fact" of language as it offers itself in its *Dass-sein* as the speaking of essence (as such, the opening of and to the movement of way-making: *that there is language*) is the access to a thought of relation. To put this schematically and to give some measure of what is happening here, we might say that Heidegger is restaging "The Origin of the Work of Art" in this penultimate movement of his meditation: he is offering— "producing," we might even say, in light of the movement of preparation — a poetic saying in which earth emerges in relation to world in precisely the way described in the earlier essay. And from the createdness of this saying, the "allegorical" character of its "that," he will move to the "nearness" that gathers the relations of the fourfold. He is staging, in other words, the thinking experience of art to which "The Origin of the Work of Art" points but which it only begins to engage. The play of art and truth presented in "The Origin of the Work of Art" is thought with much greater scope here (and much greater *resonance* considering the way of this meditation, for it is being thought out of the neighborhood of poetry and thought) as the relation between saying and nearness.

Thus, Heidegger is thinking the thingly character of language *by way of difference*, and in doing so he is aggressively avoiding an approach that takes human *Verlautbarung* as essential. But he is stepping back from the phenomena of phonetic articulation precisely in order to provide for a more concrete relation to language and a hearing that is not immediately hollowed out by the play of signification.

Once again, terms such as "thingly," "concrete," and "sensible" are all being subjected to transformation in the course of this analysis, as Heidegger reminds us in summarily dismissing all "metaphysical-technological" approaches to the physical character of language. He asks in this regard whether sound can be adequately conceived in relation to the physiological concept of the body — seeking not to divorce sound from the body, as we will see, but rather to invite us to begin rethinking the body from the basis of what happens in the sounding of language. To think vocalization and sound from the basis of the body is inevitably to introduce the metaphysical concept of the sensuous, whereas precisely the metaphysical pairings of body and spirit, form and matter are at stake here. The same metaphysical conceptuality renders problematic an approach to the sound and tones of speech through the notions of melody and rhythm (which Heidegger will nevertheless draw upon elsewhere). In general, the "metaphysical-technical approach" underwrites our everyday tendency to neglect the physical character of language — its "sounding, ringing, vibrating, hovering and trembling" — in favor of a conveyed meaning. We do so to such a point, Heidegger says, that we are not prepared to consider what it means to say that dialects are *Mundarten*, "modes of the mouth." The modes involved here are not "movement patterns of the organs of speech," just as the mouth is not the organ of an organism (metaphysically conceived): these belong, Heidegger says, "to the flow and growth of the earth in which we, the mortals, flourish" (US 194/OW 98) and out of which we receive our "groundedness."

So how are we to understand the essential determination of the *Mundarten*? Heidegger does not address this question specifically but rather cites the lines from Hölderlin's "Germanien"[26] that speak of language as "the flower of the mouth":

> And secretly, while you dreamed, at noon
> Departing, I left a token of friendship,
> The flower of the mouth behind, and lonely you spoke.
> Yet you, the greatly blessed, with the rivers too
> Dispatched a wealth of golden words, and they well unceasing
> Into all regions now.
>
> (cited in US 194/OW 99)

Presumably, the *Mundarten* receive their determination from the "flow" of words into "all regions," *In die Gegenden all* — a flow that is nothing other than the way-making Heidegger defined with his initial introduction of the notions of way and country, the stream that Laotse named *Tao*. Yet Heidegger does not really pursue what he offers here, leaving aside the motifs of sign, friendship, separation, and a solitary speaking, which will play an important role in "The Way to Language." And how do the ways of the *Mundarten* relate to the ways of the different discursive modes (the way of this meditation, we remember, is via the difference between poetry and thought)? Would the difference of these modes not itself have to be thought out of the idiomatic configurations of natural languages? And why, we might ask, does Heidegger say so little about the relation between languages?* Heidegger merely picks a flower here, marking the countering structure of earth and sky with its blossoming. A second citation then alludes to the event of the "flowering" of language that occurs as the word

---

*This fact is all the more puzzling given the importance for Heidegger of Humboldt's treatise "On the Diversity of the Structure of Human Language and Its Influence on the Intellectual Development of Mankind" (US 234/OW 116).

articulates the relation of sky and mortals in the event of *Ereignis*, marked for Heidegger with images of a glimpse and an illumination that Heidegger will develop in "The Way to Language":

> Therefore I even hope it may come to pass,
> When we begin what we wish for and our tongue loosens,
> And the word has been found and the heart has opened,
> And from ecstatic brows springs a higher reflection,
> That the sky's blooms may blossom even as do our own,
> And the luminous sky open to opened eyes.
> (cited in US 194/OW 99)

The essence of language as saying announces itself here, Heidegger says: an engagement of the heart and the tongue (the physis of mortals) in the blooming of the earth, and with these the opening of a "higher reflection" on the event of the articulation of the fourfold that occurs with the advent of the word whose "promise" Heidegger has been leading us to hear (and to hope for). The first citation named the gift of language, the second names the advent of a word that would draw forth and sound in the countering relations of the fourfold. The *exigency* attending the latter event — the need for the human word — is then named in verses that offer the *one* word that Heidegger would not have us "over-hear" in this context:

> Such is man; when the wealth is there, and no less than a god in
> Person tends him with gifts, blind he remains, unaware.
> First he must suffer; but now he names his most beloved,
> Now, now words for it must emerge like flowers.
> (cited in US 195/OW 99–100)

Again, the evocation of a separation from the divine, a bearing or enduring (the central motif in Heidegger's meditation on the threshold and his remarks on pain in "Language") and then a speaking that is demanded in the "now" of poetic exigency — a now that marks the threshold of a pure passage. The same now, presumably, marks the moment of what Heidegger once termed Hölderlin's "first lines": "But now day breaks. I waited and saw it come,/And what I saw the Holy be my word."* The "gathering" of the verses out of which we are to hear this "one word," *Worte, wie Blumen* ("words like flowers"), is marked in the "countering" of the three nows† and the tension between their imperative and what is demanded, which cannot be the product of any will. A fourth set of verses,

* "As on a holiday . . . ," in Hölderlin, *Poems and Fragments*, 373.
† The German for the last two verses reads as follows: *Tragen muss er, zuvor; nun aber nennt er sein Liebstes,/Nun, nun müssen dafür Worte, wie Blumen, entstehn.*

a variant of the latter passage, draws out this countering in another, distinctly Hölderlinian fashion (punctuating with *aber, aber, doch*):

> Lang und schwer ist das Wort von dieser Ankunft aber
> Weiss (Hell) ist der Augenblik. Diener der Himmlischen sind
> Aber kundig der Erd, ihr Schritt ist gegen den Abgrund
> Jugendlich menschlicher   doch das in den Tiefen ist alt.

> Long and difficult is the word of this coming but
> White (Bright) is the moment. Servants of the heavenly are
> However familiar with the earth, their step over against the abyss is
> Youthfully more human   but that in the depths is old.
>
> (cited in US 195/OW 100)

They name the sudden illumination of the countering saying (the *Sage*, thought from out of the *Ereignis* as the *freigebende Lichtung*) that is made possible by the "youthfully more human" step against the abyss and the relation of mortals to the earth: the countering saying that opens *in* the *Gegend* and as the *Gegend* that lets earth and sky counter one another and determines them as "world countering" (*Erde und Himmel zu Weltgegenden bestimmt* [US 195/OW 100]).

What is demanded in Hölderlin's "one word," of course, is nothing other than what the poet of George's "The Word" could not achieve, at least before his accomplished renunciation: a naming of the "most dear," presumably the gift of language itself. *Worte, wie Blumen* is not a naming in any traditional sense, but the manner of the naming to which I have just referred and the manner of its sounding as the word gathers and is gathered in its "earthly" character into the harmonious articulation of the fourfold. The latter is the attuning (*Stimmen*) of the world's jointure (*Weltgefüge*) out of which we may now think the *Bestimmung* of the *Nähe*. There is no naming and no sounding here in the sense of a phonetic *lauten*, but rather a "silent" emergence of language in its earthly character as gathered by the *Stille* of difference.

All of this must sound strange, Heidegger acknowledges; indeed, he would have it sound *strangely*. But if we follow Hölderlin's lead in thinking the word in the *Gegend*, he suggests, if we succeed in thinking the play of relations that gathers the poetic word and onto which it opens as it is "given back into the keeping of the source of its essence" (US 196/OW 100), experiencing the word, that is, out of what determines (*bestimmt*) the neighborhood in which we hear it, then we begin the step back to where we already are and think the "proper" setting under way (*eigentliche Bewëgung*) which is the *Nähe*.

I will not try to follow in detail the meditation that follows on space and time, though I would note that as Heidegger repeats the movement from received notions into a new thought of the essence of nearness, *said* in phrases such as "space spaces" and "time times," he stresses the manner in which the essence of essence *engages* mortals. Time, in its threefold simultaneity, *bewëgt* as the *entrückend zubringende*; space sets under way as the *einräumend-zulassend-Entlassende* ("throwing open," "admitting," and "releasing"). Thought out of the same that holds them, they are the setting under way of the *Gegeneinanderüber* of the fourfold in which the *Nähe* comes about. The *Be-wëgung* of the fourfold *is* the *Nähe* as the *Nahnis*. We may well find this last naming redundant, but the point would appear to be that we have acceded now to the *saying* of the event. *Nahnis* is of the same verbal status as *die Sage*. Heidegger has "translated" the unspoken in a thoughtful saying.

He has done so, once again, from out of the relation of poetry and thought — bringing the proper matter of thought (what sets thought under way, "the essence of essence") to the language of thought from *over against* the saying brought to sound in poetry. He has opened the possibility of a *thought* of the speech of essence, or so he now claims: *Die Möglichkeit ergibt sich . . .* Normally, he noted at the outset of this meditation, countering is thought only from the countering relation between two human beings (US 199/OW 103–4), whereas this meditation has limited itself to the relation of poetry and thought (obviously as the most distinguished, most distinct mode of access to the essence of language). Heidegger's reasons are convincing enough in themselves, but if we recall now Emmanuel Lévinas's doubts regarding Heidegger's subjection of the ethical relation to the ontological, we may well wonder what might have been lost. Why is it that when Heidegger thinks the particular engagement of the human in the event of *Ereignis*, he elides the engagement of two (plus) humans? I would not want to cede to the recent temptation to *claim* the ethical relation here (over against Heidegger, and in a manner that seems designed to *secure* the ethical). But I do think there is a place for wondering what might have been lost here, particularly as we approach what supposedly *distinguishes* humankind in the *Brauch* by which it is engaged for the saying of language.

The motif of the *Brauch* appears in a marginal note again as Heidegger asserts that we have reached what might transform our relation to language. We have reached the possibility of thinking nearness and saying as the same, that is, out of relation. Most immediately, this means that in thinking language as the relation of relations that sets all of the countering relations of the fourfold into play, we find *ourselves* (as mortals) within its play. This is what "bowls us over," displacing our stance in relation to language itself and all that is. But, more profoundly, we have gained a relation to the "summons" that occurs in language and by which human-kind is drawn into language for the saying of the way-making of essence.

Though he does not isolate the "contract" of humankind and *Ereignis* by which saying becomes *die Sage der brauchenden Eignis* (US 203n), as he will do in "The Way to Language," he marks the means of this contract with an abrupt introduction of the theme of death. Having passed from *die Menschen* ("humans") to *die Sterblichen* ("mortals") in his reference to the human implication in the fourfold, and then stressing the manner in which language holds itself back in its summons, Heidegger remarks upon the sudden emergence of the relation between death and language (*Das Wesensverhältnis zwischen Tod und Sprache blitzt auf* [US 203/OW 107]). This essential relation, he says, gives us a hint "as to the manner in which the essence of language summons us to it and thereby holds to itself, in the case that death belongs together with what summons us" (*für den Fall, dass der Tod mit dem zusammengehört, was uns be-langt*). What summons us is, as we will see in "The Way to Language," what essences in language, which is the way-making that involves the "contract" of *Ereignis* and humankind.

Heidegger is indeed enigmatic in this passage. He has already hinted at what he offers here in his remarks about the poet's mourning, an attune-ment, he said, to what withdraws. The relation of death and language, he says here, is to be thought out of language's withdrawal (*Wie das Wesen der Sprache uns zu sich be-langt und so bei sich verhält*). But he adds now that death "belongs together with what summons." It would seem that language summons *by way of* or *with* death. In opening to language, we open, or *have opened*, to death (mortals are those who can experience death as death), and are drawn to language by this experience. We are concerned by language *as mortals*. Thus the very joint of the *Brauch* that defines the relation between humankind and language, that *articulation* (the word *Weise*, communicating as it does with *melos*, is important here) by which mortals, as we will see, are appropriated to language and lan-guage is brought into its movement, would appear to be death. A strange "articulation" to which we will have to return in the next chapter. But here it should be emphasized that we do not "die" because language with-draws. In the withdrawal, we open to death *and* are thereby drawn to language. Death comes with language, and by death we come to language.

Of course, if death comes with language, then language's gift is strangely ambiguous. Ambiguous not only because it is the gift of mortality but also because it is not quite language's gift. In the *es gibt* of the word, an "other" gives (and this, Heidegger will tell us in "The Way to Language," is what is peculiar to language). Language's gift, Heidegger specifies here, is the "is," which is now given to thought with the word's "breaking off" as it is carried back into the *melos* it brings forth.* But with the is has come the exigency (*Brauch*) that moves the relation between language and human-kind. Death "belongs together" with what summons us, and it is via this belonging, as we will see, that we belong to language.

We might pause over the fact that Heidegger now summarizes what he has said about the *Sage* in naming it the soundless *Geläut der Stille*. Once again, death appears in relation to the soundless, motionless manner of language's gathering articulation of the fourfold. Which of these terms determines in this meditation the other? Death or stillness? Is Heidegger drawn to the possibility of stopping the noise? But we should be wary of too quick an answer. For once Heidegger *aligns* death and language as he does here, re-marking once again the relation of language and human-kind, he displaces language itself and keeps his meditation in movement. "Death" is anything but the end-term here. The reading of "The Way to Language" to follow will be devoted to this new setting under way.

*I would emphasize here once more that this is a gift *to thought* and names *what calls thinking*. Heidegger's concluding words are: "This breaking up of the word is the true step back on the way of thinking."

Free Use of the Proper

IN reading the essay "Language" in my first chapter, I gave particular attention to the relation of humankind and language insofar as it is determined by the "need and use" (*Brauch*) of human speech. Thus I came to raise a question about the possible disturbances introduced into language's articulation of the fourfold by the human word, *das verlautende Wort*. In my second chapter, I followed the movements of "The Essence of Language," focusing principally on Heidegger's "way" to language in this essay and on the manner in which the "way" folds upon the object, the *Sache* of this meditation, which is the way-making movement residing in the essence of language. Now, in approaching "The Way to Language," I will attempt to follow Heidegger's effort to think the way to (and of) language in relation to the *Brauch* of humankind.

This progression offers a formal semblance of closure, but I would not want to give the impression that these last developments will settle anything. For if this third effort at reading an essay from *On the Way to Language* offers the possibility of developing and tying together some prior concerns, it will also open further questions by pointing to a certain displacement of the problematic of *Brauch*** and thus of the question of the essence of language itself. At best, a trajectory will be completed, and the notion of the way will begin to move a bit.

Heidegger sets the stage for the displacement to which I have referred via a citation from Novalis's *Monolog*: "The peculiar property of language [*das Eigentümliche der Sprache*], namely that language is concerned exclusively with itself—precisely that is known to no one" (US 229/OW 111). In the course of his essay, Heidegger will take over these words in his own fashion. But he will not do so without questioning thoroughly the source of the identity Novalis finds in language's self-relation—or even the notion of identity that readers might have taken from his earlier discussions of language's essence (from the phrase *Die*

**As is common practice with *Ereignis* (*das Ereignis*), I will frequently elide the article that would normally accompany this noun (*der Brauch*), thereby "translating" the German into English.

Sprache ist: Sprache, for example). There is a *same* that governs the speaking of language, Heidegger will assert for his part, and this notion of a unifying same that governs what language "grants to itself" in and through human speech will allow him to assert that language speaks *alone*. But Heidegger will also complicate language's self-relation by inscribing it in his notion of *Ereignis*, unsettling thereby any temptation to take language as some kind of ground: "either the first or the last" (US 255n). He will oblige us to think the way-making of language as a movement in language and *of* language, and will come to suggest that what is proper and peculiar to language (*das Eigentümliche*) derives its peculiarity — in the sense, now, of a strangeness that marks it — from the fact that language is brought to its own in the *Ereignis* wherein the essence of mortals is appropriated to the speaking of language. Thus, while the motifs of *Ereignis* and *Brauch* will function in this text as levers for displacing the metaphysics of subjectivity that informs Novalis's *Monolog* and Wilhelm von Humboldt's treatise, they will also unsettle any interpretation of Heidegger's text that would find shelter in language and language's gathering movement (a powerful temptation for even some of the best commentaries on Heidegger). They introduce a play between the essence of language and the essence of humankind that offers this relation in a very different aspect from what we have seen thus far. Indeed, a certain "setting off" of this relation appears to be the very goal of Heidegger's efforts in "The Way to Language." We should read here again words from Heidegger's second paragraph that I have cited more than once:

If we understand all that we shall now attempt to say as a sequence of statements about language, it will remain a chain of unverified and scientifically unverifiable propositions. But if, on the contrary, we experience the way to language from out of what happens with the way itself as we go on, then an intimation [*Vermutung*] may come to us in virtue of which language will henceforth strike us with its strangeness and our relation to it as *the* relation [*das Ver-Hältnis*] will manifest itself. (US 229/OW 111)[1]

Not only will the way to language become *language's* way to speech, as opposed to thought's way to that most proximate but also distant "thing," language (we are familiar with this inversion by now); it will also be transformed in such a way as to name a movement that is the movement *of language* in the mutual play of language's "need" for human speech and the appropriation of humankind to language, a play that requires the notion of *Ereignis* to be thought as such. Thought from here, the relation constitutes both a *Fehl* (a lack, a wanting) in language, and a "bond" that delivers (*entbindet*). The point of Heidegger's meditation is to bring us to experience this relation that determines the way peculiar to language.

As in the previous two chapters, I will try to follow the full course of

Heidegger's progression in this essay, but since my primary focus will fall on motifs that only fully appear at the end of the second section (where the displacement I have evoked begins), I will move quickly at the outset, concentrating on the terms I will need for the reading of the third section. Heidegger's "way" in this essay is certainly integral to his meditation, though not as fundamentally implicated in the emergence of its object as it is in "The Essence of Language" (and the presumption is not as great). This is not to say that the essay is any less challenging in its own way — *textually* challenging, as we will see; and it is crucial to respect its "staging" and unfolding if we are to grasp how Heidegger is undoing any possibility of taking language as a foundation or subject and thereby removing the ground for the metaphysics of representation. But I do not believe we will lose too much along the way by starting briskly.

The way of this meditation is another guiding phrase, a *fil conducteur* (Heidegger calls it a *Leitfaden*, "a guiding thread," and also a *Wegformel*, "a formula for the way") that runs as follows: *Die Sprache als die Sprache zur Sprache bringen* ("To bring language to language as language" [US 230/OW 112]). In its multifold relations lies language's "proper matter" (*die eigene Sache der Sprache*) — the "same" that gathers the movement of language's essencing. But, once again, this "proper" cannot be thought apart from what contracts the relation that sets language under way. Thus, Heidegger's movement through the relations of the *Wegformel* — the way of language and of his own meditation — is to be undertaken, he suggests, in such a way as to "loosen" its weave and allow an experience of the bond that releases language in the manner peculiar to it, an experience that Heidegger links here to a kind of "glimpse."[2]

"All linguistic science, all linguistic theory and philosophy of language" (US 231/OW 112–13), Heidegger says, necessarily reside in the weave of the *Wegformel*. Thus, Heidegger's movement through it will also circumscribe these forms of reflection. Indeed, his first section appears devoted to a demarcation of language theory as it has unfolded in metaphysics, where beginning and end are marked by the names of Aristotle and Humboldt. In the passage from *On Interpretation* cited already in "The Essence of Language" but retranslated here, Heidegger points to a structure of "showing" or "indicating" that in its unthought character (specifically, the relation between showing and what is shown) lends itself to the transformation into a conventional relation between sign and signified that predominates in the Western tradition. Philosophy of language, he suggests, follows the destiny of truth, the movement from *alētheia* to rectitude; it takes language as an instrument of designation for what is present, and it takes language itself as a present being, representing it from the basis of articulated sounds conceived as carriers of meaning. This tradition finds its full accomplishment in the modern metaphysics of subjectivity in Humboldt's treatise "On the Diversity of the Structure of Human Language and Its Influence on the Intellectual Development of Mankind." In this text that has "determined the course of all subsequent philology and philosophy of language" (US 235/OW 116), language is once again thought from the basis of articulated sound and defined genetically from the basis of the activity of spirit (from something other than itself, Heidegger insists).[3] But as in the case of Aristotle's notion of showing, Humboldt's reflections on the historicity of an "inner form of language" that achieves the synthesis of subject and object in a worldview retains the mark of something unthought.[4] In speaking of the necessity of grasping language's origin as "closely intertwined with inner spiritual activity" and as exercising a "reciprocal influence" on it (US 236/OW 117), Humboldt appears to touch upon the relation between language and humankind that Heidegger will attempt to bring forth in his essay — or so Heidegger's query regarding the "interweaving" and "reciprocal influence" in his marginal notes would seem to indicate. Thus, the two limits of the metaphysical approach to language adduced by Heidegger (those defined by Aristotle and Humboldt) are open-ended and will in fact prove in the course of this meditation to mark the *same* limit: at the heart of showing, Heidegger will locate the relation that defines the historicity of language, the historial (non)ground of its "self"-unfolding.

The movement through the *Wegformel* and the elements of language that belong within it will proceed from an *Erzählung* (a relation or a narration) that weaves together virtually everything Heidegger has said about language in the preceding essays from *On the Way to Language* and that will issue in the possibility of naming the "heretofore unexperienced unity of the *Sprachwesen*."[5] In "The Essence of Language," as in "Language," it took the countering of poetry and thought to bring this word to language. Here, Heidegger's *relation* of the elements belonging to the *Sprachwesen* has sufficed to bring it to speech. Somehow, this narrative *er-zählt* as it weaves its motifs, it *marks out* (to draw from the etymology of the term) in such a way as to open beyond itself and onto that initiating incision that Heidegger names *Aufriss*. How?, we might ask. And more generally, what is a "narrative" in the language of thought? How might we characterize this departure from the language of representation, and how does it enable an initial engagement of the *Wegformel*? Heidegger provides no answers to these questions; he seems merely to propose to us a distinctive mode of articulation in a text of "thought," in the same way that he asks us to attend to the singing manner of poetry and the scarcely determinable manner of a phrase such as *es gibt* — in each case pointing to a use of language that is not simply representational or conceptual.

Aufriss, naming the design that circumscribes and composes the unity of the *Sprachwesen*, invites us to think that unity as such. From *Aufriss*, in other words, we can begin to think language's own boundaries. But before taking this step, Heidegger pauses to fill out his account and weave into the unifying design of the *Sprachwesen* the motifs of *Sagen* and *Zeigen*. *Aufriss* will remain veiled, he says, as long as we do not attend to what we mean by "speaking."

"Speaking" is defined, then, by way of a kind of transcription of the initial account in terms of both saying and showing.[6] Saying is thought from *Sagen*: "to show, to let appear, be seen and heard." Where something is said, Heidegger asserts, it is brought to language, which is to say, appearance (*Vorschein* [US 241/OW 122]). As we can begin to see from this definition, this new transcription of the forms of linguistic relation weaves saying and showing in so manifest a fashion as to call attention to the weave. But Heidegger is also working to draw the weave now into the design of the *Aufriss*, which is described as traversed or threaded (we could also say "furrowed": *durchzogen* — this would complicate the motif of the *sumplokē* in an appropriate way, unsettling any figural presentation) by the modes of saying and the said.[7] A multifold saying from different sources, Heidegger reiterates, traverses or passes through (*Das Durchgängige*, he calls it) the *Aufriss* of the *Sprachwesen*. He is evoking, of course, modes of saying such as poetry and thought, whose *Gegeneinanderüber*, as we saw in "The Essence of Language," issues from and draws out the saying that occurs in the tracing of the *Aufriss*. Precisely this *Gegeneinanderüber* constitutes the "manifold ties" (Hertz's translation of *Bezüge*) in reference to which Heidegger now names the *Sprachwesen* as a whole *die Sage* (US 242/OW 123). *Die Sage* would name, then, the "weave," or perhaps better, the "furrowed design" of language in all its modes, the totality of a differential articulation. As such it is decidedly not a kind of "monologue" in the sense that language would speak in one "voice"; rather, it is a set of differential relations drawn out in every mode of speaking that engages in some way with its source (engages in the manner of *entgegnen*). Poetry and thought are the preeminent modes for the fact that they turn repeatedly to their source; but every mode, scientific, artistic, and so on, is capable of this turn inasmuch as it is capable of speaking, of calling on the capacity to make an "is" sound. And inasmuch as this turn entails a measure of creation or invention (there is no speaking in the sense of a saying without invention), the differential structure of language's saying must be understood as being in constant movement.

Die Sage, Heidegger asserts, is not to be understood here in relation to its common signification as "rumor," nor in relation to the "essential" sense of heroic legend. In accordance with its most ancient usage (*Ge-*

brauch), it is to be thought from showing or indicating, and is thus *die Zeige. Das Wesende der Sprache ist die Sage als die Zeige* ("What essences in language is Saying as Showing" [US 242/OW 123]) he declares, adding that language's showing is not grounded in signs of any kind; rather, all signs (*Zeichen*) stem from a showing (*Zeigen*). Heidegger says little else here about the nature of this showing. He does not activate what might be suggested by the derivations to which he has indirectly pointed in calling up the ancient word *die Zeige*. For example, both *zeigen* and *zeichen* stem from *Zeihen*, which derives from the Indo-Germanic root *deik-* ("show"), appearing in the Greek *deiknynai* ("to show") or *deikmuni* ("to say"), or in the Latin *dicere*. *Zeihen* originally means "to indicate" (we noted this point above in relation to *Verzicht*) or "make known" and is used more particularly in the sense of pointing to guilt, accusing. If we link *zeigen*, *Zeichen*, and *zeihen* with *ziehen* and its derivative *Zug* via a connection with *reissen* (through *Aufriss*), we have a cluster of terms that indicate a "writing" that "moves" (sets under way) as it draws out or even "accuses" the traits (*Züge*) of what is thereby brought to appearance in the movement of appropriation. In everything Heidegger says about appearing, there is a strong pull of notions such as delineation, de-marcation, and the setting off (against) of distinctive traits (*Züge*) in the movement by which relation is established. Heidegger does little here to evoke the cluster of associations linking the tracing out and contraction of traits in the *Aufriss* to the movement of showing, but it is clear that the indicating movement of signs is to be thought within this movement by which relation is drawn out.

Thus Heidegger remains fairly allusive and seems almost more concerned here with the *complicating* effects of his weave than with the individual strands of his presentation. The principal reason for this would appear to be that in drawing out and reweaving the strands of *Zeigen* and *Sagen*, he obliges us to think each only in relation to the other, thereby disrupting any immediate apprehension (through visual or verbal associations) of what is said through the terms. This disruption and redirection into a play of language actually has the effect of opening perspectives and indeed "loosening" the web of the *Wegformel* as Heidegger moves in the direction of an increasing originariness (from speaking to saying, from saying to showing, and finally from showing to *Ereignis*—though always within the unifying "same"). We see these effects, for example, in the discussion that follows Heidegger's introduction of the term *die Zeige* and in his return to the question of the relation between the speaking of language and human speaking, where he asserts that the saying and showing that occurs in language cannot be referred exclusively to human activity. He starts here from the motif first introduced, *das Zeigen*, remarking that a *self-showing* marks the presence and absence of everything present as an appearing (*Er-scheinung*, the *er-* itself marking the movement of indicating) and that this indicating precedes all showing accomplished in human saying. From this basis, he suggests, we can grasp the sense in which all human speaking is first a listening. We are familiar now with this argument according to which all listening in the everyday sense is preceded by a more originary listening to language itself that first allows us to speak. But Heidegger has displaced the motif of listening with the motif of showing in a way that obstructs any understanding of the former with a common notion of audition. We must not privilege *any* intraworldly form of perception. We hear because language speaks, *that is to say*, because it shows. It speaks in its saying, and inasmuch as this saying is a showing, it lets things appear in and fade from all the regions (*Gegenden*) of presencing through the play of its indication. We might well say that the modes of saying (of *die Sage*) are modes of articulation of this latter play (*die Zeige*), but this articulation does not articulate in linguistic or other signs something that precedes it; the articulation of meaning (indeed *in signs*: *Zeichen* may well be the "hinge" between *zeigen* and *sagen*, though Heidegger does not seem anxious to win any new sense for the term *Zeichen* at all, being concerned only with displacing it) draws out in an originary fashion the play it points to and out of which it speaks. We hear this *articulation* between saying and showing.

Our speaking, Heidegger concludes from his statement on the precedence of hearing, is a "saying after" (*Nachsagen*) what we have let be said to us.* We let language's silent voice come to us in a *Sichsagenlassen* and thereby (US 243/OW 124) call upon the sound that is "already held open for us." And we can only allow it to come upon us, Heidegger says, insofar as our essence has been admitted to the *Sage*. We hear because we belong (*gehören*); only to those who belong is hearing granted, and such granting, Heidegger says, abides in the *Sage*.† Heidegger will take another step in defining this belonging in the third section as he develops *ereignen* out of *zeigen*, but before "accounting" for language's relation to humankind, he focuses on this relation and on the phenomenon of speaking so as to complete the initial movement through the *Wegformel*. Language's granting of a hearing, he says, allows us to attain the capacity for speech that marks us (*aus-zeichnet*, as he said at the outset) as humans. The *design* of

---

*The assertion almost effaces the human intervention in the speaking of language, but we must recall that the *Sichsagenlassen* entails in itself the anticipatory "listening" we have considered.

†*In der Sage währt solches Gewähren* (US 244) — through *währen* and *gewähren*, Heidegger is tying together a notion of giving or offering with the "lasting" or "perduring" implied by *wesen*, from which *währen* itself derives.

our being is traced out in and by language. Thus Heidegger insists that one cannot think of the relation between the essence of language as *die Sage* and human speaking as implying a separation, as though a bridge might be needed between them. Rather, in a striking image, Heidegger suggests that saying is the stream that in joining its two banks, *das Sagen und unser Nachsagen* (US 244/OW 124–25), connects them (*verbindet*).

What is the nature of this bond, he asks; where is it grounded? Language *needs* human speaking, he adds, yet is not the work of our speaking. So what is language grounded upon? The third section of this essay will make it very clear that in seeking after grounds we pass right by the *Sprachwesen*. But before taking up the ungrounded *need* to which he has referred, Heidegger recapitulates the movement of the meditation thus far and recalls the way taken and the admonition at the outset that we attend to the manner in which the way to language changes as language itself comes to light. The way thus far has taken two directions. The first (constituting the first section of the essay) traced the lines of the metaphysical tradition in its representation of language and noted the modern search for its ground. The second attempted to start from language itself and without grasping it in reference to something else; it attempted to "relate" everything that belongs to language as language. The second would seem to have reached its goal in describing all that belongs within the *Aufriss* of the *Sprachwesen* and thus would seem to have found and traversed (following the *Wegformel*) the way to language named in the title of the essay. But Heidegger declares that we have only just glimpsed a trace of the way to language. For the way can no longer be understood as a progression of thinking toward its object but must now be thought as a way proper to the object and by which we may come to it. The *Erzählung* brought language to speech, but in so doing, it just barely indicated something like the way by which *we* are brought to language and language itself is set into the movement described in the *Wegformel*. It indicated a way, but we have yet to think the way as such. Presumably, only when we think the possibility of the way itself can we truly engage with language.

The way to language, we have seen, lies in the movement by which language allows us to reach the capacity of speaking from out of a hearing. Language, in this perspective, *grants itself* a hearing and a speaking. The peculiar property of language thus appears to reside in its monological character. But Heidegger reiterates here that to think how the peculiar property of language conceals itself in this way to speech, we must attend to the way in which language's *Gelangenlassen* ("letting attain or reach") stems from a *Gehörenlassen* (a "letting belong"), for language can only grant a hearing (and thus a speaking) to those who belong to it. A letting belong to language as *Sage* holds in it what properly occurs (*das eigentlich*

Wesende) in the way to language. How does language itself come about if it is itself capable of a letting belong? (*Wie aber west die Sprache, dass sie das Gehörenlassen vermag?* [US 245]). We must allow what essences (*das Wesende*) in language to manifest itself by attending with greater instancy to what the sounding account (now referred to simply as a "sounding," to translate *Erläuterung* literally) has thus far offered.

Heidegger thus returns to *das Zeigen*, which seems to mark the limit of what we can "hear" in language and thus to offer a *glimpse* into what moves language itself. He recalls here the basic traits of saying as showing, describing saying as the "joining gathering of all appearing brought about in the in itself manifold showing which everywhere lets all that is shown abide within itself" (US 246/OW 126). And indeed, in this "self-abiding" we glimpse something of the *Eignen* of *Ereignis*, which "brings [*erbringt*] everything present or absent into its own, out of which it indicates itself [*sich an ihm selbst zeigt*] and abides in its fashion" (US 246/OW 127). But to catch sight of what thus "moves" or "stirs" in showing (to ask what showing "rests upon" would be to ask too much as yet, Heidegger remarks, but he is clearly continuing his step back to what is "closest" in language), we need a distinctive "look" — *Blick* — into something that is familiar to us but that we never seek to know. No wearisome research, merely (merely! — Hölderlin had to stay out all night for this and finally saw too much) a "sudden, unforgettable and hence always new look" into what sets into movement in showing (stirs, arouses, gives rise, excites — *das Er-regende*), that "first break of dawn, which first gives rise to the possible exchange of day and night, at once the earliest and most ancient" (US 246/OW 127). "But now day breaks!" Hölderlin writes in "As on a Holiday"; "I waited and saw it come/And what I saw, the holy be my word." May this be called, Heidegger says now, *das Ereignen*, marking with the prefix er- the impetus of the quickening in appropriation (*das Eignen*). *Ereignis* is the name for what sets into the movement of appropriation accomplished by saying as showing. It is not a ground or cause, Heidegger insists, countering the impression created by the constantly regressing movement of his meditation. It does not effect or make, rather it *er-bringt* (which without the hyphen suggests offering evidence, and with it suggests a carrying forward or into) and *er-gibt* (yields). It cannot be represented as an event or occurrence (though the *er-* brings forth strongly an eventful character), but is to be thought rather as a granting (*gewähren*). As such, it is the *Er-gebnis*: not a result — *Ergebnis* — but the initiatory granting that cannot be derived from anything else and first grants (*gewährt*) something like an *Es gibt*. It is *Ereignis* that grants the *Es gibt* that occurs in and with the saying of language — the *Es gibt*, as Heidegger remarks, that Being itself needs in order to come about as presence (US 247/OW 127).

I will try to develop the meaning of this phrase shortly, but we can see already that language's grant of a hearing and a capacity for speaking (its *Gelangenlassen*) rests upon the prior grant of *Ereignis*, which grants to mortals, Heidegger says, their "stay" (their sojourn: *Aufenthalt*) within their essence, bringing mortals into their own as those who properly belong. As such, Heidegger says, it is the gentlest law (*Gesetz* — I will return to the "gentle") insofar as "law" is to be understood as "the gathering of that which lets everything come into presence in its own, and that lets belong in what is fitting [*in sein Gehöriges gehören lässt*]."* It is the law, in other words, that speaks in the *Geheiss* of the *Geläut der Stille* (the law of the law, we might say), the *Ge-* in each case speaking to the gathering that works not by a positing or placing (*setzen* in the modern interpretation of "thesis") but by an assembling hold.

The way to language must now be thought in terms of the way *Ereignis* contracts with humankind, *in and through language*, but in such a way that language can first come to language. The way to language is both the way of humankind as it is appropriated to language (Heidegger uses the verb *vereignen* here)[8] and the way that lies in language itself. The latter, as we have seen, lies in the *Gelangenlassen* by which language gives a hearing to mortals and allows them to bring language to speech. But the *Gelangenlassen* is to be thought in its turn out of the grant by which humankind is given to belong to language. The way to language thus names a double movement: the movement of language as it is brought to speech and the engagement of humankind with language that sets the former into motion and gives it its way. Any meditation that truly follows language in thought must proceed from this double movement.

I speak of a "double" movement but must also insist again that the relation of *Ereignis* and humankind occurs *in and through language*. The latter phrase is meant to reflect the fact that *Ereignis* cannot be thought outside its relation to language — the relation (in its doubleness) being nothing other than *das Eigentümliche der Sprache* ("its peculiar property"). The saying of language "rests" upon *Ereignis*, Heidegger says, but he also asserts that saying is "the most proper way of *Ereignis*" (US 251/ OW 131). "*Das Ereignis ist sagend*," he writes. *Ereignis* appropriates the showing of saying as owning (*das Zeigen als das Eignen ereignend* [US 249/OW 130]) — sets into motion *das Wesende der Sprache* by opening its way (*be-wëgt*). Thus *Ereignis* is what properly *gives the way to language* and determines it in its saying (*Der Weg zur Sprache gehört zu der aus dem Ereignis bestimmten Sage* [US 249]). As this *er-eignend-brauchende Bewëgung*, it is the essence of the way. But this giving occurs *with* language,

---

* *Gehöriges* connotes what is proper, requisite or relevant, due or appropriate.

and thus Heidegger will come to write near the conclusion of his essay, "The saying that shows makes the way for language to reach human speaking" (*Die zeigende Sage be-wëgt die Sprache zum Sprechen des Menschen* [US 254/OW 134]) — a phrase that points again to the monological character of language and would almost seem to efface the movement of *Bewëgung* in which the *Sprachwesen* rests and to which Heidegger referred just two paragraphs earlier: "Through the experience of the essence of language as the saying, whose showing rests in *Ereignis*, the *Eigen*ümliche comes into the proximity [*gelangt in die Nähe* — the relation, as always, is to be thought as the opening of a nearness] of *das Eignen* and *das Ereignen*. The *Eigentümliche* receives from there its authentic determination [*seine urkundliche Bestimmung* — a determination that is a *writ* if we stress the *Urkunde*], something we cannot pursue here" (US 254/ OW 133). Of course, Heidegger is attempting to think precisely this determination by focusing on the *usage* of humankind that sets language under way and contracts the relation between *Ereignis* and language and by attempting to think it, as we will see, in its historicity. But what is not thought is the *possibility* of this very determination, which lies, as Heidegger says in *Time and Being*, in the *Ent-eignis* of Ereignis. It is worth underscoring that Heidegger thinks this most originary event as a kind of writing.

The apparent precariousness or even vacillation of Heidegger's formulations stems from nothing other than the unsituatable character of this *Eigentümliche* that must be thought "in the proximity" of *Ereignis* and thus out of the relation of language and *Ereignis*. The *Eigentümliche* is language's "most peculiar property," but it is something like the limit of the essence of language — that is, language's relation to an alterity (though this last term is probably not appropriate for *Ereignis*, for we are trying to think the origin of difference in its finitude), or to put this even more precisely, the alterity "proper" to it.

Once again, in thinking the way that constitutes *das Eigentümliche* of language's essence, the *er-eignend-brauchende Be-wëgung*, we are at the limit of language, thinking what determines it in its saying. And thus, to turn things about once more, it may not be quite adequate to say, as I did above, that the relation of *Ereignis* and humankind (which opens the way and *is* the way language comes to speech) occurs in and through language. For we must also say that language occurs — comes to itself — in and by this relation. The appropriation of humankind to its essence is not properly *prior* to language (in the sense of a condition), because all appropriation, including that of humankind, occurs in a showing that belongs to the essence of language. Moreover, the appropriation of humankind is to be thought as nothing other than an assigning of humankind *to* language: the appropriating of humankind to what is said in the saying and *as* capable of answering to language in a countering saying. But if the appropriation of humankind is not *prior* to language, it must nevertheless be understood as in some sense *co-originary* with it, as Heidegger indicates by isolating the relation between *Ereignis* and humankind, naming it the *brauchende Vereignung*, or simply *der Brauch*. "*Ereignis*," Heidegger says, "appropriates man in usage *for itself*" (US 249/OW 130; my emphasis). By thus isolating the relation between *Ereignis* and humankind, Heidegger breaks the apparently closed circulation of language's monologue, by which it appears to grant its way to itself, and inscribes it in (or inscribes in it) the (non)economy of *Ereignis*'s usage of humankind.

If we attempt to pry too firmly at the break or interruption I am describing, or if we attempt to detach the relation between *Ereignis* and humankind from the *Be-wëgung* that occurs *in* the essence of language (*in der Sage ereignete Bewëgung* [US 250/OW 131]), in other words, if we lose sight of the fact that we are thinking the *limit* of the *Sprachwesen*, we will hypostatize the terms of the relations involved here and lose hold precisely of the *relational* character out of which they are to be thought.[9] But we should remember at the same time that this effort to mark the limit of language and to think it from the basis of the relation between *Ereignis* and humankind is the very point of this essay (I refer again to the last sentence of the essay's second paragraph), and we should pause to consider what is at stake in this almost laborious effort. Of course, Heidegger is answering the demands of the "step back," the exigency of what calls to thinking — he is answering a "logic" of sorts. But what purpose does this emphasis on the human relation serve, or what happens with this emphasis? We have an important clue, I believe, in the citations of Goethe that furnish a precedent for the usage of *eignen* in its proximity to *zeigen* and *zeichnen*. Indeed, it would seem that only the richness of the penultimate line of the six cited (of which I will cite the last two) motivate Heidegger's curious turn to Goethe at this moment in the essay:

> Nur weil es dem Dank sich eignet
> Ist das Leben schätzenswert.

> Only because it owns [or lends] itself to thanking
> Is life estimable.[10]

Heidegger will inquire near the end of his essay about the conditions of a transformation in our relation to language, and it is clear from this text (as well as from others I will consider) that one of the conditions for such a transition involves our acceding to a comportment of thanks: *Gelassen-*

heit, renunciation, and so on. But in the context of the essay, it appears that the significant thing about such comportment is that it allows for the emergence of *physis* in language, or what Heidegger called the "earth" in "The Origin of the Work of Art": an opening to the *Natürliche der Sprache* in and through the *bodying* of language. *Das Leben* owns itself to thanks, Goethe writes. In the movement of language, this owning occurs in the *Lauten des Wortes*, which Heidegger annotates, as we have seen, as follows: *Lauten und Leiben — Leib und Schrift* ("Sounding and Body-ing — Body and Writing"). I will try to demonstrate how Heidegger gener-ates these terms, but I would emphasize here again that what distinguishes the human appropriation to language is a *bodily* answering: "The appro-priation of humans as listeners for saying has this distinguishing character, that it releases the human essence into its own, but only so that humans as those who speak, that is, those who say, may counter the saying in virtue of what is proper to them. This is: the sounding of the word. The counter-ing saying of mortals is answering" (US 249/OW 129). Thus, at the *limit* of language, thought as the relation between humankind and language — the *Brauch* — in and by which language is set under way in the movement of the *Wegformel*, Heidegger inscribes the body. The way for the articula-tion of language opens in and through the human body. Language does not come to language (*Die Sprache als die Sprache zur Sprache bringen*) except via the countering bodying of human speaking.

How much of an opening (in the circle of language's speaking) does this inscription of the body represent? If we emphasize the element of *lēthē*, the element of concealing that belongs to earth as Heidegger describes it in "The Origin of the Work of Art," would we find here the source of an irreducible opacity in language?[11] And what of questions like that of sex-ual difference? Is it possible that some kind of "bodily" determination of the latter leaves its mark on language?* It goes almost without saying that Heidegger would strictly delimit any "biological" determination of the saying of language (as we see, for example, in his interpretation of Antig-one's response to the *Brauch* in his reading of Hölderlin's "The Ister"†). The body engages with language *only as appropriated* by *Ereignis*; it comes forth only as it owns in a movement of response. But the questions still remain: What of the body is appropriated? And to what extent is this appropriation marked by a kind of irreducible remainder proper to the earth?

*Derrida has taken this question farthest in "*Geschlecht*: Différence sexuelle, différence ontologique," in his *Psyché: Inventions de l'autre* (Paris: Galilée, 1987), 395–452. I have tried to explore it in the reading of Irigaray contained in the third part of this volume.

†For this interpretation of Antigone, see Martin Heidegger, *Hölderlins Hymne "Der Ister,"* vol. 56 of *Gesamtausgabe* (Frankfurt am Main: Klostermann, 1984), 147.

Heidegger's answer to the first question is only latent in the passage I am commenting upon here, though I do not believe we would be forcing anything by drawing it out. It appears implicitly in the marginal note I have cited: *Lauten und Leiben — Laut und Schrift.** The answer, in other words, is speech and hand. Hand, here, is somewhat less evident than voice (which could hardly surprise us), but it is indicated by an entire set of motifs in this passage that I will try now to develop, starting with that of showing.

The latter motif is an appropriate starting point because it will allow me to formulate a bit more precisely the nature of the "break" to which I have alluded in describing the difference Heidegger inscribes in the essence of language (the difference introduced by the usage, the *Brauch* that gives language its movement). I emphasize *in* the essence of language, once again, because we must avoid hypostatizing the terms in relation (*Ereignis*, humankind, language) and think rather the *same* of this relation (*die er-eignend-brauchende Be-wëgung*) out of which the terms are given to be thought, and which is not *other* than language but rather the finite relationality that determines language's essence (a kind of "quasi-transcendental").

Heidegger indicates the paradoxical site of this relationality (what he calls [*die*] *Ortschaft des Zu-einander-Gehörens von Brauch und Ereignis*, "the locality of the belonging to one another of *Brauch* and *Ereignis*" [US 229n]) in two statements that would appear to bridge the opening or break we have glimpsed by suggesting, as I noted above, that the *Ereignung* of the human essence occurs through the *Eignen* that occurs in showing (which belongs, of course, to the essence of language). But Heidegger's phrasing is elliptical and could almost be said to open as much as it closes, even as it appears to assert a kind of common determining limit for the respective essences of humankind and language.† The first statement reads as follows: *Weil das Zeigen der Sage das Eignen ist, beruht auch das Hörenkönnen auf die Sage, das Gehören zu ihr, im Ereignis* ("Because the showing of saying is appropriation, the capacity to listen to saying, belonging to it, also rests in *Ereignis*" [US 248/OW 129]). The relation between humankind and language, Heidegger suggests, passes by way of appropriation. We belong to saying because showing is an appropriating. But what is the status of this "because"? Is Heidegger saying that

---

*What is the grammar of this notation? Are we to pair *Laut*, as a kind of derivative, with *Lauten*, and *Schrift* with *Leiben*? What then, is the relation between these pairs? *Schrift*, as we will see, is the "indication" of the word. But the word is not *Laut* (this discussion of writing does not fall so immediately within the logic of phonocentrism).

†But then, that is precisely what is being designated: a common limit in the sense of a boundary; the limit is the site of a relation and the inscription of a difference articulated with the preposition *gegen*.

human belonging is enabled by the fact that this showing of saying is an owning, that humankind itself owes its belonging to the showing of saying and owns by this movement of language? Or is it rather that because showing has its source in *Ereignis*, a bond is possible, because the human essence is "also" brought into its own (what is fitting, *sein Gehöriges*) by this gentle law? The former reading finds a kind of support in the normal manner of reading the statement's syntax, but its articulation is in fact paratactical and is marked, in its strangeness, by the gap at which I have been working. This gap would be too slight to emphasize, however, were it not for the fact that a similar "parataxis" appears in a second statement on the following page. Like the first, it appears to assert an articulation (via an *Also*), but in fact it merely aligns the terms of the relation asserted: *Das Ereignis ereignet den Menschen in den Brauch für es selbst. Also das Zeigen als das Eignen ereignend, ist das Ereignis die Be-wëgung der Sage zur Sprache* ("*Ereignis* appropriates humankind in usage for itself. Thus appropriating showing as owning, *Ereignis* is the setting under way of saying to language" [US 249/OW 130]). What is the relation between these two sentences? Is the movement described in the first sentence included, in some sense, in that described in the second? (Is the relation of *Ereignis* and *Brauch* part of the appropriation of showing as owning?) Is this *one* movement of appropriation? But we would still need to account for the "for itself," which picks up the developments in the preceding paragraphs about the way humankind is appropriated to language by *Ereignis* in *Brauch*.[12] Why is this distinction accorded to humankind? Could it be rather that the movement described in the first sentence is something like the condition (though the word is awkward here) of the second? Heidegger would then be suggesting that it is by way of the appropriation of the human that showing is appropriated as owning (i.e., *Ereignis* appropriates humankind in *Brauch* and *thus* appropriates showing as owning, setting language under way). This would be a stronger statement than any in this text concerning the human role in the essencing of language: it would make the appropriation of the human essence a condition of language's very occurrence as a saying in which issues the *Geheiss* of *Ereignis*. Yet it would seem that Heidegger is asserting nothing else when he states that language *needs and uses* human speaking (*braucht das menschlichen Sprechen* [US 244]) and describes this *Brauchen* near the end of his essay as resting upon a "failing" or lack in language (*Fehl* [US 254]), for he then inscribes language in a *relation* (a relation marked by its very solitude — language speaks *alone*, he says) that must be thought as determining for it. The need and use of the human *Verlauten*, in other words, is not merely an exteriorization of a (silent) sounding that might occur independently of it. Without the appropriation of humankind to language which directs language to speech, saying as showing would not be set under way at all. Language needs and uses humankind because humankind is needed and used by *Ereignis* in such a way that language is first set under way toward human speaking. There *is* no "essence" of language without the appropriation of the essence of humankind that is in some sense "other" than it.

I will return shortly to the motif of *Brauch* to justify this extension of its reach to describe not just a relation within language but a relation in which language itself is held. But I want to conclude this reading of the sentences I have cited involving the motif of showing by proposing that their ambiguity can be accounted for (if not resolved) if we both admit that showing as owning does represent something like a common limit for language and humankind (the site of their relation — *das Ver-Hältnis*) and add that showing must be thought as involving in itself an inner articulation. There is *one* movement of appropriation, we might say (issuing from what Heidegger calls "the same"), but this movement occurs through the articulation between the self-showing of everything that comes into presence in the showing of saying and the human *Zeigen* that follows it (US 243/OW 123) and counters it (in a *Sichzeigenlassen*) *from out of* the *Zeigen* of humankind that occurs in the *Brauch* of *Ereignis*. Showing would indeed be the site of the relation between humankind and language — the site of their appropriation to each other, but it would have to be thought as divided in itself. And if showing is the most originary dimension of the essence of language, *das Eigentümliche* of language would lie in the fold within showing. Did Heidegger not invite such a meditation on showing by his initial and quite provocative use of the term *zeigen* to translate the various "struts" of the structure Aristotle describes in language? The citation from *On Interpretation* marked more than the beginning of a tradition: it also marked an unthought, a question upon which the tradition closed in interpreting the relations named with the term *zeigen* with its notion of the sign.

Heidegger refers to the showing effected in human saying, as I have noted, in the second section of his essay. "A self-showing marks as an appearing the presencing and absencing of everything present of every kind. Even there, where showing is accomplished by our saying, this showing as indicating is preceded by a letting itself be shown" (US 242–43/OW 123). But I want to emphasize that if this saying *follows* what occurs in showing (as I noted above, Heidegger appears to be thinking saying as the articulation — in signs — of showing), it cannot be thought as in any way external to it (the articulation is originary) because it proceeds from the showing that occurs in the relation of *Brauch* and *Ereignis*. The showing of human saying is the drawing out of a relation of (in) showing *already contracted* (by *Ereignis*) between language and humankind, whereby showing as owning is already directed or offered to human saying.

In evoking this more originary showing, I am thinking of the movement that prompts Heidegger to speak of humankind as a *sign* in *What Is Called Thinking?* When we are engaged by what withdraws, Heidegger argues there, drawn by its withdrawal (the withdrawal that occasions *Seinsvergessenheit*, "the oblivion of Being," and that, when thought as such, first allows us to enter the domain of *Ereignis* and to experience its "draw" as *Brauch*), our essence is imprinted by this movement (this is the *Auszeichnung* of the human essence) and thus indicates the withdrawal. We *are* as indicating, Heidegger writes, and as such we *show* (*zeigen*). A being whose determination of essence is to show is a sign (*Zeichen*), and in a time when the withdrawn remains without a name, it is a sign without interpretation: without meaning or any value as a "pointer" in that it cannot be interpreted (*deutungslos*). Hölderlin writes in "Mnemosyne":

> Ein Zeichen sind wir, deutungslos
> Schmerzlos sind wir und haben fast
> Die Sprache in der Fremde verloren.

> We are a sign without interpretation.
> We feel no pain, we almost have
> Lost our tongue in foreign lands.
> (cited in WHD 6/10)

We have almost lost our relation to language in the reign of *Technik*, Heidegger avers in this text (as he does in "The Way to Language," where the aim in large measure is to recover something of the nature of language in the face of a "denatured" notion of language as information). To recover it, the imprint of our essence must discover itself; we must grasp the historial character of the essence of *Technik* and recognize in language's historicity the relation between *Brauch* and *Ereignis*. We must begin, in other words, to emerge in our *character* as signs and then undertake the transformation that will allow us to translate into and hold in our saying the name for what withdraws. The condition of such a movement is experiencing the fact of withdrawal in the fact that we are not yet thinking — to experience, in other words, the extreme form of *Seinsvergessenheit* that leaves us "without pain."

We trace signs, Heidegger comments, "presumably because humankind is a sign" (WHD 51/16). There is a showing that occurs in the delineation of our essence before any showing in signs, whether spoken or written. Humankind is first appropriated to language in this showing, but this appropriation is also such that language is released to the movement defined by Heidegger's *Wegformel*. *Die brauchende Vereignung* lets saying reach speaking, Heidegger writes (US 249/OW 131); it frees language or "delivers" it to its movement ("What looks like a confused tangle resolves itself, when glimpsed from out of the way-making movement, in the releasing [*das Befreiende*] which the way-making movement that comes about in saying brings about. It delivers saying to speaking. . . . The setting under way of saying to speech is the delivering bond that binds by appropriating" [US 250–51/OW 131]). And thus we may presume that the double movement in the *ereigneten* showing of saying is a showing in which the word itself — the soundless pealing of stillness in which issues the *Geheiss* of *Ereignis* — first opens. We "answer" the word of language that is first traced out in the "contract" of humankind and language.

I noted earlier that the extension of the notion of showing that I have proposed here in following a clue from *What Is Called Thinking?* (doing nothing more in fact than inquiring about the nature of the *sich zeigen* that marks the *human* essence in the originary showing that occurs in saying) rests upon an extension of the notion of *Brauch* — an extension that is in fact indicated by Heidegger's phrasing in the passage in which he first develops this notion. He had named it at the end of the second section as an intralinguistic occurrence ("Language needs and uses human speaking" [US 244/OW 125]); but when he describes the "contract" by which *Ereignis* allows humankind to belong to language, he nominalizes the term in such a way as to describe precisely this relation of letting belong: "The appropriation of mortals to saying releases human nature into that usage [*Brauch*] out of which humans are used [*gebraucht*]" (US 249/OW 129). The following sentence reiterates this usage: "*Ereignis* allows saying to reach speech in the using appropriation [*in der brauchende Vereignung*]." The appropriation of humankind to language is itself a *Brauchen*. And then, once again, at the bottom of the page: *Das Ereignis ereignet den Menschen in den Brauch für es selbst.* (When the word recurs near the end of the essay in the context of the discussion of the *Fehl* of language, it is used again intralinguistically: *Die Sprache braucht das Verlauten im Wort*, "Saying is in need of being voiced in the word" [US 254/OW 134] — but I will propose that the *Fehl* itself is to be thought out of *Brauch*.) *Brauch* thus names the relation toward which this entire essay has been heading, though Heidegger offers no explication of the term — just as in "The Word" (as we will see), where the term appears at the outset of the essay but is left there as a kind of threshold which this text can only approach. To develop the term therefore, we must move once more outside *On the Way to Language*. Though quite a number of texts can be called on here, I will return again principally to *What Is Called Thinking?*

Heidegger introduces the term *Brauch* in the seventh section of his lecture series (part 2) in order to translate the first word of the phrase by

Parmenides he is commenting upon. In Heidegger's initial translation of the Greek: *Nötig: das Sagen so Denken auch: Seindes: sein* ("Needful: the saying also thinking too: being: to be" [WHD 111/182]). It should be clear from the context that we are dealing with what governs the relation between thought, language, and the Being of what is, and therefore that we are touching on the relation between *Brauch* and *Ereignis*. But as in "The Anaximander Fragment," where Heidegger isolates *to chreon* as the oldest name for the Being of what is (and thus the word where a trace of the essence of Being as the presence of what is present is most likely to be preserved—a trace therefore of the *difference* between presence and what is present thought as a *relation* to what is present), Heidegger starts from the context of human activity, from "usage as practiced by humans" WHD 114/187). He first takes a linguistic indication, drawing from the verb *chrao* the word *cheir*, "the hand." *Chrao* means: "I handle and so keep in hand. I use, I have a use for." The corresponding explication in "The Anaximander Fragment" runs as follows: "I handle something, I reach for it, extend my hand to it. Thus *chrao* means at the same time to place in someone's hands or hand over, to let something belong to someone. But such delivery is of a kind which keeps the transfer in hand, and with it, what is transferred" (H 366/E 51–52). We see once again (I refer back to my last chapter) that Heidegger is thinking relation from the basis of a reaching, a giving, and a maintaining, where the given and the giving is itself "held." But he is also emphasizing here its human determination by thinking it from the basis of a distinguishing trait (*Wesensauszeichnung*) of the human essence, the hand.[13]

The human practice from which Heidegger proceeds in defining *brauchen*—that is, a way of taking in hand and handing over that maintains—is immediately distinguished from any notion of utilization or exploitation based on "mere" need. The thing is not debased (*herabgesetzt*) as it is in the commandeering of *Technik*, but is rather allowed to unfold in its being: " 'To use' means first: to let a thing be what it is and how it is. This letting [*Belassen*: also 'to leave' or 'to maintain things as they are'] requires in itself that the used thing be cared for in its essence, in such a way that we respond each time to the demands that the used thing itself manifests [*wobei wir jeweils den Anspruch entsprechen die das Gebrauchte von sich her kund gibt*]" (WHD 168/191). In the essence of usage, as we see, there speaks a demand (*Anspruch*, see WHD 124) that all usage conform to the essence of the thing used, and such conforming is thought essentially as an answering to what speaks in the essence of the thing. (This is the structure of answering that Heidegger defined in "The Essence of Language" in his discussion of essence in his third section.) It is within this structure of address and response that we must situate Heidegger's reference to the "conforming" or "fitting" of hand to thing that characterizes any "handling" in the proper sense — indeed, Heidegger reiterates that all usage as practiced by humans moves within the realm of the word. But the hold of the hand is an essential dimension of usage inasmuch as this latter is both a letting something enter into its essence (*Einlassen in das Wesen*) and a preserving or maintaining (as we can hear this word in French: *main-tenant*) of the thing in its essence (*Wahrung im Wesen* [WHD 114/187] and *Verwahrung des Eingelassenen* [WHD 169/192]). Heidegger's citation of Augustine and his concluding definition of *brauchen* in his discussion of his translation of *to chreon* in "The Anaximander Fragment" point insistently to this distinguishing trait of the *human* relation to the thing: a certain delivering hold of the hand that contracts a free relation in a movement of unconcealment. Once again, "usage," as it is thought here, is distinguished from any notion of utilization or consumption founded on need in the common sense of the term, and is also dissociated, as we will see again, from any "pragmatic" understanding of usage or custom.

In the light of this definition of "usage," we might well ask how we should read the incident in George's poem "The Word," whereby the word vanishes from the hand of the poet. The relation to the word, it seems initially, would not be a form of usage. Of course, Heidegger does propose a notion of *Sprachgebrauch* ("linguistic usage") that involves a certain *maintaining* of the word — a maintaining of the word as it is given in its withdrawal, not as something present (the relation must even be distinguished from the relation to God named in Augustine's phrase inasmuch as God remains the highest *being* in this perspective). But this example of the poetic experience with the word points again to the fact that language forms the enabling limit of human practice thought as a usage. We see this limit remarked consistently in the discussion of an aletheic comportment involving the hand — in the discussion of *Handwerk* ("craft" or "handicraft") in the transitional remarks after the first two lectures of *What Is Called Thinking?*, for example, and in Heidegger's definition of the essence of *pragma* and *prattein* as *Handlung* in his Parmenides lectures. Human *Brauchen* takes its possibility from language — it is offered with language and unfolds as an essential dimension of the *response* to language.

Though I want to emphasize the *limit* marked here (in order to pass to a broader sense of *brauchen*), it will be worthwhile to pause briefly over Heidegger's remarks concerning the relation between language and human practice, for they have immediate bearing on Heidegger's discussion in "The Way to Language" — they allow us to account, in fact, for the appearance of the motif of writing. For brevity, I will leave aside Heidegger's remarks on thought as a form of *Handwerk* and refer only to the discussion of *Handlung* ("action") in the Parmenides lectures, even though the two discussions together also reveal something about Heidegger's strategy vis-à-vis *Technik* in "The Way to Language": in each text, the hand appears to designate a distinguishing trait of the *human* relation to language (and hence to beings and Being) that is threatened by the self-veiling injunction of *Technik*.[14]

Heidegger introduces the terms *Handeln* (and *Handlung*) in his lectures on Parmenides in order to name the essence of the Greek notion of *pragma* as this term appears in a line from Pindar. *Pragma*, he says, names the unity of a comportment of unconcealing (*prattein*) and that which is unconcealed. *Pragma*, in Pindar, is not yet separated off as "thing" or "concern" (*Sache*) from praxis; rather, thing and activity are thought in the unity of a *Handeln* governed by the essence of the hand. Both things (insofar as they presence as *die Vorhandene*, "present-to-hand," and *die Zuhandene*, "ready-to-hand") and humankind *handeln* through the hand, which does not belong to humankind (and above all not, in its essence, as a corporeal organ) but rather holds in it the essence of the human. The hand, Heidegger writes,

is, together with the word, the distinguishing trait of essence of man. Only a being which like man "has" the word (*muthos*, *logos*) can and also must "have" the hand. [There follows a list of activities in which the hand manifests itself: prayer, handshaking, etc.] . . . The hand essences as hand only where there are concealment and unconcealment. No animal has a hand. . . . Only out of the word and with the word has the hand arisen. Man does not "have" hands, rather the hand holds the essence of man within it, because the word as the essential realm of the hand is the ground of the essence of man. The word as inscribed and as thus showing itself to the glance is the written word, that is to say, writing. The word as writing, however, is hand-writing. (PM 118–19/80)

A second passage from the following lecture should also be cited here. Heidegger has just defined *Handlung* as the "unitary way in which things are in each case present to and at hand, that is, related to the hand, and how each time man in his comportment, that is, in his acting [handling] by means of the hand, is posited in relation to what is at hand":

The essential belonging together of hand and word as the distinguishing trait of essence of man reveals itself herein, that the hand discloses what is concealed insofar as it indicates and in indicating marks out, and in marking out brings the indicating signs into the shape of forms [*indem sie zeigt und zeigend zeichnet und zeichnend die zeigenden Zeichen zu Gebilden bildet*]. These are called, following the "verb" *graphein*, *grammata*. That word which is indicated through the hand and thus appears is writing. Still today, teaching as concerns the construction of language is called *Grammatik*. (PM 124–25/84)

This passage actually opens more questions than it answers, despite the articulations suggested by its rhetorical structure. We may presume that the *Wesensgehörigkeit* ("the essential belonging together") of hand and word lies in the fact that hand and word draw out and preserve a relation of unconcealment by indicating or showing. But do *all* showing and *all* signifying involve the hand in some way? Is there a relation to the word that does not involve the hand? Heidegger's statement in the preceding passage I have cited might suggest to us that there is not: "only a being which like man 'has' the word . . . *can and also must* [my emphasis] 'have' the hand." The hand would be essential to all showing as effected by humans (all *saying* would involve the hand: a surprising assertion — but we should recall that Heidegger groups poetry and philosophy among the forms of *Handwerk*). And is it something of the "hand" (in its indexical movements) that effectively achieves the articulation between showing and signifying? Little in this passage will help us with such a question, including Heidegger's assertion in the immediately following paragraph that we can only begin to grasp the essence of the "showing-writing hand" by considering the relations between Being, word, reading, and writing as implied by the notions of logos and *legein*. But Heidegger does make it quite clear that when the hand draws out — manifests — its relation of essential co-belonging with the word in writing, it is drawing out what the hand preserves of the relation between word, Being, and humankind. As Heidegger puts it in the succeeding paragraph:

In handwriting, however, the relation of Being to man, namely the word, is in-scribed in beings themselves [*in das Seiende selbst*]. The origin and way of dealing with writing is already in itself a decision about the relation of Being and word to humankind and thereby about the relation of man to beings and the way in which both, man and thing, either stand in the unconcealed or are withdrawn from it. (PM 125/85)

Handwriting is nothing less than an art form — secondary with regard to poetry, to be sure (if in poetry the emergence of the word itself is involved), but nevertheless one of the sites where truth is at stake. Heidegger is not, at this point, containing writing within the bounds of a phonocentrism, for writing is co-originary with the phoneme in articulating the word ("the word by which the word comes to the word"). It is one of the essential forms by which humankind answers the saying of language — an essential form of *das Lauten des Wortes*, to cite again Heidegger's words in "The Way to Language." It is even *the* essential form, we might say, by which the *human* relation to language is made manifest: "The essential belonging together of hand and word as the distinguishing trait of essence of human-kind reveals itself herein." Thus when Heidegger remarks in "The Way to

Language" that humankind is used for the countering saying of the *Sage* through what is most proper to it, he is necessarily thinking of writing together with the sounding of the voice. He may even be thinking primarily of writing — for the hand is the preeminent dimension of the body as concerns language (*Mit der Hand hat es eine eigene Bewandtnis*, Heidegger remarks in *What Is Called Thinking?*). *Lauten und Leiben — Leib und Schrift*, Heidegger writes in his marginal note. Heidegger may well be opening the possibility of thinking other forms of the bodying of language beyond sounding, but we may surmise that he will not understand them as exceeding the reach (and the hold) of the hand.

But the hand, as we have seen, draws out the relation to the word, and for this reason, all *Handlung* must be situated within the domain that opens with the word. All human usage answers. And even though the gestures of the hand may have an initiating character (poetry and thought are among such gestures), and thus *articulate* the word in an originary fashion, drawing out the order to which they answer, they must be thought *within* a usage that first lets them occur as it sets language under way. "True usage," Heidegger writes in *What Is Called Thinking?*,

is never the affair of mortals. In the best of cases, mortals are illuminated by the radiance of usage. This is why the essence of usage can never be sufficiently clarified by contrasting it with utilization and need. We speak of usage [*Brauch*], customs [*Sitte*] and what we are used to [*Brauchtum*]. But already here, usage has not made itself. It is itself "used" from elsewhere and presumably in the authentic sense. (WHD 115/187)

So much for the pragmatism that grounds meaning in the usage of communities of interpretation.[15]

Thus to achieve the proper "elevation" for his translation of *chrao* in *What Is Called Thinking?*, Heidegger proposes the locution *es brauchet* on the model of the neutral construction *es gibt*, adding that in fact we can only begin to determine what *es gibt* means from the basis of *es brauchet*. Heidegger proposes no derivation here, but it is clear that the relation named by *es brauchet* is in fact co-originary with the essencing named by *es gibt* (as later discussions confirm). Thus we may presume that a *usage* marks all giving in the essential sense. Such usage is not defined by a relation of need or necessity, Heidegger insists, because it is a letting presence, and thus also a form of giving. But this giving is not without its conflict, as Heidegger suggests when he begins to approach (but only *approach*) the meaning of the term *Brauch* via two passages from Hölderlin. The first is from "The Ister," the second is from "The Titans":

Es brauchet aber Stiche der Fels
Und Furchen die Erd,
Unwirthbar wär es, ohne Weile.

It is useful for the rock to have shafts,
And for the earth, furrows,
It would be desolate else, unabiding.
(cited in WHD 117/190)

Denn unter dem Maasse
Des Rohen brauchet es auch
Damit das Reine sich kenne.

For measure directs that
The crude too, is needed
That the pure may know itself.
(cited in WHD 117/194)

Both passages, Heidegger proposes, have to do with the *Wesenseinlass* by which mortals are granted a dwelling on earth and by which this dwelling is secured (WHD 118/194). In other words, they touch upon the "usage" by which all custom and usage is founded.

The first passage evokes, of course, the figure of furrows that Heidegger called upon in "The Essence of Language" to name the *Riss*. Hölderlin's streams (which cut the rock's shafts) answer for Heidegger to the same determination. *Brauchen* here speaks to the relation of earth and human dwelling. But this latter opens in its turn only "under the sky," which is to say, from the human relation to the divine. The latter is implicitly named in the second citation with Hölderlin's reference to a measure. We can only think the "needed" tracing of furrows from the basis of this relation to the divine—a relation that is itself one of usage wherein the pure comes to know itself in relation to violence.

Heidegger is drawing here upon his interpretation of the historial law defined by Hölderlin when he said in his famous letter to Casimir Ulrich Böhlendorff that "the *free* use of the *proper*" (*der* **freie** *Gebrauch des* **Eigenen**) is what is most difficult, and proposes a schema whereby a chiasmic relation of the natural and the foreign allows the moderns to define themselves in relation to the Greeks.* Heidegger interprets the movement of the voyagers in Hölderlin's "Remembrance" in terms of this schema

---

*Friedrich Hölderlin, *Sämtliche Werke*, vol. 6.1, ed. Friedrich Beissner (Stuttgart: Kohlhammer, 1954), 426; translated by Thomas Pfau in *Friedrich Hölderlin: Essays and Letters on Theory* (Albany: SUNY Press, 1988), 149. I took up this schema in Chapter 5 of *Heidegger: Thought and Historicity*, "Hölderlin's Testimony: An Eye Too Many Perhaps," 199–200.

and reads the poem as describing a movement of passage between the home and the foreign (the site of exposure to an overwhelming presence of the divine) that first allows the possibility of appropriation of the natural and hence a founded dwelling. "But what remains is founded by poets," we read at the end of "Remembrance";* what they found, in Heidegger's reading, is a relation to the word as the site of an opening to the divine. "Homecoming" is in fact nothing other than *entry* into this relation — the drawing out of relation and thereby the letting occur of a *Wesenseinlass* as Heidegger names it in *What Is Called Thinking?* The pure uses violence and is used by violence to enter into the use (knowledge) of its own purity.[16]

Heidegger only alludes to the violent use of mortals by the divine. However, he concludes his commentary on Hölderlin by pointing to a "still more profound" meaning of usage in the eighth strophe of "The Rhine":

> But their own immortality
> Suffices the gods, and if
> The Heavenly have need of one thing,
> It is of heroes and human beings
> And other mortals. For since
> The most Blessed in themselves feel nothing
> Another, if to say such a thing is
> Permitted, must, I suppose,
> Vicariously feel in the name of the gods,
> And him they need [*Den brauchen sie*]; but their rule is that
> He shall demolish his
> Own house and curse like an enemy
> Those dearest to him and under the rubble
> Shall bury his father and child,
> When one aspires to be like them, refusing
> To bear with inequality, the fantast.†

The meaning of usage illuminated by these verses, Heidegger says near the end of his discussion, is one that we are unprepared to follow in thought (this is *What Is Called Thinking?*!). However, Heidegger had already commented on this higher sense of usage in the commentary on "The Rhine" proposed in the lectures of the winter semester of 1934–35, and in terms sufficiently exalted to indicate that we are moving at a suitable level of reflection. For the space of almost a page, Heidegger tells us that Hölderlin reaches in this strophe "one of the highest and most isolated peaks of

*Friedrich Hölderlin, *Poems and Fragments*, trans. Michael Hamburger (New York: Cambridge University Press, 1980), 491.
†Hölderlin, *Poems and Fragments*, 415.

Western thought, close there to the thinkers of the beginning of our Western history" (HH 269). What the poet touches upon here ("what is most highly worthy of question in the essence of Being as it has opened in our history" [HH 269–70]) is the thought of a conflict lying in the heart of Being itself—a conflict that manifests itself in an agonistic relation between the gods and mortals that is provoked by what Hölderlin describes as an excess of self-sufficiency on the part of the immortals. The gods, Hölderlin says, feel nothing but a having had enough of an immortality that manifests itself as no more than a lack of neediness (*Unbedürftigkeit*). "Immortality" thus names a lack of feeling that gives itself as a surfeit of self-sufficiency (a paradox, as I will suggest, that is perhaps homologous with that situation from which Heidegger hopes to engage reflection in *What Is Called Thinking?*: "*The most thought-provoking is, that we are not yet thinking*" [WHD 2/4]). The gods do not turn to humans to feel— they need and use mortals (or mortals are used thereby: "another must take a share in feeling, so that in such feeling what is as such might open" [HH 269]) because in their very self-sufficiency, *they do not feel*, excessively. There can be no resolution of the tension that structures this relation—no *jouissance* in this usage, whatever "intimacy" emerges in this conflict: mortals cannot find satisfaction as they are driven to tragic excess by the divine withdrawal. The *Brauch* that structures the relation of gods to mortals (a usage deriving from a lack grounded in excess) is irreducible. Thus Heidegger concludes that Hölderlin speaks of a *differend* in the ground of Being (*So wird in der grössten Härte des Sagens der Streit in den Grund des Seyns selbst verlegt* [HH 273]).

Heidegger stops short of this understanding of *Brauch* as the ground of conflict in the essence of Being in *What Is Called Thinking?* But it is clear that such an understanding of the term still underlies its usage in as late a text as "The Way to Language," because in the opening lines of "The Word," written only shortly before, Heidegger returns to Hölderlin's reflections on *Antigone* to name *Brauch* as that which governs the conflict of mortals and gods and thus the poet's saying. Heidegger starts here from Hölderlin's words in "Bread and Wine" concerning the silence of the poetic word that once sounded in Greece as the site of the approach of the god.[17]

Saying was in itself the allowing to appear of that which the saying ones glimpsed because it had already looked at them. That look brought the saying ones and the hearing ones into the un-finite intimacy of the strife between men and gods. However, that which is yet above the gods and men prevailed through this strife—as Antigone says: . . . It was not Zeus who sent me the message (but something other, that directing usage). The poetic word of this kind remains an enigma. Its saying has long since returned to silence. (US 207/OW 139–40)

Heidegger's claims here deserve a separate analysis. For while he feigns respect for the enigma of Antigone's mode of speech (her words are themselves an instance of the now-withheld poetic saying to which he alludes in opening), he has in fact *translated* them in the most presumptuous way. I refer here less to the translation itself, which merits discussion, than to the explanatory parentheses that interpolate *Hölderlin's* translation of *Antigone* in such a way as to introduce the problematic of *Brauch*.* The phrase "but something other, that directing usage" is in all probability a citation of Hölderlin's translation of Antigone's remark to Creon (line 541): *Wer weiss, da kann doch drunt' ein andrer Brauch seyn* ("Who knows, there may be another usage below"). And even if it is not such a citation, it is surely not by chance that Heidegger has cited the lines that Hölderlin himself isolated in his "Remarks on *Antigone*" to identify Antigone's engagement in the tragic conflict between the human and the divine.† With these words, Antigone begins to assume her character as a sign (*Charakter*), and thereby, Heidegger suggests, indicates the *Brauch* that governs the conflict.

"*Eigentliche Sprache des Sophocles*," Hölderlin writes in commenting on Antigone's phrase concerning a different usage. The comment may be read as saying that this is language that is proper to Sophocles — Sophocles, who knows how to "objectify" better than Aeschylus and Euripides, Hölderlin says; "the human understanding as wandering under the unthinkable." But the comment also indicates that *Eigentlichkeit* is the attribute of Sophocles' language. At the conclusion of his "Remarks on *Antigone*," Hölderlin will state: "Sophocles is right [*hat Recht*]. It is this the destiny of his time and the form of his fatherland."‡ Sophocles' language is the *proper* language, the "fitting" language for its time. It answers to the historial determination defining an authentic *Sprachgebrauch*. As such, it is true language — true language in the sense that its words are *proper* words for what is said and are thus used in their proper meaning. But it is true language also in the sense that the essence of language speaks in the words, or that they answer to this essence. It is in this last sense that Heidegger will evoke the motif of *eigentliche Sprache* in "The Way to Language."§

---

*Heidegger does not do this elsewhere. I might note here that Karl Reinhardt translates the phrase as follows: *Wer weiss, ob das auch dort geheiligt ist* (Sophokles, *Antigonä* [Godesberg: Helmut Küpper, 1949], 57).

†See Friedrich Hölderlin, "Remarks on *Antigone*," in *Hölderlin: Essays and Letters on Theory* (Friedrich Hölderlin, *Sämtliche Werke*, vol. 5, ed. Friedrich Beissner [Stuttgart: Kohlhammer, 1952], 266).

‡Hölderlin, "Remarks on *Antigone*," 115 (*Sämtliche Werke* 5: 272).

§Heidegger makes a similar claim for Nietzsche's words "the wasteland grows." The phrase is a "true word [*ein wahres Wort*], a word of thought [*ein Gedachtes*]" (WHD 14/38) — a phrase that answers to the most thought-provoking of our time.

Of course, *eigentliche Sprache* cannot mean the same thing for the moderns as it did for the Greeks: an entirely different *Sprachgebrauch* is required in modernity because the form of the *Brauch* itself has changed. Hölderlin insists upon this point in his *Remarks,* and it is essentially the point Heidegger makes when he himself evokes this notion in "The Way to Language." A language is *eigentlich,* he argues, inasmuch as it is historially destined. *In this way,* he says, every language is *eigentlich;* but only an assumption of this historicity, we may presume, would render possible something comparable to the *Eigentlichkeit* of Sophocles' language. The possibility of such an assumption is what is at stake in the notion of usage, and as we will see, Heidegger continues to follow Hölderlin's lead in thinking with this term the irreducibly historical and relational essence of *Ereignis.* While he does not evoke the theme of conflict in "The Way to Language," he does have recourse to a closely related conception of "need" for thinking the finitude of language and the structure of that usage of humankind by which language is brought to speech. It is a "need," in fact, of the same enigmatic character as that evoked in the eighth strophe of "The Rhine," and it constitutes the heart of the groundless relationality that Heidegger attempts to think from *Ereignis.* To glimpse its play in "The Way to Language," let us now return to that text.

I have noted that the "paratactical" assertions regarding the appropriation of language to its speaking mark a fold or a gap proper to the *er-eignend-brauchende Be-wëgung* that disrupts any apparent closure or immanent development in the movement named by the guiding formula of the essay: *die Sprache als die Sprache zur Sprache bringen.* The *limit* of language that is thus marked delimits the formal structure that is evoked in the formula — what Heidegger terms "the *Forma,* the *Gestalt* of the structure within which the essence of language that rests in *Ereignis* makes it way" (US 250/OW 130).* As this structure describes the unfolding of the way language comes to speech — the articulation and sounding of the *Geheiss* — the delimitation in question is also a delimitation of the form of a given destining of the saying of Being, the destiny of *Technik,* for example, whose particular character it is to seek to close upon itself and veil its historical provenance.

Thought from the *er-eignend-brauchende Be-wëgung,* the *Wegformel* describes a *release,* Heidegger says. The *Be-wëgung* holds the way free for language in *delivering* it to speech. This deliverance is the "bond" (to which Heidegger referred at the end of his second section) that links human saying to the saying of language and offers the possibility of conceiv-

---

*It is perhaps pertinent that Heidegger thinks of *Brauch* in "The Anaximander Fragment" as "what bounds," itself (as the relationality of relation) "without bounds" (H 368/E 54).

ing something like a "free" relation to a particular destiny — "the free use of the proper," as Hölderlin said. "Freedom" here is thought initially as the possibility of the assumption of a destiny *as a destiny*, and the corresponding assumption of essence. It is nowhere defined in "The Way to Language," but its appearance in the earlier essay "The Question of Technology" (1955), where the context is also the problem of a free relation to *Technik* as a destiny of Being, corresponds precisely to its evocation here. Heidegger divorces it in this latter discussion from the causality of human willing and thinks it from the event of unconcealment, from the self-concealing mystery that frees and as the appearance of that self-concealing. It names, he says, a clearing/concealing, "in whose clearing there shimmers that veil that covers what essences in all truth and allows the veil to appear as what veils. Freedom is the realm of destining that at any given time brings an unconcealing on its way" (VA 29/25). The danger of *Technik*, of course, is that it veils this appearance of the veil, thereby occluding the event of truth and obscuring the possibility of answering the injunction of *Technik* (of recognizing even that one is answering) as a mode (*Weise* [US 251]) of *Ereignis*.

In thinking this destining in "The Way to Language," Heidegger says that the *er-eignend-brauchende Be-wëgung* frees language to be concerned with itself. This is no solipsism, no oblivious "self-mirroring [*Selbstbespiegelung*]" (US 251/OW 131). Language "turns away from itself" in its appropriating-showing, freeing the shown; as such it is concerned only that we correspond to it as the saying of *Ereignis* (ultimately, that we assume our character as signs, pointing to that which withdraws). But under the reign of *Technik*, this lack of self-regard turns into a self-absorption that carries humankind into a deluded and compulsive effort to secure all resources and even itself as a "standing reserve" (VA 30–31/27). Humankind takes itself as the subject of this activity and is captured by the illusion that it encounters only itself in everything it delivers over to the command of enframing; but in committing itself to the reserve, dissolving thereby even the object as *Gegenstand*, humankind commits itself to an ever more frenzied submission and self-loss. *Brauch* is experienced (though it is not experienced as such) in the best of cases as a comfortable habitual usage (beginning with the everyday use of language); in its truest form, perhaps, it is experienced as a kind of addiction.[18]

As far as language is concerned, Heidegger suggests, humankind is ordered to a kind of techno-speak. The *Ge-stell* essences in a dissimulation of *Ereignis* and an assignment of ordering to calculative thinking and the language of *Ge-stell*, within which humankind is in-formed and fitted into the technical-calculative framework. *Ge-stell*, in which the essence of *Technik* speaks (all the while veiling its essence), commands for itself a formalized language, in-forming *itself* into information and securing itself in information theory. The drive to secure language itself as a standing reserve leads to a sacrifice of natural language (US 252/OW 132).

But the drive to formalizing meets a kind of obstacle here, a sort of irreducible, unmasterable excess. Formalization in fact *depends* on natural language. Though it seeks to deny this dependency as a merely provisional shortcoming, it is forced to concede that its formalization requires translation into natural language. *To bring its saying to language* (we should note the appearance of the *Wegformel* here — somewhat obscured by the translation [US 252]), it must pass by way of this "still unformalizable" residue. *Ge-stell* cannot come to language without natural language; its drive to self-totalization and its apparent self-sufficiency meet an unsurpassable limit here.

As long as this limit is conceived only in relation to that which it limits (as the not yet formalized or even the unformalizable), it will be determined negatively. Heidegger points instead to the possibility of a kind of sudden reversal. The "excess" represented by "natural language" must be thought out of the nature of language itself, out of *physis*, which reposes in its turn, Heidegger says, in *Ereignis*. Thought in this manner, the "natural" dimension of saying must be thought not as a residue but as what truly delimits techno-speak in the manner of an origin, preceding it and "overtaking" it. From a historial perspective, Heidegger envisions a sudden and unpredictable fulguration that would remove what is present from the hold of *Technik* (US 253/OW 133).

What is the status of this shattering glimpse (*Ein-blick*) whose possibility Heidegger offers in the mode of "What if?"* What necessity of *thought* does this mode of supposition answer to, this envisioned tearing of the veil? We may say, I believe, that this path of thinking *would not have been undertaken* unless the glimpse had already occurred (or more precisely perhaps: if the path is undertaken, the glimpse will have occurred) — thought could not have set out without this promised but unpredictable end. But it offers itself only to supposition and in supposition, as Heidegger indicates with the strongly re-marked *Wie aber* and thrice repeated *Wie wenn*, and then with a kind of qualifying retreat. For *every* language, he goes on to add here (I referred to this passage above), is appropriated in saying; every language is *eigentliche Sprache* and thus historial in character. The task in approaching the fiery horizon of this meditation is to grasp the limit of language *in its historicity* and at whatever measure possible of

*The paragraph in which this possibility is sketched is punctuated with the phrases *Wie aber, wenn . . .* ; *Wie, wenn . . .* ; *Wie, wenn . . .* Heidegger's marginal note to the first *Wie aber* suggests that the *Wie* is to be understood as containing a "how": *der Vorenthalt in dem wir uns aufhalten* ("the withholding in which we keep ourselves" [US 253]).

nearness to *Ereignis* (US 253/OW 134).[19] "In the appropriative provenance of the word," Heidegger writes, "that is to say, of human speaking from out of the saying, rests the peculiar property of language" (US 253/OW 133).

To these last words of the body of his meditation (the next line announces the conclusion), and specifically to the word "word," Heidegger appends the following note: *Wort — die verlautende Sage*. He thus evokes, once again, the intralinguistic form of the *Brauch*: language's use of human speech. He has circumscribed the "natural" with the motif of *Ereignis* and its history, eliminating any possibility of a sentimental or nostalgic evocation of the idiomatic and thus any unthinking affirmation of "natural language" over against the technical. But this evocation of the human word also prepares a redefinition of the structure of need. He has prepared the discussion thus far through a thematics of freedom versus self-absorption and dependency. He rethinks it now with the term *Fehl* and as the condition of assuming a relation to language.

The relation in question cannot be one of representation or be founded in any form of dialectical knowledge. Novalis's representation of language as a "monológue" cannot answer to the manner in which we belong to the structure (the *Gefüge*) of the design of saying. Yet language *is* monologue, Heidegger declares, designating with italics the manner in which language comes about. It alone speaks, and it speaks alone, *einsam*. *Einsam* does not mean "cut off" or "without relation"; on the contrary, Heidegger says, "in the lonesome there essences precisely the want [*Fehl*] of the common as the most binding tie *to* it" (US 254/OW 134). Linking *einsam* to the Gothic *sama* and the Greek *hama*, he argues that it bespeaks the *same* in the unity of what belongs together, returning thereby to his initial concern in this essay with the "unifying" in language. What unifies, we see now, is what is peculiar to language and what "essences" as the "want" of the common. What is the common (*Gemeinsam*) here? Are we to understand it as the everyday — the commonality of everyday usage, the commonplace? Or might the term name a triplefold unifying: *Ge[m]-ein-sam*? Would the proper of language be what the common lacks, or a wanting in/of a gathered difference, even a failing or straying with regard to such a common ground? Heidegger offers no clue, and indeed the very indeterminacy of the term in its context implies that we should understand it perhaps as no more than that commonality language *would* offer were it in fact "monologue" in the sense of Absolute Idealism. Language essences, then, as the "wanting" of such a commonality. Its essence defines in this way the finitude of Being (and perhaps the inevitability of reference to a common of some kind). But Heidegger again turns about the apparent "negativity" of such a formulation. *Einsam*, he argues, says the "same" that unifies in the belonging to one another; it thus names a relationality that Heidegger here specifies in relation to *Brauch*. Language speaks *einsam, out of relation* — the double relation of language's need of sounding and the appropriative usage of humankind: "Saying needs sounding in the word. Humankind, however, is only capable of speaking insofar as, belonging to Saying, it listens to it, in order to be able to say a word in saying after. That needed usage and this saying after [which derives from *Ereignis*'s own needed usage of humankind 'for itself'] rest in that wanting, which is neither a mere defect [*Mangel*] nor indeed anything negative at all" (US 254/OW 134). The wanting of the common is *Brauch* in its doublefold articulation, a "wanting" that is historially determined, as we saw in the line preceding this redefinition of the notion of language's "monologue."

Numerous paths open here. Stressing the link to Heidegger's words on the *Befehl*, we might pursue the notion of the law, as conveyed most immediately in the French cognate *faillir* in the phrase *il faut* ("one must"). The latter would bespeak both the historial destining of usage (*il faut* connotes fate) and the want that is its ground. Stressing the "errancy" connoted by *fehlen*,* on the other hand, we might pass to "The Anaximander Fragment" and the suggestion that within the history of Being, usage is always misusage in that it unfolds in the oblivion of Being. Without such misusage, Heidegger says, "there would be no connection from destiny to destiny: there would be no history." With every historial decision, Heidegger writes in an enigmatic phrase, "destiny tries itself against destiny" (H 337/E 26). The problematic of *Brauch* is also the problematic of history. Usage is at the origin of all epochal transformation. At the limit of the history of Being (a history where a kind of "fate," in a Benjaminian sense, seems dominant in that every struggle of the historical over the unhistorical remains committed to delusion and the inescapable movement of destiny against destiny), it is the ground of reversal once errancy manifests itself as such and humankind undertakes thinking — once it undertakes thinking, that is, as that being whose essence is used by the essence of Being.

The epochal transformation Heidegger evokes here and to which he points in "The Way to Language" names the site of a possible passage to another historial configuration, perhaps even the end of the "use and abuse" of history in the opening of an entirely different history. The relation it names offers, we might say, the "leverage," the space of freedom, for the preparation of another history. "The Way to Language" is actually

---

*Like the English "fail," the term is linked etymologically to the old French *fa[il]lir* and to the Latin *fallere* (which leads us to *falsus*).

less explicit on this point than is "The Question of Technology," which nevertheless proceeds from the same thought of usage in opening the destining of *Ge-stell* to a glimpse of what saves in it, namely a relation to what grants *Ge-stell*. In a sense, "The Question of Technology," although an earlier work than "The Way to Language," goes farther than the latter in opening the gap we have noted in the *er-eignend-brauchende Be-wëgung*; the relationality marked so precariously in the later essay is drawn out in the earlier by reference to an apportionment, to the human share (*Anteil*) in appropriation that is veiled by the injunction of *Ge-stell* but nonetheless belongs to the granting of its essence.[20] A "free" relation to *Technik* and a possible passage depend upon an assumption and harboring of this relation, which, when thought as such, allow us to speak of the ambiguity of *Technik*, a double indicating (*Technik* is *zwei-deutig*) that Heidegger goes so far as to *figure* as a constellation. The driving injunction of *Ge-stell* and the reserving hold of the saving, he says, "draw past each other" like the paths of two stars in the course of the heavens. "But precisely this," he continues, "their passing by, is the hidden in their nearness. When we look into the ambiguous essence of technology, we behold the constellation, the stellar course of the mystery" (VA 37/33). The *Blitz* that we might be tempted to read as a Nietzschean or Hölderlinian (even Benjaminian) flash of lightning gives way here to a movement in the gathering night named in the concluding pages of *Discourse on Thinking* (*Gelassenheit*) — a movement, or perhaps a tension of countermovements, that is at the source of the setting under way of thought.

"The Way to Language," as I have said, does not lend itself to such figuration, but it is thinking the *same* of the movement I have just referred to with its reference to the *Fehl* that defines the peculiar property of language. And if it does not foreground "the saving" quite as much as "The Question of Technology," it does nevertheless carry farther a thought of its harboring and growth. In some ways its figuration (it does, after all, have recourse to the *ereignisartige* thematics of sight and light) is actually poorer in suggestion; but this figural poverty answers to what I take to be a stricter thought of relationality. The question that frames the introduction of the motif of the *Fehl* concerns the possibility of a thought of language (as the "proper way of *Ereignis*") that does not pass by way of representation. Our *distinction* as mortals, Heidegger says (turning about once more the apparently negative character of the relationality he is exploring), is that we cannot escape language in order to view it cognitively: "That we cannot know the essence of language — know it according to the traditional concept of knowledge defined in terms of cognition as representation — is not a defect, however, but rather an advantage through which we are drawn forth [*vorgezogen*] in a distinctive realm, that realm where we, who are needed and used to speak language, dwell as *mortals*" (US 255/OW 134).

Two crucial points transpire here: first, the human engagement with language in usage (*Brauch*) engages us in our *mortality*; second, our relation to language, our *dwelling* as mortals with(in) language, can only be thought from our "linguistic" usage, that is, from the way we are used and engaged in usage for the speaking of language (via what Heidegger named the *Be-lang* in "The Essence of Language"). In other words, as Heidegger concludes in the succeeding lines, we must *speak* the relation to begin to think it: "Saying, in its most particular property, does not allow itself to be captured in any statement. It requires of us that we achieve by silence [*erschweigen*] the way-making movement in the essence of language — and do so without talking about silence" (US 255/OW 135). Given the context of a discussion of usage, it is difficult not to hear in this passage a subversive echo of Wittgenstein. But the reference to silence answers more immediately to the thinking we followed throughout "The Essence of Language," where Heidegger attempts to gather the *verlautende* saying in the *melos* of the relation of relations drawn out by language and thereby absorb it in the silent echo of the *Geläut der Stille*. In the last chapter, I tried to read this movement as a veritable inscription of the event thought in "The Origin of the Work of Art" within the *Denkweg* of "The Essence of Language." In this perspective, we may read the conclusion Heidegger reaches in "The Way to Language" as once again the "same" conclusion as that reached in "The Essence of Language" as well as in "The Question of Technology."* But in "The Way to Language" Heidegger is also in a position to think the saying of the "relation of relations" (which is *now* the relation in which language itself unfolds) as the manner of harboring the growth of the saving to which he referred in the "The Question of Technology." Once again, it is in and by language that the saving relation is to be drawn out: *dichterisch wohnet der Mensch* ("poetically man dwells" [cited in VA 39/34]).

The condition, Heidegger says, is a change in our relation to language. I cite at length because we should now be prepared to hear the import of the following words in their displacement of the prior reference to the "relation of relations":

The change rests upon our relation to language. The latter is determined according to destiny, that is, whether and how we come to be maintained in the essence of language as the original writ [*Ur-kunde*] of *Ereignis*. For *Ereignis*, appropriating,

---

*I refer to the remarkably strong turn to *poiēsis* at the conclusion of "The Question Concerning Technology" — remarkable for the fact that the counterplay of *Denken* and *Dichten* is played down in favor of the saving role assigned to the latter.

holding, and holding to itself is the relation of all relations. Thereby, *our* saying remains, as an answering, always relational. The relation [*das Ver-hältnis*] is thought here from out of *Ereignis* and no longer in the form of a mere connection. Our relation to language is determined out of the mode in which we, as the used, belong in *Ereignis*. (US 256/OW 135)

But in what *manner* are we appropriated in *Ereignis*, and what manner of response would correspond to this appropriation in such a way as to prepare the change? Heidegger responds, "The experience might awaken: all meditative thinking is a poetizing, all poetry a thinking. Both belong together from out of that Saying that has already bespoken itself to the unsaid because it is thought, as thanks [*weil es der Gedanke ist als der Dank*]" (US 256/OW 136) — to which Heidegger appends the following note: "as used in *das Ereignis* for *das Ereignis*, the renunciation [*Entsagen*] that owes itself to: *das Ereignis* in *die Befügnis*" (US 256).

So the question becomes, essentially, *was heisst Denken?* The text by this name defines the thinking in question precisely as a *Danc.** And to such thankful remembrance, as we have seen, *das Leben sich eignet* — the *Leben* from which we must think the *Leib* to which Heidegger refers in speaking of the appropriation of the bodily and which must itself be thought from *physis*. The cultivation and harboring of the relation to the saving is the letting emerge of *physis* and the "growth" of what saves. In language, we may presume, it is an emergence like that named in Hölderlin's phrase "*Worte, wie Blumen, entstehn*," through a human showing that emerges ever more distinctly in its relationality. It is a "free use of the proper." Free, in a sense I will gradually define, over against a freeing movement to which it owes its spontaneous thanks.

So the response is "thinking." But what of the freeing movement itself and the manner in which we are engaged? Though *What Is Called Thinking?* attempts to engage it and identifies it as its directing thought, this work offers no more than clues. But these are significant. The *experience* of *Brauch* is described in at least two ways from the basis of the figure of the drawing we have seen in Heidegger's meditation on the lines from "Mnemosyne" ("A sign we are, without meaning . . ."). What draws, he suggests, *draws us into thinking*, as he indicates with the guiding phrase that corresponds in a thinking manner to Hölderlin's poetic statement (indeed, the two forms of drawing I will describe correspond to the modes

*I refer to lecture 3, part 2, of *What Is Called Thinking?* and the examination, proceeding from the root *thanc*, of what "thinking" properly names. *Gedanc*, Heidegger writes, says "the gathered, all-gathering thinking that recalls. *Der Gedank* says as much as does *Gemüt*, *der Muot*, the heart" (WHD 92/139 — the latter phrase is omitted from the translation). Heidegger also links to *Gedank* memory and thanks, as I will note in the discussion to follow.

of thinking and poetizing in their experience of the *Brauch*).* I translate the phrase literally, because its syntax is crucial to its movement: "*The most thought-provoking is, that we are not yet thinking* [*Das Bedenk-lichste ist, dass wir noch nicht denken*]" (WHD 2/4, Heidegger's emphasis). For the fact, in the fact, by the fact, when it becomes a fact (etc.) that we are not yet thinking, the most thought-provoking *is*. The most thought-provoking *essences* in and by the fact that we are not yet thinking — it *shows*, Heidegger adds, by this fact. In the fact of our "not yet thinking," therefore, we *are* the sign of the most thought-provoking, and when we assume the impulse of this fact (for what is most thought-provoking *gives to think* as it gives itself), we are a sign that begins to take on meaning: we indicate what draws in its withdrawal, draw forth the withdrawal. Where we recognize, or perhaps say,† the fact *that . . .* , the most thought-provoking *is*. The more we assume this fact, the more its thought-provoking ground gives us to think it, and the more we are given or impelled to thought in this manner, the more we know that we are not yet thinking. The structure is precisely the same as the one Heidegger described in his Nietzsche lectures in the encounter with nihilism: thinking the essence of nihilism is a *passage* into it (ever more profoundly) and thus beyond it. It is also the structure of the relation between birth and death in *Being and Time*. Here, the assumption of the lack is the emergence of a promise and a setting under way: the more we enter the movement that gives us to think, the more we are given to think that we are *not yet* thinking — a "not yet," Heidegger tells us, that names an imminence. This "fact" has nothing negative about it; the more we confront the fact — *breathlessly*: here is the experience of the interruption or the caesura‡ — the more our waiting or anticipation grows in depth and quality and the more the promise grows. In the danger lies the saving promise — in the *Fehl* as it gives us to think in this most thought-provoking time, there is something like a gift and an impulsion.

One might wonder whether the dynamics of this movement are not the human correlate of the "godly" excess of self-sufficiency that Hölder-

---

*It is noteworthy here that *What Is Called Thinking?* once again proceeds by a *counter-ing* of thought and poetry. The relation between them that Heidegger draws with the guiding phrases (Hölderlin's and his own) constitute the distance over which the initial "practice leaps" are made.

†Implying that the thought-provoking gives itself in the phrase *dass wir noch nicht denken* (as in the case *dass es seiendes ist, und nicht Nichts*) — a possibility that I think may be heard in the phrase if it is accented properly (with the "is" stressed in such a way as to mark an "essencing," *against which* a kind of statement or declaration unfolds).

‡For we must traverse an absolute contradiction and a kind of *syncope* before the "not yet" *draws* in a temporal manner and names an imminence; what *gives* us to think is that we are *not* yet thinking: we must begin to think *that* we are not thinking, "simultaneously."

lin describes in the eighth strophe of "The Rhine." Would human "self-sufficiency" at the extremity of *Technik*, appearing to humankind as a sovereignty when it is in fact an extremity of loss and delusion, an almost total eclipse of the human essence, be the point at which "need" is engaged; would it be a kind of zero point of relation (that is nevertheless the point of advent of relation when it folds in thought) corresponding to the withdrawal of the gods?* However this may be, we find in the unfolding of Heidegger's guiding phrase a powerful commentary on the double movement of the "constellation" of *Technik*. Where *Technik* closes a future (as Heidegger indicates in *What Is Called Thinking?* with a phrase from Nietzsche: "the wasteland grows"), the essence of *Technik*, where it engages the human essence, offers a promise; and the closure of the one offers the opening to the other that opens over *against* it.

Where thought engages, Heidegger urges, it also inclines.† This is the second meaning of the drawing to which I have referred. It is a drawing in the sense of *reizen* ("to attract"): another term to add to the series that includes *ziehen* and *reissen*. Citing Hölderlin again, Heidegger underscores the manner in which the "purest" thinker thinks, so to speak, from the heart. The lines on which he focuses, from the poem "Socrates and Alcibiades," are the following:

> Who the deepest has thought, loves what is most alive,
> Who has looked at the world, understands youth at its height,
> And wise men in the end
> Often incline to beauty.
> (cited in WHD 9/20)

Heidegger does not do much with this citation. He leaves aside the relation drawn between thinking and *physis*, for example. But he indicates clearly that there is an *erotics* to usage (indeed *Brauch* is named most frequently in this text via the verb *mögen*, "to desire, to wish, to like"). Desire, where it concerns the human heart or soul, must be thought from the "need" of what calls to thinking, from its *wanting*. The point is then further developed in a manner that recalls the opening lectures of the *Nietzsche* volumes.[21] The thought-provoking, Heidegger tells us, is not necessarily something grave — it may be the beautiful (which Heidegger defines in this text as the appearance of what withdraws), the joyful, or the

---

*That human forgetting should be the correlate of godly withdrawal is close to being something of a "Heideggerian" commonplace. But here we have the dynamic of this relation: it is *Brauch*.

†"The originary word *thanc* is imbued with the original nature of memory: the gathering of the constant intending of everything that the heart lets come to presence. Intention is understood here in the sense of *Minne*: the inclination [*Zuneigung*] with which the inmost meditation of the heart turns toward all that is in being" (WHD 93/141).

graceful — all of them, we might note, manifestations marked by a "draw-ing" self-sufficiency.

There is an important crossing here of the experience of thought and what would be inappropriately termed "aesthetics." But I would like to push on and ask: in what, or how, does the "self-sufficient" *want* to be thought? On this point, Heidegger gives us relatively little to go on. He situates *Brauch* very precisely and names it, but does not think it as such. It appears in the motif of the *Verwahrung*, the "keeping" to which human-kind is given and gathered for the preserving (in the thinking that is inti-mately a memory) of the truth of Being.[22] It is the site where thought and what is to be thought contract relation,[23] and as such the site of the *Wesenseinlass* we saw described earlier, that letting-occur via *Brauch* named by Hölderlin in the passages from "The Titans" and "The Ister" that Heidegger quotes in *What Is Called Thinking?*. When it is further situated in relation to the phrase of Parmenides that Heidegger reads in the last part of *What Is Called Thinking?*, it is defined as what governs the conjunction of *legein* and *noein* in their relation to the duality (the differ-ence of Being and beings) of *eon emmenai*. In precise terms, it governs the relation between *das Vernehmen* ("perception" as "taking to heart") and *das Anliegende* ("the adjoining" [WHD 157/144]) through the relation between that which lies (already) before and the letting lie before that illuminates, Heidegger says, the essence of language (WHD 123/202).*
The essence of language, as we have seen in "The Way to Language," comes about in the contract of *Brauch*, and thus in the light of this es-say (whose logic is absolutely consistent with the earlier *What Is Called Thinking?*), we must understand *Brauch* as the origin of the call to which Heidegger refers throughout the earlier text. Speaking precisely, it is not "Being" that calls, as *What Is Called Thinking?* suggests; rather, the call issues from the difference between Being and beings that is articulated in and with language itself in the relation of *Ereignis* and *Brauch*. In the earlier text, Heidegger says merely that *Brauch* speaks through *eon em-menai* and that it is the Being of beings (thought as the *Anwesen des Anwesenden*) that keeps the human *noein*. But once we introduce *Ereignis* and think *Brauch* as such, it becomes necessary to think the duality of Being and beings itself from its (non)ground. It is *Ereignis* that *needs* for the advent of Being and by which there is a call of Being in the advent of language itself. By way of *Brauch*, thought from *Ereignis*, Being and thought may be thought as the "same."

These terminological clarifications from the basis of the later discussion

---

*This is once again, I believe, the relation between "showing" and "showing," *sich zeigen* and *sichzeigenlassen*, that I attempted to define as the limit of language.

should serve only to underscore the point that despite its explicit role in *What Is Called Thinking?*, *Brauch* is not thought there as such. So the question resurfaces: What of the truth of Being *requires* the keeping that is accomplished in *legein* and assumed in the attention of thought? The closest we have to an answer, to my knowledge, appears in words near the end of *Discourse on Thinking*.

The context is a discussion of the bearing of *Gelassenheit* as releasement to what counters. Having stressed the initiative of such a passive conjoining vis-à-vis this hidden essencing of truth,* the interlocutors go on to discuss the perseverance of this receiving com-portment. A name is offered, *Inständigkeit*, that a Heideggerian poem explicates with a variation on *Mut* evoking the patience (*Langmut*) and magnanimity (*Grossmut*) of noble remembrance (G 62/82). Such "in-standing" or "in-dwelling," it is concluded, is "the true essence of the spontaneity of thought," where the latter is understood as *Andenken*, "noble-mindedness itself."

"Noble" is defined as what abides in the origin of its nature — a belonging whose source is for thought a kind of unthinkable a priori in that thought has its beginning there. The question that frames the problematic of the *Fehl* in "The Way to Language" thus reappears here as the interlocutors acknowledge the distinctive limit of thought. The question is then raised as to why humankind is so appropriated to such belonging, to which the scholar offers a response that is "barely conceivable": "Evidently the essence of humankind is released to that which regions because this essence belongs to it so essentially that without the human essence, that which regions cannot essence in the way it does" (G 64/83). The teacher recognizes that the notion of "need" named here is inaccessible to the representation of a subject/object relation, but the scientist adds a further difficulty. Abbreviating the reference to the essencing (of that which regions) in truth, and formulating the relation of *Brauch* ("the human essence is given over to truth because truth needs humankind"), the latter asks: "But is it not the distinguishing character of truth, and indeed precisely in regard to its relation to humankind, that it is independently [*unabhängig*] of humankind that which it is?" (G 65/84). The teacher, in other words, is anxious to *preserve* difference in its "transcendent" character. The scholar interjects a caution identical to the one that appears in "The Way to Language": to think usage, we must think further the essence of truth and the essence of humankind (and once again, I must emphasize: this has always been the problem). But the teacher is still anxious to phrase (para-phrase) the statement that has been made, despite the fact that such

---

*An initiative Heidegger links back to the notion of resolve as developed in *Being and Time*, a notion defined in *Discourse on Thinking* as "the self-opening of Dasein that is *properly* taken up *for* the open" (G 61/81).

a phrasing can be no more than *Behauptung* ("assertion"). He phrases it as follows:

The essence of humankind is released into that which regions and accordingly used by it for this reason alone: because humankind for itself has no power over truth and the latter remains in-dependent of it. Truth can only essence independently of humankind because the essence of humankind as releasement to that which regions is used by that which regions in regioning [*Vergegnis*] and for the preserving of determining [*Bedingnis*]. The independence of truth *from* humankind is clearly a relation *to* the human essence, a relation which rests in the *Vergegnis* of the human essence into that which regions.[24] (G 66/84)

This is indeed "barely conceivable," but paraphrasing again schematically, it says that the "transcendent" character of truth requires, for precisely the preservation of this (finite) transcendence, a kind of assumption or access that in no way determines it but rather allows it to come about in its "independence." It can only *be* independently via a being that has a relation to transcendence, a being that by its essence ex-sists in a movement that does not *presume* upon truth in the sense of a willful determination (it presumes only its relation) but opens to it, or offers to it, in the mode of a "letting," a kind of powerlessness. To come about, truth requires a human essence that in its "character" (as a pointing sign that draws out what withdraws *as* what withdraws, as the independent) is, we might say, "= 0," as Hölderlin put it in his reflection on tragedy.[25] To say, however, that humankind is "used" in such a letting as a kind of pure condition of movement can be misleading in that one appears to ascribe an intention to truth and to turn humankind into a "means" for the event, a formulation that returns us to a subject/object relation. But truth does not subsist somewhere beyond its use of the human essence — it comes about with its engagement of the human (in *Vergegnis* — the equivalent here of what Heidegger termed *Verwahrnis* in *What Is Called Thinking?*). One might conceive, perhaps, an "in-dependence" of truth that is equivalent to the "excessive self-sufficiency" Hölderlin attributes to the gods in "The Rhine." The impetus in truth could be conceived from this basis (all of Heidegger's references to the self-reserving mystery of truth would be pertinent here). But in such a movement there would already have to be relation: humankind could not be a means for it. Truth essences only in engagement. Engagement *occurs*, we must say, because there is an opening provided by the human essence in its mortality. "Capable" of their death, humans have no "capacity" over truth, they *open* to truth and offer it the site of the passage by which it im-parts itself. Only a being that knows death may receive the gift of essence, and the gift only comes about as a gift to such a being.

Truth (paraphrasing a bit more) requires a kind of nonrelation, or perhaps a *freedom* to enter into relation. There *is* relation (in and as difference) because there is the freedom of this usage — a freedom at the heart of usage. It is not simply that truth can be independent of humankind and independently itself because it engages with the essence of humankind (that essence = o); this formulation, as I have said, turns humankind into a means and truth into a "sovereign" subject. Truth engages and comes about because there is a freedom or an in-dependence that *lets it occur*, allows it into its essence. Because there is freedom, there is relation. Once again, it is not that humankind in its receptivity allows truth to maintain its independence; it is that a nondependency, a freedom, allows truth to occur (minimally, the nondependency of a sus-pension or interruption of some kind). A freedom in *Brauch*, the freedom *of Brauch*, is the ground of all "true" relation — and not just "the" relation, but every relation opened by the latter, for as we read in "The Anaximander Fragment," *Brauch* governs the relations of all beings that stand over against one another in jointure. The freedom of *Brauch*, we might say, releases or delivers to relation. The latter releasement is enabled by the strange nonpower of the human essence in its relation to death (the human essence named *to deinotaton*, "the strangest of all," Heidegger argued in his reading of *Antigone*) — a *nicht vermögen*, or what might be termed an experience of the impossible, that in the freeing event of truth allows the latter release from/to its excessive self-sufficiency. Heidegger in fact concludes "The Way to Language" with a reference (somewhat facile, I am afraid) to the relation of *Brauch* and death.* But is the human relation to death the sufficient noncondition for this event? Does a relation to the impossible open by the "syncope" of a relation to mortality, or is the relation to death itself given in a suspension, an *arrêt de mort*† that releases to this relation even as it opens relation to the "impossible" (not death "itself" but that over which one has no power)? Might the figure of lightning employed so often by Heidegger imply that there must be a "caesura" that releases truth and the ecstasis of the human relation to death? The event of an opening is required by the logic of finitude (or at least must be figured for the conception of this logic) wherein truth essences in its independence only by usage of a human essence that occurs only where it is used and stands "freely" in de-pendence to the address that opens in this usage.[26]

However presumptuous it might be to inscribe a thought of the caesura

---

*This reference comes before the last citation of Wilhelm von Humboldt and via the citation of Alexander von Humboldt's remark that his brother worked on his treatise " 'lonesome, near a grave,' until his death" (US 257/OW 136).

†I take the phrase *arrêt de mort* from the title of the narrative I will read in my last chapter; it means literally, "an arrest of death," or "death sentence."

or interruption in the relation of usage, we must pursue this line of reflection on truth's independence by recognizing that if the (non)condition of this independence is a kind of pure releasement on the part of humans that releases truth to its advent, the condition of the maintenance and unfolding of this independence is a keeping or preserve, a be-holding-to that lets be. Such keeping has at its heart a "sensing" and an "attention," a kind of divination that is the ground of truth's original enjoining and countering (*Vergegnis, Verwahrnis*) whereby the site of its advent is prepared. In *legein*, there is reciprocally a gathering (of thought) to and a gathering by thought of what is ad-joining (*anliegend*), a gathering that originally engages all of what Heidegger unfolds in *Gedank* (memory, heart, etc.). But this gathering in thought occurs in and by a kind of fold that Heidegger develops from the motif of thanking in its relation to memory.

We owe our thinking, he says, and thereby the essence of our being to what gives us to thinking and to which thought turns in faithful recall. Thinking what we are thereby given to think (which is inseparable from the giving and the setting under way of thought), thought commemorates "what it has and is." It knows itself in this manner *as* "obedient," where obedience (*hörigkeit*) — thought's dependency on what gives it to think — is understood not as a submission but from a belonging, itself grounded in thought's interested (*inter-esse*) intention. It thanks in thinking, Heidegger says, by *devoting itself* in recollection to what gives it to think. It *owes itself to*, Heidegger writes: *Der ursprüngliche Dank ist das Sichverdanken* (WHD 93/141) — a phrase whose lack of complement initially marks the "spontaneity" of thought's turn. *Andenken* is a *Zudenken*, as Heidegger argues in a phrase that marks the fold to which I have referred: "We devote our thinking of what is to be thought [the most thought-provoking] to the most thought-provoking" (*Wir denken dem Bedenklichsten der zu-Denkende zu* [WHD 158/146]; similar phrases recur throughout this passage). All answerable, all "proper" thought is thankful for the gift of thinking, and it thanks in no other manner than by thinking what gives in *wanting* to be thought. It thanks in thinking back and in offering its thinking to what it thinks — offering in the manner of an *Entgegentragen*. The offering, once again, is a countering meeting that marks relation, that *offers* relation. The fold of this relationality is the condition of letting what is to be thought *be* in its essence. Always *offering* it thought (itself), thought provides the separateness (*Abgeschiedenheit*) of what is to be thought. A kind of closure is made possible in this manner.[27] Finding me was easy, Nietzsche said; the difficult thing is getting rid of me. The possibility of allowing a thinking its solitude stems from the same *freedom* that Heidegger attempts to think here in defining the manner of thought's devotion to what is to be thought. In its own "dependency" on this latter, its assumption of its character as beholden, thought allows what it thinks to be where it belongs: in the seclusion (*Abgeschiedenheit*) that is proper to the most questionworthy. "If a thinking were able to leave that which gives to think in each case to its own essence, then such a thinking would be the highest thanks mortals can give. This thinking would be the indebted leaving of the most thought-provoking to its most proper seclusion, a seclusion that preserves [*verwahrt*] the most thought-provoking as invulnerable in its questionworthiness" (WHD 159/146).

"The broader the dependency, the more capable is the freedom of thinking" (H 370/E 55).* In *Discourse on Thinking*, Heidegger makes the same enigmatic turn to affirm the sovereignty of thought once he has defined the "suspension" of its power. The discussion is noteworthy here for its reflection on what we have seen thus far concerning the *Stimmung* of thought. After the lines from the dialogue I cited above, the conversation continues as follows:

— If this were so, then humankind, *as* in-standing in releasement to that-which-regions, would abide in the provenance of its essence, which we therefore may paraphrase as follows: humankind is that which is made use of in the essence of truth. Abiding this way in its provenance, humankind would be en-couraged [*angemutet*] to the noble in its essence. It would presume the noble [*Er vermutete das Edelmütige*].

— This presuming could well be nothing other than that waiting as which we think the in-stancy of releasement. . . .

— Noblemindedness would be the essence of thinking.

— That thinking that does not first owe thanks for something, but only gives thanks that it might think. (G 66/84)

The folding of auto-affection as pure hetero-affection is marked in the fact that thought thanks originally only for the fact that it is given to think. Thought marks only its relationality without determining in any way that which gives relation. Only the italicization of the "as" marks a definition of this relationality (and this only by a hint in that the "as" may merely mark a consequence) in the manner of a kind of *Stimmung*: *as* the in-standing (*der Inständige*: assuming the relation in steadfastness), humankind is en-couraged to its nobility and presumes/has an intimation of it. The "passivity beyond passivity" of humankind is not subjection or a dependency on what remains independent but a sovereignty grounded in the "spontaneity" of thought's folding. In the event of usage, humankind is impelled to its own "reflective" freedom — reflective because it is given to think itself *as* the indwelling. This is why the law is "gentle." It issues

---

*This statement from "The Anaximander Fragment" is made in the context of a discussion of the relation between thinkers.

perhaps in an *il faut*, but the *faillir* must be thought from the *Fehl* of usage and thereby from freedom. The *Stimmung* that answers the *Brauch*, as Heidegger understands it, is not compliance (though we might open this word up in an interesting way to mark the countering/joining folding: com-pliance), and it is not heroism or endurance, not the *suffering* of the impossible. There is a Heideggerian piety, to be sure, but it is inseparable from "the piety of the traitor" and as such is characterized by a kind of courage, a spontaneous and "sovereign" daring that *reaches*. How free, we might still ask, is any *Vermutung* proceeding from this determination of the heart if it is prompted to its spontaneous definition of that which sets it under way? — if its spontaneity answers (though in countering) the *Befehl*? If we think in terms of causality, then we will never escape a notion of human subjection to the truth of Being (and all the *ressentiment* that follows). Heidegger is clearly inviting to another thought of relation. From where we stand at this point in the reading I have pursued of *On the Way to Language* — which is to say, from the step we have made (back) from the "intralinguistic" problematic of *Brauch* to the exigency of think-ing its "extralinguistic" form — the thought of relation to which I have referred requires a meditation on freedom and *Ereignis*: on the freedom *of Ereignis* that constitutes, we might presume, its eventful character. We have at best *touched* the logic of usage and the sudden sus-pension (the lightning of the caesura) that lies at its heart. As Heidegger would say — as he *always* said[28] — a more consequent meditation on *Ereignis* and the human essence is required. But a kind of progress has been made, perhaps, if we recognize the necessity of this meditation, beginning with the fact that the question of finitude as it engages the human essence remains *the* question for this text, at least inasmuch as it engages "*the*" relation — the relation of *Ereignis*, humankind and language — and inasmuch as Heideg-ger could not be satisfied with its formulation.

But Heidegger claims that we can only begin to think the relationality of *Brauch* and the freedom at the heart of it *from language*, from the way we are used as mortals for the speaking of language and *via* such a speak-ing. We may think *Brauch* only from a *Sprachgebrauch* that engages its own limits. What would such a *Sprachgebrauch* be? Exploring this notion of *Sprachgebrauch* (in the matter of translation, for example),[29] we would be brought again before the paradox of freedom, finding as much testi-mony to the spontaneity of thought as evidence of its "submission" in answering to language's manner of "playing" with humankind, which Heidegger at one point describes as that "slip of the tongue." We would be brought again to the fold in that call to thought wherein thought is always already implicated (implicated by *Ereignis* for showing). As for its content, the preceding pages have limned Heidegger's understanding of it and should at least indicate that any summary can only pass right by such usage and perhaps even foreclose it by reinstating the mode of *Behauptung*. But we might conclude by noting once again that such usage would be guided by the promise of what Hölderlin called "the free use of the proper," which I read now as follows.

"*Free*" names initially a manner of assuming the destiny that commits mortals to the *Geheiss* of *Technik* once this destiny is glimpsed in its ambiguity and *Technik* manifests its Janus-face. But such an assumption is always also the anticipating response (an indicating showing) to the promise of that which exceeds *Technik* as its origin — a countering, pro-voking response that is at once spontaneous and answerable, "free" in that it is released by a groundless interruption to its singular *address* (a call, but also an aptitude or adroitness [*Geschick*]), thereby proceeding from a freedom at the heart of *Ereignis* that renders possible *Brauch* itself. All usage proceeds from a freedom . . .

"*Use*" as *Sprachgebrauch* (and again, this is *how* mortals are used) is an engagement with the "common" language in what it gives or hints of a relation to the "lack" of commonality from which all speech communities proceed and to which they return whenever their essential relations are communicated (im-parted) and thereby reinvented; it is a usage impelled by an impassioned need (all the Heideggerian motifs of desire are grounded here) to im-part community in response to the opening of its promise, a desire that is known bodily in the engagement with the event(s) whereby a time offers itself to be thought in its historial character, and where what it means *to be* comes into question.

"*The proper*" was thought by Hölderlin as a capacity for representation and dictated a thought of "sobriety." Heidegger, somewhat less "sober," carries it back to the earth and *physis*, defining it as the bodily that emerges in a showing. Of the terms we have considered, it is the least approachable, its "free use" the least imaginable. It lends itself to the most suspect naturalism (metaphors of rooting, growing, etc., even an astonishing erotics: the tear, the veil, the hand, the growing again, etc.), but is also explicitly advanced as that which can never be fully appropriated and has no definable "property": no immanent movement grounds its emergence. As Heidegger said already in "The Origin of the Work of Art," the artwork uses the earth but does not exploit it in setting it forth. A kind of intervention, even a violence, is required in this *letting emerge* (we have seen this even in *What Is Called Thinking?*), but such usage never exhausts what "loves to hide." A free use of the proper will thus be impelled always to further usage, will *invite* further usage. There is an erotics here, once again, but also an ethics.

The promise of *such* usage, however, is hinted at today by *what remains* in the sense of a kind of excess vis-à-vis *Technik*. As we have seen, the "idiomatic" in the natural is what resists the commandeerings of *Ge-stell*. It is almost as though we must *start from the body* — or at least from the cultural[30] — in learning a free use of the proper, and, where language is concerned, from the *Verlautung des Wortes*: speech and writing conceived as a use of the body. Learning a free use will mean learning thought and following the heart. But at the most proximate horizon there is the bodily. The movement I have been tracing through *On the Way to Language* is in some measure a struggle with this knowledge. The problematic of *Brauch*, as we have finally seen, is the problematic of freedom, but it starts from the "fact" that language needs human speech as *Verlautbarung* (in the way that truth needs its setting-up through the earth). It is the problematic of finitude — of the "almost unthinkable" fact that truth cannot come about apart from human intervention: the daring, even exorbitant gesture of tracing a limit. Heidegger struggles to enfold this intervention within the movement that it releases and to which it will always have answered; but at the heart of the event there is the "fact" of the human — a "human" freed in its *facticity*. Thought starts from that fact and will always return to it as long as it is thought. Thought strings the bow, as Heidegger might say, of freedom and the proper, each of them equally enigmatic for it where they are thought at their limits (the *same* limit): the freedom of *Ereignis*, the furtiveness and opacity of *physis*. *Brauch* names the releasing tension of this mortal play to which a "free use of the proper" would offer no end.

PART II

Celan

4

The Realities at Stake in a Poem

IN reading Paul Celan's prose statements, particularly the speeches delivered in Bremen and Darmstadt, I cannot escape an impression Celan himself may have sought to prompt with his choice of language: *here is what must be said about poetry after Heidegger.* "Must be said" in that Celan seized the essential elements of a meditation on poetic language that still remains crucial to any reflection on the historicity of the poetic text; but "must be said" also in that Heidegger's writing on language and poetry fails to answer fully to a time after the "terrifying silence" to which Celan, evoking the Second World War, refers in his Bremen address (GW 3: 186/34). Celan recovers in these texts something of the engagement with history that initially prompted Heidegger to turn to Hölderlin's poetry in 1934 and that informed all of his thought of the late 1920s and 1930s. He recovers it through an effort to think his time *from his time* (the time given in an assumption of finitude), and in recognizing, with the later Heidegger, that such a task implies thinking from language. Yet he also recovers it *for* his time in a reflection on what poetry must be after terrifying silence and under the ever-expanding reign of *Technik.*

In the following, I will document the impression (or claim) I have described by offering partial readings of both Celan's "Speech on the Occasion of Receiving the Literature Prize of the First Hanseatic City of Bremen" (January 20, 1958) and "The Meridian" (October 27, 1960). Although I will discuss them separately, it should become apparent that the two speeches touch upon the same possibility of *passage* in language (toward oneself and toward the other, in time) and thus upon the poetic experience of history. Together, they point powerfully to what was at stake in Heidegger's meditation on language and history and to what is at stake there for us today. They mark an engagement and an affirmation to which I believe we would do well to attend—now, when the question of history assumes a new, essential urgency and is all too frequently closed by those who, for ideological purposes, evoke "history" most loudly: as though we knew where we stand today (amidst the distractions of socioeconomic systems that work powerfully to suspend a knowledge of time), as though "history" could speak for itself.

The Bremen Speech

Celan begins his Bremen address in terms that immediately evoke Heidegger. He invites his auditors to refer what he says about the path that has brought him to Bremen both to what Heidegger suggests in *What Is Called Thinking?* concerning the relations between thought, memory, and thanks and to Heidegger's development of the concept of remembrance in his reading of Hölderlin's "Remembrance."

Celan will answer the honor accorded to him by the city of Bremen by recalling the experience that has brought him to Bremen *as a poet*. Out of this remembrance, he will offer a reflection on the "realities" and (as we will see in "The Meridian") the thought at stake in the poem — for him and for those who are coming after him: "other, younger poets" (GW 3: 186/35).

He will commemorate a movement — a movement involving topographical displacements, to be sure, but more essentially an experience of time that comes to him in and through language. It begins in a region "now dropped from history" (Celan will not give its name — as though this closest name remains most distant as the "details" come back to him): a kind of literary landscape (or a landscape of the letter) from which come "many of the Hassidic stories which Martin Buber has retold in German . . . a region [*Gegend*] . . . where both people and books lived" (GW 3: 185/33). There, the name of Bremen traces its distant outline for Celan through his encounter with the names of authors associated with the city and through the shape of books published by the Bremer Presse. In the literal topography drawn in the imagination of the young Celan, Bremen is brought near but still sounds distant, "unreachable" (GW 3: 185/34). In reach (*Das Erreichbare*: Celan will use some form of the word four times) is Vienna, a literary site that Celan can hope to attain and inhabit.

But in the years to come, this imaginary topographical construction defining what is "reachable" is destroyed. We know what detours this destruction occasioned.* And we know that the fact that Vienna, for example, can no longer be attained is certainly not without relation to the possibilities of access offered to Celan by the German language. Yet language — both "his" language (the same German language in which he wrote his poetry) and, in a sense to be determined, language itself (for

---

*"Detours" is Celan's word — one that he immediately puts in question. For the history Celan is commemorating has radically altered any thought of destination or of homecoming.

Celan appears to invoke in this passage something like what Heidegger would term the essence of language) — remains reachable, "unlost." The possibility of a different kind of topography — or rather, the possibility of finding a bearing, of marking out paths and pursuing a direction — will continue to hold itself out to Celan:

Only one thing remained close and reachable amid all losses: language.

Yes, language. In spite of everything it remained unlost. But it had to go through [*hindurchgehen durch*] its own lack of answers, through terrifying silence, through the thousand darknesses of murderous speech. It went through and gave no words for what happened; but it went through this event. It went through and could resurface, "enriched" [*"angereichert"*] by it all.

In this language, I tried, during those years and the years after, to write poems: in order to speak, to orient myself, to find out where I was, where things were going, to sketch for myself a reality.

It meant, as you see, something happening [*Ereignis*], movement [*Bewegung*], being under way [*Unterwegssein*], it was an attempt to find direction. And when I ask about the sense of it, I feel I must tell myself that this question also speaks to the question as to the sense of the clock's hand. (GW 3: 185–86/34)

I cite this passage in its entirety because Celan describes in it an experience with language that is fundamental for his poetry. "The Meridian" will in fact provide a more precise description of poetic self-discovery; it will offer more precise "dates." But what Celan terms a "date" in that text — a "turning" in an individual's existence that involves an experience of mortality and of the abyss to which the singular human Dasein opens in its freedom, a turning remarked but also in some sense accomplished in the language of the poem — is not dissociable from the experience with language he describes here. And no knowledge of mortality, for Celan, can come without the memory of the losses to which he refers in the passage I have quoted. Or more precisely, all knowledge of mortality for him, after the war, entails knowledge of what became of death in the time of "terrifying silence" and murderous speech — a time for which language gave no words (thus a time where death loses *meaning*).

Yet if language gives no words for what happens in the time of murderous speech, it nevertheless gives itself. Despite its silence, and perhaps even through its silence — much as when Heidegger says that we only come to have a knowledge of language itself, that is, in its essence, through some kind of failure or suspension of speech[1] — language gives itself as the persistence of the possibility of relation. A pure possibility, we might say, for in its silence it gives no relation other than a relation to itself as "reachable" (which will offer to Celan, as we will see, another form of relation). Any other relation as Celan has previously known it is destroyed. There are no words for what is happening (no words that hold), no meaning; there is only "murderous speech," which is *of* language, certainly, but unspeaking, and of a strange negativity that destroys relation and meaning.* Still, silence and the din of "murderous speech" remark a kind of presence of language itself ("reachable, near and unlost" [GW 3: 185/34])—language remaining, persisting in its nearness, and, as Celan puts it, "going through" its own lack of answers, terrifying silence, and the darknesses of murderous speech (thus a kind of death of its own). Six times in the second paragraph of the passage quoted, Celan uses the term *hindurchgehen* to describe the survival of language. Its presence thus comes to be marked by a mode of temporality.

We should pause to consider what it might mean to try to write poems in a language that "gives no words" for what is happening and at a time when a world of signification, a world of symbolic relations, has collapsed. Such a poetry cannot signify or pretend immediately to rebuild relations as they have previously been known. It would necessarily be a poetry *of language* in a previously unheard-of form: for again, of living symbolic relations, only language remains, and as the relation language offers to itself in its survival. An effort, then, to bring a mute language into speech (but in its muteness), to work in its *proximity*, and to bring forth from this proximity (which is also a distance) what language still offers of relation, what remains. *Singbarer Rest* ("Singable remnant") Celan writes in a later poem, and then from the same poem in subsequent lines:

> Entmündigte Lippe melde
> das etwas noch geschiet, noch immer,
> unweit von dir.

> —Unmouthed lip, announce,
> that something's happening, still,
> not far from you.†

The effort to write in and from this language (to discover where he stands, to find a direction) will entail, Celan says, not a naming but a movement (*Ereignis, Bewegung, Unterwegssein*). And Celan may well be suggesting that from language's very mode of remaining or surviving, of *going through* a kind of death, there comes a knowledge of time. Relation, he discovers, is a reaching through time (*durch die Zeit hindurchzugreifen*). To project a reality and to sketch out a direction toward this

---

*Strange because it is a possibility in the logos — again, it is necessarily *of* language — that is destructive of the logos in that it turns against its capacity for holding in being. "Murderous speech" destroys the relation that it is of the essence of language to give.

†GW 2: 36. Cited by Maurice Blanchot, *Le Dernier à parler* (Montpellier: Fata morgana, 1984), 35; *The Last One to Speak*, trans. Joseph Simas, *Acts*, 8–9 (1988): 235. The lines I have cited appear in the latter in translation by Pierre Joris.

reality is to move *in time*. Continuing with the passage I have been commenting upon, we read:

And when I ask about the sense of it, I feel I must tell myself that this question also speaks to the question as to the sense of the clock's hand [*Uhrzeigersinn*].
For the poem is not timeless. True it lays a claim to the infinite and tries to grasp through time — but *through* it, not above it [*durch die Zeit hindurchzugreifen — durch sie hindurch, nicht über sie hinweg*]. (GW 3: 186/34)

Thus when language resurfaces, or returns in its naming capacity, when it begins to speak again and thus to give a relation to what is, the relation it offers is one of approach or reaching through. The notion of relation has undergone a change for Celan, and with it the nature of the poetic task. Whereas the region of his origins constituted a kind of narrative space (the space of the Hassidic stories), and whereas it was possible for the aspiring writer to construct a topological distribution of "literary" names marking distance and proximity (the reachable and the unreachable), the destruction of this essentially linguistic region and the accompanying experience of language in which this destruction issues lead Celan to conceive of an entirely different structure of relation, one that is fundamentally temporal in character.

Language is "enriched" by its passage through silence and murderous speech, Celan says: *"angereichert."* He writes the term in quotation marks — and surely not without a measure of irony.[2] For if language might be termed "richer" after passing through silence and emerging in its essence as the ground of any possible relation (perhaps in an entirely new manner in a historial perspective — in this sense, we would indeed have to do with a transformation), this enrichment involves a most paradoxical gain. Language is "enriched" by time, but not in the manner of a regeneration, or through a dialectical sublation of the "death" through which it has gone, for no *meaning* is given to this death or to the losses of the time through which it has passed — language is in no way more meaningful, no richer in any traditional sense of the term. Rather, language is enriched in the emergence of its temporal essence. Language now offers itself in its historicity and as the ground of a relation that is radically finite. When it begins to speak, its richness does not inhere in the words or the names it offers but in the manner in which these words are marked by time. Accordingly, we see that if it offers the poet a new possibility of poetic relation, namely that of an address to an other in dialogue or conversation ("A poem, being one of the forms in which language appears, and thus dialogical in essence . . ." [GW 3: 186/34–35]), this possibility is attenuated to an extreme degree — for Celan compares the poem's effort to reach across time to throwing a letter in a bottle out to sea, "with the —

surely not always strong—belief that it could somehow wash up somewhere, perhaps on a shoreline of the heart" (GW 3: 186/35). The poetic relation, we might say, is grounded in time and exposed to time: the letter may not reach its destination.

Nonetheless, language as it now offers itself does give something like "approach." It offers to the poet the possibility of a kind of self-situation in and through movement toward an other: a "reality," perhaps a "you," he writes, that is approachable or addressable (*ansprechbar*) inasmuch as it stands open in its essence and offers itself in a proximity that may be inhabited (GW 3: 186/35). In other words, inasmuch as language gives it to be approached (renders it "addressable"). For the approach, Celan says, is in "dialogue": the poem answers to what it approaches, or it broaches a "conversation" (as Celan will write in "The Meridian"), in a manner that is already response, already the answer to an opening.

In "The Meridian," Celan will develop this structure more fully in terms of his notion of encounter and a kind of countering movement. Here, Celan stresses simply that he has come to understand the task of the poet as one of seeking paths in the direction of what language gives of an opening to the other. He stresses that this opening is in no manner guaranteed, just as language itself, even if it remains "near and unlost," is in no manner a possession and is something quite other than a world of names the poet might inhabit or build upon. When Celan suggests, after comparing the poetic effort of reaching to an other to tossing a letter out to sea, that what is at stake for the poem is an addressable "you" and an addressable reality (*Um solche Wirklichkeiten geht es, so denke ich dem Gedicht* [GW 3: 186]), he clearly means that these are no more than *possible* realities. Language offers relation, it offers the possibility of approach, but this approach is not simply given, no more than the place from which this movement starts.

On the contrary, we start today, Celan suggests, in a situation of loss and exposure that requires the same kind of movement he undertook in the years of "terrifying silence." His own efforts, Celan says, are to be compared with efforts of "younger poets," "those who, with man-made stars flying overhead, unsheltered in this hitherto unanticipated manner and thus exposed in the most uncanny way in the free, carry their existence into language, racked by reality and in search of it" (GW 3: 186/35).

Following the remarkably affirmative character of the Bremen address, we may say that Celan takes the experience of "uncanny exposure" to be the condition of poetry in the second half of the twentieth century. For such exposure also exposes language, gives language as the possibility of relation and thus the possibility of a reality. In the most extreme danger,

Heidegger wrote in his meditation on *Technik*, and in memory of Hölderlin, there grows what saves (VA 32/28). Celan intends something comparable with his notion of a language "enriched." It is enriched in that it is given anew (it gives itself) in its temporal essence *as the possibility and necessity* of poetry in this time of radical loss—that is, as the sole ground of relation. Pierre Joris (following Ingeborg Bachmann, perhaps) has suggested to me that Celan turned Theodor Adorno's remarks concerning Auschwitz and poetry in such a manner as to suggest that *only* poetry is possible after Auschwitz. Celan's statements in his Bremen address would seem to bear out this reading. Furthermore, if we take "poetry" in a large sense—that is, as an approach to a reality in and through an experience with language (an approach in and through language that is also found in thought and in each of the arts, though in always specific ways)—then I think we may accept Celan's response as a decisive "counterword" to Adorno's assertion.

"The Meridian"

Celan follows tradition when he accepts the Georg Büchner Prize with a speech that situates his work in relation to that of Büchner, but he does not offer his audience a literary history. Rather, he engages with Büchner's work in a manner that Heidegger terms *Auseinandersetzung* (Heidegger's notion of *Erörterung* is also germane), taking the problem of self-situation as a kind of lever for this critical confrontation. Moreover, Celan *performs* this confrontation, rather than describing it. As he indicates with the choice of title, the speech *describes a movement* of self-situation. It demonstrates in its very structure that its concern is not with literary history but with literature and history—with the historicity of literature. The accent, as Celan puts it, is on the present (GW 3: 190/40–41).

That Celan's accent is on the present means initially that he starts from the point where Büchner's text concerns us today. Poetry, he says, must return to the question Büchner poses to art if it is to question further on its own; for in the "muted," half-conscious questioning he finds in Büchner (GW 3: 192/43), Celan hears something that evokes "the oldest uncanny things" about art—something that is also "in the air today" (GW 3: 192/43), the air we have to breath. Büchner broaches a question that concerns our historical element (breath, Celan remarks, involves "direction and destiny"), an element that Celan finds stifling.

Celan starts from Büchner, then, and if he seeks a distance and a certain liberation from the uncanny side of art to which Büchner points with his question (a muted, half-conscious question in that Büchner's own voice bespeaks, and is to some extent in the grips of, the uncanny),* he does so from within Büchner's text. This is why Celan's confrontation with Büchner is properly an *Auseinandersetzung*. He takes his distance from Büchner *from* Büchner and by carrying through Büchner's question: "I am not looking for a way out, I am pushing the question farther in the same direction, which is, I think, also the direction of the *Lenz* fragment" (GW 3: 193/44). To *carry through* the question, as we will see, is to effect a turn and to follow the text back to its most proper object of concern (what Celan will describe as *seiner eigenen, aller eigensten Sache* [GW 3: 196/48]). Here, before "Büchner"† Celan finds the place from which poetry may proceed in a step that liberates it from "art" — poetry in general, today, and his poetry. From here, and from an extraordinary statement of what poetry may "hope for," Celan will cite lines of his own, lines that mark a self-encounter and what Celan calls "a kind of homecoming" (GW 3: 201/53). The "step back" in and from Büchner's text liberates the possibility of self-citation and the poetic naming of this movement of self-situation that the speech has described.

Celan begins the confrontation to which I have referred after introducing the "eternal problem" of art (in its uncanniness) and after describing the interruption of art by poetry, illustrated by Lucile's "counterword" in *Danton's Death*. The "turn" begins when Celan locates Büchner's question regarding art in his evocation of the means by which art serves "the natural and the creaturely" (GW 3: 191/42). Celan foregrounds in Lenz's description of the scene he has witnessed of "two girls sitting on a rock" a kind of disjunction or incongruity between the admired natural beauty and the expression of a desire to capture it: "Sometimes one would like to be a Medusa's head to turn such a group to stone and gather the people around it" (GW 3: 191–92/42). The strangeness, even the perversity of Lenz's expression (perverse already by virtue of the figural transactions occurring between the Medusa's head and the girl on a rock "putting up her hair") allows Celan to remark the distance implicit in Lenz's — and Büchner's — aesthetic effort, which is "to seize the natural *as* the natural by means of art" (GW 3: 192/42 [my emphasis]). Such an effort, Celan remarks, "means going beyond what is human, stepping into a realm which is turned toward the human, but uncanny — the realm where the monkey,

*Celan writes: "This is not the historical Lenz speaking, but Büchner's Lenz. Here we hear Büchner's own voice: here too art holds something uncanny for him." And shortly thereafter: "But you see: we cannot ignore the 'rattling' voice Valerio gets whenever art is brought forward. These are — Büchner's voice leads me to this supposition — old, the very oldest uncanninesses" (GW 3: 192/43).

†Which I write in the manner of Heidegger when he describes the object of his *Auseinandersetzung* with Nietzsche's thought: "Nietzsche" (see *Nietzsche* [Pfullingen: Neske, 1961]), 1: 9.

the automatons and with them … ah, art, too, seem to be at home" (GW 3: 192/43). Büchner's question would seem to involve the extent to which the human can be served by such a transcending movement, and perhaps even the extent to which art is even about the human or the "creaturely," in the sense of the naturalism evoked by Lenz.

Celan draws out this question by further remarking the uncanny form of Lenz's reference to art's uncanny means. For as I have noted, Celan hears in Lenz's words "Büchner's own voice" (GW 3: 192/43). Here, the mimetic character of the *Lenz* fragment betrays itself in such a way as to reopen the questions about the uncanny nature of art already posed by Plato ("the old and oldest uncanninesses"). Philippe Lacoue-Labarthe has identified what is essentially at stake in this implicit reference to the uncanny aspect of mimesis — namely its alienating character, its capacity to make the person involved in it (the artist and the commentator, reader, listener, or observer) "forget" about themselves.[3] Büchner has forgotten himself, Celan suggests, and this is why his questioning is "half-conscious." But he has engaged with the question of mimesis enough, or has gone far enough with art's anti-mimetic means, to have exposed another possibility in art. The very instability by which the *Lenz* fragment betrays its mimetic character points to a presence of the artist that cannot be grasped with any notion of representation.

At the outset of his speech, Celan had located such a presence of the human in the figure of Lucile: Lucile, who does not listen to what is said but who, as Celan remarks, "hears the speaker, 'sees them speaking,' who has perceived language as a physical shape and also — who could doubt it within Büchner's work — breath, that is, direction and destiny" (GW 3: 188/39). He now listens to Büchner's text as Lucile might ("I think of Lucile when I read this," Celan says, speaking of the way the artist forgets himself [GW 3: 193/44]) and seeks Büchner as a "person" in the figure of Lenz.

Lucile testifies to the presence of the human with her defiant "Long live the King" — an act of freedom, Celan writes, a step that draws its force from its mortal character inasmuch as with this "counterword" Lucile commits herself to death. Celan finds an indication that the *Lenz* fragment is also written out of an experience of mortality (Lenz's experience of mortality as grasped by Büchner) in its interrupted last sentence: "His existence was a necessary burden for him. — Thus he lived on …" (cited in GW 3: 194/45). By reading this final sentence in the light of Lenz's end (the historical Jakob Michael Reinhold Lenz), he gives it a kind of Heideggerian — or more appropriately, perhaps, a kind of Hölderlinian — tonality. In other words, Celan inscribes the fragment under the sign of poetry, which, he says, "rushes ahead" and seeks to "see the figure in its direction"

(GW 3: 194/45); that is, as it emerges as a figure, as a "sign," advancing under the unthinkable, as Hölderlin says, and toward death. From this end, Celan can find the "person" of Lenz ("that is — Büchner") in lines that appear near the beginning of the fragment — his presence as an " 'I' become strange" (GW 3: 195/46) in an opening upon the abyss whose condition, as Heidegger tells us, lies in an authentic confrontation with mortality. Lucile's words, honoring the "majesty of the absurd," and thus testifying to the presence of the human, now find their counterpart in a line expressing Lenz's regret that he cannot walk on his head. Celan remarks: "A man who walks on his head, ladies and gentlemen, a man who walks on his head sees the sky below, as an abyss" (GW 3: 195/46). Lenz ("that is — Büchner") has gone farther than Lucile, however, in that his "step" is no longer a word: it is "a terrifying silence [*ein furchtbares Verstummen*]," Celan writes, that "takes away from him — and us — breath and the word" (GW 3: 195/47).

In the Bremen address, Celan had used the same words to describe the suspension through which language had passed during the war. It had gone through "its own lack of answers, through terrifying silence, through the thousand darknesses of murderous speech." As we saw, for Celan this silence was something like the condition of poetry as he came to practice it. Here, in "The Meridian," poetry is identified with a turn back to such a suspension of the word and of the breath:

Poetry: this means perhaps an *Atemwende*, a turning of our breath. Who knows, perhaps poetry goes its way — the way of art — for the sake of just such a turn? And since the strange, the abyss *and* Medusa's head, the abyss *and* the automaton, all seem to lie in the same direction — it is perhaps this turn, this *Atemwende*, which can sort out the strange from the strange? It is perhaps here, in this one brief moment, that Medusa's head shrivels and the automatons run down?

Perhaps, also with the I, estranged and freed *here, in this manner*, some other thing is also set free? Perhaps from there the poem can be itself ... can in this now artless, art-free manner go its other ways, including the ways of art, time and again. (GW 3:195–96/47)

Büchner's phrase (" ... only, it sometimes bothered him that he could not walk on his head" (cited in GW 3: 195/46), thus *remarks a silence* that echoes beneath Lenz's steps in the mountains, a silence in which the poetry of the *Lenz* fragment takes its own step. *Against this silence*, "Büchner" appears in the shape of Lenz. The event (*Ereignis*) marks a date: the 20th of January. Celan notes that perhaps every poem is marked by such a date and that what constitutes the "newness" of poems today is that they seek to be "mindful" (*eingedenk*) of such dates (GW 3: 196/47). But this "newness" is not what he referred to as "in the air." On the contrary, it is what interrupts the ubiquity of art and the spread of the uncanny.

It would be worthwhile to pause at greater length over Celan's treatment of the uncanny. He tells us near the end of his address that he set out
to counter the contemporary demand for an extension of art, and it would
seem to follow that he is attempting to counter a contemporary form of
art's alienating tendencies. Celan may be referring to a specific movement
or movements, or he may be thinking more generally of *la société du
spectacle* (a reference that may be justified by Celan's allusion to the reign
of *Technik*);* most likely, he had both possibilities in mind. But whatever
his specific reference, we should observe that Celan's concern is with art's
uncanny character *in relation to the human*. His stated purpose is to free
poetry from art, but it must be emphasized that this also means freeing art
from its subservience to a notion of representation that is indissociable
from a representation of the human and "what is natural for the creature"
(GW 191/142), a representation no less stifling today than in 1960. By
freeing the possibility of recognizing poetry in art, and thus the presence of
the human — in other words, by delimiting art (and the uncanny) and
making art possible to approach from another direction ("Perhaps after
this the poem can be itself . . . can in this now artless, art-free manner go
other ways, including the ways of art, time and again" [GW 3: 196/47]),
Celan is able to entertain the possibility of relaxing the distinction he has
attempted to achieve between the strangeness proper to poetry and the
strangeness of the uncanny and assert that "art, the uncanny strangeness
which is so hard to differentiate and is perhaps only one after all — art lives
on" (GW 3: 200/53). Carrying through Büchner's question in the *Lenz*
fragment and finding "Büchner," Celan can consider the uncanny side of
art as the way of access to the strangeness from which poetry takes its
departure, and thus as the way of access to self-encounter: "Take art
with you into your innermost narrowness. And set yourself free" (GW 3:
200/52). The uncanny both alienates *and* affords a poetic experience of
mortality and the abyss.

Jacques Derrida has remarked in his reading of Celan that we learn
about death and mourning from language, not the other way around,†
and in *Shibboleth* he has gone far in defining the potential in language that
creates the ambiguity of the uncanny around which Celan's speech pivots.
To carry Celan's question any farther, it would be necessary to dwell
further on this question of language and the strangeness of art. At this
point, however, I want only to emphasize the "pivoting" movement itself
and to suggest that it makes possible the essential turn in Celan's text, a

---

* "'Speed,' which has always been 'outside,' has gained yet more speed" (GW 3: 197/48).
† "One cannot say that we know [about the spectral quality of words] *because* we have
the experience of death and mourning. This experience comes to us from our relation to this
ghostly return of the mark, and then of language, of the word, of the name" (Derrida,
Schibboleth, 96).

turn away from the aesthetic, mimetic tradition by which art is conceived as the imitation of reality. This turn is a movement back from the transcending (albeit "uncanny") movement by which the natural is seized as natural and in which the existence of the writing subject is effaced; it is a turning back in which the poetic self situates itself in relation to a reality toward which it "reaches" in its otherness and *in its time*.

In a discussion of this movement "back," Celan will evoke an attention to "detail, outline, structure, color," and to the "tremors and hints" (GW 3: 198/50) of the creature described by Lenz. In other words, Celan will describe a no less precise — indeed, a far more "realistic" — attention to the "natural and the creaturely," but he will do so from the perspective of the finitude or "finite transcendence" of the singular (writing) Dasein. He will describe a poetry that would proceed from the turn of an *Atemwende* and thus a poetry that would proceed from *difference* in its approach to the other. In so doing, he will describe how poetry effects the "push" into historical existence that Heidegger described in *Being and Time*.*

I will try to stress essentially two points in Celan's remarkable statement of his poetics and what he hopes to add to the "old hopes": these concern the time of the poem and the structure (also temporal) of the encounter it seeks. I will stress the first point, because I believe we find in Celan's statement a forceful appropriation of Heidegger's description of the structure of the work of art. By emphasizing the second point, I hope to bring forth the way in which Celan begins to depart from Heidegger by pushing Heidegger's thought of the singularity of existence (or of the work of art) in the direction of a very radical understanding of the relation to the other.

The time of a poem, of course, is that of an *Atemwende*; and as we have seen, every poem marks a date, even commemorates a date (it is "mindful," Celan says), as it proceeds from this pause of the breath and the word. It speaks from out of this date, "its date," and as such it speaks of its own concern (*in seiner eigenen, aller eigensten Sache*). As Celan will emphasize, this concern, or "matter," is the concern of an individual; indeed, in these pages in which Celan exposes his poetics, he will return repeatedly to the fact that the poem is "the language become shape of a single person" (*gestalt gewordene Sprache eines Einzelnen*) (GW 3: 197–98/49). In doing so, however, he will also always return to his notion that the self comes to itself in relation to an other. The poem thus marks the advent of a self to itself in the "present" of the poem — but this is the presence of a self as open to an other and as heading or reaching toward it. In his descrip-

---

*Martin Heidegger, *Being and Time*, trans. John Macquarrie and Edward Robinson (New York: Harper and Row, 1962), 435.

tion of the poem's structure and "object," Celan will move back and forth between the presence of the solitary "I" and the other toward which the poem moves, but in the interweaving of these motifs, he will make it clear that the poetic self comes to itself and comes forth or steps forward in its finitude only in and by this movement. Poetry, Celan writes in identifying "Lenz," "rushes ahead" and "tries to see the figure in its direction." This direction is the direction of the figure in its mortality. Yet in the opening given in and by this "being toward death," the movement is also toward the other. Thus, Celan adds that in its *Atempause*, in the present of the poem opened by its "pause for breath," the poem also "heads straight for the otherness" which it considers "reachable." Its movement from its date is also to an other (date) — it marks its date *in this movement*.

The time of this movement is the time of hope and thought. The poem has always hoped, Celan claims, to speak from a different matter (*in einer Anderen Sache* [GW 3: 196/48]) even as it speaks only its own; once again, to speak its own concern is to give a "voice" to the other. Celan "merely" adds to the "old hopes" a different understanding of this other (a notion that leads him to speak of an "altogether other" [GW 3: 196/48]) and speculates that the poem "dwells or hopes" (*verweilt oder verhofft* [GW 3: 197/48]) with the thought of an encounter between this entirely other and a quite close other (which we may take, I believe, to be the freed and estranged "I"). The poem commits itself to a thought (with hope, "a word for living creatures," Celan adds, indicating that the time of the poem is distinctly human [GW 3: 197/48]) — it is the poem *of a thought* (the conception of a relation between self and other) that is "conceivable, perhaps, again and again."[4] The poem gives its thought to be thought repeatedly, just as it goes its way "time and again." Its time, the time of a pause of breath ("Nobody can tell how long the pause for breath — hope and thought — will last" [GW 197/48]) is one constituted in repetition.

The repetitive character of the poem's particular presence is remarked again by Celan when he recognizes that the poem "shows a strong tendency to silence" (GW 3: 197/48) but then asserts — as if to characterize more precisely the poem's "abruptness" — that the poem "holds its ground on its own margin": "In order to endure [*um bestehen zu können*], it constantly calls and pulls itself back from an 'already no more' into a 'still here' [or 'yet still,' *ein Immer noch*]" (GW 3: 197/49). These are difficult lines, but I believe we may understand them by remembering that the poem commemorates an event (a date) that *has happened*, an event that is nothing other than the emergence of a singular Dasein in its finitude. The poem proceeds from this event ("we all write from such dates," Celan observes [GW 3: 196/47]), but the event only happens in the language of the poem. It happens in the poem, as Heidegger says of the event of truth in the work of art, as *having happened*.[5] The poetic self steps forward *against* the difference that opens with this step and that is ontologically prior to it, as a kind of origin. In structural terms, we may speak of an originary delay in the human Dasein. But this stepping forward as it occurs in the poem *draws out the event* that is the opening of difference, or the opening of a relation between the human Dasein and everything that is, including other Dasein. It draws it out (makes it come about, makes it perdure) and brings it forth (remarks the date: this manifest re-marking constitutes what Heidegger calls the "createdness" of poetry) in an initiatory fashion. The repetitive structure of the poem derives from the fact that the poem re-marks its origin in such a way as to bring it about as having been. And the more forcefully (the more "abruptly") it asserts itself (*sich behauptet*), the more it remarks the origin from which it proceeds, thereby standing out or standing forth more distinctly against this origin. It stands out, then, as Celan observes, through the singularity of the poet's language: "The still here can only mean speaking. . . . In other words: language actualized, set free under the sign of a radical individuation" (GW 3: 197/49).

"Still here," or "yet still" — a phrase that corresponds to the *Dass* ascribed by Heidegger to the work of art — marks the presence of the poem. The essence of the poem, Celan claims, is the presence of something present (*seinem innersten Wesen nach Gegenwart und Präsenz* [GW 3: 197–98/49]). It marks a here and now ("Even in the here and now of the poem — and the poem has only this one, unique, momentary present — even in this immediacy and nearness" [GW 3: 198–99/50]) that in its repetitive structure turns both forward and back, anticipating and recollecting (recollecting forward to the other, back to its date), in such a way as to remark relation and a movement, a passage in time. I should perhaps reemphasize that the presence in question is not the presence of the metaphysics of presence, for the presence is that of a sign that does not signify, but rather a presence that, in its very distinctness (Hölderlin spoke of its "firmness"), points beyond itself in an allegorical mode — thus marking relation to an alterity.

Celan remarks that the "yet still" is language "corresponding," language that is *Entsprechung* — "and not simply verbally."* This last qualification, "and not simply verbally," refers undoubtedly to what he has said about Lucile's perception of language, for he goes on to emphasize that the language of the poem is the language of a "radical individuation," the

---

*An *Entsprechung* is a "corresponding case or instance," or can be an analogous or equivalent word. The poem's *Entsprechung*, we might say, is its "ana-logy." The verb *entsprechen*, which Celan is activating here, means "to answer to," "to conform to," "to correspond to," or "to be commensurate with."

language of poets "who do not forget that they speak from an angle of reflection which is their own existence, their own creaturely nature" (GW 3: 197/49). This is a language, then, that "corresponds" to the person (though not in the mode of signification, since the person first emerges in this language). But while Celan's focus in this paragraph is on the singularity and solitude of the individual, as of the poem, the turn of the paragraph ("Does this very fact not place the poem already here, at its inception, in the encounter, *in the mystery of encounter?*" [GW 3: 198/49]) reminds us again that the "correspondence" of the poem's "still here" must also be conceived more broadly. "Corresponding," the language is *commensurate* with the event that has happened (that it draws out) and *answering to* something to which it gives itself over, which it "needs" and which it addresses as an other "over against it." Once again, this is simultaneously recollection and a reaching forward — a reaching forward out of recollection:

The poem intends another, needs this other, needs an opposite. It goes toward it, addresses it.

For the poem, everything and everybody is a figure of this other toward which it is heading.

The attention which the poem pays to all that it encounters, its more acute sense of detail, outline, structure, color . . . all this is achieved not, I think, by an eye competing (or concurring) with ever more precise instruments, but, rather, by a kind of concentration mindful of all our dates. (GW 3: 198/49)

We have seen that the date marks the emergence of the poetic self in its mortality — against the possibility of its death and thus against the opening that occurs in this assumption of mortality. For the human Dasein, this is the opening of a spatiotemporal disposition that defines its time and its place, and hence the opening of the possibility of relation to an other (in other words, the event of truth). The poem thus bespeaks the movement of an individual existence *in and from its time.* Yet this time is given to it (the event is drawn out in the poem) only as this existence emerges in its movement *toward an other* with which it seeks to engage. In seeking the other, then, the poem is seeking its own (and its author's) truth: its truth, in relation, understood always temporally.

For the poem, Celan writes, everything and everybody is a figure of this other. The altogether other is u-topic — for it is other than every other (everything that is). It is precisely what gives the other to be perceived in its precise outline — in other words, it is its essence or what is most proper to it: most fundamentally, Celan states, its time ("Even in the here and now of the poem . . . even in this immediacy and nearness, the poem lets the other speak with what is most proper to it: its time"). Yet we might ask here: if Celan is insisting so markedly on the singularity of the self that emerges in the poem, would not every "you" be a singular "you" in the same manner, and would not that which is most proper to it also have the same unique character? In which case, how could every other be a figure of the altogether other that the poem seeks?

The answer to this question, I believe, derives from Celan's elaboration of the notions of finitude and singularity. The essence sought by the poem, what constitutes the "otherness" of the other, has its origin in what must be understood not as a substantial ground but as difference. This difference is the "same" out of which beings emerge in their difference — "over against one another," *gegeneinanderüber*, as Heidegger puts it. Thus we may speak appropriately in these terms of *the* other or *the* difference the poem seeks. But Celan underscores the radically temporal character of this difference, and in view of his emphasis on the solitude of the poem (and its author), as well as the radical individuation of the poet, we may conclude that he is pushing Heidegger's thought of finitude to the point of recognizing that the difference can only be thought as occurring or opening *in relation*, in always singular relations (and thus thought as always differing from itself). The difference, then, is to be understood in the manner of what Jean-Luc Nancy refers to as a *partage* (both a sharing and a division). It is other than any other — "transcendent," one might say (thus it is the u-topic out of whose "light" the poem seeks "the human being" and "the creature") — but other *only in relation*, thus a "quasi-transcendental," to use Gasché's term. Truth, Heidegger argued in "The Origin of the Work of Art," happens nowhere other than at the site where it is drawn out, in always singular articulations; that to which the poem points (allegorically) is other than it, but also occurs nowhere other than in it.

We may understand better now what it means to say that the poem is seeking its truth — its truth, in relation. Its truth is the opening of a possibility of relation realized in the movement of reaching poetically for an other. This is not its truth in the sense that this possibility would be something it brings to the other or institutes *from itself*. Rather, it would be something that comes about or occurs as it proceeds, in and from an experience of mortality, toward the other (other beings in their singularity). The poem *seeks* its truth in going to the other, it *draws out* a relation, a relation that is open-ended like the question posed by the poem: "Whenever we speak with things in this way we also dwell on the question of their wherefrom and their whereto: a question that 'remains open' and is 'without resolution,' a question pointing to the Open, Empty, and Free — we have ventured far out" (GW 3: 199/50).

Once again it is difficult not to hear Heidegger in these lines. Also, it is difficult, in this context, not to recall another one of Heidegger's terms for the site of difference or what Celan calls here the "Open," *das Gegend*, a term that also appeared in Celan's Bremen address. In its engagement or encounter (*Begegnung*) with the other, the poem would be pointing with its "question" to the *Gegend*. The word *Gegend* does not in fact appear in this passage, but it comes immediately to mind when we recognize the extent to which Celan is following Heidegger in thinking relation with the preposition *gegen — working* the term in such a way as to subvert its dialectical determination. Let me recall here Heidegger's words in "The Essence of Language" as he proposes to move from the neighborhood of poetry and thought (defined in relation to the "divergence" of their modes of saying and the relation that opens out of the tracing of this difference, a relation that Heidegger defines as a *Gegeneinanderüber*) back to the "region," the *Gegend* in which this neighborhood stands. The way back is provided by the region itself, Heidegger observes, because all encounter (as in the relation between poetry and thought, taken in this essay as an exemplary case of the "face to face encounter of things") takes its possibility from the countering, the way-making movement of the region:

Speaking allusively, the country, that which counters, is the clearing that gives free reign, where all that is cleared and freed, and all that conceals itself, together attain the open freedom. The freeing and sheltering character of this region lies in this way-making movement, which yields those ways that belong to the region. To a thinking so inclined that reaches out sufficiently [*hinreichend gedacht*], the way is that by which we reach [*was uns gelangen lässt*] — which lets us reach what reaches for us by concerning us, by suing us.[6]

What concerns and summons, what puts under way, is essence, understood in its temporal character: "*Es west* means it presences, in persisting it regards us, moves us and concerns us [or 'sues' us: *be-wëgt uns und belangt uns*]. Essence, so understood, names the persisting, what concerns us in all things, because it moves and makes a way for all things" (US 190/OW 95). Heidegger then adds that if essence can thus summon or "sue" us, this is because language is what is most proper to it. Essence "counters" in speaking. All encounter with what concerns us or regards us (in the manner of the other that *in its otherness* — in its essence — is "turned toward the poem," as Celan says) is made possible by language, understood in its most originary manner as a "saying" that opens "ways" and thus articulates the "region," the *Gegend*, as the differential relation structuring all relations of things as they stand "over against one another" (*gegeneinanderüber*).

Yet essence counters, Heidegger says, only as it is drawn out in and by a "rejoining" (*entgegnende*) word — a word that "corresponds" to what it draws forth (the speaking of language itself). For Heidegger, such a rejoining word occurs in all language where truth is at stake, but it occurs most manifestly in poetry. Might we say, then, that this "rejoining word" is equivalent to Lucile's "counterword" (*Gegenwort*) and Lenz's silence ("his 'Long live the King!' is no longer a word. It is a terrifying silence" [GW 195/47])? Explicitly designating Lucile's word as "poetry," Celan suggests that all poetry has its source in the turn, the turning against (art) that occurs with such a speaking (even Lenz's silence is a kind of "speaking" — it is the same as a "Long live the King"). To the extent that all poetry is encounter, for Celan, we may presume that it proceeds from and embodies such a countering word which opens the possibility of relation by opening to the other in its otherness.

The detour I have taken through Heidegger's meditation on relation by way of the preposition *gegen* should throw light on the structure of what Celan understands by poetic relation. Yet most importantly, perhaps, it should underscore the point that the relation in question is a relation *in and of language*, for the relation to the other toward which the poem moves and which it seeks to bring to speech is given essentially in language and in what Heidegger calls the speaking of language. As we saw already in his Bremen address, Celan conceives of poetry as *engaging with language* — with the essence of language understood as that which gives relation. With its "counterword," the poem opens the paths that are the ways of relation given by language itself (as saying) when it is brought to "speak," that is, when something other is brought forth in its singular presence "over against" a "speaking I" as something that "concerns and sues" in its otherness. The way is opened in the tracing of what Heidegger calls the *Riss*, a differential relation that both separates and draws together — it is the *difference* that "lets us reach what reaches for us by concerning us, by suing us." We have seen that the poem traces out such ways with its initiating counterword, but this counterword must be understood also as a response, or understood as *becoming* a response in the time of the poem (as it is poised between recollection and advance toward an other) — a response that allows the unfolding of a poetic relation that is *given* by language. It is in this sense, finally, that the poem is "conversation" — it is a conversation *in and from language*.

Such a conception of poetic conversation does not — or should not — elide the "creaturely" existence of the speaking subject or that of the other (thing or human being) over against which the "I" comes to stand. But it is true that Celan succeeds in "The Meridian" in carrying a thought of the singularity of existence — as Heidegger himself began to develop it in *Being and Time* — into a meditation on poetic language that Heidegger perhaps only approached in his readings of Hölderlin (we do not find it, for example, in "The Origin of the Work of Art"). He does so in a manner that effectively challenges in its very radicality the thought of finitude and historicity that Heidegger pursued in the existential analytic, because he thinks singularity *always in relation.* Heidegger, by introducing his concept of *Mitsein* ("being-with"), recognized the necessity of thinking Dasein in relation, but he failed to carry through this concept in any manner adequate to his own description of the facticity of Dasein. He failed, in effect, to think through sufficiently the relation to the other in its otherness and to take the measure of what this might mean for a thought of the historicity of Dasein.[7]

This last assertion will have to stand without development, for it would require a lengthy commentary of the section of *Being and Time* entitled "The Basic Constitution of Historicality." If we consider Celan's own description of poetic "conversation," however, it is possible to hear something of the radicality to which I want to point in the very *questioning* character of the conversation as Celan understands it:

The poem becomes — under what conditions! [a reference, apparently, to the "increasing speed" of *Technik* in a time after the "terrifying silence"] — the poem of one who — yet still — perceives, one who is turned toward what appears, questioning and addressing what thus appears. The poem becomes conversation — often desperate conversation.

Only in the space of this conversation does that which is addressed constitute itself, gather itself around the naming and addressing I. But this addressed, also become a "you" through naming, brings its being-other into this present. Even in the here and now of the poem — and the poem has always only this one, unique, momentary present — even in this immediacy and nearness, it lets what is most proper to this other, its time, speak along with it.

Whenever we speak with things in this way, we also dwell on the question of their wherefrom and whereto, a question "remaining open," "coming to no end," and pointing toward the Open, the Empty, and the Free. — We have ventured far out.

The poem also searches for this place. (GW 3: 198–99/50)

The relation is tenuous, this passage seems to suggest, because it is a relation in time: the "abyss" for Celan, lies in time itself. I have said that the poetic "I" seeks its truth (and thus its time — the time in which it situates itself, mindful of its dates) in relation to the other, in and from the difference between self and other. But this difference in which time occurs for Dasein can only be thought, if we follow Celan's text, in such singular relations, in always singular instantiations (single "instants," *Augenblicke*) and cannot be thought as *gathering* the terms it draws into relation (as would a third term that provides a common measure).[8] To put it schematically: the time I must assume as Dasein is not your time, though I know my time only in opening to yours, in relation. Properly speaking, this is not "my" time but a time given in this relation, "our" time, shared. Yet as "shared," this time differs from itself with each occurrence in which it is drawn out and instantiated (your time is not my time). I ask "wherefrom and whereto" in this encounter in order to situate myself in a present, a "shared" time — I can know (encounter) myself only by going beyond myself in search of this time. But the time I seek will never constitute a grounding destiny or even a shared condition, precisely because it is "shared" in an originary fashion and because the other remains other, even as relation is drawn out.

Hence, the conversation is "often desperate," for I may situate myself only in relation to an other, but my reach is toward an otherness of the other that I can never appropriate and that exposes me always to an alterity (*La poésie ne s'impose plus, elle s'expose* [GW 3: 181/29]). This alterity is marked in the poem — brought to "speak" there — but its voice is fundamentally unsettling *because always other*.

I believe we hear something of the unsettling character of the relation to the other in the quatrain Celan offers as an example of poetry written from his own "20th of January." Of this quatrain, and of "Conversation in the Mountains," Celan affirms (with the same sureness with which he announces that he has "touched" a meridian with his audience): "I had . . . encountered myself" (GW 3: 202/53). Both texts are about being under way and about encounter; they each evoke in some manner "the paths on which language becomes voice." Indeed, "Conversation in the Mountains" contains a reflection on language that complements the turn against naturalism that Celan develops in relation to Büchner's aesthetics. The "encounter" in this text unfolds in a linguistic space that is declared to be incommensurable with the "language" of nature, a language "without I and without You." This text also mirrors the assertions of "The Meridian" in that the encounter unfolds through a movement of recollection that allows something like an opening by which the speaking "I" comes to describe itself as "accompanied." I will not try to read the text any further here, however, because its complex linguistic structure and its densely allusive texture require quite lengthy analysis — an analysis that could well force us to reconsider in depth the somewhat "Greek," Heideggerian character of the phenomenology "The Meridian" seems to offer, but which could only reinforce my suggestion that Celan is trying to think a less gathered essence of time than the one developed by Heidegger and thus necessarily a very different kind of "homecoming." Rather, and by way of conclusion, I will focus on the quatrain Celan chooses to cite in "The Meridian." Its irony might be said to reflect some of the instability he finds

in Büchner's *Lenz*, and it points to the uncertainty out of which Celan —
"Celan" — proceeds in seeking relation to the other in its otherness.

In German, the quatrain reads:

> Stimmen vom Nesselweg her:
> *Komm auf den Händen zu uns.*
> Wer mit der Lampe allein ist,
> Hat nur die Hand, draus zu lesen.
>   (GW 3: 201 [GW 1: 147]/53)

In a literal translation:

> Voices from the nettle-path:
> *Come to us on your hands.*
> One who is alone with the lamp
> Has only the hand to read from.

The irony at play in the quatrain derives in part from the way in which
it echoes its context in "The Meridian." It recalls to us, for example, the
line regarding Lenz's desire to walk on his head: to walk on one's head is,
after all, to walk on one's hands (the figures are of course very different,
but Celan seems to be working with this echo in order to point back to
Lenz, as he will do in referring to his use of "a man like Lenz" in "Conversation in the Mountains"). Moreover, the abruptness of the quatrain
cannot but prompt us to look to it as a *Gegenwort*. Yet is the *Gegenwort*
in the challenging, italicized call, or is it in the sardonic character of
the second couplet, which might evoke for us an absurdity that "bespeaks
the presence of human beings" but this time in anything but a majestic
manner?*

Within the quatrain and through the ironic play of *both* couplets, we
find a rather sharp reflection on the unsettling character of encounter and
on the difficulty experienced in moving toward the other. I am amplifying
the tone of the quatrain somewhat, but I believe one cannot avoid hearing
the one addressed as the object of a kind of teasing aimed at dislodging it
from a solitude to which the second couplet refers; indeed, I would suggest
that the subject of this quatrain — actually elided in it — is a subject "dis-
lodged" but barely under way, or under way only hesitantly. The call, we
might say, evokes the hesitancy of the addressed subject; it speaks to that
hesitancy in asking that this subject undertake with his or her hands what

---

*Here, I suspect that "countering" can only be thought as occurring *between* the two
couplets. The countering challenge of the first couplet comes forth in its unsettling character
when it is answered with the irony of the second — the challenge occurs *with* the answer.
Only with this second couplet does it emerge as *having been heard*, thereby marking the
presence of the other.

is hardly a tempting path. We may well read the path as the path of poetry "on which language becomes voice" (GW 3: 201/53): a path that *the poet* is invited to undertake inasmuch as poetry is a craft and thus "a matter of hands" — "the hands of one person, i.e., a unique, mortal soul searching for its way with its voice and dumbness."* But there is something mildly cruel or mocking in these voices that invite the poet[9] to proceed by hand over a path through *nettles*. Had Celan written "thorns," for example, this couplet would have taken on a far different tone in that the poet would be called to a kind of ritual suffering. To be sure, "nettles" are also not without their ritual connotations, but their *annoying* character upsets any possible gravity in their appearance in this couplet.

Of course, the voices are calling for either trust or humility, or both, inviting the one addressed to follow the voices by feeling his way along a "blind" path (where sight will somehow not suffice to direct an erect gait), or inviting the one addressed to come in a kind of supplication or even humiliation. They require a kind of openness or exposure, and a form of self-renunciation. Yet obeying this call (at least as it is heard from the position of the one addressed) will be something more than difficult — it will also be irritating and unpleasant. In this way, "nettles" undoes or unsettles any too pious or easy evocation in this context of the attention to which Celan refers in quoting Malebranche by way of Walter Benjamin: "attention is the natural prayer of the soul" (GW 3: 198/50).

After the first couplet, the second also takes on something of an ironic, stinging character. The couplet could be read as part of the address by the voices, but the italics distinguish the second verse in such a way as to suggest that the couplet is spoken by one who has heard their call (in which case — which is certainly the most probable and interesting — the quatrain embodies a movement of self-reflection). In either case, in the image of those who in their solitude have only the lines of their hands in which to read a figure of their destiny ("solitary" in that they are proceeding under what we might call the light of conscious understanding), there is a subtle but quite effective inversion of *finding one's way with one's hands* (poetically). The "reader" (the poet) is impoverished, and somewhat pitiful, not because they have no book with them but because they are following the solitary path of reflection and interpretation, along which no lines will ever confront them with a destiny. In this solitude, they will never see or hear the trace of the other — they might as well read their hands. They can know their destiny only by going out toward the other in a mode of encounter that exceeds any traditional hermeneutic relation.

*In a letter to Hans Bender from which this line is taken, Celan continues: "Only truthful hands write true poems. I cannot see any basic difference between a handshake and a poem" (GW 3: 177/26).

They cannot "read" the other; they must "invent" the other by reaching poetically for the other in a language that projects a reality and is thus "under way" toward an addressable "you."

In "Engführung" ("Stretto") Celan writes:

> Liess nicht mehr — schau!
> Schau nicht mehr — geh!
>   (GW 1: 197)
>
>   Read no longer —
>   look!
> Look no longer — go!

The quatrain, I would suggest, embodies such an invitation — an invitation and a *response* that draws out the invitation as an invitation coming from an unsettling alterity. The irony of the quatrain remarks the otherness of the voice and the necessity of a movement toward the other, even as it evokes its difficulty. It remarks that the other *has been heard*; thus it marks a date.

Beyond *Nesselweg* and "voices," there is no "figure" of the other here, and the speaking "I" is all but elided, appearing only in a turn. The quatrain offers no more than a sketch of encounter and a movement that is no more than the condition of conversation (a movement of self-reflection *in response to the other*). Nonetheless it underscores the fundamentally unsettling character of exposure to the other; thus it gives some sense of the instability of the opening from which poetic questioning proceeds. When Celan invokes the presence of the person and the distinctness of the figure it takes as an image of the other, we must not forget that this image is traced out against *such* a date.

The irony at work in the quatrain, I want to suggest, cannot but spill over into the argument of "The Meridian" and prevent us from any too triumphant celebration of the possibility of self-discovery. Through its re-evocation of Lenz, it reminds us that the freedom of the estranged "I" lies in the opening to an abyss: "only, it sometimes bothered him that he could not walk on his head." If the obscurity and strangeness of this last phrase — deriving from its opacity as the "actualized language" of an existent being — appears "for the sake of an encounter," the encounter occurs only over this abyss. The abyss, we have seen, is time as it is given *with* the possibility of relation to the other, that is, *with* language when it is brought to speak in the "actualized speech" of the individual (language, once again, that is a *sign*), tracing a difference that holds one over to another (but as other). Language, the language that Celan experienced as "near and unlost" and to which the poem turns in its *Atemwende*, gives relation only in and through time. More simply, it gives time: the irreversible time of a singular existence as it seeks itself in reaching to an other. Here, then, is what I wanted to suggest must be said today about poetry (after Heidegger): its language gives time, and only in this time — a time we know today as irreversible and disjunctive — can we speak of something like an encounter with reality. What is at stake in poetry is the possibility of a reality: from language and in time.

An Exquisite Crisis

WE know the limit of language bodily, Heidegger suggests. Might this experience be conceived as a touch?

Luce Irigaray proposes such a notion in *Speculum* when she poses the question of sexual difference at precisely the point where this question is indissociable from the question of ontological difference — at that point, we might say now, where body and language are articulated in "usage" at the *limit* of language and difference is articulated in a relation of language, *Ereignis*, and humankind. Irigaray, for her part, speaks of an *ex-schize crise de la différence ontico-ontologique* (S 181/145), remarking thereby, thrice over, and in full continuity with Heidegger, that the ontological difference is articulated in a kind of "crisis," a chiasmic crossing of empirical and transcendental, material and ideal that leaves none of these terms intact. Her writing *is*, I believe, *or would be* such a passage in its engagement of the question of sexual difference. It cannot be reduced to an "essentialism." In what she calls *parler femme*, she is attempting to think and practice that bodily usage whereby humankind opens to itself and to the play of difference, entering a pure experience of relation (what Heidegger calls "the" relation and Blanchot "the absolute relation") that has nothing pure about it inasmuch as it is the opening of a site that is always *of* the earth. Thought enters this crisis only in leaving it; it cannot dwell there. But in this passage whereby thought touches the "material" nonground of its finite transcendence, the question of sexual difference (among others) communicates with the question of ontological difference. Where thought touches the question of sexual difference, once again, it touches the question of difference itself, and where this touch occurs, meaning, "the meaning of meaning," is at stake.

This is why the fundamental prohibition of phallogocentrism, for women at least, is "don't touch" (or so the argument of *Speculum* implies). The prohibition bears on the body, of course; but, most fundamentally, it bears on autoaffection and the articulation of desire. The prohibition is "don't touch your self." Since a self is touched only in language (in a remarking of the relation of same and other), the prohibition works essentially by denying any language to a woman's touch that is not already appropriated to a phallic economy. "She" (the marker of a latency in the light of this disappropriation) is not allowed to touch *in language*: herself, the other, and, above all, language. To touch the self at its limit, its bodily limit in the relation of same and other, is also to touch language. The prohibition is: "don't touch language," don't touch the logos.

Irigaray is attempting to transgress precisely that prohibition, and I believe she stages such a transgression in a brief text from *Speculum* entitled "La Mystérique." In this chapter, I propose to follow the movement of this text and draw forth some of the dimensions of the experience with language presented in it. I will focus in particular on what she indicates about mimesis, for the experience with language she describes proceeds by a mimesis of the body that has not been recognized thus far, at least to my knowledge, in readings of her work.

There are at least five levels at which the topic of mimesis might be addressed in "La Mystérique." The first lies in the very presentation of the text, in Irigaray's miming of a mystic discourse — *the* discourse, she says, in which "woman" has spoken and acted most publicly in the history of the West. This staging or enactment (at virtually the center of *Speculum*) takes on a kind of narrative form that moves fluidly between direct and indirect presentation as it proceeds through an autoerotic experience that issues in an encounter with "her 'god' "* as well as something like a language for these relations. The narrative, in fact, is a narrative of being under way to language.

I will not dwell on the complex mimetic form of this presentation, on Irigaray's *style* in this case.† I note simply that in the gap between the narrating voice of this theoretical *Darstellung* and a first person, there is space for following the movement she is presenting — and sufficient space to make it indeterminable *who* follows, male or female. The lines preceding the actual staging of the movement are in fact devoted to the masculine effort to descend into this "cryptic" other scene of consciousness where "she" (*la conscience, elle*) speaks of a source of light and a burning embrace beyond (masculine) understanding. To speak to her, write to her, sermonize her, take her confession, Irigaray notes, "man" has gone so far as to allow himself to fall into the trap of miming her and pretend to her ecstasis: "To the point of no longer finding himself again as 'subject' and

*See Luce Irigaray, *Ce sexe qui n'en est pas un* (Paris: Minuit, 1977), 75; *This Sex Which Is Not One*, trans. Catherine Porter (Ithaca, N.Y.: Cornell University Press, 1985), 77.

†The topic is addressed in a marvelous essay by Elizabeth Weed, "The Question of Style," in *Engaging with Irigaray*, ed. Carolyn Burke, Naomi Schor, and Margaret Whitford (New York: Columbia University Press, 1994), 79–110.

letting himself be led where he wanted above all not to go: to his 'loss' in this a-typical, a-topical mysteria." So when Irigaray asks a few lines later, without any intervening identification of the subject of this question, "But how is this to be done?," her question not only extends to the dilemmas of the mystic but also folds back upon those who would follow and even upon the one (narrating) who follows *here*: any subject proceeding from philosophy (recalling that any theoretical subject has been appropriated to the masculine) . . . even Irigaray herself. It also leads into a second question: If a "male" subject can mime and be taken in this movement, can this movement involve something "essentially" feminine? Or does it, at some point, suspend such differentiation (rendering it possible, perhaps, in a new form)?

In a provisional answer to these questions, I would observe that the mimetic space Irigaray opens with her quasi-narrative form makes it possible to follow the experience presented (and if it is necessary for me to justify my reading such a text, the answer lies here); further, and more fundamentally, the mimetic character of what Irigaray is presenting renders engagement possible. I can only develop this last point in the discussion to follow, but the questions tied to the matter of "essentialism" weigh so heavily in such a scene of reading that they must undoubtedly be addressed if we are to proceed. Thus I would offer the following hypothesis. Irigaray is carrying her reader in this text back to the material site of differentiation that is the "origin" of a feminine sexuality. She will offer an originary figuration of feminine desire from this material (non)ground that is a body "proper" *only by this figuration*. To be sure, she will locate at this site a "feminine" reflexivity (and of a distinctively fluid nature). But if it is feminine in essence, it is such only as it *offers relation* in its fundamentally mimetic character.[1] This is the ground of the engagement to which I have referred. And it must be added that this reflexive structure "folds" *only* in relation, a relation that is not necessarily heterosexual or homosexual, but that necessarily involves an *other* ("entirely" other — difference, in relation) and thus the possibility of other movements or articulations than the one figured here. "The feminine" names here a historically possible experience of finitude, and as an open-ended experience of relation, it marks a first step in a new thought of sexual difference. It is in part for this reason that Irigaray names the feminine a "threshold" in *An Ethics of Sexual Difference*.[2]

Irigaray, I want to emphasize, is presenting in this text a movement of heteroaffection: the appropriation of self in relation to alterity and the appropriation of the possibility of signifying this self-presence, which is nothing less than the appropriation of language. It proceeds bodily, as I have suggested, and is figured, from its "fluid" ground, in bodily terms that connote an essentially feminine experience. There is no denying that Irigaray is celebrating in this text a particular (bodily) configuration of feminine sexuality and that she is giving an irreducible role to the "biological." But the ecstatic experience presented here is not *determined* by this configuration; it is de-fined by it, but also exceeds it in such a way as to mark the possibility of its own refiguration or reconception. This bodily heteroaffection, as we will see, is fundamentally the experience of *nothing*—the nothing, to begin with, of human sexuality. Indeed, I would propose that the experience of heteroaffection staged here is devoted in large measure to clearing the space of representation. In three successive modalities, we will follow an identification with (almost) nothing. The "opening" that is figured bodily and never quite loses its physiological connotation *also* takes on a transcendental character, and thus the assumption of finite transcendence becomes the condition for the emergence of a "free" use of the proper and a free sexual relation. Irigaray traces a path in this text (a path given historically), not a destiny; she traces the site of a passage.[3]

Let me attempt to follow now the movement to which I have referred. It begins in a flight of the "soul" from the prison of the subject's self-representation, proceeding by a "method of meditation" that can only be called blind since it involves an ex-centric movement beyond the horizon of the eye/I of Cartesian consciousness. The trajectory of this "inner experience" is through the center, but also beyond in an ecstasis that transgresses the very distinction between inside and outside (S 240/192).[4] The method is blind, once again, because she must traverse "the very shadow of sight," and do so without any foreseeable goal or telos. Moreover, the path must be repeatedly tried by reason of the ideological (theological) constructions that will lead her back to an ideal unity ("To resembling what she would be ideally in her proper form or substance" [S 240/193]). Hence the need for a method in this meditation, and tact. She must find this path entirely by feel.

Desire is the motor of this autoerotic (spiritual) exploration, but it has no object other than a touch that it has been priming yet also repeating in this originary repetition of a primal scene. "Where can it be fixed?," the question emerges,* "if not farther ahead in the night until it becomes a transverberating beam, a luminous shadow. . . . In a *touch* that opens the 'soul' again to a contact that is divinely wounding in its blow and its radiation" (S 240/193). What she seeks, again, is a touch, or more precisely a being-touched; she seeks to expose that site where she is (has nec-

*The referent of "it" here is probably "gaze" or "look," as the English translation indicates, but "it" might also refer to the desire that directs this gaze.

essarily already been) touched: "Reached in that subterraneously shimmering expanse [*nappe*] that she has remained without knowing it. And that she will never know (for herself) distinctly when she begins (again) to burn, in a sweet confusion" (S 240/193). *Nappe* is translated in English as "fabric," but it is crucial to recognize that here *nappe* names a liquid expanse that will become (as it is touched and remarked) the ground of her (self) reflection, a *mirror*, as we will see shortly.[5]

But it is known at this point only in a pain ("the tearing apart imposing its pain . . . above any other feeling" [S 240/193]) of which she can only demand more: "Delight and longing in this torment, if she has entrusted herself to a dexterity sufficiently subtle in its force. Asking for more ... But without being able to specify what she wants. Failing in words. Sensing a *remaining to say* [*un rester à dire*] that resists all words, that one could hardly stammer out, that all terms are too worn out, too weak, to translate in a sensible manner" (S 240/193). Words fail her now. The fact that she has traditionally been denied a language presents itself in a failure of words (but then *all* language will "fail" here) before the possibility she now approaches of saying something. Or not some *thing*. What is to be said is no more than this sensible exposure (the *nappe étincelante*) that opens, as marked, to nothing, that is, beyond every *thing* she might have to say, suspending her relation to the whole of what is. "Nothing" is what she has to say, or more precisely, *un rester à dire* — a something still to be said which is her own remaining as a remaining *to say* out of this deferral/suspension of what is; nothing more than the opening of a space and a time that is to become a saying and that is not yet signifiable, though a translation of a "sensible" nature, a translation of this nascent *sense* or *thought* is *called for* (as we see by the fact that a suitable translation is wanting). "For it is no longer a matter," Irigaray writes, "of longing for some determinable attribute, some mode of essence, some visage of presence. What is awaited is not a *this* or a *that*, not even a *here* any more than a *there*. Without a designatable being, time, or place. Best to refuse oneself to all discourse, go silent, or hold to a sound so little articulated that it barely forms a *song*. Directing the ear to any shiver announcing a return" (S 241/193).

To touch the self — its limit in the form of a sense or (material) thought that is the opening of same to other and thus the ground of any reference whatsoever — is to touch the "origin" of language: to open to language. The movement we have seen thus far is nothing other than the beginning of what Heidegger calls the tracing of difference, the *Riss*, as he first named it in "The Origin of the Work of Art." But this (re)beginning of a heteroaffection and of (its) language has only begun to occur and has yet to be drawn out so as to subsist. There is as yet only response, in anticipation, and without any preestablished direction or sense. ("But how to go about it, even if one has a passion for such trials, if one has not been 'called' to it? No perceptible end to reach toward, no assignable cause to refer to" [S 241/193].) No "reach" is possible yet—a spacing must be drawn out, a spacing that we begin to see already in the fact that this movement is *back* as much as forward: "What is beginning to come about taking place in so profound and inaccessible secrecy that no intelligence or common sense can have precise knowledge of it. A distant and distancing solitude of this tact that is nevertheless moved most intimately" (S 241–42/194). Touched "most intimately," this sensibility is at a distance and creates distance—it is at a remove and it removes, it opens a remove that will become the space of solitary reflection that exists only in the *proximity* of the other. No decision, no act of the will can resolve this paradox, the "suspense" of this *ex-schize crise* where coming is a distancing and the anticipation of and opening to something (no *thing*: "grace") that cannot even be projected (the only pro-ject [*Ent-wurf*], as yet, lies in the manner in which she addresses herself to an other), only awaited in the form of an unrepresentable memory, or perhaps at most the "dream" of such a "memory."* What comes with the touch comes only as having come—to no one. It comes with an opening: "Abyss that opens still further (ahead), moves apart, forces itself open without knowing (itself) or imagining (itself) in its unfathomable nudity. Abyss in which all persons and all names that are still proper disappear" (S 242/194). The touch marks an opening without property, attribute, or determination, an opening that in its desire to open further gives itself in complete abandon. This opening to the other cannot even be called a "love" to the extent that this affect involves some return for the self. Here, the "self" gives beyond the self in an expenditure beyond economy, beyond even the calculation of a potlatch, for the calculating "I" that would draw benefit from this movement is consumed. An excess opening always to more excess.

But it cannot last without the touch to which and in which it opens. She cannot feed her own consumption/consummation, still voiceless, still, in fact, without a hand (S 243/195). The between of this waiting has no icon to mollify it, no image that would mediate the absence, allowing remembrance and anticipation. We are still prior to a "mirror stage," in an imagining without image:

No image, no figure to divert so mortal an absence. No picture, no portrait, no visage would suffice to appease the delay, even should they subsist in the lack of all defined form. Finding (herself) again demands a *proximity* that knows no aspect,

---

*"Unless it be an ungraspable memory that hides from its representation, re-presentation, repetition. Its dream even" (S 242/194).

mode or figure. No metaphors to designate the burning brilliance of this touch. No *intermediary* to defer it in the ungraspable *instant* of its event. Not even a *milieu* that sustains, prepares, or recalls its intuition. (S 243–44/195)

The touch is mortal and brings about what Blanchot, in commenting on his own presentation of a *scène primitive*, also calls a "dying"; for, once again, there is no self here to synthesize or schematize what comes. This primal scene (though "scene" may be misleading) occurs before it can be imagined, in an im-mediacy that is prior to any lived experience. If the term "imagination" is even appropriate (and I believe it may well be),[6] then we have to do here with the opening of what Blanchot names the imaginary. Thus "death" (effraction) alternates with death (absence) in a time that cannot even be described as punctuated with the violence of im-mediacy. "Implacable rigors of summer noon, of winter's midnight that mingle their extremes without the calm of a more neutral between that would regulate their alternations. *Immediacy of the whole* imposed in this marriage with the unknowable" (S 244/196). She knows a unity that is not a speculative synthesis but an abyss and that proceeds from a union with "God" alone, without mode or attribute. The soul opens "only to one who also gives themself in their nudity . . . it joins [*s'épouse*] only in the annihilation of all power, all having and all being that are founded elsewhere and otherwise than in this embrace of fire whose end is inconceivable" (S 244/196).

A union, then, beyond being, otherwise than being—a union with "nothing" we might say—but not without a trace: "Each becoming the other in consumption, the nothing of the other in consummation. The other, whose identity they will not have known in truth, having thus lost their own, but whose imprint they retain, so slight it is barely perceptible, in order better to join to it in an entwining that is already, finally, close" (S 244/196). A reciprocal identification ("co-identification"), even a fusion, but again, not without a trace that renders possible a memory. Nothing would subsist of these transports were it not that each takes the image of the other (the "nothing" of the other) in a reciprocal reflection/writing. "Identification" here is a *mirroring* made possible by the fact that the "center," the site of the soul's infinite exposure and infinite joining, is made up of a reflective matter so fluid and subtle (that "subterranean shimmering expanse") that even the greatest depths are already "specularized." Here is the bodily mimesis to which I have referred: "Thus I have become (in) your image in this nothing-ness, and you reflect mine in your absence of being. This *tain*, at least, would retain *being*—that we have perhaps been, that we will be again—though our image has failed at present or has been covered over by alien speculations. A living mirror am

I thus (in) your resemblance as you are mine" (S 245/197). Each mir-
rors/becomes the "nothing" of the other in this originary mimesis, each
takes the image of nothing but the other's very exposure, ex-posing this
reciprocal exchange, this *partage* (division/sharing) that is the difference
of Being. Being, the logos communicated and divided, is re-marked and
thereby subsists in this infinite mirror-play, this "graphy" of the tain that
produces light(ning) in its writing.

The first mimesis, then — a mimesis constitutive for identity and con-
sisting not in the borrowing of positive attributes but in an identification with and inscription of *nothing* — is the tracing of difference, difference "itself."[7] Assuming the limit (the material site of receptivity that is
"touched," the "there" of this singular being) as it is marked with the trace
of the nothing of the other, the soul captures its transcendence, its ecstatic
exposure. It knows transcendence — the (always forgotten) condition of
self-reflection — as it draws out this photo-graphy that captures a relation
to Being: "Thus have I become (in) your image . . . thus am I (in) your
resemblance as you are mine." Being *is* in this graphic inscription that
comes to the word ("This *tain*, at least, would retain *being*"). And thus we
may say that this originary mimesis is the *partage* (communication, sharing, division) of the logos.[8]

A question I touched upon at the outset now emerges. Does the material ground of reflection, the reflecting surface that marks her transcendence in taking the image of the "nothing" of the other, already prepare a
sexual determination, and is the logos, in this way, already divided along
these lines, however multiple they might be? Is the reflection here (of
nothing) already "feminine"? Of course, its mirror-play constitutes the
very definition of essence, the de-marcation that sets all difference (including sexual difference) under way; thus it would be reductive to say without
qualification that its "liquid" character makes it essentially feminine.*
The reflective movement we are considering, once again, is "before" essence. Moreover, if this mirror-play only subsists as a mutual reflection
where "[neither mirror] exceeds the other in grandeur and quality," it is
difficult to see how there could be a differentiation already at work.[9] To be
sure, she starts from a gendered configuration in finding her path. But does
the material support of this passage predetermine its shape and direction?
Is the threshold irreducibly "hers" in some sense? And if difference (and
language itself) only opens at/over such a bodily threshold, is the way-

---

*I noted above that Irigaray's thought is not an essentialism. Part of my aim here is to
demonstrate that she is posing the question of the "essence of essence" — that is, at a level
where all of the terms of the essentialism/anti-essentialism opposition (all of them held by a
very traditional meaning of essence) break down.

making of difference always materially determined in a way that involves "biological" difference?

I have nothing like an answer to this question. Nonetheless let me suggest that this bodily ground will never be hers in the sense of a "property" but will become her singular path of knowing, necessarily "hers" in this sense, to the extent that we are dealing with a structure of finite transcendence. The very possibility of a touch lies in a singular configuration defined, or rather *defining* itself, bodily. The material substrate we are considering is constitutive for the identity fashioned but not determinative for it. To abstract it from the process (neutralize it, neuter it) would be to fall into another form of essentialism: it would be to assume that language (and eventually gender definition) could ever be free of the body. The chiasmic structure of the "crisis" we are reading opens any number of possibilities in gender identification, but all of them pass by way of that material ground that *limits* them only in the sense that it is an irreducible part of their number. There is transcendence, but it is from/of the body, and always singular.

The body comes about as gendered in a remarking of the limit we have traced. But for "woman," according to Irigaray, this reflection is particularly difficult to achieve inasmuch as theology has already interpreted this limit as the division between ideality and materiality and has already assigned woman her place in this division. Thus, the theological, teleological interpretation of her passion will find a mutual attraction between the father and the son in a loving breast (thereby preserving the soul of "man" from confusion in this encounter). And while this same interpretation may allow that He has preferred her body for an inscription of His "will," it finds her too burdened with matter to know "the most perfect *jouissance*."

The problem is thus one of resisting the historical weight of this interpretation. Appropriation of her knowledge will require, first, a primary reappropriation of her body, a reinscription of her body as the proper site of her knowledge. She cannot truly touch herself, give a substance to the nothing she "is," without passing by way of a violent demarcation of a body she has never really known. The limit she has traced must be re-marked, cruelly. Her first step thus takes the form of a kind of masochism: the reclaiming of a body she cannot distinguish as her own except "by a certain number of cuts," a *scission* through the pain of which she can begin to feel herself again and gather her forces. Her forces will gather in this movement; in fact, they will gather excessively in her transports. But she must overcome not only the horror of onlookers but also the weight of centuries of interpretation before she can *know* herself in them.

It is worth following the movement Irigaray stages here closely because the masochism to which I have referred will pass through two stages, the first far less reflective than the second. The violence the mystic practices against herself (S 248/198) is only partially contained (by which I mean not only controlled but also hidden to onlookers) and constantly leads beyond consciousness into a lapse of some kind. The self-punishment and the forces it releases exceed any method or economic calculation; the last line of this passage reads, "Still without knowledge." But with the accession of these forces (in French, we would have *accès*), she begins to know—in her "fainting," Irigaray specifies—the approach of her God. She awakens to doubt, but the masochistic movement that follows will serve to win a now latent knowledge. This is the mystic's version of the overcoming of the ascetic ideal and the morals of the priest that Nietzsche describes in accounting for the birth of the philosopher from the shape of the priest in his *Genealogy of Morals*. The cruelty practiced here lacks the wickedness of the philosophical turn of will by which the philosopher exposes the will to the *nihil* in an act of creative overcoming, but it is no less an overcoming of the system of ascetic ideals and a reclaiming of the body, what Nietzsche calls a "translation" of humankind back into nature in *Beyond Good and Evil*.[10] It takes the form here of a second form of mimesis, the one most frequently identified as such in Irigaray's text.[11] In dis-covering her body, reigniting and appeasing her passion in the same movement, she assumes the negative judgment of her maculate being— re-proving her bodily knowledge of His love:

How could "God" manifest himself in all his magnificence and waste his substance in/to as weak and as vile a creature as a woman? She who has so often been humiliated. . . . Thus she will abase herself over and again in order to try this love that is supposedly offered her and to retraverse those imaginings that prohibit her response. She takes on the most slavish tasks, affecting the most shameful and degrading behavior so as to force the disdain that is felt toward her, that she feels toward herself. To rediscover, perhaps, at the bottom of the abyss, her purity . . . pure at last for having dared push to extremes the repetition of this abjection, this revulsion, this horror to which she has been condemned, to which, mimetically, she had condemned herself. (S 248/199)

By drawing the condemnation upon herself in acts of ever greater abjection, she effectively neutralizes the judgment passed upon her, undoes the negation of her material being. Each act, now, has become an act of auto/ hetero-affection, each act re-proves the love, the presence of her "companion," the presence of her (embodied) self. There is no idealism in this movement, and certainly no dialectic. Every act of "self-negation" neutralizes the moral condemnation that defined it as ab-ject, and the movement, in its totality, undoes the history of representations that have defined her, even as it reaffirms the presence of the divine love. She achieves a "nothingness of representation," a "nothing" of soul (S 249/199), so that she may know herself beyond good and evil: "And if God still loves her, she who has thus reestablished the proof of her non-value, it is because she nevertheless exists beyond everything one might think of her. . . . And that one man, at least, has understood her to the point of dying for it in the most atrocious suffering. This most feminine of all men that is the Son" (S 249/199). A nothing of representation achieved in her mimetic trials clears the way for a new form of identification. She now sees in the suffer-ing body of the Christ a figure of her own passion. A first mimesis, as we have seen, prepared the ground for this figuration with its graphics of the nothing — a writing that *figures nothing*, demarcating only an outline for the self that is a relation of self and other, sketching the *Da* of existence. A second mimesis begins a "transvaluation" by overturning a historical weight of negative judgments and by re-marking, bodily, the material site opened by this initial form. But the latter appropriation of this "ground" of her being lends itself to figuration — a third form of mimesis — only now in the visible figure of an exposure or an opening, almost nothing. She gazes upon the suffering Christ in his nudity, "offered for all to see" in his wounds and the extension of his crucified body, "in his suspense, his passion, and his abandon." She loves herself, Irigaray says, in what is now a *model* for her redemption.* She recognizes herself in him, positively re-presenting (the material ground of) her passion and with it the object of her desire:

Not every wound, then, would be unavowable, every laceration shameful? . . . Ecstasies there . . . where she reposes (herself) as if she had found her home — and He is also in her. Bathing in a blood that she feels as warm and purifying in its generous flow. And what she discovers in this divine passion she neither wants nor can translate. Finally authorized to remain silent, hidden from the prying glance in the intimacy of the exchanges where *she sees* (herself as) what she could not say. Where she sees nothing and sees everything. (S 249/200)

She achieves here something like a "specular" recovery in an "aletheic" movement that is an appropriation of her origin[12] — an imaginary figura-tion that phallogocentrism, as Irigaray demonstrates firmly in the first part of *Speculum*, has always foreclosed. She sees herself, touches herself "(al-most) immediately" in the contemplation of the abyss where she finds her meaning.

---

*"Inundated with love for him/herself. A model, which, in its crucifixion, opens a path of redemption for her in her fallen state" (S 249/200). It is striking that Gill omits the word "model" in her translation, and thus the crucial reference to the appearance of a nascent identification.

And the word? The presence to self via this image of an offering/opening, almost nothing (but not "nothing" or a "lack" in regard to the stature of the phallus — there is a figuration here that is not referred to the latter morphology)[13] issues in a kind of self-sufficiency that she has no desire to translate, even if she could. She is authorized in her silence because her ecstasy is also a reception and assumption of the Word. She has touched the word in her transports, but now it comes with the opening of her eye/I:

And in the rapt vision of the place from which you flow out, in a mortal ecstasy, *a lightning flash has lit up the sleeping understanding within me.* Resisting all knowledge that would not find its/my meaning in this abyss. . . . And if in the view of the transpierced body of the Son I drink a joy of which I cannot say a single word, let one not conclude too quickly that I take pleasure in his suffering. If the Word was made flesh in this way and to this point, it could only be in order to make me (become) God in my jouissance now finally recognized.* (S 250/200)

Irigaray started by noting that *la mystérique* is the only discursive site in the history of the West where woman speaks so publicly. But we recognize now that to accede to speech is to accede to silence. Nowhere in the history of the West, we should say, does woman achieve this silence in her speaking — nowhere does she so fully engage the word. She becomes the word, *is* (in) the word. Her word is this (holy) communication.

I borrow the last phrase from Hölderlin, in recollection of lines that Heidegger considers the prerequisite for thinking the advent of poetic language. In Heidegger's own terms this prerequisite is thinking together *Ereignis*, earth, and the abyss, all of which are drawn together in the ecstatic *measuring* of the abyss that the subject of *la mystérique* knows bodily. This is not "psychosis," as a more modern, more technically minded confessor might conclude in witnessing this accomplished identification with "God"; rather, it is the marking and crossing of the threshold in a bodily ec-stasis:

But that the Word should have been made flesh in this way and to this point, this could only be in order to make me (become) God in my jouissance now fully recognized. Engulfed now in my self, no longer cut in two contrary directions of elevation and fallen depths. Knowing now that height and depth give birth — incise — each other in(de)finitely. And that the one should be in the other and the other in me matter little since it is in me that they engender one another in their trans-ports. *Outside any self (as) same.* Never the same, always new. (S 250/200)

*I have elided the following line: "Now I know it/Him/me and in knowing it/Him/me I love it/Him/me and in loving it/Him/me I desire it/Him/me." The French gives *le/me*, and Gill prefers "it" to "him"; but I would emphasize that the "it" here — meaning — is the "/" between these pronouns — i.e., the meaning that emerges in the *partage* of the logos, in the encounter of Him/I and *only* in this encounter with the other.

Ex-schize crise of the ontico-ontological difference: the "synthesis" of ideality and materiality, essence and existence in an ec-stasis of the body that is an embodiment of the word. An experience with language in the *saying* of finite transcendence. Repeatedly new because repeatedly an exposure of and to an in-finite alterity in each exchange, each time she touches, is touched at the site of this reciprocal sharing (*partage réciproque*) of the abyss between her and God. A *sublime* transport that is perhaps specifically feminine (if only in the perspective of the discursive history of this concept from Kant onwards) because there is no self-protection in this exposure to a mortal immensity ("Uncountable in their enumeration for being determinable without measure, moreover eternal by reason of being immense" [S 25l/201]), no anxious distance converting freedom into negativity. And if this inmost site of her transport is "secret" or "cryptic," it is so only for the prospecting gaze of theoretical consciousness, for it reveals itself (in ecstasis) only to the touch that lets her be, in-finitely. And where she accedes to her innermost being, she is wholly outside: exposed at the limit that no theory can know.

"*A strange economy, this specula(riza)tion of woman*, who in her mirror seems always to refer to a *transcendence*. Who parts (for/at) the approach [*Qui (s')écarte (pour) qui approche*]" (S 251/201). There is no translating this (auto)erotics of *Entfernung*, this *pas* of relation in which a distance for self opens in encounter. "She" translates it, however, in play, in a final miming (the fourth form we see in this autoconception) of her relation to the other — a first presentation of self to other. Outrageous and exquisite — the miming of an *ex-schize crise*:

Thus (re)assured of the complicity of her all-powerful partner, they/she play(s) at courtship, in abasement at one moment, but only to adorn themselves with gold and diamonds the next, touching, inhaling, listening, seeing, embracing each other, devouring, penetrating, enflaming, consuming, melting each other ... Her divine companion never tires of praising her and encouraging her for her (auto)eroticism that has been so miraculously rediscovered. . . . And if one should object that, with the Good thus within her, she no longer needs to receive it, she would reply in her ateleo-logic that, for her, the one does not prevent the other. (S 251/201)

To which we might add, perhaps, the one is the other, the one *needs* the other, assuming the finitude of difference as a threshold and an invitation.

From this threshold, the (figurative) play of desire is infinitely open, its possible metamorphoses unlimited. Indeed, if we were to fall into taking this experience as a *model* (as though Irigaray were promoting *one* figuration of sexual desire in its biological and spiritual determination, as though this scene captured the truth of feminine desire), we would miss the play of mimesis that has been engaged here. *La mystérique* is a *passage* that offers itself to a particular sociocultural imaginary by virtue of its historical density, a density of language and usage. Irigaray has traversed it (staged it) in order to mark in it the conditions of a (sexual) freedom. We (are scare-quotes needed here?) are implicitly invited to engage with these material/spiritual conditions in an entirely different elaboration of the ethics of sexual difference. Ultimately, one cannot approach (and leave) this scene except in play.

PART IV

Benjamin

Translation as a Concept
of Relation

WALTER Benjamin's assertions in the opening paragraphs of "The Task of the Translator" (1923) are now famous: The translation of a literary work does not serve the reader (who cannot understand the work in its original language); it serves the work. And no literary work is intended for a reader. These uncompromising assertions rest upon two related claims. The first founds the dismissal not only of any consideration of reception in the critical appreciation of the work of art but also of any "bourgeois" notion of translation (where translation is conceived as a means for conveying the "signified" of a work — whether this be statement, information, or even the particular "poetic" genius or sensibility expressed by the work).* It entails the notion that the "essential" (GS 4.1 9/I 69) in a work of art involves a realm of meaning that transcends the signifying order Benjamin described in 1916 in "On Language as Such and on the Language of Man" as proper to fallen language, a realm that ultimately escapes even that language produced by humankind (in translations) that exceeds the limits defined in the early essay.[1] Not only does a literary work not "communicate" anything in the sense of this term presupposed by most reception theory; it is not even finally addressed to its human readers. It is addressed to language. Ultimately, to a language that will redeem it: the pure language to which all "purposeful" manifestations of life (GS 4.1 11/I 72) are directed as "the expression of its nature" (*Ausdrück seines Wesens*) or the "presentation of its significance" (*Darstellung seiner Bedeutung*) (GS 4.1 11–12/I 72). But since such redemption cannot be immediately and absolutely attained by any finite language, its address is necessarily to other language: language that will "complement" it in its striving toward the "inner relation" between languages that alone con-

*Benjamin characterizes the philosophy of language presupposed by such a notion of translation as "bourgeois" in "On Language as Such and on the Language of Man" (GS 2.1 144/R 318).

stitutes the "language of truth." The language of translation is such a complementary language; indeed it is the preeminent one.

But to be precise, we should say that the work *addresses itself* to such language. This is the second claim to which I have referred, and it suggests that the assertion from which we started should be rephrased: the translation (a "true" translation) *answers* to the work rather than serving it. A work *requires* its translation, Benjamin says. It speaks, we could say (this is language, after all), and its speech contains a "law" for the translation. This law, constituted by a certain ideality in the language of the work, allows us to speak of the translation that answers to it as a "form":

Translation is a form. To comprehend it as a form one must go back to the original, for that contains the law governing the translation: its translatability. The question of whether a work is translatable has a dual meaning. Either: will an adequate translator ever be found among the totality of its readers? Or more pertinently: does its nature [*Wesen*] lend itself to translation, and, therefore, in accordance with the significance of this form, require it [*verlangen*]? (GS 4.1 9–10/I 70)

The first part of the question asked here is dealt with summarily. It is of less importance in that it can be decided only "contingently," whereas the second part, bearing on an ideal structure, may be decided apodictically. Of course, we have seen that the first part of the question involves more than empirical considerations, for a strict concept of translation actually provides a negative answer ("would they not really be untranslatable to some degree?"). But even a *de jure* negative answer to the first part of the question does not appear to disqualify the possibility of speaking of a work's translatability (and thus Benjamin definitively sets aside human subjectivity in the consideration of the relation between work and translation). For translation *is* a form, as Benjamin asserts in the lines I have quoted. And as he writes at the conclusion of his paragraph, "if translation is a form, translatability must be an essential feature of certain works" (GS 4.1 10/I 71).

Thus certain works lend themselves to translation and *call* for it "in accordance with the significance of this form." I stress the motif of this call because it recurs in a crucial fashion in Benjamin's notion of the dialectical image. If we are to understand the past as "claiming" the present, then we must posit as inherent to language (in its essence) some form of "communicability" (to borrow a concept from the essay of 1916 [GS 2.1 142/R 316]) or some form of relation — some "concept of relation"[2] — that does not involve the mediation of signification. But I would also underscore here the concept of the work's *need* for translation. For while I may be forcing the phrase "in accordance with the significance of its form" by hearing such a need expressed in it, Benjamin's later reference to "the great longing for linguistic complementation" (GS 4.1 18/I 79) indicates that the "call" of the work marks the work's finitude and its need for a supplementing echo.

But it is important to add here that the "significance of the form" is not immediately of significance (*bedeutend*) *for the work* but rather for a significance (*Bedeutung*) latent in the work that emerges only in the work's "afterlife" (GS 4.1 11/I 71). Benjamin's argumentation on this point is quite perverse (I refer both to the manipulation of the term "significance" and to the fact that the paragraph in question is devoted to a concept of life, all the while describing a certain death).[3] It is coherent, however, if we recall Benjamin's constant recourse in his critical theory to a concept of "mortification." A text must perish in its apparently "organic" form for its truth content to emerge. Thus Benjamin argues here that the connection (*Zusammenhang*) between work and translation, to which the original text may well be indifferent (GS 4.1 10/I 71), is all the more "intimate" (*inniger*) if the translation is no longer significant for the original (*nicht mehr bedeutet*). "Intimate," a distinctively Hölderlinian term, describes a relation that is perhaps ultimately other than one of signification (this would render the passage all the more coherent) — it names, in any case, a proximity in difference that is founded, as we will see, in the differential relation between languages and that in fact *manifests* this relation ("signifying" in the mode of a resonance). Tracing Heidegger's own very similar appropriation of this term in "The Origin of the Work of Art" and in his readings of Hölderlin, we would produce an important convergence between the two texts: in both cases, the indication of the essence of language is produced through the remarking of difference, in the "drawing out" of a proximity.

But for my purposes here, I want to stress the temporal basis of the connection in question. Benjamin, as we see, inscribes the ideality he ascribes to the work in a history, arguing that translatability only emerges *after* the time of the work's initial emergence, its *Entstehung* — that is to say, in the time of its "survival" or "continued life": when the connection between translation and work "is no longer significant for the original" (GS 4.1 10/I 71). Benjamin is extending the term "life" here in such a way as to encompass the "natural" death (of organic form) to which I have referred, as well as the unfolding of everything that has a history — "The philosopher's task [*Aufgabe*]," he writes, "consists in comprehending all of natural life through the more encompassing life of history" (GS 4.1 10/I 71) (it is "life" in this extended sense whose meaning is presented by the "most inner relation" between languages). And though he appears to fall back upon an empirical determination of this history as concerns the work and its translation — relying both upon the contingent existence of a translator

("For a translation comes later than the original, and since the significant works of world literature [*bedeutende Werke*] never find their chosen translators at the time of their origin, their translation marks the stage of continued life" [GS 4.1 10–11/I 71])* and upon the public's response to the work ("Translations that are more than transmissions of subject matter come into being when in the course of its survival a work has reached the stage of its fame" [GS 4.1 11/I 72]) — he in fact refers it to a historical movement in language that transcends any human determination:

For in its afterlife — which could not be called that if it were not a transformation and a renewal of something living — the original undergoes a change. Even words with fixed meaning can undergo a maturing process. The obvious tendency of a writer's literary style may in time wither away, only to give rise to immanent tendencies in the literary creation. . . . To seek the essence of such changes, as well as the equally constant changes in meaning, in the subjectivity of posterity rather than in the very life of language and its works, would mean — even allowing for the crudest psychologism — confusing the root cause [*Grund*] of a thing with its essence [*Wesen*]. (GS 4.1 12/I 73)

The "fame" in which the work's "afterlife" may come to the surface (though presumably this "in principle eternal" afterlife might also *not* manifest itself: "Where this last [fame] manifests itself, it is called fame" [GS 4.1 11/I 71]) is perhaps the *cause* of the emergence of the work's ideal structure of meaning, and thus of the fact that it offers itself to translation; but "fame" does not define the *essence* of the historical movement that makes a translation possible at a certain moment in the life of a work. "Fame" is a kind of secondary, "surface" manifestation (like history itself when read in terms of cause and effect) in relation to a more essential process that Benjamin describes elsewhere in "The Task of the Translator" as "the hallowed growth of languages" and that he situates, as we will see, in what is perhaps best termed a "historial" order. This more fundamental process is described later in the essay when Benjamin writes the following:

In all languages and their formations, there remains, in addition to what can be communicated, something noncommunicable; depending on the context in which we come across it [*in dem es angetroffen wird*], it is something that symbolizes or something that is symbolized. It is symbolizing only in the finite formations of language, symbolized, however, in the becoming of the languages themselves. And that which seeks to present, to produce itself [*sich darzustellen, ja herzustellen sucht*] in the evolving of languages is that very nucleus of pure language [*jener Kern der reinen Sprache selbst*]. Though concealed and fragmentary, it is present

---

*The term "chosen" saves Benjamin from contradiction here: the translator is in fact called forth by the work; the call is the condition of possibility for the "existence" of the translator.

in life as the symbolized, whereas it inhabits linguistic formations only as symbolizing. While that ultimate essentiality, pure language, in the various tongues is tied only to linguistic elements and their changes, in linguistic creations, it is weighted with a heavy, alien sense. To deliver it from this latter, to turn the symbolizing into the symbolized, to win back the formed pure language of the movement in language, is the powerful capacity of translation alone. (GS 4.1 19/I 79)

The emergence of translatability in a work must ultimately be traced, we may presume, to that moment when "pure language" seeks its presentation (*Darstellung*).*

An explication of this proposition will take us to the core (the seed, the nucleus, the germ, etc.) of Benjamin's notion of translatability and translation itself. But the proposition is anything but self-evident, at least in the context from which it has been drawn. For while the concept of pure language arises elsewhere in the essay, the passage I have just cited is the only one in which Benjamin refers to this ultimate essentiality as "symbolizing" or "symbolized," and his use of these last terms raises several questions. Is the pure language of the becoming of languages "symbolized" by virtue of the *selbst-Darstellung* Benjamin describes here? And does the "translation" of the "symbolizing" dimension of the finite formations of language into the "symbolized" accomplish this movement in some way? Is translation, in its own *Darstellung*, a kind of *mimesis*, in the realm of linguistic creations, of the self-presentation of the essence of language (itself the expression of the essence of life)?[4] If Benjamin's definitions were not strictly linguistic — always involving a relation of language to language, always involving *translation* in some way — we could speak of translation's task as one of a "reflection" of pure language. But to approach what Benjamin is saying here, let me start with the notion of pure language.

The concept is named for the first time several pages before the passage in which Benjamin refers to it as "symbolizing," and it is called upon implicitly at least twice before this explicit definition. It appears in an implicit manner first in Benjamin's initial description of translation as "the latest and most abundant flowering of the life of the original" (GS 4.1 11/I 72). As a special and high form of life, he says, translation is governed by a special, high purposiveness. And he continues:

All purposeful manifestations of life, including their very purposiveness, in the final analysis have their end not in life, but in the expression of its nature [*Aus-*

*For consistency, I will translate *Darstellung* always as "presentation." The discussion in this and the succeeding chapter of the character of this "presentation" should reveal why "representation" (which should probably be reserved for *Vorstellung*, in any case) would not be an appropriate choice even if it sometimes works unobtrusively.

druck seines Wesens], in the presentation of its significance [*Darstellung seiner Bedeutung*]. Translation thus ultimately serves the purpose of expressing the most inner relation of languages to one another. It cannot possibly reveal [*offenbaren*] or establish [*herstellen*] this hidden relationship itself; but it can present it by realizing it in embryonic or intensive form [*aber darstellen, indem sie es keimhaft oder intensiv verwirklicht, kann sie es*]. (GS 4.1 11–12/I 72)

Could we translate this passage in the light of the earlier quotation and say that all purposeful manifestations of life "symbolize" in that they are directed to the expression of the essence of life — which is in fact nothing other than pure language itself according to the essay on language of 1916? We could do so only if such symbolization (where the realm of linguistic formations is concerned) is understood to signify in some way the "inner relation between languages." For while Benjamin's argument remains elliptical, it nevertheless suggests strongly that the expression of the essence of life lies in the inner relation of languages to one another that translation, as one of the highest and most purposive forms of life, "realizes" in an embryonic and intensive form. Benjamin's later definition of pure language will in fact confirm this suggestion and make it clear that pure language is *only* attained (in linguistic creations, once again) in this relation that translation draws forth. Thus, if there is a latent purposefulness in the original work that translation accomplishes as this work's "latest and most abundant flowering," it inheres in that dimension of a work's language that belongs to this relation and indicates it (if only latently) — in other words, it inheres in the work's very call to translation. The latter would be the "seed" of pure language that seeks its presentation and production in the course of the growth of a language.

Benjamin's reiterated reference to the "embryonic" character of translation underscores this point. The *Darstellung* of pure language realized by translation as it draws forth the kinship of languages is *keimhaft oder intensiv*, as we read in the passage I have cited. And Benjamin continues, "This presentation [*Darstellung*] of something signified [*Bedeuteten*] through the embryonic attempt at its production is an entirely singular mode of representation [*Darstellungsmodus*] that can hardly be met with in the sphere of nonlinguistic life" (GS 4.1 12/I 72). The seed of pure language "germinated" by translation is not to be understood as a hidden, self-subsisting element in the individual languages and their words that awaits development (as the very image of a hidden seed, kernel, or nucleus would suggest). Rather, it is that trait by which languages, in their essence ("a priori and apart from all historical relationships" [GS 4.1 11/I 72]), relate to one another. It is their very *finitude*: marked by the way in which a language *requires* complementation as it intends the pure language that would redeem it.

The notion of complementation (or supplementation: *Ergänzung*) to which I have referred appears in the passage in which Benjamin names pure language (GS 4.1 13/I 74). Every language, he tells us in his definition of the "kinship" (*Verwandschaft*) of languages, intends pure language; every language is seeking to say the "same thing" in its particular, finite manner (this "same thing" being once again the absolute linguistic expression of the spiritual essence of what is—there is no "object" expressed, as Harry Zohn's translation suggests [GS 4.1 13–14/I 74]: the object of any given language is the logos). But while the structure of signification of each language is determined by this language's relation to the "true" language (GS 4.1 16/I 77), no language, taken singly, ever says what it thus intends. "Suprahistorical kinship" inheres in the fact that in each of the languages as a whole, "one and indeed the same thing is intended; however, none of them on their own, but only the totality of their mutually supplementing intentions can reach this: pure language" (GS 4.1 13/I 74). Pure language never speaks in the individual languages on their own, or never emerges there in any formed manner. It is never "symbolized" or presented in any unsupplemented language. As Benjamin writes later in the paragraph from which I have just quoted: "In the individual, unsupplemented languages, the intended is never found in relative independence, as in individual words or sentences; rather it is in constant change—until it is able to emerge as pure language from the harmony of all the modes of intention. Until then it remains hidden in the languages" (GS 4.1 14/I 74).

We might try to understand this statement by assuming that pure language is never present in any word or sentence because it inheres in the symbolizing dimension of a language *in its totality*, in the relation between a language's mode of intending and the intended (*die Art des Meinens zum Gemeinten* [GS 4.1 14]). The expression of pure language would therefore involve the remarking or manifestation of a language's order of meaning as such: what structures the divergent and even *conflicting* meanings of words such as *Brot* and *pain*.[5] No isolated element of a language could achieve this expression of the essence of the language itself (the kind of expression Wittgenstein imagines in his "Lecture on Ethics" when he entertains the question of what it would mean for a language to say the fact of the existence of the world). But it is still insufficient to say that pure language inheres in a language's finite manner of "symbolizing" its intended. For while there must indeed be some such symbolization—Benjamin clearly posits a relation between the mode of intention and the intended—pure language "itself" (what Benjamin in fact designated as the "symbolized") lies *only* in the relation between the modes of intention of the various languages. Pure language *is* only where it speaks—how else could it be called language?—and it speaks only where a language's call for complementation (what I have identified as the "seed" of pure language) is drawn forth as such — that is, as the "relationality" of a language, as that dimension of a language's relation to the "intended" that "wants" or "requires" complementation by the modes of intention of all the other languages. It is translation that draws forth this call, and it draws it forth in a "resonance" that participates intensively in what is ultimately a harmony — in what can only be conceived as a differential relation between languages: not a simple complementation of modes of intention in the sense that these might be added together to form the "total," that is, cumulative expression of the essence of what is, but an "inner relation" of these modes by which *alone* each may be heard as participating in the symbolization of pure language.

Two descriptions of translation in "The Task of the Translator" establish the point I am making here. In the first, Benjamin tells us that translation involves precisely the kind of remarking of the signifying order of a language as a whole that I described above as the expression of the essence of a language (but we must now understand this essence to be the "symbolizing" dimension of a language as it gives itself *in its finitude*). The task of the translator, he says, is to direct his or her effort at their language in its totality in such a way as to make it echo with the language from which they are translating. I cite at length here because the published English translation requires some adjustments:

The task of the translator consists in finding that intention toward the language [a relation to a language's own relation to the "intended"] into which he is translating from out of which the echo of the original can be awakened. This is a trait of translation that basically differentiates it from the poet's work, because the intention of the latter is never directed at the language as such, at its totality, but solely and immediately at determinate linguistic connections of content. Unlike poetry [*Dichtung*], translation does not find itself in the center of the language forest itself, but on the outside facing [*ihm gegenüber*] the wooded ridge; without entering, it calls the original into it, aiming at that unique spot where the echo in its own language can give back the reverberation of a work of the foreign language. The intention of translation is not only directed at something other than that of poetry, namely at a language as a whole, taking an individual work in an alien language as a point of departure, but it is even entirely different: that of the poet is spontaneous, primary, graphic; that of the translator is derivative, ultimate, ideational. For the great motif of integrating many languages into one true one is at work. (GS 4.1 16/I 77)

The second description of translation to which I have referred (and to which I will turn shortly) makes it clear that when Benjamin refers to the totality of a language, he is referring to that language's mode of intention: what will be drawn forth in what he calls the *intentio* of a linguistic work ("the language of a translation gives voice to the *intentio* of the original not as reproduction but as harmony . . . as its own kind of *intentio*" [GS 4.1 18/I 79]). A work of high quality is eminently translatable in that it engages with the symbolizing dimension of a language in a particularly immediate fashion — it draws most powerfully on what we might call the "idiom," even though it works in this idiom in an immanent fashion, directing its intention to the expression or representation of content ("the intention of the poet is spontaneous, primary, graphic"). The higher the quality of a work, however, the less it will consist of communicable "information" and the more its content will be suffused with the language's "symbolizing" character. Translation will deliver the original of its "surface content," its "alien meaning" (GS 4.1 19/I 80), and render that dimension of the poet's intention that engages with the mode of intention of the language as a whole. But it will not reproduce it in this manner in a sublated form; it will "render" it only in the form of a reverberation. The translator, Benjamin tells us, seeks to make the governing mode of intention of his own language echo in such a way as to bring forth a resonance in the original. An echo is to make the symbolizing dimension of the original reverberate in a kind of sympathetic vibration. Once again, translation is concerned with the *relation* between languages, not a core of meaning latent in the original; or rather, it is concerned with the original's core meaning *as* it lends itself to complementation and ultimately a harmony. A little work is required to justify the passage from a notion of harmony to one of resonance and sympathetic vibration,* but the essential point here, once again, is that the aim of translation is to bring forth the kinship of the languages involved in the process of translation: the relation between the essence of the language of the original and its complementary language in the translation.

Of course, there is only one language in a translation (one *estranged* language). To represent the relation of kinship, Benjamin tells us, a translation brings forth its own language in its complementarity — it presents the symbolizing dimension of the original work as complemented or in complementation. Let me cite now at greater length the second description of translation to which I have referred:

As regards the meaning, the language of a translation can — in fact, must — let itself go, so that it gives voice to the *intentio* of the original not as reproduction but as harmony, as a supplement to the language in which it expresses itself, as its own kind of *intentio*. Therefore, it is not the highest praise of a translation, particularly in the age of its origin, to say that it reads as if it had originally been written in that

*A passage that Benjamin makes in his reflections on Ritter in the "Epistemo-Critical Prologue," to which I will refer in my next chapter.

language. Rather, the significance of fidelity as ensured by literalness is that the work reflects the great longing for linguistic complementation [*die grosse Sehnsucht nach Sprachergänzung*]. (GS 4.1 18/I 79)

I will not try to explore here how the manner of proceeding word for word in a translation—a procedure of which Benjamin takes Hölderlin's translation of Sophocles as an exemplary case—entails an engagement with the "symbolizing" dimension of the translator's own language. Suffice it to say here that the estranging effect of such a procedure (the translation has "its own kind of *intentio*" but does not sound original) breaks the relation between signifier and signified in this language and renders the language of the translation allegorical: "For it signifies a more exalted language than it is itself and thus remains unsuited to its content, overpowering and alien. This disjunctiveness [*Gebrochenheit*] prevents [further] translation at the same time that it renders it superfluous" (GS 4.1 15/I 75). It is precisely as broken or fragmentary that the language of the translation is allegorical.* I have suggested that the symbolizing dimension of a language (that by which it symbolizes pure language or that element of pure language in it that symbolizes) must be understood as the mode of intention of a language in its finitude or relationality. Translation essentially remarks this finitude of the symbolizing character of a language—it presents its own symbolizing dimension as a fragment, as a *symbolon*. Shortly before the passage in which Benjamin evokes the harmony of *intentio*, he presents the well-known comparison of the relation between translation and original to that between fragments of a broken vessel: "The demand for literalness . . . must be understood in a more meaningful context . . . a translation, instead of resembling the meaning of the original, must lovingly and in detail incorporate the original's mode of intending, thus making both the original and the translation recognizable as fragments of a greater language, just as fragments are part of a vessel" (GS 4.1 18/I 78).

In its fragmentariness, the language of the translation reflects "the great longing for linguistic complementation." It effectively re-marks the call for complementation that defines the translatability of the original by repeating this call *en différance*, remarking its own symbolizing dimension in its relation to the original. It must be emphasized that this sonorous "reflection" of the symbolizing dimension of the translating language (a self-relation produced by the "lever" of the language of a foreign work) also produces a reflection of the relatedness of the translation to the origi-

---

*I might note that Benjamin's reference to the folds of a royal robe (GS 4.1 15/I 75) also evokes strongly the material of the German *Trauerspiel*, wherein the allegorical mode finds an extreme mode of self-reflection.

nal. Self-relation *and* the relation to the other appear in the "estranged" language of the translation. The translation appears *as* a fragment that fits another fragment; it sounds as a "supplement" to this other language and in harmony with it. Once again, its very *complementarity* appears, and in this manner it points to pure language, which is the *relationality* of languages: the order of their relations, or the relation of relations. In remarking its own essence via the other, it remarks intensively the differential relation between languages. And in so doing, it marks, and perhaps contributes to, the "growth" of languages toward their messianic fulfillment. For this growth consists in the developing emergence of the complementarity of each language. Let me now complete a citation I introduced earlier:

In the individual, unsupplemented languages, the intended is never found in relative independence, as in individual words or sentences; rather, it is in a constant state of change — until it is able to emerge as pure language from the harmony of all the various modes of intention. Until then, it remains hidden [*verborgen*] in the languages. If however, these languages continue to grow in this manner until the messianic end of their time, it is translation that catches fire on the eternal life of works and the perpetual renewal of languages. Translation keeps putting the hallowed growth of languages to the test: how far removed is the truth hidden in them from revelation?; how present can it become in the knowledge of this distance?

Inasmuch as pure language inheres in the harmony of the modes of intention of the various languages, the growth of these languages toward the revelation of what is hidden in them must entail an emergence of their inherent complementarity, and to some extent a gradual *definition* of their complementarity (for what is hidden in them, the relation between languages, is in "constant change," Benjamin says, until the messianic moment of revelation [GS 4.1 13/I 74]).*

Revelation would be the complete subsumption of a language in the harmonic relation that constitutes pure language — the manifestation of a general resonance throughout the language. Or, in other words, the total manifestation of the essence of the language (its symbolizing character) *in its relationality* and thus the harmonic manifestation of the essence of language in general (language becoming song). Might translation actually effect or participate in a *Bestimmung*? Would this be part of the *task* of the translator? Benjamin tells us that translation "catches fire" on the eternal life of the works and the perpetual renewal of language (GS 4.1 13/I 74).

*They are related "a priori and apart from all historical relationships in what they want to say," and they stand in need of complementation — but the relationality expressed by their call to complementation (in translatability) remains not only obscured but to some extent undefined, "untuned."

As a kind of spontaneous combustion, translation would appear to be marked by a growing and finally critical intensity of that which "seeks to present, to produce itself": the seed of pure language. The time of a translation is marked by the emergence of a dual need for complementation: that of the original language as it expresses itself in the afterlife of the work, and that of the target language that seems to need translation for its very vitality. In its faithful re-creation (*Umdichtung*), the translation seeks to "free" the pure language imprisoned in the work of the original language, and in its freedom, the translation seeks to "break through the decayed barriers" of its own language. Translation at least liberates something that is constantly pressing for expression or symbolization, presumably at always higher levels of articulation (for the growth of the languages is characterized by an ever higher development toward harmony), itself seeking in this process "a final, conclusive, decisive stage of all linguistic creation" (GS 4.1 13/I 75). If it does not actually contribute to bringing this about through its intensive signification of the goal (both an intensive realization and a pointing), that is to say, if it does not actually define in any determining manner the complementarity of the language whose relationality it draws forth, it at least *marks* the development of this complementarity: "Translation keeps putting the hallowed growth of languages to the test: How far removed is their hidden from revelation?; how present can it become in the knowledge of this distance [*Entfernung*]?" (GS 4.1 13/I 74–75).

Would a translation somehow mark this distance by the very brokenness of its language? This historical marking, as we have seen, presents "intensively" the language to which it points. Assuming the most active understanding of the manner in which language draws out complementarity in its broken language, we might ask whether the very "existence" of pure language is a function of *Entfernung*, whether it *is* only in a distancing, and whether translation's intensive *Darstellung* consists in a kind of measuring of the pure language it signifies. However this may be, I would underscore in a final observation concerning the "intervention" represented by translation that Benjamin understands this mode of signification as a *writing*—a writing that defines the philosophical interest (in the strongest sense) of translation. Describing the "language of truth" that is hidden "intensively" in translations (*sie ist intensiv in den Übersetzungen verborgen*), Benjamin writes:

There is no muse of philosophy, nor is there one of translation. But despite the claims of sentimental artists, these two are not banausic. For there is a philosophical genius that is characterized by a yearning [*Sehnsucht*: the same word will be used for language itself and its longing for complementation] for that language which manifests itself in translations. "*Les langues imparfaites en cela que plusieurs, manque la suprême: penser étant écrire sans accessoires, ni chuchotement mais tacite encore l'immortelle parole, la diversité, sur terre, des idiomes empêche personne de proférer les mots qui, sinon se trouveraient, par une frappe unique, elle-même matériellement la vérité.*"* If what Mallarmé evokes here is fully fathomable to a philosopher, translation, with its seeds [*Keime*] of such a language, is midway between poetry and doctrine. Its products are less sharply defined, but it leaves no less of a mark on history [*Ihr Werk steht an Ausprägung diesen nach, doch es prägt sich weniger tief ein in die Geschichte*]. (GS 4.1 17/I 77)

In his "Epistemo-Critical Prologue" to the *Trauerspiel* study, Benjamin will define truth's mode of presenting itself as a form of *typography*: the impression of the word on empirical phenomena. Here, Benjamin, following Mallarmé, thinks the "intensive," allegorical presentation of truth in terms of a similar imprinting, a similar *frappe*. And as in the "Prologue," this finite language of truth is the writing of history. Or, to put this more precisely, a writing *in* history. The latter history, in Benjamin's presentation, has a transcendental horizon, to be sure, but Benjamin may well recognize — the "perversity" of his writing suggests such a recognition — that the reference to fulfillment is first a function of the structure of "need." Redemption is promised in the very structure of meaning, and such a horizon is perhaps the condition of thinking its relationality. But there is no ground for saying that pure language inheres in anything more than *Entfernung* (just as there is no ground for denying the assertion that the messiah might enter the gate at any time). However we assess Benjamin's reference to fulfillment, in any case, the recognition of the finitude of the essence of language (ours or his) does not dissipate the thought of a dimension of language exceeding the play of signification of human intentionality. It "deconstructs" it perhaps, but this term does not name a neutralizing or a suspending. It names rather the opening of a thought of historicity. The next two chapters on Benjamin's philosophy of language will follow his attempt to historicize this thought and will continue to entertain seriously the notion of pure language.

*"*The languages imperfect in that they are several, the supreme one lacking: thinking being to write without accessories, or whispering, but still tacit the immortal word, the diversity of idioms, on earth, prevents anyone from proferring the words that would otherwise find themselves, by a unique stroke, the truth itself, materially.*"

7

The Presentation of Allegory

THE task of the critic, Benjamin indicates in the "Epistemo-Critical Prologue" to his study of the German *Trauerspiel* (1928) is to read language — not a signified meaning, but *language*, where it gives itself as such. Language *as such*, however, is not an object of knowledge, at least not an object of conceptual apprehension by an intending consciousness. It gives itself only im-mediately to a form of philosophical contemplation that is "sovereignly" receptive of its communication. The problem for a philosophically founded criticism is one of articulating this offering as it is presented in literary form, in what Benjamin terms the *Formensprache* of a work (GS 1.1 225/O 44).

The task for the reader of Benjamin's *Trauerspiel* book is to determine not only whether such a criticism is conceivable but whether and how it occurs in Benjamin's analysis of the German *Trauerspiel*. For while we may well suspect a certain amount of philosophical fictioning in Benjamin's "Prologue," perhaps even a bluff to some degree, it is offered as a methodological statement and cannot be avoided in any serious reading of the volume.[1] The task is therefore to think the relation between the "Prologue" and the exemplary piece of philosophical/historical criticism it introduces, a task that comes down to thinking the relation between the claim for criticism as a form (no less of an "objective instance" [GS 1.1 109] than translation) and the formal analysis of the linguistic structure of the German *Trauerspiel*. In that the former pursues Benjamin's speculations on the language of names and the latter analyzes an extreme reflection of the signifying mediations of subjective consciousness, it will be a matter of assessing Benjamin's historical instantiation of the formal relation defined in his essay of 1916, "On Language as Such and On the Language of Man," between a language of names and the fallen, human language of signification. A matter, ultimately, of assessing Benjamin's attempt to delimit a structure of subjective reflection from a "sober" stance of philosophical contemplation — his claim to read one possibility of language from another in what should perhaps finally be called an allegory of allegory.

Of course, a thorough approach to the task I have outlined here would require a volume. In lieu of such an undertaking, I propose to start with a single latent thread connecting the "Prologue" and the body of the study, introducing by this means the question of presentation (*Darstellung*) as Benjamin treats it in his opening statement, and then moving rapidly to Benjamin's presentation of the German *Trauerspiel* as a historically grounded linguistic form. The thread I will follow is no more than latent, and I certainly do not want to suggest that it is the essential one. But since I am particularly interested in Benjamin's historicization of the reflections on language contained in the essay of 1916 and the essay on translation (no less than in the continuity of his reflections on "language as such"), it should provide a useful lead. Once I have followed it into the body of Benjamin's study, I will turn to Benjamin's *theological* interpretation of his formal analysis and attempt to read the relation between this analysis and the "Prologue."

I start from Benjamin's appropriation in his "Prologue" of the "Platonic theory of Ideas" (GS 1.1 210/O 30) and his assertion that the romantics of the "older generation" were frustrated in the attempt to renew this theory by virtue of the fact that they gave truth the character of a reflective consciousness rather than conceiving it as language (GS 1.1 218/O 38). The latter claim is one that Benjamin would appear, at first glance at least, to have amply supported in his thesis of 1919, "The Concept of Aesthetic Critique in German Romanticism," and does not immediately present a problem. But the strong presence of this earlier discussion in the "Prologue" might also give us pause, for it is clear that Benjamin's argument for the possibility of conceiving a philosophically founded criticism as a *form* draws heavily from the notion of critique he had developed in his thesis from the basis of the "fundamental philosophical conception" (GS 1.1 103) informing the romantic philosophy of art. The distance he takes from the romantics would seem to require a bit more justification than he offers; in the case of Hölderlin, in fact, it seems downright questionable. The thread on which I want to draw is that of Hölderlin's presence in the methodological statements of the *Trauerspiel* study, both in the "Prologue" and in the body of the text.

The distinction Benjamin implicitly draws between Friedrich Schlegel's manner of thinking the work's "medium of forms" (GS 1.1 107) from the basis of a philosophy of reflection and his own attempt to think such a notion in relation to the self-presentation of the Idea *as language* is clear (though subject to qualification as regards Schlegel). The Idea is something *vorgegeben*, Benjamin says (GS 1.1 210/O 30). It gives itself "in advance" in an immediate unity that is prior to any reflection and, of course, prior to the mediated connections proper to conceptual knowledge. It is a transcendental in the Platonic sense, Benjamin says, and in the Platonic sense it offers itself as the essential content of beauty. But the self-presentation of the domain of Ideas that constitutes what Benjamin terms the "impulse to presentation" (truth's *darstellendes Moment*), this "truth content" of the beautiful, does not take the form of an appearance or any kind of phenomenal manifestation. It presents itself in an order "superior to that of the beautiful" and any empirical manifestation. It is never given in experience (as defined in Kantian terms). Like the "purposiveness" of life functions to which Benjamin refers in his essay on translation (and indeed we are in the same order of meaning, i.e., that of the presentation of essence), it must be sought in a higher sphere, a "fundamentally different domain" from that of the phenomena whose virtual, objective order it defines by way of what can only be described as a form of *typography*. "Truth," Benjamin asserts, "is not an intention that finds its determination in empirical reality, but rather consists in the initial imprinting power of the essence of empirical reality. The being beyond all phenomenality to which alone this power belongs is that of the name. The name determines the given character of Ideas" (GS 1.1 216/O 36).

The reference to truth as a power is worth noting here, for it will also mark Benjamin's descriptions of the dialectical image. But I would emphasize two other points, beginning with Benjamin's uncompromising elimination of subjectivity for the constitution of truth. We see this gesture here as he removes truth from any phenomenal determination, and we see it in his dismissal, a few lines earlier, of any recourse to an intellectual intuition: "The being of Ideas cannot be thought as the object of vision, not even an intellectual one. . . . Truth is the death of intention" (GS 1.1 215–16/O 36). Benjamin departs decisively here from the modern metaphysics of the subject and the structure of representation it presupposes (or within which it unfolds, as Heidegger demonstrated in his Nietzsche lectures). Truth is not an object for a representing subject and is not in fact present to consciousness at all. It is not constituted in a structure of representation but rather gives itself, once again, im-mediately, in its imprinting configuration of reality.

As such an offering (and this is my second point), it is essentially *sprachlich*, "linguistic." Truth is given, and it is given in the word: *Es, das Wort, gibt.* This translation of Benjamin's argument in Heideggerian terms must be done cautiously in that the concept of essence is far less developed in Benjamin than it is in Heidegger. Nevertheless, *es gibt*, naming the mode of presencing of essence for Heidegger, might properly characterize the "offering" of truth Benjamin describes inasmuch as this offering occurs in language and as language and, in the *name*, as the presentation of the essence of language. Heidegger's guideword *Das Wesen der Sprache —* :

Die Sprache des Wesens is quite appropriate to the movement Benjamin describes in defining the given character of truth, as is the phrase *Die Sprache als die Sprache zur Sprache bringen* to the task of philosophy as Benjamin defines it in the passage where he describes the originary form of perception to which philosophy must return in its translation of the self-presentation of truth, an offering that is thought from what Benjamin termed, in his essay on language of 1916, the "communicability" of language (GS 2.1 142/R 315).

I am using the term "translation" from the basis of the same essay of 1916 (GS 2.1 151/R 325) and will conclude this introduction to Benjamin's understanding of the linguistic character of truth by summarizing some of that essay's basic assertions regarding the language of names — assertions that clearly underlie portions of the "Prologue." The spiritual essence of things, he affirms in this early essay, *is* their language — which is to say (and I am doing a little translating of my own here) that language is the movement by which something *is* inasmuch as the spiritual essence (*geistiges Wesen*) of a thing is identical with its communicability. Benjamin defers the latter equation at the outset of his essay, stating explicitly that philosophy of language must start by differentiating between spiritual essence and linguistic essence; their identification, as expressed in the ambiguity of the word "logos" (GS 2.1 141/R 315) is the "abyss" over which language philosophy must hover, at least at its outset, Benjamin says. But in naming humankind as the site where the essence of language (the communicability of spiritual essence) communicates itself absolutely, and in thus producing, halfway through his essay, the concept of revelation (Benjamin's reference to the theological perspective and his reading of *Genesis* will follow immediately upon the definition of the spiritual essence of humankind as language itself — language as such and in its totality), Benjamin cedes fully to the speculative temptation and proceeds to identify language and being. Humankind is the site of the revelation of the linguistic being of what is. It is of the essence of all beings to communicate their essence. The communicability of essence (the essence of language itself) communicates itself absolutely in the name, by which humankind expresses its own spiritual essence. Humankind expresses its essence not *by* the word, Benjamin emphasizes, but *in* the word and *as* language itself.[2] All beings communicate their essence (in its communicability) to humankind, and the essence of humankind is to express this communication, and thus itself, in the name, in a *presentation of the fact of language* — a presentation that is not a self-reflection but a communication of language before God.* The name, once again, does not designate something beyond

* Benjamin insists that "this is not anthropomorphism" (GS 2.1 144/R 317).

language, as the "bourgeois" view of language holds (GS 2.1 144/R 318); it is the expression of the essence of what is in the expression of the essence of language itself — the saying of language in its intensive totality (its immediate, infinite expression, de-fined only by its own being) and in its universally extensive character as the *address* of all that is in its linguistic being: "Name, however, is not only the last utterance of language, but also the true call of it. Thus in the name appears the essential law of language according to which to express oneself and to address everything else amounts to the same" (GS 2.1 145/R 319).

We are a long way from a philosophy of reflection and any notion of critique that involves an accomplishment or systematization of the work, as documented in "The Concept of Aesthetic Critique." Yet it is clear, as I have noted, that Benjamin's description of a philosophically founded criticism as "an original form of prose" (*eigenbürtige prosaische Form* [GS 1.1 209/O 29]), a "sober prose," is deeply marked by the earlier discussion. Criticism, he demonstrates in the thesis of 1919, achieves legitimacy as an objective instance in the romantic philosophy of art by virtue of its presentation of the prosaic "kernel" of the work (GS 1.1 109), a "medium of forms" that is the ground of the work's "criticizability" (GS 1.1 110). Benjamin's demonstration that this "medium" is conceived by the "older generation" as a medium of reflection is clearly justified (if partial). But he also seems quite aware that *at its limit*, the philosophical conception of a prosaic kernel involves a notion of the linguistic presentation of truth. This limit is attained by Hölderlin.

Benjamin actually seems to signal that he is reaching a limit-concept for his thesis when he introduces the notion of prose as a "new foundation" (GS 1.1 100) for the early romantic philosophy of art and its concept of critique. In the light of this "fundamental philosophical conception" (GS 1.1 103), Benjamin argues, it is possible to enlarge the circle of individuals he has described as romantic and include the person who stands at the *center* of this enlarged circle from a philosophical point of view. Hölderlin is thus introduced under the sign of "philosophy" — a designation that seems virtually shorthand for what Benjamin means by "philosophy of language."* Benjamin would appear to be indicating clearly here that he has reached the limits of the romantic philosophy of reflection to which he points in his "Prologue."

The notion that establishes the "singular philosophical unity" of Hölderlin's thinking with that of the early romantics is the principle of so-

---

*The remarks preceding the citation of Mallarmé in "The Task of the Translator," the concluding statement of "On the Coming Program of Philosophy," and the strong claim made for philosophy's concern with the problem of presentation in the "Prologue" all point to this synonymy.

briety, which Benjamin names "the fundamental thought of the romantic philosophy of art" (GS 1.1 103) and describes as "the *proper* meaning of the romantic notion of prose as a principle of reflection" (GS 1.1 103). Though Benjamin's remarks on this "fundamental notion" are remarkably spare here (another sign that he knows he is touching the limits of his thesis), he suggests that it names a form of reflection that is to be contrasted with a poetic *mania* or enthusiasm (GS 1.1 104). Sober reflection is a form of calculation, even a "mechanical reason" that any aesthetics based on the notion of the beautiful will fail to recognize, not only by reason of the limitations of its concept of form but also by reason of its reference to aesthetic pleasure (two consistent targets in Benjamin's attacks on aesthetic ideology). Sober reflection is a form of reason permitting an objective form of linguistic usage that would allow poetry, for example, and in the words of Hölderlin cited by Benjamin, to attain the surety of the *mēchanē* of the ancients (GS 1.1 104).

Read in its context (which includes the famous remarks about the "caesura" and the "pure word"), the citation from Hölderlin to which I have just referred indicates clearly that "sober reflection" has its ground in language, thereby belying or at least problematizing Benjamin's claim about the limitations of the romantic reflection on truth. Moreover, it seems to offer a basis for the historical and phenomenological grounding of what Benjamin terms in his "Prologue" the *Formensprache* of the work. Here is the Hölderlin passage cited by Benjamin (I cite at length because this passage is so central to the concerns of this volume):[3]

It will be good, in order to secure a civic experience for poets, even our own, if poetry is raised, even our own, and allowing for the difference of times and institutions, to the level of the *mēchanē* of the ancients. For other works of art, too, compared with those of the Greeks, the conditions of reliability are lacking; up until now, at least, they have been judged more according to the impressions they make than according to their lawful calculus and their other mode of procedure through which the beautiful is brought forth. Modern poetry, however, is especially lacking in schools and craft, namely what would enable its mode of procedure to be calculated and taught, and once learned to be repeated always reliably in practice. One must, where humans are concerned, and in relation to every thing, see above all that it is Something, i.e., that it is recognizable through the means [*moyen*] of its appearance, that the mode, the way in which it is conditioned, can be determined and taught. For this, and for higher reasons, poetry is especially in need of surer and more characteristic principles and bounds. To this belongs precisely that lawful calculation.

Several lines later, Hölderlin adds the following regarding the phenomenological dimension of the work's "calculus":

The law, the calculation, the mode, the way in which a system of sensibility, the entire man develops as under the influence of the element, and the way in which representation, sensibility and reasoning arise one after the other, in different successions, but always according to a sure rule — in the tragic this is more an equilibrium than a pure succession. For the tragic *transport* is properly empty, and the least bound.

He then continues with a statement on the rhythmic structure of the work's *Formensprache* and its presentation of this language itself.

Thereby, in the rhythmic succession of representations wherein the *transport* presents itself, there becomes necessary *what in meter is called caesura*, the pure word, the counter-rhythmic interruption, in order to counter at its highest point the rending alternation of representations so that it is no longer the alternation of representations that appears, but representation itself.

Now, when Benjamin implies that the task of criticism is to *read language* in a work, and proceeds to read baroque allegory as a possibility given by "the spirit of language" itself, he may well be remembering Hölderlin's last words here. I suspect too that when he gives a historical grounding to the form of baroque *Trauerspiel* in his "Prologue," he is recalling Hölderlin's "lawful calculation."[4] Evoking his notion of form as a structure that transcends any empirical instantiation but that necessarily emerged in its time, Benjamin writes: "And just as every speech form, even the unusual or isolated, can be seen not only as a testimony to the man who coined it, but also as a document in the life of the language and evidence of its possibilities at a given time, so too does any art form — and far more genuinely than any individual work — contain the index of a particular, objectively necessary artistic structure" (GS 1.1 230/O 49). One could conceivably read the last phrase as a reference to the ideal history that Benjamin describes as governing the rhythmics of the origin (GS 1.1 226/O 45). But the previous references in this paragraph to the *Trauerspiel* as a product of its epoch, and the subsequent discussion of the historical determination of this form, clearly suggest that Benjamin is seeking to define a history of forms that is grounded phenomenologically in the historical *presentation* of ontic reality (a presentation, once again, that is always thought *from language*).

Benjamin's effort to ground literary form historically is crucial for his study and bears emphasis. We could well interpret it from a theological perspective and attempt to show how Benjamin is translating a kabbalistic understanding of the relation between truth and history in philosophical terms. But this philosophical translation (references to Being, essence, etc.) also offers another way of presenting Benjamin's effort. The thought of the origin, I would suggest, strives to preserve what is perhaps best defined as an ontico-ontological difference. On the one hand, the history of the origin (and literary form in the "Prologue" is read as an "original" phenomenon) is inscribed in the history with which Benjamin thinks the concept of life in "The Task of the Translator" (GS 1.1 227/O 47). As the form in which the Idea impresses the essence of historical phenomena, its history is the history of essence or essential Being (*wesenhafte Sein*) (GS 1.1 227/O 47) and as such is redeemed in "the world of Ideas." The dialectic of the origin does not involve any fundamental historical determination of the Idea. Ideas are the "objective interpretation of phenomena," their "virtual objective arrangement" (GS 1.1 214/O 34) that is to be read in a differential configuration of "unique extremes" (GS 1.1 215/ O 35). But the Idea belongs to "a fundamentally different world" (GS 1.1 214/O 34) from that which it apprehends. In its historical realization of the origin, it *rewrites its difference* from empirical reality (GS 1.1 226/O 45) — setting itself apart anew (*auseinandersetzt* is the term Benjamin uses) each time it configures the essence of the empirical.* Benjamin is thus anxious to preserve the transcendent character of the meaning he seeks to read in originary phenomena. On the other hand, he is committed to anchoring the Idea in historical facts. The category of the origin is not "purely logical," Benjamin argues; it is historical. Demarcating it from a Hegelian form of idealism, he asserts that its "central kernel" (again!) inheres in the necessity that the philosopher be able to define the *authenticity* of the origin, its inscription in fact. This does not mean, Benjamin hastens to add in a characteristic turn, that the philosopher starts from a given fact, seeking in it a constitutive moment of essence (*wesensprägendes Moment*). A fact is only a fact if its inner structure (a differential relation) appears in such a way as to reveal it as a fact. But the object of philosophical discovery is the "seal of the origin" in phenomena (GS 1.1 227/O 46).

So we might say that Benjamin is holding firmly to both ends of the ontico-ontological difference — that he wants it both ways; and we could add here that a notion of the finitude of truth would have given him what he was seeking. By assigning the origin a quasi-transcendental character (as he does implicitly with his notion of the dialectical image), he could have collapsed the distinction between the *quaestio juris* and the *quaestio facti* as he seeks to do (GS 1.1 226/O 46). This might have meant, perhaps, a slightly friendlier relation to Heidegger and a bit more philosophical sobriety (indeed, this is where I find Benjamin's speculative flights — the full-blown invocations of the Platonic Idea, for example — most troubling). But however much the ontico-ontological difference *resists* a true historicization in Benjamin's philosophical statement in the

---

*Heidegger thinks of Nietzsche's "will to power" as precisely such a movement.

"Prologue," his aim and practice dictate a grounding for his method in historical reality, and it is for this reason that the recollection of Hölderlin I am reading in the *Trauerspiel* book seems so important to his methodological statement. Not only does Hölderlin offer Benjamin a hint for conceiving the possibility of a "sober," objective criticism (in effect, a kind of science) via his notion of a lawful calculus; he also points to a way of thinking an "existential/phenomenological" grounding of art that Benjamin finds lacking in Nietzsche's aestheticization of experience in *The Birth of Tragedy*.* Once again, the passage from Hölderlin I have cited — specifically, his description of a kind of calculus of human finitude offered by the "soberly" determined relation between subject and object — seems to inform Benjamin's remarks about the "laws" governing *Trauerspiel* as a form whose affective basis is melancholy. Introducing the topic of mourning, Benjamin writes:

Every feeling is bound to an a priori object, and the presentation of this object is its phenomenology. Accordingly, the theory of mourning, which emerged unmistakably as a pendant to the theory of tragedy, can only be developed in the description of that world which is revealed under the gaze of the melancholy man. For feelings, however vague they may seem when perceived by the self, respond like a motorial reaction to an objective structure of the world. If the laws which govern the *Trauerspiel* are to be found, partly explicit, partly implicit, at the heart of mourning, the presentation of these laws does not concern itself with the emotional condition of the poet or his public, but with a feeling which is released from an empirical subject and is intimately bound to the fullness of an object. (GS 1.1 318/O 139)

The proximity to Hölderlin here seems strong. But we have now reached the body of Benjamin's study and Benjamin's documented reflections on melancholy and allegory in their historical manifestation in the baroque *Trauerspiel*. I will only regain my *fil conducteur* (what Hölderlin may have offered to Benjamin for a thought of the work's criticizability) once I have defined how the *Formensprache* of *Trauerspiel* involves a presentation of a mode of representation — in other words, how the "philosophical truth" of *Trauerspiel* concerns language. This last step, however, will take us into a theological reflection that is quite different from anything Benjamin drew from his study of the romantic notion of critique. The relevant prior reference is rather the work on language of 1916 — not only "On Language as Such" but also "*Trauerspiel* and Tragedy" and "The Signification of Language in *Trauerspiel* and Tragedy," the texts to

---

*"Where art so firmly occupies the center of existence as to make man one of its manifestations instead of recognizing him above all as its basis, to see man's existence as the eternal motif of its own creations instead of recognizing him as its own creator, then all sober reflection is at an end" (GS 1.1 282/O 103).

which Benjamin evidently refers in the epigraph to the *Trauerspiel* study: "conceived in 1916, composed in 1925."

*

"The object of philosophical criticism," Benjamin writes, "is to show that the function of artistic form is as follows: to make historical content, such as provides the basis of every important work, into a 'philosophical truth'" (GS 1.1 358/O 182). The historical content of baroque *Trauerspiel*, Benjamin demonstrates, is essentially the religio-political configuration determining the "concrete structure of the world" to which Benjamin refers in his statement on the phenomenology of mourning. Lutheranism, in the context of the Counter-Reformation, had effectively stripped natural existence of any transcendental source of meaning, leaving the contemplative with an experience of something like a *horror vacui*:

> For those who looked deeper saw the scene of their existence as a rubbish heap of partial, inauthentic actions. Life itself protested against this . . . it is overcome by deep horror at the idea that the whole of existence might proceed in such a way. The idea of death fills it with profound terror. Mourning is the state of mind in which feeling revives the empty world in the form of a mask, and derives an enigmatic satisfaction in contemplating it. (GS 1.1 318/O 139)

The form proper to such an experience and such a "revival" is allegory. "It is only thanks to its [allegorical] structure," Benjamin says, "that the *Trauerspiel* can assimilate as its content the subject which contemporary conditions provide it" (GS 1.1 390/O 216). Allegory is suitable to such content because it is the form that expresses the relation between death, nature, and signification, which is part of the "philosophical truth" conveyed by the German *Trauerspiel*. Referring to allegory's representation of the *facies hippocratica* of history as a petrified landscape, Benjamin writes:

> This is the form in which man's subjection to nature is most obvious . . . This is the heart of the allegorical way of seeing, of the baroque, secular explanation of history as the Passion of the world; its significance resides solely in the stations of its decline. The greater the significance, the greater the subjection to death, because death digs most deeply the jagged line of demarcation between physical nature and significance. But if nature has always been subject to the power of death, it is also true that it has always been allegorical. Significance and death both come to fruition in historical development, just as they are closely linked as seeds in the creature's graceless state of sin. (GS 1.1 343/O 166)

Here is the "knowledge" of *Trauerspiel*—a knowledge of nature as marked by original sin. The historical act, like the natural context that is its setting and to which it finally returns inasmuch as it is always determined by natural forces, can have no redemptive significance and can only signify, finally, its own subjection to the power of death. Historical reality and the natural object do signify in this sense ("natural history" is part of "signifying nature") — or rather, they offer themselves to a play of signification that inevitably signifies the same thing: death as the sign of original sin. Thus the object's very "emptiness," as Benjamin described it in referring to the "phenomenology of mourning," is also, for the allegorist, the source of its allegorical potential: the "negative" is the source of an "enigmatic contemplative satisfaction" (GS 1.1 318/O 139) that is converted into pleasure as the allegorist speculates on the significance of the object delivered to his gaze.

But this conversion is only possible because the allegorist is drawing upon the very power that emptied the object and marked it with the sign of death, offering it thereby to an infinite play of signification. The baroque allegorist speculates on the cognitive relation that opened, according to Benjamin's theological interpretation, with the subjective act of judgment concerning good and evil. The ultimate ground of his own melancholy (for this act of judgment recoils upon itself and provokes its own judgment) is the very source of the pleasure he derives in what appears to him as the only possibility of redeeming fallen nature: the allegorical interpretation that in its baroque extremes (where "any person, any object, any relationship can mean absolutely anything else" [GS 1.1 350/O 175]) realizes absolutely the signifying relation that opened with the fall.[5] The allegorist speculates on the power of the negative that defines his relation to the object — hence the (ultimately abyssal) experience of an *infinite* potential and the *fascinating* quality of the object delivered to contemplation, known initially only in a subjective delusion of freedom and mastery. The following lines capture this delusion nicely. Forgetting the origin of his melancholy, the allegorist arrogates the power of the negative to himself:

Allegories become dated because it is part of their nature to shock. If the object becomes allegorical under the gaze of melancholy, if melancholy causes life to flow out of it and it remains behind dead, but eternally secure, then it is exposed to the allegorist, it is delivered up to his mercy or displeasure. That is to say, it is now quite incapable of emanating any meaning or significance of its own; such significance as it has, it acquires from the allegorist. He places it within it, and stands behind it, not in a psychological but in an ontological sense. In his hands, the object becomes something different; through it he speaks of something different and for him it becomes the key to the realm of hidden knowledge; and he reveres it as the emblem of this. This is what determines allegory as a form of writing. It is a schema. (GS 1.1 359/O 183–84)

In the following lines, Benjamin develops the scriptural character of the conventional schema that makes allegory, as a practice of language (like writing, like speech), not a convention of expression but the expression of convention. He then continues on the theme of the allegorist's extravagance and arbitrariness, which he terms "the most drastic manifestation of the power of knowledge": "The voluptuousness with which significance rules, like a stern sultan in the harem of objects, is without equal in giving expression to nature. It is indeed characteristic of the sadist that he humiliates his object and then — or thereby — satisfies it. And that is what the allegorist does in this age drunk with acts of cruelty" (GS 1.1 360/O 184–85). There follows a remarkable description of the degradation of the object expressed in the motif of the "opening of the eyes" in baroque painting and through the baroque manner of stripping the object of any suggestion of immanent meaning by assigning a caption to it: the writing affixed to the image functions as a kind of exposure of the image's purely allegorical significance (this practice of exposing allegorical meaning explains why the scenes of the *Trauerspiel* are like print, and why it could be assumed that they were never staged but only read — their very staging is a writing). He then concludes this description in the following paragraph with a description of the way the allegorist's pleasure inevitably pales as the object loses its fascinating quality: "It is true that the overbearing ostentation with which the banal object seems to arise from the depths of allegory is soon replaced by its disconsolate everyday countenance; it is true that the profound fascination of the sick man for the isolated and insignificant is succeeded by that disappointed abandonment of the exhausted emblem, the rhythm of which a speculatively inclined observer could find expressively repeated in the behaviour of apes" (GS 1.1 361/O 185).

If the reader is tempted to read in Benjamin's inspired description of the allegorist's sadism a certain celebration, the last image should provide the necessary counterbalance and underscore the fact that the very exuberance of this description is meant to point out the excessive and finally deluded character of the interpretive behavior he is describing. The allegorist is in a certain sense correct in thinking that he is the master of signification — his allegorical activity is the manifestation of a pure play of subjectivity. But what the melancholic baroque allegorist does not grasp, or will grasp only at the limit of his allegorizing, is that he is doing nothing more than exploiting the cognitive relation and thus (ultimately) the very linguistic structure that initially offered the object to his signifying play. The allegorist knows the relation between death, nature, and signification. But he does not fully grasp (at least at the outset) that this knowledge is implicated in the fall it reflects to itself, that his allegorical play indulges in the fall into signification that constitutes the very essence of the fall and that offers fallen nature to him as "signifying." Thus he redoubles the fall and precipitates into an abyss. Only at the limits of allegory will the allegorist discover the theological "truth" of this movement, a truth that Benjamin reads in the final part of his study in relation to his own theological speculations on language.*

Benjamin begins this last section of his study by linking baroque and medieval Christian allegory. Christian allegorical exegesis, he argues, essentially established the demonic character of the ancient divinities in their relation to matter and read both in terms of a notion of guilt. The effect of this interpretation is a kind of silencing of nature — for its mortification and for its redemption. "The allegorically significant," Benjamin writes, "is prevented by guilt from finding fulfillment of its meaning in itself" (GS 1.1 398/O 224). This notion already guided Benjamin's initial description of *Trauerspiel*, as I have noted, in 1916. In a brief text from this same year entitled, "The Significance of Language in *Trauerspiel* and Tragedy," Benjamin argues that the essence of *Trauerspiel* lies in the expression of mourning by a nature betrayed by language, or more precisely by *signification*. In this brief text, he reproduces (or produces?) as an "ancient wisdom" the same "metaphysical truth" to which he refers in "On Language as Such," from the same year: "The essence of *Trauerspiel* is already contained in that ancient wisdom according to which all nature would begin to lament if it were endowed with language" (GS 2.1 138). In "On Language as Such," Benjamin develops this notion by arguing that this proposition has a double meaning: nature would lament its very speechlessness (the language of things *requires* the name), and its speech, if given language, would be lament. Nature mourns, Benjamin concludes this first point, because it is mute. But grasped more profoundly, he continues, its muteness must be understood from the basis of its mourning. "In all mourning there is the deepest inclination to speechlessness" (GS 2.1 155/R 329) — a proposition Benjamin explicates in virtually the same words that appear in the *Trauerspiel* study itself after the statement I cited above concerning allegorical signification and the inhibition of self-expression.[6] I will cite this last passage because it leads directly into the problem of subjectivity:

In all mourning, there is a tendency to speechlessness, and this is infinitely more than inability or reluctance to communicate. The mournful has the feeling that it is thoroughly known by the unknowable. To be named, even if the name-giver is god-like and blissful — perhaps always brings with it a presentiment of mourning. But how much more so not to be named [Benjamin leaves off citing himself here], only to be read, to be read uncertainly by the allegorist, and to have become highly

---

*Most immediately, this is the theology of history we have evoked in relation to the knowledge of good and evil and the fall into the language of signification (a theology outlined in the essay of 1916 on language). But as I will suggest, this theology may well figure another.

significant thanks only to him. On the other hand, the more nature and antiquity were felt to be guilt-laden, the more necessary was their allegorical interpretation, as their only conceivable salvation. For in the midst of the conscious degradation of the object, the melancholic intention keeps faith with its own quality as a thing in an incomparable way. (GS 1.1 398/O 224–25)

Thus far, we have seen melancholy attributed only to the subject. Here Benjamin suggests that this latter sentiment is in fact nothing other than the sentiment of all natures delivered over to signification and judgment (hence the reference to "life" in the passage I cited above, and, as a figure of it in its most spiritually degraded form, the reference to the repetitive behavior of apes). This is the ground of the allegorist's "faithfulness" — though it is a divided fidelity since the allegorist is involved in carrying forth the prior interpretation of nature as guilty, effectively articulating the consequence of the fall. The allegorist's implication in the fallen character of what he reads only begins to discover itself in a kind of collapse of the allegorical relation (as a relation of subject and object), a collapse that occurs as the allegorist cedes to the temptation of absolute knowledge, an absolute realization of allegorical meaning. For in this movement, the allegorist finds the reflection of his activity in matter: in the visage of the devil. The muteness of nature is thus overcome in diabolical laughter:

If it is the creaturely world of things, the dead or at best the half-living, that is the object of allegorical intention, then man does not enter its field of vision. If it sticks exclusively to emblems, then revolution, salvation, is not inconceivable. But scorning all emblematic disguise, the undisguised visage of the devil can raise itself up from out of the depths of the earth into the view of the allegorist, in triumphant vitality and nakedness. (GS 1.1 401/O 227)

This reflection appears in baroque *Trauerspiel* in the diabolical figure of the intriguer who essentially represents earthly knowledge in its material aspect:

In the devil . . . [matter] scorns its allegorical "significance," and mocks anyone who believes he can pursue it into the depths with impunity. Just as earthly mournfulness is of a piece with allegoresis, so is devilish mirth with its frustration in the triumph of matter. This explains the devilish jocularity of the intriguer, his intellectuality, his knowledge of significance. The mute creature is able to hope for salvation through that which is signified. The clever versatility of man expresses itself and, in a most basely calculating act, lends its material aspect an almost human self-confidence, so that the allegorist is countered by the scornful laughter of hell. Here, of course, the muteness of matter is overcome. In laughter, above all, mind is enthusiastically embraced by matter, in highly eccentric disguise. . . . The inner madness is conscious of it only as spirituality. (GS 1.1 401/O 227)

Benjamin is delighting here in the dialectic of allegory. The emblem remains mute — in a certain sense, *allegory* itself remains mute (though it is allegory that itself renders nature mute) — until the mode of knowing that it embodies begins to reflect itself as the allegorist cedes to the speculative temptation. It reflects itself in the *Trauerspiel* initially in the intriguer's intellectuality, his knowledge of significance, which is nothing but a free use of the kind of signifying activity that is at the heart of baroque allegory. His intellectuality, Benjamin says, is an *expression* (*spricht sich selber aus*) of "the clever versatility of man"; he is the emergence of allegory into speech. This versatility, however, is a kind of material consciousness, a spirituality wholly committed to the significance of matter and ultimately reflective of it. In a dialectical reversal, Benjamin describes it as matter masquerading as spirituality and so precipitate in its self-reflection that it bursts forth in mad laughter. Spirituality and matter exchange masks. Several pages later, Benjamin will describe this as an illusory mediation between matter and spirit: "The purely material and this absolutely spiritual are the poles of the Satanic realm; and the consciousness is their illusory synthesis, in which the genuine synthesis, that of life, is imitated" (GS 1.1 404/O 230). In "On Language as Such," Benjamin described the knowledge of good and evil borne by the human, judging word in precisely the same way: as an "uncreated imitation" (GS 2.1 153/R 327) of the divine word — not its image (the Adamic language of names is a reflection of the divine word: as the knower, man is the image of the creator), but its parody. His description of Satanic knowledge here follows the same argument. It is a knowledge that is essentially abstract — fallen knowledge in the sense that it falls away from the true and into the mediations of subjective judgment. A judgment that is not without its own magic, its own apparent immediacy and infinity (GS 2.1 153/R 328), but that represents in its abstraction an ever more precipitate distancing from the true essence of things. Benjamin's description of the temptation of this knowledge is also worth citing here. Again we see the play of reflection between spirit and matter, spirit finding its reflection in the "external" light of matter:

It is not an inner light, a *lumen naturale*, that shines forth in the night of mournfulness as this knowledge; rather, a subterranean phosphorescence glimmers from the depths of the earth. It kindles the rebellious penetrating gaze of Satan in the contemplative man. This confirms once again the significance of baroque polymathy for the *Trauerspiel*. For something can present itself as allegorical only for the man who has knowledge. But on the other hand, if contemplation is not so much patiently devoted to truth, as unconditionally and compulsively, in direct meditation, bent on absolute knowledge, then it is eluded by things, in the simplicity of their essence, and they lie before it as enigmatic allegorical references, they continue to be dust. (GS 1.1 403/O 229)

Of course, the allegorist could never have a relation to things in the simplicity of their essence as long as he works with the perspective of good and evil and from the presupposition that nature is essentially guilty. The only contemplation devoted to truth and the "simple essence of things" (a phrase we saw in the "Prologue") is the Adamic one. The allegorist's very mode of knowing separates him from being, however much he restrains his knowing and stays within the limits set by theology (but how can he not at some point cede to the temptation of absolute knowledge since the significance this mode of knowing reads in matter is fundamentally *its own*?). In the concluding paragraph of his treatise, Benjamin states this "theological truth" explicitly:

Knowledge of good and evil is the opposite of all factual knowledge. Related as it is to the depths of the subjective, it is basically only knowledge of evil. It is prattle, in the profound sense in which Kierkegaard conceived the word. This knowledge, the triumph of subjectivity and the onset of an arbitrary rule over things, is the origin of all allegorical contemplation. In the very fall of man the unity of guilt and signifying emerges before the tree of knowledge as an abstraction. The allegorical lives in abstraction; as a faculty of the spirit of language itself, it is at home in the fall. (GS 1.1 407/O 233–34)

Allegory does nothing other than realize a possibility in language co-eval with the fall. In its extreme form in the baroque *Trauerspiel*, it becomes a kind of speculation on this possibility, which is itself nothing other than the signifying structure that is the basis of what Benjamin termed in 1916 the (fallen) human word (GS 2.1 153/R 327). *At its limit*, and in its ostentation, it is a manifestation of language in its fallen state: an *exhibition* of the possibility of allegory itself.

This limit is reached as baroque *Trauerspiel* pushes the dialectic of death and significance toward its ultimate figure. Here, its precipitate, infinite signifying progression suddenly turns about and reveals its truth:

For it is precisely visions of the frenzy of destruction, in which all earthly things collapse into a heap of ruins, which reveal the limit set upon allegorical contemplation, more than its ideal. The bleak confusion of Golgotha, which can be recognized as the schema underlying the allegorical figures in hundreds of engravings and descriptions of the period, is not just a symbol of the desolation of human existence. In it, transitoriness is not signified or allegorically represented, so much as in its own significance, displayed as allegory. As the allegory of resurrection. (GS 1.1 406/O 232)

Death (transitoriness, etc.) is not the signified of the landscape of Golgotha; the death represented there itself points to redemption. The melancholic contemplation of the object marked by death had taken this fallen state of things for their truth. It had effectively lost itself in contemplation, forgetting its origin in subjective judgment and the opening of the play of signification. By pushing this play to its limit, however, allegory loses the object ("the phantasmagoria of the object") and its illusory position of subjective mastery. It rediscovers thereby its origin in a groundless subjectivity: "Left only to its own devices, [allegory] rediscovers itself, not playfully in the earthly world of things, but seriously under the eyes of heaven. And this is the essence of melancholic immersion: that its ultimate objects, in which it believes it can most fully secure for itself that which is vile, turn into allegories, and that these allegories fill out and deny the void in which they present themselves" (GS 1.1 406/O 232–33). Allegory ultimately points beyond itself — it points beyond itself by pointing to itself as allegory and by drawing the subjectivity that informs it into self-appearance (thereby "filling the void"):

> Evil as such, which [allegory] cherished as enduring profundity, exists only in allegory, is nothing other than allegory, and signifies something different from what it is. It signifies precisely the non-existence of what it represents. The absolute vices, as exemplified by tyrants and intriguers, are allegories. They are not real, and that which they represent, they possess only in the subjective view of melancholy; they are this view, which is destroyed by its own offspring, because they only signify its blindness. (GS 1.1 406/O 233)

The figures of evil in which melancholy thought to secure its own mastery signify only the allegorical meaning of evil and the delusion of the contemplation that took them for a self-subsistent reality. They reinscribe this vision in the divine order as a work of the highest wisdom and love, "as hell . . . as the real reflection of empty subjectivity in the good" (GS 1.1 407/O 234). In evil, subjectivity grasps what is "real" in it (nothing other than its *Nichtsein*) and sees it as the mere reflection of itself in God, glimpsing thereby the "tain" of its specular relation. More strictly, melancholic subjectivity knows its finitude and translates this self-discovery, this *exposure* — perhaps nothing more than a knowledge of judgment* — into a "knowledge" of divine transcendence. Melancholic immersion dis-covers itself, Benjamin says, "not playfully in the earthly world of things, but seriously under the eyes of heaven" (GS 1.1 335/O 158). It "confronts itself," as Benjamin says of Hamlet (the sole figure in *Trauerspiel* who realizes this turn at the limit of melancholic subjectivity) and experiences what Benjamin had described as the ground of melancholy.

The Christian resolution of the dialectic of allegory (certainly appropriate to the material but hard to reconcile with Benjamin's own theologi-

---

*If we were to be strict here, we might conclude that what it knows in its finitude is judgment: it knows its own form of cognition in the "recoil" of judgment. This would be the true limit of its transcendence: it knows judgment.

cal inclinations) may well mirror another that is sketched in Benjamin's "Theological-Political Fragment."[7] Both forms of redemption involve an ecstatic knowledge of finitude — an ecstatic assumption of the limit of knowledge itself (*over against* a posited transcendence). From this perspective, we could account for the strangely affirmative character of Benjamin's conclusion — a conclusion that unsettled Benjamin himself, to say nothing of his critics.[8] But Benjamin also makes a step beyond the ec-static nihilism that we might find reflected here at the extremes of allegory (subtracting, of course, the figure of transcendence). For the discovery of the limit of melancholic allegorical contemplation is also a discovery of the limit of signifying language and a delimitation of abstraction: "In the very fall of man the unity of guilt and signifying emerges before the tree of knowledge as an abstraction . . . ; as a faculty of the spirit of language itself, it is at home in the fall." Benjamin's own theological translation — in the form of a philosophical/theological speculation on language that makes it possible to read what Hölderlin described as the presentation of representation itself — appears in this reference to the spirit of language. Benjamin is no less prepared than the baroque allegorist to translate the experience of finitude into a knowledge of transcendence, "transcendence" naming here the possibility of "expression" that he defined in his essay on translation. Benjamin, of course, foregrounds the Christian doctrine of original sin in presenting the "theology of history" with which he situates the historical and philosophical "truth" of the baroque *Trauerspiel*. But within the larger framework of the *Trauerspiel* study, this doctrine of original sin is to be read as an "allegorical" account of the interruption of the possibility Benjamin described as a language of names — an interruption of meaning by (signified) meaning that Benjamin describes in the section preceding his final "theological" interpretation of *Trauerspiel* as the "philosophical basis of the allegorical" (GS 1.1 389/O 215). Benjamin's theological account of mourning in the final pages of his study ("The allegorically significant is prevented by guilt from finding fulfillment of its meaning in itself") effectively restates and completes an (absent) philosophical reflection of the division between "signifying written language" and "intoxicating spoken language" that is at the heart of the baroque mode of expression, a form of "staging" that "only represents [*repräsentiert*] — that is to say, represents the nature of language — and as far as possible avoids profane communication" (GS 1.1 384/O 210). Where sound, for the baroque, represents an expression of creaturely spontaneity ("the harmless effusion of an onomatopoeic natural language" [GS 1.1 384/O 210]), the written word represents its interruption and binding by a petrifying meaning:

For the baroque, sound is and remains something purely sensuous; signification has its home in written language. And the spoken word can only be afflicted by signification, so to speak, as if by an inescapable disease; it breaks off in the middle of the process of resounding, and the damming up of the feeling, which was ready to pour forth, provokes mourning. Here, signification is encountered, and will continue to be encountered as the basis for mournfulness. (GS 1.1 383/O 209)

The problem, again, is the interruption by signification of the communication between the language of nature ("the harmless effusion of an onomatopoeic natural language") and, ultimately, the equivalent of a language of names. Baroque *Trauerspiel* stages this interruption (in its bombast, in the "forced logicality" of the pattern of the alexandrine, in its ostentation, in a fragmentation of language, etc.), never resolving the "tense polarity" of sound and writing (GS 1.1 376/O 201). On its horizon, however, is a potential resolution in music that only "the musical philosophy of the romantic writers, who have an elective affinity with the baroque" points toward (GS 1.1 387/O 213).*

Benjamin's discussion here is itself interrupted, proceeding largely by citation — anything more, he says, would be "irresponsible improvisation." But the "virtual romantic theory of allegory" to which he points (GS 1.1 388/O 214), requiring accomplishment in a "fundamental discussion of language, music, and script," is worth noting here in that it seems to reflect in a significant way Benjamin's own philosophical meditation in the "Prologue." Proceeding from a series of reflections by Johann Wilhelm Ritter, Benjamin envisions a synthesis of word and script in a universal language of creation where every image and indeed every form of language (in the broad sense given to the term in the opening pages of "On Language as Such") is a form of writing, a "signature," or "monogram" of essence, that is not external to it but is rather its "figure" or "pattern," as the figures of sand on glass formed by different notes in Chladni's experiments (GS 1.1 388/O 214). Benjamin finds in a phrase by Sigmund von Birken the same understanding of a universal language founded in rhythm: "Every natural occurrence in this world could be the effect of the materialization of a cosmic reverberation, even the movement of the stars" (GS 1.1 389/O 215). "This finally establishes," he writes, "the unity, in terms of a theory of language, between the verbal and the visual manifestations of the baroque" (GS 1.1 389/O 215).

In his "Prologue," Benjamin described truth's self-presentation as a "dance" of Ideas (GS 1.1 209/O 29), each of which presents in monado-

---

*This resolution is also named in the early text "The Significance of Language in *Trauerspiel* and Tragedy," where we see again clearly the link between the theory of mourning and the philosophical question of the relation between sound and meaning, natural feeling and signification.

logical form the totality of the world of Ideas but remains nevertheless in a state of autonomy and perfect isolation, separated by an "unsublatable distance" that forms a relation comparable only to that of the "spheres." Harmony again — as in the translation essay. This link between the "virtual romantic theory of allegory" and Benjamin's theory of Ideas (a link that is fully completed once we recall that the Idea's self-presentation takes the form of a typography and the task of philosophical criticism is to read the "seal" of the origin in phenomena) is perhaps enough to allow us to conclude that the "Prologue" offers an accomplished theory of allegory. But if we consider also the disintegrating, mortifying procedure of this mode of reading, we will recognize that the "Prologue" is actually mirroring certain descriptions of baroque allegory (or vice versa). Philosophical criticism, as Benjamin explains in his "Prologue," reads a configuration of "elements" via an inter-cession and inter-cision of the "concept." The Idea is not given in phenomena; the latter must be articulated (redeemed) conceptually in their basic elements:

Through their mediating role, concepts enable phenomena to participate in the being of Ideas. It is this same mediating role that fits them for the other equally originary task of philosophy, the presentation [*Darstellung*] of Ideas. As the salvation of phenomena by means of Ideas takes place, so too does the presentation of Ideas through the medium of empirical reality. For Ideas do not present themselves in themselves, but solely and exclusively in an arrangement of thingly elements in the concept: and indeed they do so as their configuration.

The set of concepts that serves the presentation of an Idea makes this Idea present as a configuration of them. . . . The concern of concepts is to group phenomena together, and the division that is brought about within them thanks to the distinguishing power of the intellect is all the more significant in that it brings about two things at a single stroke: the salvation of phenomena and the presentation of Ideas. (GS 1.1 214/O 34)

Only the fact that elements seem to *offer* themselves to this distinguishing intellect distinguishes this *Zerteilung* ("division," "decomposition," or "analysis") from the abstract distinctions of subjective judgment (*Urteil*), though Benjamin is treading a fine line. He is giving a fundamental initiative to philosophical reading that will become, as we will see, a distinguishing trait of the work of the dialectical materialist, but he is attempting to make this initiative *answerable* and ground it in that original contemplation of words that makes philosophy a *legein* of the Idea (both a laying out and a collection of phenomena in a kind of "spelling"). The distinction is precarious. But if we grant Benjamin the communicability of the word by allowing that the "elements" of the Idea rooted in the word (GS 1.1 407/O 234; cf. GS 2.1 154/R 328) indicate or signal themselves in their differential relations and offer their relationality via (perhaps) something like a fundamental play of mimesis (a similarity in difference),[9] then we may recognize in philosophical contemplation a fundamentally different procedure from that of baroque allegorizing. We could conceivably allow Benjamin his claim that his own reading of baroque allegory is an allegory of allegory that subsumes a subjective mode of reflection in an objective apprehension of language.[10] In which case, Benjamin would be performing in his study the delimitation of reflection he pointed to in his critique of the romantics in the "Prologue" and presenting a founded mode of criticism. Such a conclusion presupposes, once again, that the reading of baroque allegory is not a cognitive apprehension of linguistic phenomena, or any form of hermeneutics, but a response to a presentation of language (the presentation of allegory as "a faculty of the spirit of language itself") — objective, sober, and sovereign. "Objective" in that it is grounded in a structure of meaning that transcends subjective intention; "sober" in that its mode of reflection (thought, once again, in terms of an apprehension of linguistic laws) constantly preserves a distance from the potentially captivating character of its "object"; "sovereign" in that its mode of reading (a *legein*, once again) proceeds from a "de-cisive" initiative that helps to articulate the structure it presents in an originary manner and constantly maintains its freedom before the spectacle it allows (a freedom, as we will see, that is the condition of a new historical posture).[11] I will return to the structure of this active *legein* in the next chapter, but to conclude the present discussion and prepare for the next, I would note the following by way of summary. The melancholic contemplation proper to baroque allegorizing represents an immersion in subjectivity and a capture by the false magic of mediation. At stake in its presentation is the possibility of transcendence, a transcendence offered not just in the distance of reflection (the reflection offered in this staging of allegory's self-reflection, what I have transcribed as a discovery of finitude) but in a "free" recovery of meaning, beginning with the meaning of the present that reads its prehistory in baroque literature.

8

The Claim of History

IN the notes to the *Passagen-Werk* grouped in "Konvolut N," we read the following statement linking the historical approach of the *Trauerspiel* study to the later work on nineteenth-century Paris that absorbed Benjamin in the last decade of his life: "Much as the baroque book illuminates the seventeenth century through the present, so the nineteenth century should be treated here in analogous but more distinct fashion" (GS 5.1 573/B 45–46).

This statement underscores a crucial point regarding the methodological reflections we followed in the last chapter. It indicates that even if we read the *Trauerspiel* study as a thoroughgoing historicization of the speculative reflections contained in the essay on language of 1916 ("On Language as Such and on the Language of Man"), our approach remains formal. For we have still to grasp the historical character of the study itself: the fact, as I suggested at the end of the last chapter, that Benjamin is writing from his present and, to some extent, *for* this present — a present intimately *interested* in the truth offered by the form of the German *Trauerspiel*. As a form of *Geschichtsphilosophie*, literary critique involves an act of historical engagement.

The point was made clearly (if allusively) near the end of the "Epistemo-Critical Prologue,"[1] and it is reasserted in the notes to the *Passagen-Werk* and the "Theses on the Philosophy of History." Thesis 7, in fact, recalls the prior discussion explicitly by renewing the attack on the methodology of modern historians, describing their "pathological suggestibility" this time in terms of a melancholy. Historicism, he argues here, can only seek to deny its knowledge about the course of the history it studies and then empathize with the era if it has accepted this history as given and renounced any idea that the present might in some sense be *at stake* in historical interpretation. In such renunciation, Benjamin argues, historical researchers have effectively empathized with the rulers who have defined the cultural tradition in relation to the telos of their own victory. In their passivity, they "despair" of grasping and holding the genuine historical image as it flares up briefly (GS 1.2 696/I 256). They have lost the strength and the will (the "presence of mind") to *invent* history in an act of reading that will secure an objective relation to it.

The claim for the necessity and the possibility of such a historical posture is essentially the same as the one made a decade earlier. But it is better founded, in some respects, and more urgent.* History writing, as Benjamin defined it in the 1930s, bears a charge of political responsibility that renders *critical* the task of historical engagement—an engagement with the past that is thought, as before, as an engagement with language, but is now more concretely grounded and fundamentally more historical, thought more fully in its *historicity*. A decade of reflection on dialectical materialism in increasingly trying circumstances did not represent, despite some detours, any compromise of Benjamin's philosophical and theological commitments; on the contrary, it seems to have defined them by historicizing them.

The aim of the following discussion will be to mark this historicization via a reading of a lengthy note (N 3.1) from "Konvolut N." My approach will be somewhat schematic and summary (proceeding frequently by review of points made in the prior chapters), because I would like to draw forth the continuity in Benjamin's reflection on language while marking the step made in his thought on the dialectical image. I will focus rather specifically on the structure of the "call" of history and of the dialectical materialist's response, leaving aside much of the context of these methodological reflections (their historical and biographical context and the richness of the materials to which they answered).[2] I have eschewed "concreteness" (and resisted its lure: there is also a risk of capture here, as we see in some commentaries) in order to focus on its philosophical conditions and draw forth one side of Benjamin's famous remark on the "tense" connection between his "very particular standpoint in philosophy of language, and the approach of dialectical materialism."† I would want to emphasize, however, that one loses the meaning of Benjamin's reflections (and the "tension" to which Benjamin alludes) if one pretends to divorce speculation (theological or philosophical) from politics. The thought of finite transcendence that Benjamin pursues with the dialectical image is devoted precisely to the articulation he names in thesis 17, where each half of the following sentence deserves equal weight: "In this structure [the historical materialist] recognizes the sign of a Messianic cessation of happening, or,

---

*We see this throughout the last remarks on fascism and social democracy in the "Theses" (GS 1.2 691–704/I 253–64).

†Letter from Benjamin to Max Rychner, Walter Benjamin, *Briefwechsel*, vol. 2, ed. Gershom Scholem and Theodor W. Adorno (Frankfurt am Main: Suhrkamp, 1966), 523.

put differently, a revolutionary chance in the fight for the oppressed past" (GS 1.2 703/I 263).

Note N 3.1 reads as follows:

What differentiates images from the "essences" of phenomenology is their historic index [*historischer Index*]. (Heidegger seeks in vain to rescue history for phenomenology abstractly, through "historicity.") These images must be thoroughly marked off from "humanistic" categories, such as so-called habitus, style, etc. For the historic index of the images doesn't simply say that they belong to a specific time; it says above all that they only enter into legibility [*Lesbarkeit*] at a specific time. And indeed this 'entering into legibility' constitutes a specific critical point of the movement inside them. Every present is determined by those images that are synchronic with it: every Now is the Now of a specific recognizability [*Erkennbarkeit*]. In it, truth is loaded to the bursting point with time. (This bursting point is nothing other than the death of the *intentio*, which accordingly coincides with the birth of authentic historical time, the time of truth.) It isn't that the past casts its light on what is present or that what is present casts its light on what is past; rather, an image is that in which the Then [*das Gewesene*] and the Now [*der Jetzt*] come together into a constellation like a flash of lightning. In other words, an image is dialectics at a standstill. For while the relation of the present to the past is a purely temporal, continuous one, the relation of the Then to the Now is dialectical: not of a temporal but of an imagistic nature. Only dialectical images are genuinely historical, i.e., not archaic images. The image that is read, that is, the image at the Now of recognizability, bears to the highest degree the stamp of that critical, dangerous impetus [*kritischen, gefährlichen Moments*] that lies at the source of all reading. (GS 5.1 577–78/B 50–51)

However tempting it is to take up the gesture toward an *Auseinandersetzung* with Heidegger here,[3] I will move directly to three basic points concerning the "theory of knowledge" that is asserted in this note. The first of these concerns the "legibility" of the dialectical image. Legibility is what Benjamin terms in "The Task of the Translator" a *Relationsbegriff*, a "concept of relation":

Certain concepts of relation retain their meaning, and possibly their foremost significance, if they are not referred exclusively to man. One might, for example, speak of an unforgettable life or moment even if all men had forgotten it. If the nature of such a life or moment required that it be unforgotten, that predicate would not imply a falsehood, but merely a claim not fulfilled by men, and probably also a reference to a realm in which it *is* fulfilled: God's remembrance. (GS 4.1 10/I 70)

Benjamin will define the dialectical image as a singular occurrence that *can* be forgotten inasmuch as it flashes "in the moment of its recognizability, never to be seen again" and threatens to "disappear irretrievably" if it is "not recognized by the present as one of its own concerns" (thesis 5, GS

1.2 695/I 255). But the "legibility" of this image is no more "referred exclusively to man" than is the "translatability" for which Benjamin introduces this notion of a *Relationsbegriff*. That is to say, legibility names a structure that is independent of any mediation by an intending consciousness. It is fundamentally historical inasmuch as it depends upon its realization in a given present (though it still posits something like the promise of God's remembrance, and there are enough allusions to a final redemption in Benjamin's late work to make us question whether this promise is not something more for Benjamin than a formal characteristic of the structure in question), but it remains an objective structure of meaning, an *event* of meaning, that is not essentially determined by human subjectivity and to which human subjects *answer* in the initiative by which they write their history.

Why *Relationsbegriff*? Benjamin introduces this notion shortly before describing the relation between a translation and the original work, and before defining the ground of this relation with his notion of the kinship of languages. Drawing, as we have seen, on the Hölderlinian term *Innigkeit*, Benjamin defines the relation of translation and original in terms of an intimacy: "It is plausible that no translation, however good it may be, can have any significance as regards the original. Yet, by virtue of its translatability, the original is closely connected with the translation; in fact this connection is all the more intimate [*inniger*] insofar as it is no longer significant for the original" (GS 4.1 10/I 71). The connection to which Benjamin refers is a differential relation between languages that translation draws forth from the basis of their "innermost relation" (*innerstes Verhältnis*)—a relatedness ("a priori and apart from all historical relationships" [GS 4.1 12/I 72])—in their fundamental intention vis-à-vis what is perhaps best defined as the logos. Thus, translatability could be understood as a *Relationsbegriff* inasmuch as it issues from and in some sense realizes an a priori relation (like the notion of legibility, which, as we will see, involves a "secret agreement" between the past and the present).

But Benjamin's introduction of the notion of a *Relationsbegriff* in reference to his concept of translatability in fact stresses the *opening* and *communication* of relation. Translatability, as we have seen, is that structure by which a work *calls* for translation and in relation to which a translation may be said to answer faithfully to the original. Whether a work is translatable, Benjamin says, depends on "whether, following its essence, it lends itself to translation, and, therefore, in accordance with the significance of this form, also calls for it [*ob es seinem Wesen nach Übersetzung . . . verlange*]" (GS 4.1 10/I 70). The language of a literary work (or that dimension that issues in the work's "afterlife") *offers* itself to translation: it offers the possibility of relation, much as the work of art, in Heidegger's account, sets forward in its "createdness" (also a *Relationsbegriff*) the conditions of its reception, the possibility of a relation to it and indeed the possibility of relation in general. A *Relationsbegriff*, I would argue, defines the structure of the *opening* of relation.

The relation in question is not mediated by signification in the traditional sense of this term (and in this sense, translation, like criticism, like history writing, is not a form of *interpretation* insofar as interpretation presupposes the deciphering of some signified meaning). Indeed, one might ask whether signification as understood traditionally (what Benjamin calls the "bourgeois conception of language" in "On Language as Such" [GS 2.1 144/R 318]) is even a structure of *relation* for Benjamin, or anything more than an abstract relation, and therefore no true relation at all. The very notion of a *Relationsbegriff* is clearly proposed in order to differentiate the communication that occurs in the essence of language (where language communicates *itself* and not some signified content) from any act of signification or communication effected by an intending consciousness or depending in any way on such a consciousness. The essence of language, once again, is defined by its "communicability" (*Mitteilbarkeit* [GS 2.1 146/R 320]): in its essence, language is the communicable nature of the "spiritual essence" of what is, and its nature is to communicate itself *immediately* in the name, which is thought as the revelation of language itself, the "speaking" of language, we might say. A name does not designate a thing external to it (it does so only after it has fallen into the structure of signification, which for Benjamin is the fall itself). It is rather the im-mediate expression of the essence of the thing.[4] Inasmuch as Benjamin finally identifies linguistic essence and spiritual essence, it is the self-expression of the essence of language: "All language communicates itself" (GS 2.1 142/R 316) — that is to say, all language in its *essence*.

Throughout his reflections on language, Benjamin posits the identity of language and Being, or simply "truth," as he most often writes, and will ascribe to truth an "impulse" to presentation. In "The Task of the Translator," he tells us that the "seed" of pure language (of the language of truth, which can only emerge in the full harmony of the various languages at the "messianic end" of their history [GS 4.1 14/I 74]) "seeks to present itself, to produce itself" (*sich darzustellen, ja herzustellen sucht* [GS 4.1 19/I 79]) in the evolving of languages. This is the source of the work's "call" in its afterlife, its "translatability"; translation, as a form, consists in remarking this call in such a way as to present (*darzustellen*) pure language in an "intensive" fashion (GS 4.1 12/I 72), in the complementarity of its own language vis-à-vis the original. In the "Epistemo-Critical Prologue," he will ascribe to truth a *darstellendes Moment* (GS 1.1 211/O 31), an "impulse to presentation" or a "presentational moment" (both translations work) that occurs in and as language — in a writing or a kind of imprinting of the essence of phenomena. (The essay on translation, as we have seen, also attributes such a "typography" to translation: the "intensive" presentation of the language of truth occurs in a "concealed" writing that is "less sharply defined than poetry or doctrine, but leaves no less of a mark on history" [GS 4.1 17/I 77]). The latter notion of truth's *darstellendes Moment* is then taken up in the meditation on the dialectical image when Benjamin describes the image as "legible" and refers to the "stamp" of "that critical, dangerous impetus that lies at the source of all reading." The "impetus," once again, is the impetus of truth: "in it [the Now of recognizability offered in the dialectical image] truth is loaded to the bursting point with time."

The source of all reading, then, is the address of truth — of truth as it offers relation in and as language. The relation is im-mediate: it is an abyssal opening. Benjamin will insist upon the im-mediate character of truth's self-presentation throughout the initial pages of his "Epistemo-Critical Prologue" in defining the *given* character of truth in its linguistic character. He develops this same notion of the immediacy of truth's offering in the description of the dialectical image in N 3.1 when he suggests that what is "legible" in the dialectical image (once again, we have to do with a "typography") is a constellation of the Then and the Now. It is not a matter of the Now reading the Then; it is a matter of reading the Then *in the Now*, of reading the Then Now. In the dialectical image, the Now, strictly speaking, is prior to our present, which must constitute itself in this reading or forget itself in myth. We are already engaged by the dialectical image when we begin its reading and thereby act in the authentic historical time to which it opens us (delivering the present to itself or offering it the possibility of self-relation in a relation to the past that it must elaborate). To read is to have been engaged by the object of our attention and to read it as our interest *Now*.[5]

We might pause here to ask, if truth gives itself in language in an im-mediacy that is prior to any visibility (for an intending consciousness), why does Benjamin speak of a dialectical *image*? Even "legibility" is a problematic concept, since we are dealing with an offering of meaning that does not take a constituted form for consciousness before it is "spelled" in what Benjamin refers to in his "Prologue" as an "originary apprehension of words" (GS 1.1 217/O 37). Are we dealing here with a form of schema, and hence an interpretation, after Kant, of the schematism effected by the imagination (*Einbildungskraft*)? This specific question requires separate treatment, but to underscore the character of the structure of meaning Benjamin is describing, I would note that I believe it is possible to link the late reference to an "image" with Benjamin's description (in "On Language as Such") of the communication of the divine word in the language of things. Borrowing an image from Friedrich Müller, Benjamin speaks of "the image of a sign" (GS 2.1 152/R 326) by which this "communicating muteness" of animals offers itself to the Adamic name. However we eventually interpret this "image of a sign," it is clear that we are dealing with a form of presentation that is prior to any signification in the broad, semiological sense and to the constitution of a visible form. We find in Blanchot a comparable effort to think the "origin" of language with a notion of the image, but Blanchot takes this thought in a very different direction from Benjamin.

The topic of history, the relation of Then and Now to which I referred above, brings me to my second observation, which concerns the "historic index" of the dialectical image, though not immediately in its indexical or referential character. "For the historic index of the images doesn't simply say that they belong to a specific time; it says above all that they only enter into legibility at a specific time." The historic index marks an image as being (indissociably) *of* and *for* a time. But it is the former characteristic that I want to stress initially in noting that the dialectical image essentially fuses two concepts: that of the *Relationsbegriff* (conceived as an im-mediate address of language) and that of the "origin." I would say formulaically that the dialectical image is the origin conceived as a *Relationsbegriff*, though to complete this definition we will also have to return to the temporal determination of the address in question; legibility, like translatability, occurs only with time.

My point here is to stress the historical determination of the address of truth as it occurs in what Benjamin calls in his "Epistemo-Critical Prologue" an "origin." Like the dialectical image, translatability emerges only with time and at what would appear to be a specific conjuncture in the development of two languages ("translation catches fire on the eternal life of the works and the perpetual renewal of language" [GS 4.1 14/I 74]). A growing intensity of the need for "linguistic complementation" and for the expression of pure language is matched, apparently, by a need for linguistic renewal. But while the "intensive" expression of pure language effected in the concealed writing of the translation is said to leave a mark on history, what is marked in this manner is no more than the growth of the languages in relation to the "messianic end of their history." Taking a cue from Heidegger, as I have argued, one might draw this messianic horizon into the historical movement Benjamin is describing by interpreting this marking as a measuring of the distance of pure language from revelation, and by understanding pure language itself as inhering in nothing other than a certain distance (*Entfernung*), in which case the measuring in question might be conceived as having a determining function, and pure language might be understood as a "quasi-transcendental." But the writing of history to which Benjamin alludes in "The Task of the Translator" remains the marking of the distance of a language's "symbolizing" dimension from revelation and redemption. The history evoked in "The Task of the Translator" is the history of truth, oriented entirely toward a final, messianic fulfillment.

In the "Prologue" to the *Trauerspiel* study, history is also described as a history of truth, indeed of the "same" truth as the one alluded to in "The Task of the Translator." As Benjamin says on the first page of his "Prologue," philosophical writing (and this includes a philosophically founded criticism like that of his study) is concerned with "the domain of truth intended by the languages" (GS 1.1 207/O 27). But it is a truth containing a historical content that is itself doubly articulated. On the one hand, it offers itself, where it seeks its representation, as the "objective interpretation" of the historical conditions of existence, offering thereby "access" to an epoch. Where it is given in the *Formensprache* of the work, it may be read as the ground of a phenomenology, and accordingly the "index" of this form marks a "determinate, objectively necessary figuration," a "contemplative necessity" in relation to a determinate historical situation.

On the other hand, the historical character of the origin is founded in the history of the Idea; history is not an event for truth but rather is immanent to it, and ultimately gathered in the accomplished world of Ideas. The origin is a dynamic configuration of "unique extremes," a "vortex" of differential relations that is itself to be read in a rhythmics that is temporally determined, the "dialectic of the origin." Might the incompleteness of the origin inhere in the fact that the meaning of this linguistic event requires time for its full emergence, as is the case with the "translatability" of the literary work? Benjamin does, after all, suggest that the history he is sketching is the fore-history of the present. But he never hints in his *Trauerspiel* study that baroque allegory only offers itself in its truth to a modernity expressed, for example, in Baudelaire's allegorizing (a new determination, perhaps, of the form in which an Idea confronts the historical world). The allegorical vision of the German *Trauerspiel* represents an original phenomenon for the present in Benjamin's study and will be read as such (making Benjamin's approach a truly historical and political one), but the origin as conceived in the "Prologue" is not quite the dialectical image inasmuch as the former does not bear the temporal determination and indexical character of the latter. There is no sign in the "Prologue" that the origin is incomplete by virtue of its "latency" and that it requires a kind of linguistic maturation in order to achieve the "higher concretion" of the historical object of interest in its "Now-being." In "Konvolut K," and in discussing the dialectical image, Benjamin refers to "a growing condensation (integration) of reality in which everything that is past (in its time) can obtain a higher degree of actuality than it had at the moment it took place. This higher actuality expresses itself [*prägt sich aus*] through the image in which it is understood" (GS 5.1 495). Benjamin will identify his notions of the origin and the dialectical image (see N 2a4 and N 9a4, as well as N 2a3, where the dialectical image is described as *sprunghaft*), but the earlier conception of the origin does not incorporate the still earlier idea of linguistic maturation, which Benjamin will come to define in N 2.3 as "the foundation of history itself" (GS 5.1 575/B 47). Nor does it really incorporate the idea of the past *addressing* the present, which Benjamin will develop in his reflection on the dialectical image with his notion of a "historic index."

The dialectical image, as I have suggested, is the origin conceived as a *Relationsbegriff*. We must now recover in the earlier concept the idea of an a priori (though temporally determined) structure of meaning and define the fully *historicized* character of the dialectical image. The latter concern will constitute my third observation about N 3.1.

"For the historic index of images *doesn't simply say* that they belong to a specific time; *it says above all* that they only enter into legibility at a specific time. And indeed this entering into legibility constitutes a specific critical point of the movement inside them" (my emphasis). The phrase "it says . . . that" is sufficiently colloquial to pass by without drawing attention to itself. But it is somewhat opaque. For whom does the index speak? On what calendar does it date the image? On the one hand, Benjamin is almost certainly saying that the dialectical image bears a "signal" ("Konvolut K," 1a6, GS 5.1 493) or a "sign" (*Zeichen* [thesis 17, GS 1.2 703/I 263]) that indicates the image *to the time* in which it can be read. The historic index of the image says to a specific time that it is legible *now*, can be read *now*. It signals the image's entering into legibility at and for a specific time: it is the signifying structure of the call to which Benjamin refers in defining "translatability" (though as we have seen from the "Prologue" and N 3.1, it takes the form of a writing or an "impress"). Yet the phrase "it says . . . that" also suggests that the index speaks beyond the time to which the image addresses itself (or before that time by anticipating that time). It marks the image for another time—in structural terms, that time described in "The Task of the Translator" as "God's remembrance."

Is it possible to think together the a priori character of this signifying structure (a structure that implies a temporal order beyond that of *human* history) *and* Benjamin's claims for the historicity of this event in which, as Ernst Bloch says of the dialectical image, "History flashes its Scotland Yard badge" (cited by Benjamin in N 3.4, GS 5.1 578/B 51)? The a priori structure of the event cannot be explained away by the ambiguity of Benjamin's phrasing in N 3.1. In the second thesis of his "Theses on the Philosophy of History," he refers to the image's "temporal index" and describes the relation it signifies in terms of a "secret agreement between generations":

The past carries with it a temporal index by which it is referred to redemption. There is a secret agreement between past generations and the present one. Our coming was expected on earth. Like every generation that preceded us, we have been endowed with a *weak* messianic power, a power to which the past has a claim. That claim cannot be settled cheaply. Historical materialists are aware of that. (GS 1.2 693–94/I 254)

The past "carries with it" a temporal index: the date of its emergence and of its expiration (not "must sell by," but "must read by" and "will not be readable before"). Moreover, when it designates *this* present with its temporal index (the image is dated but also indicated to a time), it calls upon a debt. The present's "weak messianic power" comes to it from the past and carries with it an obligation by virtue of a "secret agreement." The present has already contracted with the past in a historial order that clearly exceeds any human temporality. Is it on the calendar of this order that the index dates the image?

Is the dialectical image, in other words, a fundamentally theological or metaphysical concept whose apparent historicity is subsumed in a transcendental order? This possibility cannot be denied, and it does not necessarily deny the political import of the dialectical image (particularly if the messianic order is conceived as subject to history). But it may also be possible to think the structure of the image without reference to a transcendental scheme — that is, to think the a priori structure of the dialectical image as the structure of a historical *event*. A kind of transcendental order is implied in the fact that the past calls upon a power with which it has already endowed the present. But the "secret agreement" implied here does not necessarily involve a prior negotiation in the time of God's remembrance. It might well be thought as an agreement that occurs in the structure of speech. The possibility of speaking/acting in the present — the possibility of speaking the truth of the present — comes out of the past. To begin to speak truly in the authentic historical time of the present is to realize a contract with the past to which one has necessarily already agreed. The contract is the condition of speech: to "recognize" the contract is to *have assumed* it; otherwise there can be no true act of recognition. With the dialectical image, to speak is to have recognized the past in its recognizability, to have recognized the past's *binding* gift. Every time we speak (historically and truly), we have contracted with the past.

Every time. The past *has endowed* the present with its "weak messianic power" to speak/act, but this endowment is perhaps to be thought as occurring or as being realized *in the moment* of the dialectical image and as it presents itself in a historical (ahistorical: this is the quasi-transcendental condition of human history) caesura. All of Benjamin's figures for the communication of power in the dialectical image suggest that the "weak" messianic power of the present comes to it as it is addressed. The dialectical image, we recall, bears "the critical, dangerous impetus that lies at the source of all reading." But the communication only comes about *with the answer* (the debt is not contracted until we answer, though it is the condition of the answer). We *read* our ability to read in a strong, almost transitive sense. For the image is radically subject to its realization in the present, and in this sense radically historical. If the "expiration date" borne by the dialectical image is not read at the moment when it indicates the image to the present, the date itself expires. It is irretrievably lost, Benjamin says (thesis 5, GS 1.2 695/I 255). The address of the past in all its power *will have been* if it is read by the present that it enables; if it is not, it disappears without a trace (that is, without the trace it bore).

Thus, if the moment of the caesura is a *critical* moment for the present (cf. "Konvolut N," 7a5), it is no less critical for the past and its possible redemption. It is critical, once again, by virtue of a movement in language. Criticism occurs in language, Benjamin suggests, and it is to the same notion that Benjamin appeals when he speaks in N 3.1 of a "specific critical point of the movement inside" the dialectical image, alluding to the "stamp of that critical, dangerous impetus that lies at the source of all reading." The stamp of truth is critical and dangerous because it puts the present fundamentally in question (like the *Stoss* of truth in Heidegger's description of the work of art) and indeed *destroys* it as the present of a consciousness that conceives itself in relation to the linear continuity of the representation of historical time. But the past is no less at stake. Both past and future hang in the balance. In N 7.2 (GS 5.1 587/B 59), Benjamin writes that "the dialectician can't see history as anything other than a constellation of dangers." This constellation is formed by the threat posed by the reigning ideologies to the constellation of past and present offered by the dialectical image. But the moment is also dangerous in that it is critical for the past: if the present does not read the past (and *itself* as implicated in this past) — if it fails to read and write itself — the constellation of past and present will simply flit by.

The reading of the dialectical image in *Geschichtsphilosophie*, provided it is truly historical, is thus *critique* in the strongest sense. It engages with the conditions of "authentic" historical understanding and indeed the foundation of history itself. It engages with them, moreover, in an active fashion (hence my reference to a writing). Its initiative plays a *constitutive* role in the critical moment. In N 10a1, Benjamin virtually reproduces the phrase about truth's "critical, dangerous impetus," but ascribes it to the intervention of "materialist history writing" (which he describes at several points in "Konvolut N" as a "blasting" (see, for example, N 10.3, 10a1, 10a3); "The destructive or critical impetus [*Das destruktive oder kritische Moment*] in materialist historiography [*Geschichtsschreibung*] comes into play in that blasting apart [*Aufsprengung*] with which the historical object first constitutes itself" (GS 5.1 594/B 66). I noted above that we read our ability to read in the dialectical image (the entire complexity of its temporal structure is expressed in this phrase). Reading, as we see, releases the critical power that is its own "source" — it is essentially a writing of the origin (*Ursprung*) in a writing of its own present.[6] It is as much active as receptive, though without quite being a transitive verb.

Throughout Benjamin's descriptions of the presentation of truth (or the descriptions of truth's self-presentation), there is in fact a moment of something like translation and thereby the recognition of a kind of "invention" in the act of reading/writing. Reappropriating Benjamin's terms, we might say that the text is not just the thunder rolling afterward; it helps to ignite the spark. This "active receptivity" in reading/writing appears already in "On Language as Such," as we have seen in reference to a notion of translation: the communicability of the essence of language offers itself immediately but requires translation from language to language (from the "mute" language of things, for example, to the language of names). In "The Task of the Translator," translation is a writing that "leaves its mark on history" as it draws out the seed of pure language in answering the address of the work. In the "Prologue" to the *Trauerspiel* book — and not without some risk for his statement about the immediate unity of truth's self-presentation — Benjamin posits a kind of mediation of the presentation of truth with his notion of the concept: truth requires the concept for this self-presentation. The same notion will appear in "Konvolut N" in the repeated image of setting sails for the wind of history. And Benjamin will note that the presence of mind required in a political context for the reading of the dialectical image requires a form of anticipation (Heidegger will invoke precisely the same necessity in defining the "presumption" of the thinker): "Presence of mind as a political category is beautifully brought out in these words of Turgot: 'By the time we come to discover that things are at a given juncture, they have already changed several times. Hence we always perceive events too late and politics must always foresee, as it were, the present' " (N 12a1, GS 5.1 598/B 70).

This is not prophecy, as the "Theses" would indicate clearly. It is something more like a translation of the present, a delivery of the present to itself in an act of anticipation. A kind of naming, we might say—in any case, a performance by which the present *writes itself*. It is neither a purely passive transcription nor a subjective imposition in the form of what is commonly (but mistakenly) understood as a Nietzschean form of history writing. It is something closer to an "invention" of history that does justice to the past. It is an *event*.

Benjamin argued in his "Prologue" to the *Trauerspiel* book, as we have seen, that the dialectic of the origin does not involve any fundamental historical determination of truth: history is a content for it, not a determining event. The dialectical image, on the contrary, is (as read) an event for truth, and in this sense it has a radically historical character. With the dialectical image, Benjamin effectively historicizes the address of truth and draws it into historical experience as its quasi-transcendental condition. Truth not only requires its realization in a reading (at the risk of disappearing irretrievably if it is not seized); it is constituted in the reading/writing of the image by the dialectical materialist.

One might well argue that Benjamin always thought the address of truth in historical (or at least temporal) terms; translatability, after all, comes about only in time and for a time, and translation is not a mere transcription. But one cannot say that translatability involves the *times* in question (as times) in quite the way the dialectical image does (even though the life of a language appears to be involved)—or at least not in such a fundamentally political fashion. With the dialectical image, it is a matter of the present's capacity to define itself: to *be* and to be *historically* (from the basis of concrete historical conditions whose truth is offered to it out of the sudden dialectic of past and present). The notion of the origin introduced such a historical determination of the address of truth, but only the thought of the dialectical image fully historicizes the latter notion and makes the response truly *critical* for the occurrence of truth.

PART V

Blanchot

Crossing the Threshold

ON "LITERATURE AND THE
RIGHT TO DEATH"

LITERATURE begins, Maurice Blanchot says, when it becomes a question, when the language of a work becomes literature in a question about language itself (PF 293/21). This question concerns the source of literature's ambiguity, its "origin" in an irreducible "double meaning" that is a movement not between irreconcilable meanings but between meaning and a "meaning of meaning" that is itself irreducibly ambiguous: material and ideal, neither material nor ideal—a "point of instability," a "power of metamorphosis," an "imminence of change" (PF 330–31/61–62) that gives itself in language beyond either the meaning language takes on or its "reality."

The question, as Blanchot stages it in "Literature and the Right to Death," opens in both a temptation and an obsession, a "torment." Only the latter will provide my focus here, since my aim is to bring forth the way the ambiguity of literature constitutes an offering of the *il y a*, and to read the relation (the *pas* of relation) marked by this offering as the site of what Blanchot will later thematize as the encounter with *autrui*. But to approach this second dimension of this essay and the infinite movement onto which it opens, I will start with a few notes on the first, and what Blanchot describes as the temptation of the negative.

"Any writer who is not led by the very fact of writing to think: 'I am the revolution, freedom alone makes me write,' in reality is not writing" (PF 311/40). Blanchot makes this statement categorically in the first moment of his movement through what we might call "the two versions of the imaginary." The declaration introduces the Marquis de Sade, whom Blanchot identifies as "the writer par excellence," and this by virtue of his identification with the French revolution and the Terror—his engagement with the passion of death as a negativity that gives itself up to the *jouissance* of an "absolute sovereignty" (PF 311/41). Blanchot will lean to

Mallarmé (and others — Flaubert, for example, and the surrealists) in subsequent references to literature's drive to realize the negation inherent in language. Along this first slope of literature's double movement (PF 321/51), we find the prosaic search for a transparent meaning, and beyond this the tropological movements by which literature seeks the flower that is "absent from all bouquets," or the ground of essence itself in the movement of thought (though when this movement reaches Mallarmé's "Igitur" we are clearly on the "second slope," where we have in fact also already been with Flaubert). But in seeking to illustrate the irreducibly *imaginary* dimension of this negation (the "imaginary" ground of its very opening) and its "irrational," even "aberrant" character as the passion of that "life that bears death and maintains itself in it,"* Blanchot turns to Sade.

The reference is undoubtedly dictated in part by the subversion of the Hegelian dialectic to which Blanchot dedicates himself in the first half of this essay; to release a kind of excess in the negative, Blanchot writes Sade into a very particular moment offered by Hegel himself (one that communicates with moments signaled by Georges Bataille in "Hegel: Death and Sacrifice").† The Terror, Blanchot suggests, represents for literature that specular, speculative moment where literature "contemplates itself," "recognizes itself," and "justifies itself" (PF 311/41) in the realization of absolute freedom. In the Terror, literature passes into the world. It becomes "real," we might say, it embraces existence, but only inasmuch as existence has become fabulous in giving itself over to the absolute character of the word wherein all finite determinations dissolve.‡ What is terrible about the Terror is its abstraction, the fact that its incarnation of absolute freedom, its synthesis of the universal and the singular, the ideal and the real, remains "ideal (literary)" (PF 310/40). The "life that bears death and maintains itself in it" represents the sacrifice of "life," if life names existence as it is given in the always singular experience of human finitude. To put it more succinctly, it is the sacrifice of "our" dying.

Once again, Blanchot's subversive aim is to write Sade into the dialectic at a moment indicated by Hegel himself, to draw forth the "imaginary" character of the negation from which literature proceeds when it works to

---

La vie qui porte la mort et se maintient en elle (PF 324/54) — both "the life that brings death" (as in a murder) and "the life that bears death" (the death it can never murder or be done with, not even in suicide).

†A translation of Bataille's "Hegel, la mort et le sacrifice" by Jonathan Strauss is published in the issue of *Yale French Studies* devoted to Bataille, no. 78 (1990): 9–28.

‡"At this moment, freedom pretends to realize itself in the *immediate* form of 'everything is possible, everything can be done.' A fabulous moment — and no one who has known it can completely recover from it, for he has known history as his own history and his own freedom as universal freedom. Fabulous moments indeed: in them, fable speaks, in them, the speech of fable becomes action" (PF 309/38).

offer a presentation of the meaning of being in its totality, or the world as such; "the meaning and absence" of the whole of what is (PF 308/36). The finite, "imaginary" character of the transcendence offered by language (and the possibility of its uncontrollable passage into the *jouissance* of "absolute sovereignty": "life elevated to the point of passion, passion become cruelty and folly" [PF 311/41]) haunts the negativity of meaning no less than the becoming image of the word, as we will see, haunts its material presence. Ultimately, Blanchot argues (this is the conclusion of his essay and its challenge), the one veers into the other and is even indistinguishable from it; the ambiguity of literature lies in the communication of the image and the imaginary (the word, in its "reality" and "significance," doubly *limiting* this communication). Nevertheless, the foregrounding of the Sadian temptation is striking. "I am the revolution." Could this phrase *also* characterize Franz Kafka and Francis Ponge? (Kafka perhaps, but Ponge?) Or has Blanchot allowed himself to be carried into the movement he is describing when he claims that every writer knows such delirium? And could he be capturing something that not only haunts his own more literary writing but also constitutes a temptation he has known in seeking to pass from literature to reality? Could he be thinking here of his own past political passions? This would be to point to something more than a "national aestheticism," something far more profound (where identification or "mimesis" is concerned) and more unsettling.

This last question is not without interest for Blanchot scholarship, but it certainly points beyond his person. Blanchot notes that in literature's specular and speculative identification with that historical moment where " 'life bears death and maintains itself in death itself' in order to obtain from it the possibility and the truth of speech" (PF 311/41), the question of literature itself opens. Without transition, Blanchot writes: "That is the 'question' " (PF 311/41). The question, we may presume, has to do with the abstract character of the negation to which literature commits itself, possibly even the delirious character of this engagement when it is undertaken without reserve, but equally with something that escapes its murderous power: something that haunts its movement of negation and becomes an obsession.

Blanchot returns to Hegel here, a young Hegel, "the friend and neighbor of Hölderlin," who recognizes in the "right to death" (PF 309/39) afforded by the negation borne by language a "strange right" (PF 312/42) (they are "friend and neighbor" more by this recognition than by their physical proximity at the *Stift*). Adam's act of naming, Hegel wrote in a text prior to the *Phenomenology*, is an act of annihilation — an act, Blanchot adds, to which every instance of naming or designation alludes. "The meaning of speech requires . . . that before any word is spoken there be a sort of immense hecatomb: a prior deluge, plunging into a total sea all of creation" (PF 312–13/42). All of being must be given over to death for speech to be possible. Language itself brings this death, and we speak only *from* it. Blanchot's words are worth following closely here:

Of course, my language does not kill anyone. And yet: when I say "this woman," real death is announced and already present in my language; my language means that this person, who is there right now, can be detached from herself, removed from her existence and her presence and plunged suddenly into a nothingness of existence and presence. My language essentially signifies the possibility of this destruction; it is, at every moment, a resolute allusion to such an event. My language does not kill anyone. But, if this woman were not really capable of dying, if she were not threatened by death at every moment of her life, bound and united to it by an essential bond, I would not be able to accomplish that ideal negation, that deferred assassination that is my language. (PF 313/42–43)

Most will be familiar now with the argument that says that for a word to be a sign, it must signify beyond any concrete context in which it might appear. Signification presupposes the possible absence of a referent and the absence of the speaker who might initially claim this language as their own. But Blanchot also appears to be saying something more that should be noted here, something on the order of an ontological claim. It is not only that language signifies in the possible absence of its speaker and its referent; it is that a "real death" has occurred. The woman negated when I say "this woman" must have been "really capable of dying," bound *essentially* to death. Language is thus constantly referring back to its origin in the essential bond between the existent being and the possibility of the death that offers this being to language. How do we think this offering or opening — in what manner does the living being give itself to language? How does death mark itself? I will not try as yet to answer this question, but I would note that this mark is what Blanchot names (in much of his earlier writing) "the image."

Before any speech, there is the offering of a dying and the offering of my own dying. ("I" speak from my power to distance myself from myself, to be other than my being — in other words, from my death.) Might this help to explain why Blanchot figures the effort to return to what exists *before* language as the effort to recover a corpse? (As we will see, Blanchot will argue in "Two Versions of the Imaginary" that the becoming-image of the thing is best figured by the cadaver.) If what is "before" language is not life but life bound to death, life offering itself to language in the image (and in this, already language, at least as "the image of a sign," to borrow Benjamin's phrase [GS 2.1 152/R 326]), is the before not already an "after" (life)?

The question of the "before" torments language. Were literature to cede to the temptation to gather to itself its very separation from existence, to attain and offer negation in itself and make the nothing (as the ground of meaning) everything, it would already have "a strange and awkward task." But literature cannot forget the initial murder:

It recalls the first name that would have been the murder of which Hegel speaks. The "existent" was called out of its existence by the word and it became being. The *Lazare, veni foras* made the obscure cadaverous reality leave its original depths and gave it, in exchange, only the life of the spirit. Language knows that its realm is the day and not the intimacy of the unrevealed; it knows that for the day to begin . . . something must be excluded. Negation realizes itself only from the basis of the reality it negates; language draws its value and its pride from being the accomplishment of this negation; but what was lost at the outset? The torment of language is what it lacks by the necessity that it be the lack of it. It cannot even name it. (PF 315–16/45–46)

Since the first "slope" of language's movement is the slope of negation and the assumption and accomplishment of the murder from which meaning proceeds, one would expect the "before" to be figured under the names of life. And indeed much of Blanchot's language in this passage points in that direction (everything surrounding the evocations "this woman," "a flower," "the cat"). But the living reality evoked by these words is unavoidably *idea*—entirely a product of language; and how can one avoid thinking the before without reference to some Eden? Blanchot's move is to substitute a figure of death where we expect life, and a figure of the "after" for the before. Literature, seeking what it has lost, wants not the living Lazarus but the dead Lazarus. The Lazarus resurrected is short-changed in the tropological movement of negation—he gets only the life of spirit, not the death of material existence.[1] The (un)revealed Lazarus would be Lazarus in his death. In a "commensurate" exchange, he would be brought forth *as* death; or, beyond metaphor (as we read in *Thomas the Obscure*), he would *be* death (an absolute aporia), the death that is the nondialectical *other* of living existence:

The language of literature is the search for this moment that precedes it. Literature generally names it existence; it wants the cat as it exists, the pebble in its *siding with things*, not man, but the pebble, and in this pebble what man rejects to say it, the foundation of speech and what speech excludes in order to speak, the abyss, the Lazarus of the tomb and not the Lazarus brought into the day, the one who already smells bad, who is Evil, the lost Lazarus and not the Lazarus saved and resuscitated. (PF 316/46)

"The foundation of speech"—could this be, once again, the "real death" of the existent "really capable of dying" and bound to death by an "essential bond"? And what abyss lies in this "real"? For Blanchot's evocation of the corpse of Lazarus suggests, I believe, that literature's torment drives it actually beyond the threshold that is the opening of language and toward what, for spirit, appears initially as a tomb ("appears" in the sense that spirit knows here a lure — as Blanchot consistently indicates, spirit sees its outside first as something tempting). For the cadaver presents a materiality that refuses itself to language and gives only its refusal. The cadaver in effect, is "exemplary" in this way; a strange "non-thing," it is of the earth, as Heidegger might say, but in the extreme form of the ab-ject, a residue that has always fallen from signification as inassimilable (in *cadaver* we should hear the Latin *cadere*). What "object" is more other, more *unheimlich*, more charged in its obtrusive but fleeting presence, and what leaves a more indelible image when we chance upon it? A material (non)presence that is not quite of nature, no longer of the world and given in the absence of life, the corpse presents the inassimilable other of spirit and meaning that has in fact always been there.

That has also always been there in words. Literature's chance for returning to what language has left behind lies in the materiality of language. Its way back lies in the abandonment of meaning and a flight into the physical character of the word: "rhythm, weight, mass, shape, and then the paper on which one writes, the trail of the ink, the book" (PF 316–17/46). It finds there not only the thingly character of the word but its primitive force: "The word acts not as an ideal force but as an obscure power, as an incantation that coerces things, makes them *really* present outside themselves. It is an element, a part barely detached from its subterranean surroundings: no longer a name, but a moment of the universal anonymity, a brute affirmation, the stupor of a confrontation in the depths of obscurity" (PF 317/46–47). The word is a thing, and it draws forth the thing in its "hidden intimacy" (PF 312/41), leaving behind ideality and the consciousness of the writer in its negative force. Literary language communicates the presence of things *before* consciousness:

[Literature] is not beyond the world, but neither is it the world: it is the presence of things before the *world* comes to be, their perseverance after the world has disappeared, the stubbornness of what subsists when everything is effaced and the dazedness of what appears when there is nothing. This is why it cannot be confused with the consciousness that illuminates and decides; it is *my* consciousness *without me*, the radiant passivity of mineral substances, lucidity in the depths of torpor. It is not the night, it is what haunts the night; not the night but the consciousness of the night that lies awake ceaselessly in order to catch itself and for this reason dissipates itself without respite. It is not the day, but the side of the day that the day rejected to become light. And it is not death either, for in it there shows existence without being, the existence that remains beneath existence like an inexorable affirmation, without beginning and without end, death as the impossibility of dying. (PF 317/47)

I cite at length for the beauty of this passage (this night that dissipates itself in a vain effort at self-reflection) and because the movement of Blanchot's argument as he follows literature's way back must be followed with the greatest care. Sinking into its physicality, Blanchot suggests, literature communicates an uncommunicating presence that is not quite self-presence and never quite posits itself but nevertheless stirs and persists ("moment," "affirmation," "presence," "perseverance," "stubbornness," "appearance," "passivity," "lucidity"). The "nature" of words, "what is given to me and gives me more than I can grasp" (PF 316/46), thus communicates something of what Blanchot, following Lévinas, terms the *il y a*: "The anonymous and impersonal current of being that precedes all being: being as the fatality of being" (PF 320/51). Given that Blanchot thinks the *il y a* as an abyssal opening, we could in fact have more grounds for comparison with Heidegger's *es gibt* than one might at first assume (inasmuch as Hegel appears to be the determinant philosophical reference in Blanchot's essay). One might in fact stage the confrontation between Heidegger and Blanchot around precisely these words of "thought" that normally serve as translations for one another but also *resist* with the diversity of the idiom. For Blanchot as for Heidegger, *il y a/es gibt* names the opening of essence; but the *pas* of this opening in Blanchot (to which I will return) also paralyzes the setting under way and turns the way itself into an endless detour. The *il y a* is a name for what might be called the "underside" of the hermeneutic circle, the abyssal opening from which Heidegger consistently turns away even as he remarks its presence. But rather than pursue Blanchot's relation to Heidegger directly, let me continue to follow the movement of Blanchot's meditation, for it is the "signifying" structure of the communication we have seen that most interests me here (and precisely in its bearing on Heidegger's reflections on language).

The paragraph following the one from which I have cited at length appears to take back what is given in the first: the effort to return to what is before revelation (which by all "appearances" has been a success) is now labeled "tragic." Literature may well have succeeded in abandoning a signified meaning, but it cannot avoid signifying this abandonment: its language continues to show its own intention and expose its pretense:

[Literature] says: "I no longer represent, I am; I do not signify, I present." But this will to be a thing, this refusal to mean that is immersed in words turned to salt, in short, this destiny that literature becomes as it becomes the language of no one, the written of no writer, the light of a consciousness deprived of self, this insane effort to bury itself in itself, to hide itself behind the fact that it appears — all this is what literature now manifests, what literature now shows. Should it become as mute as stone, as passive as the cadaver enclosed behind this stone, the decision to lose the capacity to speak would continue to be read on the stone and would be enough to awaken this false corpse. (PF 317–18/47)

The "death" that literature thought it could find (and by all appearances did find: nothing of the preceding paragraph was qualified as illusory) turns out to be "false." But then we recognize in retrospect that it was not exactly the "death" of the cadaver or the silence of the stone in which it is enclosed that was supposedly found. If literature set out to find the "real" beyond language in the form of a materiality that gives itself only in refusal, it actually found something else: the obscure reflection without reflection of the *il y a*, that affirmation that is a failure of negation to negate itself, the fatality of the day. The turn in Blanchot's argument from the first to the second paragraph remarks the traits of reflection (without reflection) in the first paragraph only to recover them in a third paragraph in a more affirmative manner. It is as though the ineradicable reflection of language's intention and self-offering remarks the prior reflection in such a way as to offer its "truth." For when Blanchot summarizes the movement that has just occurred in the first two paragraphs, this movement changes sign once again. Literature knows that it cannot go beyond itself; "it is the movement by which what disappears appears" (PF 318/47–48)—a statement that recalls the first slope but is also already ambiguous since what "disappears" is also what refuses itself. He then goes on, summarizing the second movement:

When [literature] refuses to name, when it makes of the name an obscure, insignificant thing, witness to the primordial obscurity, what has disappeared here—the meaning of the name—has indeed been destroyed, but in its place signification in general has come forth, the meaning of the insignificance encrusted in the word as an expression of the obscurity of existence. So that, if the precise meaning of the terms has been extinguished, the very possibility of signifying now affirms itself, the empty power to give a meaning, a strange impersonal light. (PF 318/48)

The word's inability to avoid signifying its intention (its *vouloir dire*) has become the presentation of signification in general, the very possibility of signifying. Words that *would* become things, that offer themselves *as* things, remain *words* that offer themselves in this way; but the persistence of the word as word (*qu'il y a — ici — langage*) becomes the indication or expression of the *il y a* itself. All of the ambiguity of this movement is expressed in the phrase "in its place . . . has come forth . . . the meaning of the insignificance encrusted in the word as an expression of the obscurity of existence." "The meaning of the insignificance" may be read, after the preceding paragraph, as referring to the marking of the fatal destiny of the word in its effort to be a thing (PF 317/47), the ineradicable designation that this insignificant "thing" is a word offering itself as insignificant. But "meaning" here also takes on another meaning: for it is the obscurity of existence appearing *as* insignificance: the appearance of insignificance *as such*. The self-reflection or self-offering of language becomes the showing of the *il y a*. The tragic undermining of literature's endeavor has become a *discovery* of the fatality of the day (tragedy itself changing meaning with a new sense of "fatality"):

Negating the day, literature reconstructs the day as fatality; affirming the night, it finds night as the impossibility of the night. That is its discovery. . . . If we call the day to account, if we reach the point of pushing it away in order to find what there is before the day, beneath the day, we then discover that it is already present, and that what there is before the day is still the day, but as a powerlessness to disappear and not as the power to make appear, an obscure necessity and not the light of freedom. (PF 318/48)

The inability to avoid signifying, become the "empty power to give a meaning," is the expression of the "powerlessness to disappear" of the being of what is before the day, the existence from which one must turn away to speak and to understand.

Has Blanchot worked a kind of dialectical sleight of hand here — have we read something more on the order of a slippage than an argumentation? It may well be a slippage, but Blanchot would suggest, I believe, that this is the "slippage" that makes dialectic possible (and impossible). Blanchot will return to it once again after a summary of his two slopes in what seems an effort to catch more precisely the movement we have just followed. Summarizing the second slope, Blanchot affirms that literature's effort to refuse to say is not in fact tragically undermined. The metamorphosis in itself has not failed, he says:

It is quite true that the words are transformed. They no longer *signify* shadow, earth, they no longer represent the absence of shadow and earth that is meaning, that is the shadow's light, the transparency of the earth; opacity is their response; the rustle of closing wings is their speech; material weight presents itself in them with the stifling density of a syllabic accumulation that has lost all meaning. The metamorphosis has taken place. (PF 319/49)

But in this metamorphosis, he continues, and beyond the solidification of words, there reappears (like a *revenant*, a kind of spectral return) "the meaning of this metamorphosis which illuminates them and the meaning they draw from their appearance as things, or even, if this should happen, as vague, indeterminate, ungraspable existence where nothing appears, the heart of depth without appearance." The meaning of the metamorphosis refers us back once again to language's inability not to present itself as language offering its abandonment of meaning, an inability not to show itself *as* language offering itself *as* thing. But the appearance of the meaning language draws from its appearance as a thing, or, "if it should happen," as nonappearance, is also the appearance of meaning itself, or more precisely, "signification in general," the "empty power to give a meaning." The possibility of the "as such" of meaning is given as the word gives itself as a word giving itself as a thing. Once again, these are *words* appearing *as things appear*, offering this *as* by which a thing may appear as a thing, or even by which insignificance may appear *as* insignificance, but doing so by their own self-giving, which is a giving as. This is a presentation of the possibility of the as such via a self-presentation that is irreducibly a marking of dissimulation. The word gives (itself) as, thereby giving "meaning" as "detached from its conditions, separated from its moments, wandering like an empty power with which nothing can be done, a power without power, a simple powerlessness to cease to be, but which, because of this, appears as the proper determination of indeterminate and senseless existence" (PF 320/50). The word showing itself offering itself as (existence in its refusal to signified meaning) — giving itself giving as — is the condition of signifying or offering to understanding (or better, thought) what escapes signification. *Qu'il y a — ici — langage* — a remarking of the fact of language, but in its irreducible figurality: this is what literature produces as a "question" (or perhaps a stunned discovery: something related to Kafka's joy when he writes, "He was looking out the window" [cited in PF 298/26]) as it says the fact of being — as it says "is" — in its fundamental dissimulation. Literature, on one of its slopes at least, is language remarking an irreducible figurality, its own, but as a saying of the dissimulation that belongs, as Blanchot asserts, to being itself. "Mimesis," we might say, "figuring" (itself) like a wandering corpse.

The image, once again, is from "Two Versions of the Imaginary." Borrowing this title and summarizing the movement we have followed thus far, we might say that the two slopes of literature's ambiguity are constituted by the movement between the "imaginary" point of view literature adopts in seeking to give expression to the world that is the meaning of things in their totality ("I am the revolution") and the becoming-image of the word ("I no longer represent, I am"). As Blanchot suggests in his concluding footnote to "The Essential Solitude" (EL 28/34), the language of literature is language that has become entirely image. Not a language full of images, but a language that has become the image of language, figuring by this nonreflection the dissimulation of being itself, which is the condition of appearance in general and which appears when the thing is absorbed by its image. The damaged tool offers such an appearance, Blanchot remarks (recalling Heidegger) in "Two Versions": "The category of art is linked to this possibility that objects have of 'appearing,' that is to say, of abandoning themselves to pure and simple resemblance behind which there is nothing—except being. Only what has surrendered itself to the image appears, and everything that appears is, in this sense, imaginary" (EL 352/259). The corpse, again, is most "exemplary" here, though it figures this time (on another "slope") not only a materiality that offers its refusal to signification via the absence of life but an "ideality" that has grown thick with "the elemental strangeness and formless heaviness of being that is present in absence" (EL 351/258)—it figures, in other words, the very possibility of appearing, vacillating between ideality and materiality and marking their point of confusion (which is also the "confusion" of the idealism of classical art, as Blanchot notes with a certain perverse irony). As a cadaver falls from the hold of our affective interests and the world of names and identities, Blanchot writes, it will come to resemble itself, and in this "self"-reflection that reflects no one and nothing (it is not "simply" a corpse, nor is it a human being, for the being that appears is "impersonal," a monumental double of the one we have known: "the apparition of the original—until then unknown—sentence of last judgment inscribed in the depths of being and triumphantly expressing itself with the help of distance" [EL 350–51/258]) it will offer resemblance itself, resemblance absorbing the thing:

The cadaver is its own image. It no longer has any relations with this world, in which it still appears, except those of an image, an obscure possibility, a shadow present at all times behind the living form and that now, far from separating itself from this form, transforms it entirely into shadow. The cadaver is the reflection becoming master of the reflected life, absorbing it, identifying itself substantially with it in making it pass from its use and truth value to something incredible—unusual and neutral. And if the cadaver is so resemblant, this is because it is, at a certain moment, resemblance par excellence, entirely resemblance, and also nothing more. It is the like, like to an absolute degree, overwhelming and marvelous. But what does it resemble? Nothing. (EL 351/258)

Perhaps it would suffice to stop here with the observation that with his thought of the image, Blanchot has effectively generalized the *Verstellung* that Heidegger recognizes as belonging essentially to truth and that art offers in its own withdrawal and thingly quality. Heidegger's "that"— what the work of art *says* as it offers the event of truth in a movement of simultaneous approach and withdrawal—has been rethought as the "that" of language (which in fact it was for Heidegger inasmuch as the essence of art is said to reside in language). But here the "that" marks an irreducible figurality that undermines any stability in the pose. The representation of language is the remarking of the "imaginary" dimension of truth — the remarking of the dissimulation of being.

Could we go further? Is this not a limit for thought? It is a limit, but a limit of a very particular kind. For we might observe in each of Blanchot's descriptions of the becoming-image of the word that it marks a "meaning of meaning" (or perhaps better, a meaning *without* meaning) that is neither material nor ideal, but something prior to each of these categories that embraces both while *inclining* toward an "elementary depth" in an infinite movement toward what Blanchot names the "neutral."* The image is a threshold — a limit, as Blanchot will emphasize in asserting that it has a protective function,† but a limit that marks an infinite abyssal relation and that is therefore already a crossing toward what Blanchot calls in *The Space of Literature* the "other" night. For the consciousness that undertakes this crossing (though initiative will reveal itself always to have been the fatality of desire), it will be a movement toward the other of consciousness — toward itself as other:

The *other* night is always the other, and he who hears it becomes the other, he who approaches it departs from himself, is no longer the one who approaches, but the one who turns aside, goes hither and yon. He who, having entered the first night, seeks intrepidly to go toward its profoundest intimacy, toward the essential, hears at a certain moment the *other* night — hears himself, hears the eternally reverberating echo of his own progress, a progress toward silence, but the echo sends it back to him as the whispering immensity, toward the void, and the void is now a presence that comes to his encounter. (EL 224/168)

The noise at the threshold is the echo of approach,‡ but an echo that reverberates with an otherness that itself becomes approach. What consciousness hears is its own absence, *itself* becoming other in opening to the other — something that can be "known" only as a kind of madness. Or as a kind of exposure. Here is the same movement across the threshold I have just followed as it is described in "Literature and the Right to Death":

In this effort, literature does not confine itself to rediscovering in the interior what it wanted to abandon on the threshold. For what it finds, as the interior, is the outside which, once an exit, has now changed into the impossibility of leaving — and what it finds as the obscurity of existence is the being of the day which has changed from an explicatory light, creative of meaning, into the harassment of

---

*See, for example, the opening paragraphs of "Two Versions of the Imaginary" (EL 345/254).

†The point is suggested in "Literature and the Right to Death" (PF 328/60); for a reference to the image as a limit, see "Two Versions of the Imaginary" (EL 345–46/79).

‡"An imperceptible whispering, a noise one can hardly distinguish from silence, the sandlike seeping of silence. Not even that: only the noise of some activity, some foraging or burrowing" (EL 223–24/168).

what one cannot prevent oneself from understanding and the stifling haunting of a reason without principle and without beginning, which one cannot account for. Literature is that experience by which consciousness discovers its being in its powerlessness to lose consciousness, in the movement in which, disappearing, tearing itself from the punctuality of a self, it reconstitutes itself, past unconsciousness, in an impersonal spontaneity, the desperate eagerness of a haggard knowledge, that knows nothing, that no one knows, and that ignorance finds always behind itself as its own shadow changed into a gaze. (PF 320/50)

This is consciousness become the gaze of fascination, a blind seeing that is *contact* with the outside and the impossibility of not seeing what obtrudes with the collapse of the separation that is constitutive of consciousness. Consciousness become a passivity or an opening that proceeds from an effraction or a touch: thus it is the *passion* of the image when the thing becomes image in withdrawing from the world and the passion of writing when the word veers toward the image and opens onto the outside — the passion of the outside:

To write is to arrange language under fascination and, through language, in language, remain in contact with the absolute milieu, where the thing becomes an image again, where the image, once an allusion to a figure, becomes an allusion to what is without figure, and where, once a form sketched on absence, it becomes the formless presence of that absence, the opaque and empty opening on what is when there is no more world, when there is no world yet. (EL 27–28/33)

It is a seeing that is at once a suspended self-reflection ("a lost neutral glimmer that does not go out, that does not illuminate, the circle, closed upon itself, of the gaze" [EL 25/32]) and a *being seen* — once again, an exposure. In "solitude," Blanchot writes, "I am not alone, but in this present I am already returning to myself under the form of Someone [*Quelqu'un*]" (EL 24/31). And then further on the same page: "Where I am alone, the day is no longer anything but the loss of an abode, intimacy with the outside that is placeless and without repose. The coming, here, makes it so that he who comes belongs to dispersion, to the fissure where the exterior is a stifling intrusion, the nakedness, the cold of that in which one remains discovered, where space is the vertigo of spacing" (EL 24/31). *My* consciousness *without me*, appearing *as other* in the form of an impersonal anonymity that is less a presence than the presence of an absence, the intrusion of the outside, *relation* with an irreducible alterity. Fascination is heteroaffection, "self"-affection that is an infinite becoming-other in a fundamental passivity. The coming of *on*, *il*, or *quelqu'un* is an infinite opening to the outside, not a "human" presence but the presence of the other to a self that is no longer the "same," no longer a "self." Where Blanchot names the other — "Eurydice," for example — this name is a figure for a nameless other dissimulated by the night, the "other" night or "dissimulation itself," an infinite, abyssal movement.

Thus the image is not a limit, if by this we mean a point where reflection — or thought — must stop. Rather, it is a site of engagement and passage where reflection halts, but in becoming the approach to/of the outside. It is a threshold, in this sense, but a threshold already marked by a crossing, a passage, that Derrida has identified and engaged in exemplary fashion by tracking the *pas* (both adverb of negation and noun: "step") that echoes throughout Blanchot's text.* I will not try to subject this extraordinarily rich demonstration to summary, precisely because it works to demonstrate *pas*, describing the movement in question both in a thematic manner and in a trajectory (like the *Viens*, "Come," which it attempts to think while making it sound). But I would like to note the point of juncture with the current discussion by observing that in Derrida's reading, *pas* names and "is" what happens in the becoming image of the word. *Pas* is what is marked (or marks itself) in the powerlessness of the word to efface its own re-presentation of its effacement of meaning, in this remarking of the very possibility of meaning that inhabits it as a wandering, empty power whose "ghostly" presence Blanchot figures as a movement, "a walking staircase, a corridor that unfolds ahead" (PF 323/54).† Together with *sans*, as Blanchot uses this term almost formulaically to mark the same effacement of meaning and a passive opening to the other, it is the *re-trait* — at once remarking and withdrawal — of a movement of distancing that infinitely suspends the "as" given in language's re-presentation of its possibility, rendering this "giving as" abyssal.[2] If the "as" I have isolated marks the very possibility of metaphor or figurality in general, the *pas* that marks it is the *re-trait* of metaphor, and, as set to work in the text, the marking of what exceeds the order of the signifiable — or the signifier — in a movement beyond meaning and beyond Being. The step (not) beyond that occurs in and with the opening to the *il y a* in the becoming-image of the word is the *opening* (and closing) of a thought of Being. Here is Derrida's inscription of *pas* in this becoming-image that we have followed in "Literature and the Right to Death":

To remain near oneself in one's effacement [the movement from *je* to *il* we have seen], to sign it still, to remain in one's absence as remainder, there is the impossible, death as the impossibility of dying on the basis of which death without death announces itself. The remainder without remainder of this effacement that no

*See Jacques Derrida, "Pas (préambule)" in *Gramma*, nos. 3/4 (1975): 111–215. A slightly modified version of this essay appears in Derrida's *Parages* (Paris: Galilée, 1986), 19–116. I will cite the original version.

†These phrases mark what Derrida identifies as the labyrinthine topology — or tropology? — of *pas*: the vertiginous *spacing* of pas.

longer effaces *itself*, here is what *there is* perhaps (by chance) but that *is* (not) *pas*: here is *pas* under the name of forgetting as he uses it, as one can no longer think it, think it that is, starting from [*à partir de*] a thought-of-Being. If "Being is another name for forgetting," it names a forgetting of forgetting (that it violently encrypts) and not a synonym of forgetting, exchanging itself with it as its equivalent, giving it to be thought. Or naming it, it unnames it, makes it disappear in its name. This *thought* which is no longer of Being or of the presence of the present, this *thought* of forgetting tells us perhaps what was to be heard under this name (*thought*), which named, as you remember, without declaring her name, she [*elle: la pensée*] to whom *Death Sentence* said "eternally: 'Come,' and eternally, she is there"; or the unique *word* to which, in *The One Who Did Not Accompany Me*, "Come" is said so that it [*elle: la parole*] should cry its name. "When I say 'this woman ...'" That's you, that's your name."*

Derrida (or more precisely, one of the interlocutors in this dialogue — the "counterpart" to the one marked as feminine: "Derrida," as Blanchot might put it, only to the extent that he is not "himself") goes on to say here that this forgetting that gives forgetting to be thought (*pas d'oubli*), this forgetting that gives (thought) is *il y a*. To which he adds: "this *il y a* enjoins *Viens*."

The becoming-image of the word is the opening to a call, Derrida suggests, that must have already occurred for the *pas* to have been engaged in the first place. *Viens* is the "invitation" that provokes the *pas* of approach but that this step provokes in its turn in such a way as to allow it to sound for a first time as the word of the other. *Viens* is the word of approach, the word that is written in approach (on the body) as the word of/to the other that comes to our encounter (never "our" encounter). This other, once again, is not another human being (or not simply, as we will see). What approaches is the other night, an infinite alterity whose coming is the opening of what is named in *Thomas the Obscure* "the supreme relation which is sufficient unto itself."† *There is* (*il y a*) joins in approach, en-joins itself in a giving prior to the law that is the birth of the law. The call is wholly anonymous, wholly other.

Blanchot will emphasize later, however, that this joining of relation occurs only in engagement with the other as *autrui*. As one of the voices from his own dialogue in *The Infinite Conversation* asserts, "All alterity presupposes man as *autrui* and not the inverse." This voice then continues:

Only it follows from this that, for me, the Other man who is "autrui" also risks being always Other than man, close to what cannot be close to me: close to death,

*Derrida, "Pas," 196–97.
†See Maurice Blanchot, *Thomas l'obscur* (Paris: Gallimard, 1950), 125; *Thomas the Obscure*, trans. Robert Lamberton (Barrytown, N.Y.: Station Hill Press, 1988), 105.

close to the night, and certainly as repulsive as anything that comes to me from these regions without horizon.

—We well know that when a man dies close to us, however indifferent his existence might be to us, in that instant and forever he is for us the Other.

—But remember: the Other speaks to me; the decisive interruption of relation speaks precisely as infinite relation in the speech of the Other. You are not claiming that when you speak to *autrui*, you are speaking to him as though to a kind of dead person, calling to him from the other side of the partition?

—When I speak to the Other, the speech that relates me to this other "accomplishes" and "measures" that inordinate distance (a distance beyond measure) that is the infinite movement of dying, where dying puts impossibility into play. And in speaking to him, I myself speak rather than die, which means also that I speak in the place where there is a place for dying. (EI 103/72)

The address comes from the other (human being) as the address of the other. *Viens* marks an infinite relation to which the other (human being) gives itself up in giving itself to language. This is "real death," as Blanchot emphasizes in "Literature and the Right to Death"—a "real" dying into language that Blanchot defies us in *The Writing of Disaster* to distinguish from a murder (ED 110–15/65–71). But this death is infinite. The other, in its dying, "knows" the *il y a*, the "absence of being" ("such an absence that everything has forever and for always been lost in it, to the point that the knowledge affirms and dissipates itself there that nothing is what there is, and first of all nothing beyond" [ED 117/72]). This is what they "give" in their dying: "the absence of being under the mortifying gaze of Orpheus" (EI 53/38). This is why Derrida can assert that behind the "thought" to which *Death Sentence* addresses itself, or behind the "word" addressed in *The One Who Did Not Accompany Me*, there is the "thought" of the *il y a*. The presence of others in their infinite dying, in the "infinite" of their dying (and which "I" approach only in forgetting), is the presence of an infinite absence.

Literature happens, we noted at the outset, when its language becomes a question addressed to language itself. We may add now, perhaps, that literature becomes a question *in response*, in fascinated and repeated response to the speaking that occurs as language remarks "that there is . language." That there is language is the *opening* of the question (in response)—the question of Being or difference, we might say now (recognizing how abyssal this question is for Blanchot), but also, and only, as it comes to us from a "real dying" Blanchot persistently assigns to the self (though it is prior to the self) *and* to another. Not the dying of "this woman," but of "she" whom this designation returned to the night. A distinction, I would have to add immediately, that is crucial but ultimately untenable, as Derrida suggests, I believe, when he takes up the question of

citation and repetition in Blanchot's narratives, arguing that writing introduces what he calls an irreducible contamination in the address of the
other.[3] The deconstructive move in literary criticism would be to stress the
contamination to which Derrida refers. Such a move is in no way a falsifi-
cation; indeed, it has been a necessary one both in the context of the politics of criticism and in relation to the matter at hand. But this emphasis on
the "contamination" of writing and its citationality has served to purify
the recitation of contamination by what I am tempted to call a reference,
that is, a relation to the other that opens in the singular event of address.

When we figure this speaking in relation to "Literature and the Right to
Death" and give it a word (*Viens*), we undoubtedly precipitate a movement that will only be made thematically by Blanchot in subsequent texts.
But is not the condition of writing *Viens* (with or without quotation
marks) something like the haunting "real" presence of an other? And can
it be called a new departure when Blanchot draws out the thematics of
autrui in *The Infinite Conversation*, for example (disregarding for the
moment what he offers in his fiction, where the question of *autrui* is
almost always present)? Has he not drawn out something of the relation
already marked in his text?

It is undeniable that a step is made when Blanchot takes up overtly the
problematic of *autrui* in *The Infinite Conversation*. And though I am
hesitant to use the same language in comparing narratives, I am tempted
to say, and will have to demonstrate elsewhere, that a step has been made
between texts such as *Thomas the Obscure* and *Death Sentence* with
regard to the question that has furtively appeared here. But the insistence
of what I am prompted to call the question of *reference* in Blanchot's
thought on literary language marks out the site of the problematic of
autrui. Literature becomes a question, Blanchot seems to suggest, because
a "touch" of some kind has occurred. Literature's origin is the "signifying"
of that touch: the writing of an infinite relation that opens there, the
writing, for example, of *Viens*. Here is one version of its structure (one
that I find particularly useful for approaching *Death Sentence*):

In the room: When he turns back toward the time when he signaled to her, he
senses clearly that he is signaling to her in turning back. And if she comes and if he
grasps her, in an instant of freedom of which he has nothing to say and that for
some time he has marvelously forgotten, he owes to the power of forgetting (and to
the necessity of speech) that grants him this instant the initiative to which her
presence responds.*

Here we have "*pas*," "forgetting," and "*Viens*" unfolding in the space
of writing. It goes without saying that we must not reduce the touch to an

---

*This passage from Blanchot's *L'Attente l'oubli* is cited in Derrida, "Pas," 128.

empirical event. The event *would only have happened* in writing. But it would only have happened had it already happened in a past that is no less "real" for being immemorial. There has been a touch. A text such as *Death Sentence*, I want to suggest, remarks it as the "real" condition of the infinite relation in which it is given and lost. The step Blanchot makes (has always made) draws it out as the touch of *autrui*.

10

On 'Death Sentence'

THE EXIGENCY OF
ANOTHER RELATION

LET me start by sketching out a kind of schema for *Death Sentence*. To begin, it is a narrative in two attempts: the *same* narrative ("I will go on with this story" [A 54/31]) in each of its two parts, though the events implicate the narrative in such a way as to necessitate an interruption and a second approach of an entirely different mode (this second part involving new "facts"). The first attempt is too direct, it seems, even naive in its unguarded approach to what it takes to be a truth that might be disclosed ("I will write freely, sure that this narrative concerns no one but myself" [A 8/2]). A forgivable naïveté, we might say, because this narrative proceeds (supposedly) from documented events.* But if the first attempt proceeds from flawed premises, still it would probably be inappropriate to speak in terms of "failure." For something happens in the narrative, or through it. The narrator is overwhelmed by what lies on the border of his words: "The extraordinary begins at the moment I stop. But I am no longer able to speak of it" (A 53/30).

Let me suggest that what happens in the first attempt at narrative is an event, an event of language, of "saying," that the second attempt will bring to language in the form of what Blanchot describes in *The Infinite Conversation* as the "narrative voice." The first attempt, "failed" as it is, traces — retraces: the narrative has already begun — the circle of the narrative space ("that circle where, in entering, we enter incessantly into the outside"); it marks the threshold.[1] The second *returns* across this threshold, but in such a way as to transmute the narrator's relation to the "origin" of his narrative. We have seen such a circling before, such a move-

---

*"Facts" that become extraordinary only after the extraordinary has overwhelmed the narrator and necessitated a second approach: when the narrator has made his peace with the fatality that prompts him to write and has accepted that the story would be the same regardless of the "facts" — when the death/murder of the first section becomes a necessity, in other words, the *fact* of that death/murder takes on its mysterious force.

ment of bringing a saying to language (even such a transmutation of a writer's relation to language), but the movement in question here is infinitely more complicated, more abyssal. Its vertiginous movement is described, I believe, near the start of the second part, in a scene that takes place on the metro:

Two steps away, there was a great affliction [*malheur*], as silent as a true affliction can be, beyond all help, unknown, and which nothing could cause to appear. And I, who sensed it, was like a traveler walking off to the side along a road; the road has called him and he advances, but the road wants to see if the one who is coming is indeed the one who should be coming; it turns back to see if it recognizes him, and in one somersault they both tumble into the ravine. (A 63/37)

*

A schema, even when it sets a rhythm, is nothing more than a precaution. Let me now try to approach the event of the first part of *Death Sentence*, beginning immediately with the occurrence that is most immediately named by the title: the death and revival of "J."

The narrator has held out for this expected death, and has been held away until its occurrence ("Go away," J. tells him on the telephone from her sickbed in a moment of crisis [A 13/25]), remaining absent even after he is informed that her death is imminent and that his presence is the only thing that could render J.'s relations to the world bearable.[2] Why will he only come when she is on the edge of defeat—only to her *dying*? Is the wait only here—hers as well as his? The narrator is himself puzzled by his absence, which he claims was "responsible" for the events to follow (A 24/12)—as though the space of relation they will occupy is prepared here, as though he commits her to that waiting.

The narrator comes to J.'s apartment only after her death is communicated to him—communicated in words that do not report it after the fact but say it or speak it immediately, *as* it is happening, without even the delay of observation or her own acquiescence to the words—as though she dies *with these words*, which are, of necessity, spoken by another (over the telephone).* The narrator's first response in seeing her (without seeing her—the anonymity of relations around the deathbed obscures his view) is to lament that she had not been able to hold on a bit longer. An astounding response: had he not held out for this defeat? Nevertheless, the distress that grows in the narrator is such that J.'s sister sees in his eyes the imminence of "something she did not have the right to see": something like his exposure before J.'s death, from the space of which will come the infinite movement of his address. Out of this infinite exposure, then, he calls her name—to which she responds, immediately (the communication does not

---

*Derrida comments on this temporality in his rich discussion of *Death Sentence* in "Survivre," collected in his *Parages* (Paris: Galilée, 1986), 165.

follow the temporality of address and response, cause and effect). Her sigh (as though she had indeed been waiting and this is indeed relief) gives way to a look: "At this moment her eyelids were still completely shut. But a second after, perhaps two, they opened abruptly, and they opened upon something terrible of which I will not speak, on the most terrible look a living being can receive, and I believe that if I had shuddered at that instant, and if I had felt fear, everything would have been lost" (A 36/20).

The eyelids "open" upon a look—as though this is not an intentional act, but the exposure of another gaze. It is hard not to rediscover here a scene that Blanchot has described many times in his meditations on the myth of Orpheus and Eurydice. Of course, each of these descriptions is unique, each one bearing on a different dimension of Orpheus's quest, and no explication of the scene at hand by any given instance of commentary would be justified (for it would turn that scene into an illustration).[3] But one reference to the myth seems particularly rich in its implications for this scene in *Death Sentence*, and a textual interruption at this point where identificatory pathos most threatens reading may not be inadventitious. The reference comes in the context of an essay entitled "Reflections on Hell," in *The Infinite Conversation*. Orpheus's look, Blanchot remarks, is the look of death, the killing look that would seize the presence of Eurydice in the absence of her death. But the moment of encounter, he notes, also precedes this encounter. Before the look, already the look, there is Orpheus's song, the movement of speech when "it speaks outside all power to represent or to signify . . . a language that does not push hell back, but makes its way into it, speaking at the level of the abyss and thereby giving word to it" (EI 274/183–84). This speech, Blanchot writes, exposes the naked face of Eurydice (which is the face of absence, of what Blanchot calls the *other* night, but also the face of Eurydice always veiled by the world: Eurydice's face, in other words, *as* dissimulation, the dissimulation of absence). It is a speaking before the look that is already the look, already delivering this "non-transparency that escapes being" (EI 275/184) to the power of being and dispersion,

as though the proximity of absolute power, that of death, were necessary in order to strip, through speech (a certain speech), the clothed figure of living beings— always dressed by the world—in order to lay this figure bare and assure an encounter with it; but also, at the same time, in order to discover that this nakedness is what one encounters but does not seize, it being what slips away from every hold. As though the exercise of absolute power were required, therefore, in order to encounter the limit of this power, no longer solely in its negative form, but as the strange affirmation that escapes being and the negation of being. (EI 275/184)

At this limit, Blanchot writes, the absence of relation becomes, in speech, the experience of the outside. *Between* the violence of the empty night and the violence of the word that renders death possible, *seeming* to suspend them, Orpheus's word delivers Eurydice.

Because his infinite movement proceeds from what is already a relation, not yet relation (or because her waiting is still relation, already no longer relation: she has also called him), the narrator's call and look give J. the possibility of a kind of memory of the generous violence of that exposure. "How long have you been there?" she asks after returning to life. The words are anxious, for a reason the narrator finally interprets as follows: "In asking how long I had been there, it seemed to me that she remembered something, or was close to remembering it; at the same time she felt an apprehension linked to my person [if he has come, she must be dying] or to my tardy arrival, or to the fact that I had seen and surprised what I should not have seen" (A 37/21). The narrator has effectively violated the solitude of her dying. Indeed, he has not simply surprised her at a moment when she is exposed ("defenseless"), he has *exposed* her in her dying. Later, as she passes into a kind of coma from which the narrator feels excluded (she is "attracted," he suspects, "by something terrible but perhaps also seductive, tempting" [A 44/25]), he attempts to reach her once more: "I took J.'s hand gently, by the wrist (she was sleeping), and scarcely had I touched her when she raised up with her eyes open, looked at me furiously and pushed me away saying, 'Never touch me again'" (A 45/25). Does this defense not reflect on the prior "touch"? This episode may be saying at least as much about the narrator's desire (which we must never forget in this sequence) as about the solitude essential to dying. But I suspect it points to the terrible responsibility the narrator has assumed in "touching" J. when he calls her back from her death.

But what is this "responsibility"? The narrator has J.'s life and death on his hands, and it will indeed become his responsibility (though it is shared)* to take her life. But prior to this last act—which may not finish anything: her second death is offered only as a citation of the first (her pulse is said once again to "scatter like sand" [A 52/30], and the phrase appears in quotation marks)—the narrator experiences his responsibility as a situation in which he can *do* nothing. Here, in fact, is the "origin" of the narrative (both sections), on which I want to focus briefly.

After the crisis I have just recounted (where J., from a place close to the one into which she had slipped in dying the first time, tells the narrator not to touch her again), J. recovers—though her present sadness now marks a knowledge—only to return to a sleep in which she is struggling with

---

*The mode of this sharing, as it is phrased, is worth noting, for it is a *common* responsibility that they do not share in common (there is no articulation of their wills): "I was persuaded anew that if she didn't want it and if I didn't want it nothing would ever get the better of her" (A 51/29–30). Will and decision are part of the narrator's central concern throughout the first part. We will see the meaning of these terms transmuted in the second.

"terrible things" and in which he plays "a role that is perhaps terrifying" (A 45/26) — presumably "death," which he would represent for her, or the impossibility of dying (since he is liable to call, or touch her, again). Her face takes on here an extraordinary youth even as it is bathed in tears, but the tears soon dry as she moves from sleep to waking, and her face takes on a severity of aspect that is also reflected in an unfeeling grasp and the jealous words of a struggling ego. Then sleep again. I will cite much of this paragraph:

Around two or three o'clock, I became convinced that the same terrible thing [*malheur*] that had happened the day before was in danger of occurring. It is true that J. was no longer waking. The nurse must have dozed off too. As I listened without pause to her slight breathing, faced by the silence of that night, I felt extremely desperate and miserable just because of the miracle I had brought about. Then, for the first time, I had a thought that came back to me later and in the end won out. As I was still in that state — it must have been about three o'clock — J., without moving at all, woke up, that is to say, she looked at me. That look was very human: I don't mean affectionate or kind, since it was neither; but nor was it cold or marked by the forces of that night. It seemed to understand me profoundly; that is why it appeared friendly to me, though it was at the same time frighteningly sad. "Well," she said, "you've really done it now." She looked at me again without smiling at all, as she might have smiled, as I have since hoped she had, but I think my expression did not invite a smile. Moreover, that look did not last very long. (A 46–47/27)

The narrator is desperate and miserable as they approach the same *malheur* as that of the preceding night. Is it the repetition that oppresses him — his sense that he has delivered her over only to a repetition of the same agony and that he must perhaps repeat his own act of calling her back (and how could he not, without her absolution)? J.'s response to him, which is a response to his distress,* coming first in a look that reveals her sleep to have been a vigil and conveying no more than a "human" understanding, expresses precisely the *impossibility* of their situation — their powerlessness in this interim state between deaths, a survival that can go nowhere beyond itself (for they know that there is no moving beyond this state: no future beyond a possible repetition, or its repetition of itself in this absolute presence). Her *Eh bien, vous en avez fait du joli* is both "You've really done it now" and "So what do we do now?" It is the infinite character of that state that causes the narrator's *malheur*, and it is the knowledge of that infinity that produces (for the first time, here) the "thought" that will return, as the narrator says near the beginning of the second section, "perhaps a thousand, ten thousand times" (A 55/32) be-

*The French, after the phrase concerning the thought, reads as follows: *Comme j'étais toujours dans cet état.* I have translated that *comme* as "as" in order to capture both the temporality evoked and the hint of a logical conjunction.

fore triumphing in the infinite victory over life that is recounted near the
end of *Death Sentence*. I have named this moment the "origin" of the
narrative, because *Death Sentence* is essentially the tale of that triumph,
the transmutation of the narrator's relation to the *affliction* he experiences
here as an oppressive powerlessness in this in-finite, suspended present
(which can only affirm itself in its very powerlessness to become anything
other than itself: more than life, less than life). The tale, in other words, of
the narrator's relation to a *thought* which is nothing other than an experience of an infinite relation — a relation that *opens* in the encounter with J.
but also exceeds infinitely the subjects of that relation.

I am tempted to reiterate that what is extraordinary about these events
is that *they happened* (according to the narrative). To combat the anonymity of this thought (for there is something terrible about this narrative
in its apparent sacrifice of figures for the sake of the *thought* that is affirmed), I would indeed be tempted to insist again that there would be no
cause for this story (but we must carry this back to *causa, chose*) were it
not a story that, according to the narrator, can be documented — the story
of a thought, but of a thought that only opens in an encounter. But is it
possible that J., in her "excessive" youth ("the sickness had made of J. a
child" [A 18/8; cf. 12/4]) and with her face "bathed in tears," *must* have
something of the dead child of whom Blanchot writes in *The Writing of
the Disaster*? That even if this experience allows an astounding transformation of the narrator's relation to life/death, and a version of what I can
only describe as an ethical affirmation, this "child" must die (or live its
death) in *secret* — that her necessarily *anonymous* dying is the saying from
whose avowal *Death Sentence* speaks? Does "J." figure the "impossible
necessary death" that can never come to language because it is the condition of coming to language?

On tue un enfant, "a child is being killed" — the phrase itself, Blanchot
tells us, is the avowal of such a saying.[4] An avowal that mirrors another
that Blanchot comments on in the passage immediately following his evocation of the myth of Orpheus and Eurydice in "Reflections on Hell," and
that will return us to the question of responsibility. It is Kaliaev's phrase
from Camus (*The Rebel*), the words he speaks in describing his inability
to murder the Grand Duke Serge in front of his children: *Je ne peux pas*, "I
cannot." The phrase, Blanchot tells us, says the moment of encounter with
the "face" in which the indestructible character of the human at its limit
point of impossibility (escaping the possible as what is in human power) is
revealed. The phrase is the phrase of death, "death in person," Blanchot
writes, arrested before this extreme impoverishment that exposes the limit
of its power — death recoiling from itself in a moment of suspension or
deferral that marks the very opening of speech, the opening of a site where
it can unfold:

This second [in which the visage is revealed]: here is what remains to us. Here is the *time* of speech, the moment where speech begins, lays bare the visage, says the encounter that is this nakedness and says man as the encounter with the extreme and irreducible limit. . . . *Je ne peux pas* is the secret of language where, outside all power to represent and to signify, speech would come about as what always defers from itself and thus withholds itself as difference. . . . *Je ne peux pas* is the word of *death in person* [my emphasis], an allusion it formulates, in the act of killing, to the evidency of the visage which it runs up against as against its own impossibility, a moment that is death's own drawing back before itself, the *delay* that is the site of speech, and where speech can take place. (EI 279/187)

L'arrêt de mort ("the arrest of death"): an event of speech (the event of language's essence) experienced in an extreme of powerlessness. Blanchot goes on to ask in this passage: "Why the exigency of such a language?" An impossible question, since it concerns the origin (an imperative issuing from the origin to which I will return), but a question to which Blanchot offers what is apparently an answer:

This is a speech, assuredly, of which we are not directly aware and, it must be said again, a speech that is infinitely hazardous, for it is encompassed by terror. Radical violence is its fringe and its halo; it is bound to the obscurity of the night, to the emptiness of the abyss, and so doubtful, so dangerous that this question incessantly returns: Why the exigency of such a language? What have we to do with it? What does it bring us in the frightening silence that announces extreme violence, but that is also the instant at which violence goes silent, becomes silence. What is this communication without community that no power, that is to say, no comprehension, no human or divine presence precedes? Would it not be an attraction without allure, *desire* itself, the desire become song that opens hell to Orpheus, when the absolute of separation *takes on body*, all the while remaining the depth and detour of the interval? (EI 279–80/187)

Death Sentence, I want to suggest, will become the narrative of this desire. Returning from that point where language defaults (after the experience of the extra-ordinary onto which it opens in the *interruption* of its saying),[5] returning, in forgetting, to the impossible that opens there, *Death Sentence* will become the recounting or recitation of that arrested speech (and the infinite relation it marks) in an infinitely repeated "*Viens*."

*

Only a finite self (having finitude for its sole destiny) necessarily comes to recognize, in the other, its responsibility for the infinite. — *The Writing of the Disaster*

Near the end of *Death Sentence*, at a moment marking a kind of denouement, the narrator voices a distress very similar to the one we have just considered from his first attempt at narrative. This is a moment of defeat for the narrator, defeat so thorough that words have finally failed him in his feverish effort to build a verbal scaffolding (a veritable tower of Babel) over the "cold, implacable truth" (A 122/77) of his relations with N.; he *sees* her speaking here but cannot grasp her words, his own ability to speak suspended with his accession to a knowledge from which he has been hiding for over a week, and even much more. N., seeking absolution for the act that links her fate with that of J. (the act that also finally seals the narrator's fate for him: she has had a cast made of her hands and face), attempts to reengage him with a childlike tone and a gesture of the hands "of a marvelous innocence" (A 123/77). The narrator's response is suffering, followed by acceptance: "I think meanness — which remains when everything else is gone — made me shrug my shoulders; but perhaps it's because I was beginning to suffer again. She looked so human, was still so close to me. . . . — 'It was probably necessary,' I murmured" (A 123–24/77–78). The "again" is what is striking here. There has been "suffering" in the preceding pages, to be sure, but the word has not appeared; and the suffering described here is far more reminiscent of the distress the narrator felt in the night after his revival of J. than of the affliction he experiences with N. (which occurs in a presentiment and discovery of disaster). Could this actually be a recollection of the earlier distress or at least a point of contact between the two narratives (marking, if not a continuity of lived experience via memory, at least something like a point of vertical intersection between two cycles infinitely separated by the interruption in the narrative)?

However strong the echo may be, it is impossible to demonstrate that there is an actual reference between narratives here; to the contrary, there is quite a bit of evidence against it. First, and on the most immediate level, it is difficult to get by the impression that the narrator of the second part has effectively *forgotten* the experiences recounted in the first (or since it is the same narrator but a different mode of narrative, that the second narrative forgets the first). Moreover, even if talk of a continuity of experiences is warranted, there is no ground for interpreting the reference of the sentence beyond its immediate context. Thus, even though N. would seem to have forced an (unacknowledged) recollection by repeating the operation carried out on J. shortly before her death, the narrator's suffering is to be read, in this more probable perspective, as recalling not his prior experience of an extreme of powerlessness but rather the affliction that surfaces every time he approaches the truth of his relations with N. (after the event in the theater, for example, or at the moment of discovering the loss of his key, where he experiences "a certainty of misfortune [*malheur*] so great that I could taste the affliction in my mouth and have kept the taste ever since" [A 107/66]).

Even if we recognize that the "truth" of the narrator's relations with N. involve a fatality (and a forgetting) that is indissociable from his experience with J. (for the affliction out of which the narrator writes *both* parts is an experience of that fatality), this very "fatality" is known only in forgetting—*at least* until the lines I have cited from the end. It exceeds lived experience infinitely and suspends any possibility of linking in terms of "memory" the experiences of suffering that appear at the ends of both parts. *Death Sentence recounts forgetting* in the very precise sense of the term Blanchot gives to it in "The Narrative Voice" when he defines narration *as* forgetting and writes, "to recount is to put oneself to the trial of that first forgetting that precedes, founds, and ruins all memory. Recounting, in this sense, is the torment of language, the incessant search for its infinity" (EI 564/385). "Reflections on Hell" refers to "the movement of forgetting: the infinite that opens, closing upon itself with forgetting—on condition that it be received not by the lightness that frees memory from memory but, within remembrance itself, as the relation with what hides and no presence can hold" (EI 288/192),[6] and it is clearly with such a forgetting that the narrator engages when he awakens from his silence and allows himself to be tempted (into writing) by a superb thought that he attempts to bring to its knees. What prompts him to write (and then against which he writes: this strange muse he calls a "thought") is an experience in and of language that transcends any experience of self-affection that could be ordered by memory in something like a traditional narrative.

So while the narrator's experiences with J. and N. are clearly linked in some manner (at the level of the narrative itself), this link involves a suspension of relation that makes the "again" in question fundamentally ambiguous. There remains, however, the fact that *Death Sentence* is also the tale of an *event* by which the narrator's experience of what exceeds experience is transmuted and affirmed. The assumption of affliction in the victorious concluding statement involves a reversal by which forgetting becomes a form of remembrance. "I have loved it [*la pensée*] and loved only it, and everything that has happened, I willed" (A 127/80)—a "yes," the narrator declares, has preceded all of the agonistic relations he recounts in his narrative and is now assumed in a kind of *amor fati*. The condition of the emergence of this "yes"—itself the condition of everything that has occurred, including the catastrophe that releases it—has been the narrator's final surrender ("it was probably necessary") after the moment of distress in which he finally *suffers* the knowledge of fatality. There is no way, once again, to demonstrate that he is remembering at this moment his prior experience of powerlessness. But it is intriguing to note that this passage into a kind of *Gelassenheit* (surrender and the opening to a saying) occurs immediately after N. refers to a document—the sculptor's card — that evokes the events of the first part, and just before the narrator is able to affirm, for the first time, that he has *always* loved and willed the thought with which his writing (in both parts) has engaged. The repetition of suffering (is it a recollection of the "same" suffering then?) works as a hinge that links parts one and two of *Death Sentence* and allows the narrative to turn toward the magnificent conclusion by which the saying that occurs in part one comes to language (infinitely suspended) in the infinitely repeated "*Viens*" (though we will have to ask, whose language?).

The narrator tells us in his concluding declaration that what he has recounted seems to him, the question of dates aside, *vraisemblable* ("probable": an indication that we are dealing with the narrator's understanding of fiction). The facts are unimportant, he says, for in the eternally recurring call of "the all-powerful affirmation that is united with me" (A 126/79) others arrive in their place, and in response to this affirmation they take on the same meaning and the story is the same. The story, it seems, is playing itself out endlessly in the space of the exchange we see released after the narrator's final acquiescence — a space we may now call the space of the narrative.[7] The echo we have been entertaining may indeed point to this sameness and be subsumed by it. But if this echo is in fact a reference from one part to another, a reference *back* by a narrative carried out in a quite self-conscious mode of fictioning (I will return to this point) to one marked by an anxious documentation of the "facts," then we must say that the story is the "same" in a somewhat different and very intriguing sense. The difference between narrative modes effectively collapses at the point where they recount the "same" experience (the same experience of suffering by one who can say, "I began again to suffer"). What would be the status of the recounting (in the time of this "I began again") that remains the same between shifts in narrative approach, and what is the status of the recounted (as it persists in this "ruined" narrative space)? A kind of *experience*, we would have to say, insists in the multifold space of these narratives: in an eternal affirmation where facts and events ceaselessly substitute for one another, a kind of "lived" time persists and makes it possible to speak of something like the "same" story. What is the status of this experience?[8]

I find it difficult to carry this question much farther (and it rests already on very thin grounds — for again, there is no way to demonstrate the reference from one section to another). But I have been unable to resist following it as a kind of heuristic introduction into the second part of *Death Sentence* because it dovetails into what is perhaps the central question of this part — at least the question that most preoccupies the narrator: that of the relation between "thought" and "person," between an infinite desire and its finite repetition. It also relates in this manner to a second concern, one that must especially preoccupy the reader inasmuch as it involves the status of the event of narration. The narrator may well be telling the "same" story, as he asserts in his concluding declaration, but it seems that only the retelling of it, and, in a strange way, the substance of this retelling (a narrative content that seems to run counter to the narrator's efforts in his act of narration), makes this assertion possible. The story *becomes* the same — in the narrator's understanding of the term — as it brings its eternally recurrent affirmation to language. The narrator must know defeat (in relation to what he sets out to do in narrating — that is, bring it to an end and die alone) before he can make his triumphant declaration, and the catastrophic event that produces this defeat is a (recounted) coalescence of thought and person that exceeds the narrator's grasp: the finite repetition, once again, of an infinite desire.

"Desire" is not a word used by the narrator as he begins his second attempt at narrative and describes his undertaking. The word that recurs instead is *malheur*, a *malheur* the narrator feels in his seduction into speech by a thought. But I would suggest, once again, that this "thought" is something like the figure of a relation with the impossible,[9] and that the impossible experienced by the narrator takes precisely the form of "desire," as Blanchot defines the term in "Reflections on Hell." The relations with N. that form the substance of the second part clearly point to this term.

Lines I have already cited from "Reflections on Hell" are pertinent here, but I would add to them a passage that follows Blanchot's remarks on Orpheus and Eurydice and concerns the relation of Tristan and Isolde, specifically, that "relation without relation" that persists in forgetting after the lovers separate and return to their respective worlds:

When the absolute of separation has become relation, it is no longer possible to be separated. When desire has been awakened through impossibility and through night, desire can well come to an end and the empty heart turn away from it; in the void and in this end, in this surfeited passion, it is the infinite of the night itself that continues to desire itself, a neutral desire that takes neither you nor I into account, that appears therefore like a mystery wherein the happiness of private relations founders, *a failure [échec] that is nevertheless more necessary and more precious than all triumphs if it holds hidden and reserved in it the exigency of another relation.* (EI 287/192, my emphasis)

"Desire" is relation with "what does not concern," as Blanchot writes in the dialogue that opens *The Infinite Conversation.* Or, to put this in a way that accords more strictly with Blanchot's most frequent usage, it *is* what does not concern, or "the supreme relation that suffices to itself," as Thomas puts it in his erotic transports of the penultimate chapter of *Thomas the Obscure*.* It is a neutral, infinite relation that needs no terms in its self-relation but nevertheless forms the exigency of "another relation" (the relation, I would suggest, assumed by the narrator at the end of *Death Sentence* after his "failure": "more necessary and more precious than all triumphs"). As an infinite self-sufficiency and as an exigency, it has its source in what Heidegger terms *Brauch* (drawn out here, as always in Blanchot, by the hand that writes).

The narrator, once again, speaks of *malheur* rather than desire in the second part, and specifically of a *malheur* that opens as he begins to speak.[10] His aim in writing, it seems, is to end this affliction, though writing simply redoubles it: "Who makes it so that now, each time my tomb opens, I awaken there a thought strong enough to make me live again? The very derisive laughter of my death. But know this: where I am entering, there is neither work, nor wisdom, nor desire, nor struggle; where I am going, no one enters. That is the meaning of the last combat" (A 86/52–53). A thought appears each time he approaches his death (in writing) in an effort to put an end to the events that have gripped him and from which he seeks to free himself. His aim is to die (finally) and to die alone, as he reiterates in his very last statement (removed in the second edition [p. 81 in the English]). Or we might say that his desire is to be one with himself in his dying (to bury himself in the manner of Thomas). But every act of speech reawakens the thought and makes his solitude reecho. His response, we learn at the outset of this second part, is a kind of loyal struggle with this thought, loyal in that it involves no ruse, just the "precaution" of fiction.[11] "Safe narration," we might say, but it is not without its risks. For when the narrator casts about for his story, it does not take him long to return to the affliction that haunts him and that now presents itself in the form of engagement with another. *Malheur*, as it initially appears, is linked to a "solitude" known in writing (or "speaking"), but it is an "impossible" solitude, always haunted by a thought. Its cause or object, here, seems to be the infinite that opens in the relation with another, and hence desire. These threads begin to come together (*malheur* in losing silence, *malheur* in engagement) in the lines I have already cited concerning the *malheur* the narrator recognizes on the metro.

"It doesn't matter, I decided to follow that path," the narrator says after commenting obliquely on what it means to "lose silence." The path, it seems, is narration, and it begins, in this second part, with a fairly distracted account of the narrator's relations with a young woman who is his

---

*Maurice Blanchot, *Thomas l'obscur* (Paris: Gallimard, 1950), 124; *Thomas the Obscure*, trans. Robert Lamberton (Barrytown, N.Y.: Station Hill Press, 1988), 105.

neighbor in a hotel on the *rue d'O.** Of her background information, he notes, "perhaps this was a novel [*roman*]" (A 59/34). What he will recount, perhaps, is *not* a novel; these notes are meant only to get him going. The narrative then begins to take as he recalls a mistaken entry into her room and an unpleasant moment where she shows him a scar on her hand with an air of morality (weak echoes of his relations with both J. and N.). Its movement starts fully with another form of recollection — "I just thought of her" — and then a vision: "Now I see this scene."[12] These states of recollection (or "vision") are a kind of *engagement* of the event of narration whose essential story (now) is the relationship with N. and whose opening is announced with the scene on the metro from which I cited at the outset of this chapter:

This scene appears to be now. I was in the metro. I think I was on my way home. By chance, I found myself sitting across from someone I knew. She told me she was married or was going to be married. After one or two stops, she got off. This encounter made me think of my neighbor C[olette]. In that moment I had the extraordinary impression that I had completely forgotten this woman whom I saw almost every day. (A 62/36–37)

The narrator further reflects on this forgetting and then continues:

This ride on the metro left me with the memory of a great sadness. This sadness had nothing to do with my short memory. But something profoundly sad was happening there in that car, with all that noonday crowd. Two steps away, there was a great affliction [*malheur*], as silent as a true affliction can be, beyond all help, unknown, and which nothing could cause to appear. And I, who sensed it, was like a traveler walking off to the side along a road; the road has called him and he advances, but the road wants to see if the one who is coming is indeed the one who should be coming; it turns back to see if it recognizes him, and in one somersault they both tumble into the ravine. (A 63/37)

   The fact that this scene occurs in the metro (in a means of transport) may perhaps link the *malheur* to which he refers here with the *malheur* that attends the loss of silence ("It doesn't matter, I decided to follow that path"). But of course, there will be another metro scene where the narrator himself invites a relation like marriage, and the invisible and silent *malheur* that announces itself here may be doing so in a time of anticipation (for the "tragedy" is close to beginning, and he is close at this point to knowing everything that will be "necessary"). But in the immediate con-

---

*We will see that what he is narrating here is how he came to lose silence. A new form of narration is engaged in this second part, a far more self-conscious form, but this is not the beginning of "writing" (which of course has already occurred — he has recently written the first part). I will try to suggest that the writing of both parts begins at a moment the narrator is only now approaching in his account of these "events."

text of his account, the *malheur* appears related as yet only to the announced marriage of another and the way this fact calls to his mind his forgetting of C. *Malheur* seems to have to do with a form of relation (that despite everything, he appears to have known with C.),* a relation that is betrayed by the kind of marriage S. is entering. As he says of this marriage later, "I had had a foreboding that an invisible betrayal was about to take place, one of those rending acts of which no one knows anything, that begin in obscurity and end in silence, and against which the unrecognized affliction has no weapon" (A 76/46).

Affliction, to repeat, is betrayed by marriage — at least that marriage for which the narrator shows "little regard" and that helps individuals to forget precisely the impossible of human relation. N., whose uninvited entry into his hotel room occurs immediately after the scene on the metro (as though the recollection of this scene marks a threshold of sorts), is also considering marriage, as we later learn when the narrator tries to explain how insignificant the circumstances of this entry were. But her entry into the room marks her choice of the opposite path and her entry into the space of desire.[13]

I will not review the excessive circumstances of this first visit by which N. enters the trap constituted by this space† and experiences the "irremediable" (literally, "what cannot be cured": there are several echoes of J. in this passage — N. is like a "statue" in her fear; she also seems drawn by a light, much as J. was in her deathbed — but the reference to sickness is surely most significant). I will note only how the narrative doubles or splits in such a way as to involve the present of narration and, apparently, the "real" circumstances of narration.

There are many things I could say about the impression I had, but that impression is the one I have now as I look at that same person, from behind, *arrested a few steps* from the window and just before the table; it is about the same hour, she has come in and *she is advancing* (the room is different). To see her in this way, now when she is no longer a surprise, I am seized in a much greater way. I experience a feeling of dizziness and confusion that I never had then, but also something cold, a strange tightening of the heart, to the point that I would like to beg her to go back and to remain behind the door, so that I too might leave. But such is the rule, and

---

*From the distance, even the lack of respect, he shows vis-à-vis C., one might conclude that he does not experience with her the kind of "affliction" he knows with N. But as the narrative proceeds, the meaning of "forgetting" changes (he will say of N. roughly what he says of C.), and the despair he knows the morning after hearing (with indifference) her "perpetual chagrin" bears all the traits of the infinite he names *malheur*.

†"I once saw a squirrel get caught in a cage hung from a tree" (A 65/38) — one of the great figures of the trap that Blanchot elsewhere describes in relation to the space of fascination and especially in relation to the act of reading. See, for example, Chapter 4 of *Thomas the Obscure*.

one cannot free oneself of it: as soon as the thought has arisen, it must be followed to the very end. (A 66/39; my emphasis)

Clearly, this present, however actual, however arresting, does not constitute a "present reality" — its space no less subject to torsion than is the space of the first encounter (I have italicized the most salient signs of this: the person arrested before the writing table is advancing in that strange time of narration that is marked by Blanchot's *pas*). The narrator would appear to be describing, in fact, one of those "thousand, ten thousand times" where the thought has risen in the space of narration, a space of unending repetition. The narrator may well be describing the "real" context of his writing, but this "real" is infinitely suspended in the time of narration.

I retain the word "time," however, even though any relation to the present of consciousness is suspended in this space. For at this point in the narrative/narration (I will try to distinguish these indissociable levels further in a moment — here, I am referring to the time of the act of narration), the narrator is still *suffering* the fatality that has presumably opened after the account of his experience with J., a fatality he knows as an implacable law. (Transgression has given way, it seems, to the emergence of a law that he feels obliged to serve.) He tells us clearly that at this point *he would like to leave the room*. However, the concluding declaration will manifest the opposite inclination: not flight, but invitation and affirmation. The time of narration to which I have referred includes the time of this reversal (though it is a reversal that may be happening, as we will see, in an endless repetition, and we will have to ask *who* accedes to that final affirmation).

In the time of the "narrated," we also observe at this point a kind of service to a law. The narrator seems to consider it his role to guard his room and the "spirit of terror" that lives there (what at this point in the narrated events of the second part has not yet emerged as a "thought"). There is apparently no prohibition against entry in N.'s case; but flight, where it represents a refusal to submit, is intolerable. The narrator will invite N. back to the room after his sickness, and she will know the same "irremediable." But he will regret that invitation (made most liberally, it seems, in his answer to her question "Do you know other women?") and close the room to her. When she subsequently invites him to move in with her, he grows suspicious of her invitation. The relation to the room is one of a jealous guard (and we might note that a certain jealousy will never disappear from the narrator's relation to this space) — presumably all of the agonistics of his relation to others derive from this jealousy.

What is he guarding? The narrator will call it his "life." We might more easily call it his death, though its most distinguishing characteristic is its *earthly* nature.[14] When N. seeks to flee the first time, she releases a "furious force" that he compares to an earthquake and a tempest — images that are recalled again in the catastrophe in the metro (A 99/61) and in his approach to the room after this event. Mounting the stairs, he says, "a kind of strange draft descended toward me, a cold odor of earth and stone that I knew perfectly because in this room, it was my life itself" (A 106/66; elsewhere, he asserts that he spends his nights in an "open tomb" [A 91/56]). What he is guarding here, it seems (if we follow the motif of the earth), is that life that is properly called neither life nor death, as we saw when those terms grew interchangeable past the threshold described in "Literature and the Right to Death." It is the place of a self proximity (in dying) that is also, irreducibly, a place of exposure (and this is the narrator's problem). It is the site of a touch.

The narrator vows after N.'s second visit (after his sickness) that he will never open his room to the outside. This is a statement that comes after his declaration that no one goes where he is going (a declaration of his intention to die alone) and immediately after he describes his relation with the thought that lives there with him: his thought, but other than him,[15] and appearing here *for the first time* in the second part. The latter point bears emphasis. Though the thought has appeared in the time of narration ("as soon as . . ."), it manifests itself in the time of events narrated only during this second, "fatal" visit of N. — first in his frank and loyal response to N.[16] and then "manifestly" in the armchair. N.'s visit, which has been marked by a major indiscretion and too free a response on the part of the narrator ("Do you know other women?" — "Yes, of course"), has represented a "violation" of the room and has awakened the thought that he will now try to "bring to its knees" as he closes the room and begins to write — or at least "loses his silence."

We have here, in other words, the onset of the narration (in the time of the narrated). The narrator tells us that after the experiences of the night of N.'s second visit (after the "accident" that overcomes N.), he changes. "It was a grave misfortune [*ce fut un malheur*]," he says; "I spoke of this earlier" (A 90/55). Would the *malheur* to which he refers here not be that *malheur* to which he refers in speaking of being "tempted" by the thought and beginning to speak? The emergence of the thought to which he awakens (not sleeping that fatal night) represents the emergence of an immemorial past. He knows it as a repetition that he wants to put an end to and that he will attempt to end by embarking on the narrative of the first part. We have followed the "failure" of this attempt and the emergence of the thought that now, after this first attempt, attends his writing (hence the redoubling we have seen). What writing would put an end to, it draws out, obliging him to live again when his aim is only to die (and it should be noted that he is sick and "at death" when the events of N.'s second visit unfold). Once again, it would appear that when the narrator closes the room after N.'s visit, he begins the narrative of what has brought him to writing. Everything we have read is written from this point: from the narrator's knowledge, after the violation of his solitude, that it is starting over. Needless to say, this interpretation of the narrator's remark *ce fut un malheur* introduces a singular fold into the narrative, for it implies that now, in the time of the narrated, *he is writing*, and that what we read after this point is a narration of what (also) happened with the onset of narration (and of course, what happened has also always been happening in what we have read). Are there traces of the fold? There are perhaps two: the narrator "loses his silence," and the tragedy begins.

The narrator's description of "losing silence" is so obscure and playful that I can hardly pretend to capture its meaning with the following observation (and as I have suggested, it is almost certain he is also referring to "writing"). But I would note that the narrator becomes singularly voluble after the "engagement" that occurs after the exchange in the room (he speaks of "getting involved," *en me liant* . . . [A 90/55], with Nathalie immediately after recounting this exchange). Or rather, he begins the (deluded) construction of relations that will eventually shatter in the metro (in what can itself only be described as a kind of linguistic event—an *excessive* volubility) and in the hours afterward, only to be reconstructed in a no less deluded verbal scaffolding during the week following the "consummation" of the engagement in the room after the event in the metro. After the fatal events of N.'s second visit when he closes the room, the narrator seems to enter a space of fiction, attempting, until the scene on the metro, to construct a relation with N. that is of the day, and attempting, after the night in the room, to contain her with his words, preserving a "natural life" (A 115/72). But his fictioning is also always doubled by a movement toward his truth (and the defeat of his narrative endeavor: to end it and to die alone). The most dramatic violation of the room will occur well after the night when he decides to close it indefinitely. But the decision only marks the fact that it has already been violated, and the movement of the narration will now be toward an event in the room (for which N. has stolen the key and in which she is waiting) that "had already happened long ago, or for so long had been so imminent that not having brought it into full daylight, even though I experienced it in my existence of every night, was the sign of my secret accord with this premonition" (A 107/67; this is the first sign of the narrator's "yes"—a "yes" that was already latent in the answer to the question "Do you know other women?"—"Yes, of course"). The presentiment is there as soon as he sees N. at grips with the irremediable. To touch her at this point, he says, would be "against the law" (the law, it seems, comes with the thought), and he looks on as though he is watching a tragedy (under glass).[17] "But it seems to me," he continues, "that I had reason to fear something horrible: in one moment, that horror was almost there. The needle is advancing, I thought after her departure" (A 87/53). *Incipit tragoedia.*

What is this horror? The narrator approaches it slowly, but after about ten pages, he gives us a clue as to the nature of what he dreads: it is the union of N. and the thought. After a kind of infidelity ("without excuse, but not without pretext") and a broken engagement, he sees her at the theater to which his work has taken him:

At the theatre, during the intermission, she was there, accompanied by a young man I did not know. She seemed very beautiful to me. I saw her passing in front of me, coming and going in a place that was very near yet infinitely separated and as though behind a window. This idea struck me. No doubt I could have talked to her, but I didn't want to, and maybe I actually was not able to. She maintained herself in my presence with the freedom of a thought; she was in this world, but in this world I was only encountering her because she was my thought; and what connivance was being established between them, what horrifying complicity. I must add that she looked at me like someone who recognized me perfectly well and even regarded me in a friendly way, but it was a recognition from behind the eyes, without a look and without a sign, a recognition of thought, friendly, cold, and dead. (A 97–98/60)

This union of thought and person is the disaster that exposes the narrator (in that life/death that is his most intimate being) to encounter with N. and eventually to a *sharing* of the fatality that joins them.

The narrator has "almost nothing more to learn" (A 98/60), but his approach to the "inevitable" is still guarded: almost as much a flight as it is an approach. The scene of proposal that follows the incident in the theater is so multifold in this manner that it defies any account. The narrator plays at a proposal of marriage — "which proved how fictitious my words were, given my aversion to marriage (and my little esteem for it)" (A 100/62) — that nevertheless occurs *in her language* ("but I married her in her language" [A 100/62]), yet whose acceptance is infinitely suspended by N.'s refusal to allow the narrator to translate, a refusal that stems from a fear that he might just hit upon the *correct* translation. N., a professional translator, does not want to translate the engagement, attempting to preserve, it seems, the "novelty without precedent" (A 102/63) of the words that speak in him via her language (if they can be translated, as Derrida observes, their novelty is not absolute) and the "absolute" of her response, which may be affirmative or negative (because it is surely not "marriage" in any traditional sense that she is agreeing to in her acceptance or rejection).* But the narrator's commitment to the truth of his proposal is not without its complications:

The more they were excessive, I mean alien to what might have been expected of me, the more they seemed true to me because of this novelty without previous example; the more I desired, since they could not be believed, to give them credit, even in my eyes, especially in my eyes, putting all my strength into going farther and farther and building, on what might have been a rather narrow foundation, a pyramid so dizzying that its ever growing height dumbfounded even me. Still, I can put this down in writing: this was true, there cannot be illusion in such great excesses. My error in this state, an error in which I see best its character as a temptation, was much more a result of the distance from her I imagined I was preserving through these completely fictive means of approaching her. (A 102/63)

Are the narrator's indirections "precautions," like those in which this entire second attempt at narrative unfolds? He will go on to say here that his frenetic attempt to make his words true characterizes all his efforts of the next week — all of them efforts to escape the "truth" of this engagement, which has a "more terrible origin" (the union of thought and person). Yet the envelope of falsity, like the envelope of this narrative, perhaps, shelters a movement of approach: the more he approaches, the more he must take a distance, but the movement of *Entfernung* — as always in Blanchot — entails a passage. Under the cover of falsity and avoidance (in a foreign language, then in his own, spoken as though it were a foreign language, but all the more immediate for its redoubled strangeness), and in a movement by which an *excess* of (false) engagement converts into a violent passion beyond what he can know — beyond all the second thoughts and inhibiting or complicating folds of self-awareness† — the narrator traverses the distance he has figured thus far with the image of the glass. Here again, the *crime*, which seems almost the immediate consequence of the apparently incestuous union of thought and person, takes on a *physical* character. His language converts from a medium to a force:

No doubt I went extremely far the day of the shelter [a wonderful phrase pointing to the thematics of *alētheia* and *éloignement*]. It seems to me that I was driven by something furious, a truth so violent that I suddenly broke apart all the frail supports of that language and began speaking French, using insane words that I

---

*Affirmative or negative, this is in all probability an "affirmation" — the voicing of that affirmation to which the narrator refers in his concluding words: "at the call of the all-powerful affirmation that is united with me" (A 126/79).

†The narrator returns repeatedly to this theme, contrasting his own heightened self-awareness (cf. A 85–86/52) with the truth of N.'s answer to the question as to why she came to his room: "I've forgotten." One could perhaps say that the whole narrative is unfolding at various levels of distance from that truth: for the narrator, the "truth" of his relation to the impossible.

had never dreamt of using before and that fell on her with all the power of their madness. Hardly had they touched her when I was physically aware that something broke. At the same instant, she was swept away from me, borne off by the crowd, and as it hurled me far away, the unchained spirit of that crowd struck me, battered me, as if my crime, turned into a mob, was determined to separate us forever. (A 103/64)

The proposal of marriage translates the horrible union of thought and person into a physical act that seems to release the possibility of entering the room (though it will take the narrator at least eight hours to recover his composure and achieve the "clairvoyance" that leads him back to her: "Now it is time to do what must be done," he says, setting out on a path that is still almost comically indirect). The approach once again passes by way of his awareness of the "life" that is in the room in which she is waiting; beyond the glass and in the unbreathable air (cf. A 57/33) lies a relation to something of the "earth."

"Where I am entering, no one enters" (A 36/53) the narrator declared. Where he goes now, there is supposed to be no one:

I knew everything about this room, plunged as it was into the greatest night; I had penetrated it, I carried it in me, I made it live, with a life that is not life, but stronger than it and that no force in the world could vanquish. This room does not breathe, there is neither shadow nor memory in it, neither dream nor depth; I listen to it and no one speaks; I look at it and no one inhabits it. Yet the greatest life is there, a life that I touch and that touches me, absolutely similar to others, which presses my body with its body, marks my mouth with its mouth, whose eyes open, the most living, the most profound eyes in the world, and that see me. May the person who does not understand that come and die. (A 107–8/67)

As readers of Blanchot, we are perhaps all destined to this room (we would not be reading otherwise). For the narrator himself, it is already occupied. The space in which he wanted to bury himself alone (alone with the obscure double with which he lives: himself, in his dying) is already shared. But writing, as we will learn (and what is this room other than the "there" of writing — the there of his existence?), has always already been an assent to this encounter, an affirmative abandon to the fatality it holds.[18]

The complexity of this passage, again, calls for a line-by-line commentary, but I will focus simply on its stages. It is an approach, again, to a thought, and via this thought to a person, the thought subsisting as a kind of opening to the other through an infinite distance. The narrator first knows a frightening darkness (the other night) and the exigency of this darkness ("It is frightening because there is something in it that scorns man and that man cannot endure without losing himself. But he must lose himself; and he who resists will founder, and he who goes forward will become this very darkness: this cold, dead and scornful thing at the heart of which the infinite resides" [A 108/67]). The narrator had lived in "the proud intimacy of terror," and terror is still his emotion, but in his surrender to this inevitable, he now gradually allows the thought to emerge:

A great deal of patience is required if the thought, when it has been driven down to the depths of the horrible, is to rise little by little and recognize us and look at us. But I, I still feared this look. . . . All of a sudden, the certainty that someone was there who was searching for me was so strong that I drew back from it, knocked violently against the bed, and immediately, three or four steps from me, I saw it distinctly, that dead and empty flame of her eyes. I had to stare at her, with all my strength, and she stared at me, but in a strange way, as if I had been in back of myself, and infinitely far back. Perhaps that went on for a very long time, even though my impression is that hardly had she found me before I lost her. (A 109/68)[19]

Orpheus, we might say, receiving Eurydice's look — a scene that Blanchot now pursues further, pursuing also thereby the look that he had exchanged with J. As in the moments following the revival of J., the narrator does everything he can to retain the opening and not allow the fear of this moment to convert into violence. In extreme calm (this, once again, the place of the *arrest*), he approaches what he now calls "this solitary night" bending down on his knees in order "not to be too large," and reaching toward her hand. J. had refused such a touch when the narrator attempted it in distress after her revival, but here the touch is successful, occurring in a space at an infinite distance from the narrator's consciousness (a distance that expresses all the precariousness of a relation traversing the impossibility of relation: an impossible relation between consciousness and what is beyond experience and the capacity to say "I"):

All this was taking place at an infinite distance, my own hand on this cold body seemed so far away from me, I saw myself to such a degree separated from it and pushed back by it into something desperate which was life, that all my hope seemed to me to be in the infinite, in that cold world where my hand rested on this body and loved it, and where this body, in its night of stone, welcomed, recognized, and loved that hand. (A 111/69)

There is the touch, the limit of this narrative (where finite and infinite meet and dissolve), to which the narrator will return after recounting the call by which he attempts to draw her back — a call in which there is still relation (he will receive the look once again), but already loss, since he is calling her to life (what "rises up in him" is part of this movement, and when he proposes to breath onto her face [warmth?, life?] he loses her). The touch, he tells us in returning to it, is not a contact between surfaces but an entry into the *cold* of the body, a penetrating, enveloping cold. "One must follow it," he says (an *il faut* rings throughout this passage), and with it enter a "thickness without limit, an empty and unreal profundity where there is no possible return to an exterior contact." "Death" (or desire), we might say now, but he continues: "That is what makes it so bitter. It seems to have the cruelty of something that gnaws at you, that seizes you and draws you, and indeed it does seize you; but that is also its secret, and he who has enough sympathy to abandon himself to this coldness rediscovers in it the kindness, the tenderness and the freedom of a true life" (A 112/70).

As we saw with Blanchot's description of desire, passage into this infinite space that has grown thick with cold, space that has "taken on body" ("Would it not be, alluring without attraction, *desire* itself? . . . when what *takes on body* is the absolute of separation, all the while remaining the depth and detour of interval?" [EI 280/187, cf. also 67–68/47]), opens onto "another measure," a "true life." But "life" here must not be confused with the life of consciousness and desire (in the sense of an appropriative movement); it is not the life the narrator experiences in his distance from the touch ("I saw myself . . . repelled by it into something desperate that was life"), the life that raises up in him when he wants to breath onto N.'s face, or the life into which he tries to escape in the days following their "consummation" of the engagement ("a natural life," or an impetus that he summarizes when he says, "I wanted above all to retain this name Nathalie" [A 115/72]). "True life" *excludes* life, and names something other than life, beyond life: a death mask is its most living token (or the narrative itself).

A veering in the narration signals this point. The touch, it seems, constitutes again a kind of threshold, a limit that is marked by the *Viens* that follows it and that recites and liberates the *Viens* that has opened the space of this encounter. As the narrative folds back upon the touch after the account of the narrator's *Viens*, the narration redoubles in such a way as to engage the act of narration: the hand that touches is also the hand that is writing. Before the lines I cited above, the narrator intervenes quite demonstratively:

I would like to say that the cold of these bodies is something very strange: in itself, it is not so great. If I touch a hand, as I am doing now [*maintenant*], if my hand lies under this hand, this hand is not as icy as mine; but this little bit of cold is profound, it is not a slight radiation from a surface, but penetrates, envelops, one must follow it and with it enter an unlimited thickness, an empty and unreal depth where there is no possible return to contact with the outside. (A 112/70)

Main-tenant. How do we understand this conjoining "now"? Is the narrator offering us a demonstration, or is he suggesting (as seems probable if we recall the first redoubling of this kind in the scene where N. first enters his room) that the hand that is writing, *maintenant*, is touching, is even joining hands — that writing has become a touching? The struggle with the thought, we might say, has ended in bed (like the struggle with literature Blanchot describes in "Literature and the Right to Death" via Kafka).

But the redoubling in narration is also accompanied by a kind of ironic turn — though "irony" is probably not the right term here inasmuch as the narrator is in some sense also losing his grip in this touch. How seriously can we take the reference to a "true life" in light of the words that immediately follow it?

It must be said, because it would certainly be useless to shrink from it now: the coldness of a hand, the coldness of a body is nothing, and even if the lips draw near it, the bitterness of that cold mouth is only frightening to someone who can be neither more bitter nor more cold, but there is another barrier which separates us: that of the lifeless material on a silent body, these clothes which must be acknowledged and which clothe nothing, steeped in insensitivity, with their cadaverous folds and their metallic inertness. This is the obstacle which must be overcome. (A 112–13/70)

Blanchot's humor is never far off, even in the most solemn moments — for reasons that have to do with the very essence of the narrative act (which has reached its limits in the touch). The instability that marks the description of the consummation of the narrator's engagement with N. (and the engagement with the thought that occurs in what I have called the present of narration) is another version of the plus/minus that attends every narrative moment. It is extreme here, or beginning to grow extreme, because a threshold has been crossed. "There's no going back," he remarks, but there is also no going forward for the narrator, at least not immediately. The narrator will now recount his inability to assume the fatal conjunction of thought and person (in the manner of a true life), and the narrative itself will grow more and more tenuous, even failing to hold with the interruption of a markedly unstable narrative voice.

The narrator is not prepared to assume the loss to which he refused himself at the beginning of this passage ("but he must lose himself," and, at the beginning of the second attempt at narrative, "It would demand of me what a man cannot concede" [A 56/32]). The week he recounts that follows the encounter we have been reading will consist of a constant flight from the surrender to which he is called by N.'s absence and strangeness (A 103/63 and 115/72), a reserve he interprets as "feverish" in relation to his "limitless impatience" in building a "common time" (A 115/72) and space (A 116–17/73) with meaningless words. Yet the falsity of his excesses envelops a truth of which he is also aware (driving him, in fact, to ever greater extremes doubled with a kind of hysterical knowledge of their precariousness): "All this may seem childish. No matter. This childishness was powerful enough to prolong an illusion that had already been lost and to force to be there what was no longer there. It seems to me that in this chatter there was the gravity of a single and unique word, the reminiscence of that 'Come' that I had said to her, and she had come, and she would never be able to go away again" (A 117/73).

What is no longer there? What has *ever* been there with N. (this person "less than someone") that has not been the product of the narrator's guardedness and his fictive approach, "these entirely fictive means of approaching her"? There has never been a relation with N. that has not been marked by the "terrible origin of her absence": the fatality of their relations, or quite simply, "desire." The acceptance of this fatality means total defeat: the destruction of any relation to the "world" (as exemplified by the narrator's involvement in the "intimate affair" recounted in the last pages), the destruction of any "living" impetus, including "hope," and finally the destruction of any ruse, precaution, or even fiction ("and besides, all these circumstances and my interpretations of them are only a way for me to remain a little longer in the realm of things which can be recounted and lived" [A 118/74]). Whatever else N.'s gesture of having a mold taken of her hands and face might signify (and I can hardly pretend to exhaust this mystery), it marks the assumption of a relation that eternally suspends any shared "life."[20] If there is a sharing—and I have suggested that I believe there is something like a sharing, a *partage*: in a sense of this term that involves *division*—it is the sharing of a kind of death, or perhaps better, "another relation" that is neither death nor life, and to which each gives the other access from out of the fatality between them. What can be seen in the cast, he says (prompted by the superb power in her to which he has lent his voice), is "alive for all eternity, for yours and for mine" (A 125/79). It is not until the narrator can surrender to this relation that transcends his person and that of N.—a relation that opens upon *nothing beyond*—that he can accede to what he will claim to have always affirmed. He must effectively *lose* "Nathalie's name" in order to gain access with her to that relation that forever seals their relations.

I would not want to temper in any way the import of the imperative to which the narrator accedes and eventually cedes, acceding in this way to "another measure." This magnificent transmutation of the relation to life and death represents a kind of "telos" in Blanchot's fiction that I can do no more here than indicate.* But in approaching this horizon, we must still ask: who gains access to this "true life" if it indeed represents such a defeat, such a loss of anything to which we might attach the name of life

*Though I would not hesitate to call it ethical. We find it echoing, I believe, in the narrator's opening words in *The Madness of the Day*: "I see the world, an extraordinary happiness. I see it, this day outside which there is nothing. Who could take this away from me? And when this day is effaced, I will be effaced along with it, a thought, a certainty that transports me" (Maurice Blanchot, *Madness of the Day*, trans. Lydia Davis [Barrytown, N.Y.: Station Hill Press, 1981], 6).

(or simply the name). "True life" is relation with a thought that effectively submerges the person in its infinite exigency. The word of that relation is *Viens*, as the narrator tells us in his concluding declaration. It is *his* word, but his word in response to the word of that thought that he will claim to love, a word that is something like the opening of language itself, its "origin." Even if it is still possible to speak of a "he" after the defeat he recounts, the question remains, *who* can affirm (what subject, what kind of subject) that in every relation his or her only relation has been with this origin. *Who* can bring that affirmation to language if it is an affirmation of something like the "inhuman" condition of the touch we have witnessed?

The strangeness of the narrator's voice, a strangeness that *is* (in part) the narrative voice, begins to emerge as the narrator breaks into his narrative a second time to anticipate the defeat he is recounting and the triumph that will emerge from it. Having noted his inability to dwell with N.'s absence in his feverish effort to perpetuate what has been lost (an effort that he claims is "true," in some sense unavoidable: "pushed by such a movement and such an affection that I did not have the time to feel anything other than the truth of this movement and the force of this affection" [A 115/72]), he claims he is certain N. was attached to him, then *sublates* that assertion (in a movement marked by a distinctively Blanchotian distance):

Besides, and this is certain, she was extremely attached to me and was becoming more so every day; but the word attachment, of what does it speak? And the word passion: what is its meaning? And the word delirium. Who knows the greatest sentiment? I alone, and I know that it is the most glacial of all, for it has triumphed over an immense defeat, and it is even now triumphing over it, and at each instant and always, so that time no longer exists for it. (A 115–16/72)

Any account of the movement here would belie it, but I would suggest that we witness something like a passage from delirium to delirium — from the account of a desperate construction, written in a kind of memory (for the narrator's qualification, "*en outre*," "besides," seems to salvage something from the false movement he is describing, almost as though he is justifying himself), via a collapse of that construction at the moment the narrator makes his qualification (for the word "attachment" strikes him as almost meaningless in remembrance of the truth with which he has engaged, even in the prior delirium), to a no less delirious assertion that effectively effaces N., or *definitively* effaces her. It is as though the narrator's sense of the impossibility of the construction (pushing it to ever greater extremes) communicates, as a delirious knowledge of defeat, with the "madness of victory" that the narrator will share with N., the one veering into the other, infecting the other. But I would insist that the "madness" at this point is truly delirium — for the narrator begins to speak like a "shadow" who *alone* knows the truth that lurks in the heart, and the heart's greatest sentiment. Is this a momentary defense on the part of the narrator himself (in the present of narration) as he replays his surrender in these last pages, or does the murderous jealousy (marked in his elision of N. — his inability to bring her to the narration now complete) communicate something of the "inhuman" character of the voice that speaks also in the last declaration? Is it superseded by the last declaration (the scene of defeat, the acquiescence from which we started, will follow, and the last declaration must be seen as issuing from it), or does it reflect immediately in that declaration, marking it with a sonorous reflection that undermines the generosity and abandon of its engagement and reveals something of its "true" character?

What the narrator says here will in fact reecho in the concluding declaration, no less than will the insistence of the "I." He will speak there of a voice in him that is always "reborn," a "jealous voice" that is of a sentiment "incapable of dying."* These echoes, I would suggest, are indelible — however much the sweep of the released voice seems to carry the narrator beyond his earlier guard. However admirable this declaration might be in its abandon, in other words (and I say this unqualifiedly, reminded also of Derrida's response to it), it is marked by an irrevocable strangeness. The earlier interruption continues to echo here. Moreover, and more fundamentally: even if we allow that the echoes of the earlier interruption are effectively effaced by the passage through suffering and defeat and then the movement that ensues, we cannot ignore the strangeness of what is said. For even if this is a voice of acquiescence and an assumption of the engagement that has always been (the condition of the narrative that has been recounted: requiring the tale for its emergence and affirmation), the engagement in question remains inextricably an engagement *in* language and even *with* language, thus infinitely suspending any relation to lived experience. The narrator's problem, the source of his *malheur*, has been engagement: he knows impossibility via the responsibility he assumes in entering the space of J.'s dying. The narrative is an attempt to close or escape that space and to make dying possible. But the effort only precipitates a violation of the death he seeks (and to which he has been committed — he too under a death sentence). He would die alone in this "literary space," but the effort to do so only accomplishes a repetition of engagement. The transmutation of his relation to that fatality will require an assumption of that fatality, an assumption that only occurs via a kind of catastrophe brought on when N. joins with this thought that has required the narrative. N. gives this thought body (herself a figure, of course, and even as such "less than someone," requiring the flow of his

---

*"It might be that she herself obeyed a mysterious commandment that was my own and that is in me the voice forever reborn, it too a jealous voice, of a sentiment incapable of dying" (A 126/79–80).

words to retain a "physical solidity" [A 117/73]): she provokes a kind of ontico-ontological crisis that produces the narrative denouement. She realizes the relation of desire (a relation that infinitely exceeds her, even if she represents the necessary site of its advent) and forces the narrator's submission, which is the condition of the release of the submission (the "yes") that has necessarily already occurred and has let what has come unfold. But with what has the narrator engaged when he submits other than with language itself (at its limits); with what does he engage other than the saying in which the thought opens and of which it is a figure, a saying that is something like the opening of language (which the narrator draws out with his *Viens*)? The eternally recurring engagement reiterates that opening (that approach, that exigency) endlessly. Can a *subject* enter into such an engagement? Even if every engagement of the order we have considered, every event of encounter, presupposes such an engagement, even if this is the *truth* of engagement ("the truth will be said"), *who* could make this engagement in language and *sign* it without precipitating into what might have to be called madness (or the narrative voice)? Could this be anything more than the simulacrum of a self, the remainder of a self abandoning its *self*?[21]

I believe there is no avoiding the fact that there is something terrible about what is staged in *Death Sentence*. The sacrifice of the person is terrible, as is the violence of the one who makes that sacrifice in answering the infinite exigency to which he is called (an ethical imperative that ruins all "ethics"). Blanchot is uncompromising in this staging, pushing the burden of finitude to its extreme and offering no release (something Lévinas, for example, cannot bear, as we see in his reading of *The Madness of the Day*). And one could go perhaps even farther (bracketing, necessarily, perhaps forgetting the force of that event at the threshold that is the touch, losing the juncture of the finite and the infinite): one might assert that Blanchot has actually sacrificed the "human" to the experiment of writing, that in drawing upon and drawing forth the speaking that *gives* the human in the strangeness that makes it human, he has rendered the person no more than a figure, a kind of figural necessity for language (the language that has claimed and uses "us"). The poignancy of his narration, one might argue, the astounding and implacable "truth" of his descriptions of the movements of consciousness, redoubled with an omnipresent humor that facilitates its passage and our identification, are only the more terrible for their inevitable suspension in writing. To which I would only respond (vainly holding to that touch that is accomplished and lost) that such is the price of the exposure of the human that is offered by language at its limit.

The Lightning Field

The Lightning Field (1977) contains 400 polished stainless
steel poles. Located in west-central New Mexico, this piece of
land art by Walter de Maria measures one mile by one
kilometer and six meters. Visitors (never more than a small
group) stay for at least 24 hours in a farmhouse adjacent to the
installation.

from the vantage point of the house, it is difficult to get beyond statement
and beyond the formal apprehension offered by the distance of representation and by the fact that one has come to an art installation. Of course,
the house is itself absorbed in the landscape, and the fluidity of relations is
almost enough, in the course of the day, to defeat the solemnity of the
installation, its statements.

Thus, according to the hour and the play of light, the poles will either
cede to the landscape or claim it. We would speak in familiar (aletheic)
terms of emergence and veiling, perhaps, if it were the landscape that were
given in this way to our vision. But in fact our attention is held principally
by the poles and *their* relation to the landscape and sky, which varies
between one of play and confrontation, reception and aggressive resistance. This installation is about art and *technē*.

At sunrise, the poles gradually draw definition from the sun as fine lines
of light, needles that emerge from the indistinct dawn and finally glow
with the sun's rose and orange. Here, their character as *receptors* is dominant — they exist, it seems, to testify to the light, to bear witness in their
reflection. Monumental waiting that has nothing of an *aesthetic* offering.

As the sun ascends toward noon, they recede again and virtually disappear into the landscape. Lying in the midday sun, the desert suffers the
needles as hardly more than an ignored fencing. The installation barely
stands, barely holds as a setup.

But past midday, the rods begin to assume their posture as gleaming, sharpened poles. Here, an aesthetic begins to assert itself, and a purpose. The aesthetic is principally that of the sublime, both dynamic and mathematical — at this hour their extension seems unlimited (at sunset, the borders will appear as the poles interact more directly with the sky and its declining light). In its appeal to the negative, this aesthetic communicates a range of statements about the relation between humankind and nature: statements evoked by the menacing character of the sharpened poles, by the strict delimitation of their measure, and by what they recall of modern technology and its command of energy (in electrical installations, first of all — though the *minimal* character of these rods, their insistent but mysterious purpose, also points to that other installation in a desert landscape of New Mexico that defined the modern relation to power). The statement about technology here *insists*. This installation is telling us about its mythic resonances, its reach and its capabilities. And it is hard to forget the "false" telos of these lightning rods and abandon hope for the Promethean spectacle they promise — though one knows by the very solemnity of these rows that the point of this installation is not spectacle.

but if we leave the house and enter the field in mid-afternoon, we enter a field of signification that absorbs time and space, and even any statement. We may have glimpsed it before, *a veil of intention* that covers the landscape. But we must confront the poles obliquely and from within their range, so that they lose their order and their statement. Where their *direction* is so interrupted, where intention, in this manner, becomes *mere intention*, the poles blanket the landscape; from this angle and in the advancing afternoon, they seem to have *no end.* They stand in mute testimony, witness to nothing except the relation they mark in a pure offering of the mark. There is a temporality here because there is a kind of address, or perhaps nothing more, in fact, than a witnessing; *anticipation,* we could say, if all destination were not interrupted, if this address could project for itself some accomplishment. These sentinels *wait* and seem to indicate only an intention to enter into relation, a kind of offering, "indicating" in this way an otherness they do not present to themselves or to us. They mark relation without another term, they mark an opening. Perhaps the evocation of the sacred comes primarily from the fact that they face the sky and offer themselves to light. But we might wonder whether such a testimony does not occur wherever signification is interrupted and *signification itself* is offered (and wonder if the divine does not come down to this); we might wonder whether all appearance of the fact that there is language is accompanied by the effect of an offering to an otherness, or this indicating to . . .

Notes

Following the style of Stanford University Press, I have divided my notes into footnotes and endnotes. I have used footnotes for brief remarks or citations in order to avoid interrupting the flow of the text. The endnotes contain more substantive discussions.

Introduction

1. My first work on Heidegger turned upon the question of the relation between Being and human being (*Heidegger: Thought and Historicity*, expanded edition [Ithaca, N.Y.: Cornell University Press, 1993]), a relation that contained for Heidegger what he called a "distressing difficulty" (H 74/P 87). This study explores the same "difficulty."

2. I have cited Foucault partly in view of his recognition in *The Order of Things* (New York: Random House, 1970) that the question of the being of language, as he puts it, is irreducibly linked in modern thought to that of the being of humankind. In fact, I could well situate the current project in relation to a citation from this volume by suggesting that it explores the "task" of thinking this relation *from* the hiatus or discontinuity that lies there: "Is the task ahead of us to advance towards a mode of thought, unknown hitherto in our culture, that will make it possible to reflect at the same time, without discontinuity or contradiction, upon man's being and the being of language? — In that case, we must take the very greatest precautions to avoid anything that might be a naive return to the Classical theory of discourse. . . . But the right to think at one and the same time the being of language and the being of man may be forever excluded; there may be, as it were, an ineffaceable hiatus at that point (precisely that hiatus in which we exist and speak), so that it would be necessary to dismiss as fantasy any anthropology in which there was any question of the being of language, or any conception of language or signification which attempted to connect with, manifest, and free the being proper to man. It is perhaps here that the most important philosophical choice of our period has its roots — a choice that can be made only in the test of a future reflection" (338–39). The Heideggerian notion of *Brauch* ("usage") that I will explore here opens a path other than the "choices" to which Foucault refers, but I am intrigued by what appears to have been a choice in *The Archaeology of Knowledge* (where the problematic of finitude recedes in relation to the meditation on the *énoncé*) and by what must have been a resurgence of the question of finitude in the latter parts of Foucault's project on the history of sexuality. I would not try

to legislate at the point of the limit marked by Foucault in the passage I have cited from *The Order of Things*, but I continue to believe that it is only from the relation between language and the human (and that is to say, from the interruption that marks it) that the question of language becomes an opening for a thought of something like the "ethico-political." Whatever "choice" we might make, in any case, it proceeds from the straits of the discontinuity to which Foucault alludes. In this regard, I would argue that if the question of language has proven so difficult of access for modern philosophy and theory (despite widespread acknowledgment of the irreversibility of the linguistic turn), this is because it requires a real assumption of the question of finitude or "existence" — something more than a mere suspension of the prerogatives of the subject. This is why a simple valorization of the "later Heidegger" in accounts of contemporary thought on language (in vague contradistinction to the "earlier") is deeply misguided.

Let me add that I have discussed the viability of recourse to a notion of "the human" in my response to a query from Derrida in "The Question of the Human (Geschlecht 1bis)," forthcoming in a publication of the proceedings of the colloquium "Futures for Jacques Derrida" (ed. Richard Rand; Johns Hopkins University Press). A term such as "the human" carries significant baggage, but I risk it here in an attempt to deliver it to its strangeness.

3. How so much contemporary reflection could rest satisfied with such a reductive reading of a precursor's text (and not just any precursor) remains a troubling mystery to me. It says a great deal, I fear, about modern historical understanding, to say nothing of modern philosophy (and as I tried to demonstrate in the added chapter to *Heidegger: Thought and Historicity*, reference to the political question will not suffice to explain this phenomenon, for it also involves a failure to think the political). But the inadequacies of contemporary reflection are of less import, even as symptoms speaking to a historical situation, than what they consign to obscurity, which is an engagement with language that explores the historical grounds of self-understanding. The task of learning to read this text *as* such an engagement has seemed highly urgent to me.

4. I am using the term "culture" in the light of remarks by Gérard Granel in *De l'université* (N.p.: Trans-Europe-Repress, 1982) that I comment on in an essay devoted to his work and the question of the university ("But Suppose We Were to Take the Rectorial Address Seriously: Gérard Granel's *De l'université*," *Graduate/Faculty Philosophy Journal* [New School for Social Research], 14, no. 2/15, no. 1 [1991]: 335–62). I will not try to develop this problematic here, and I must acknowledge that I only point to it in this essay on Irigaray. But I believe that Irigaray is engaging the question of "existence" at the level Granel evokes when he names "culture" that excess of Capital and Modernity (as these two are thought by Marx and Heidegger) that "appears" at the time of their full accomplishment, and as "the immediate element of history" (91). Granel approaches this "element" from a thought of the finitude of the subject and that "totality" that is its world, its *pragma* ("the genre of the whole that is involved here is comparable only to that which forms for each individual that inevitably missed totality they call their 'life,' and to whose want one must try to be 'adequate'" [65]). I have attended to this

fundamental "matter" or "concern" of the Dasein in its *relational* structure in part because I believe that cultural studies, and more generally, cultural politics, urgently require a thought of relation if any articulation of a "common" concern is to be won beyond what is offered by liberalism. Identity (or "essence") must be thought *in relation* at a far more fundamental level than that offered by the various models of historical determination (where identity, despite everything, remains abstract). What is at stake in such a thought is, of course, the question of community.

5. I think of Jean-François Lyotard, for example (and principally of *The Differend: Phrases in Dispute*, trans. Georges Van Den Abbeele [Minneapolis: University of Minnesota Press, 1988]). I also think of Jacques Lacan, another reader of Heidegger who speaks directly to the Heideggerian motif of "usage" and recognizes not only the question of the essence of language but also the question of the relation between the human and language. I have sketched Lacan's engagement with these questions in an essay entitled "Between Ethics and Aesthetics" (*L'Esprit Créateur*, 35, no. 3 [Fall 1995]: 80–87). Derrida deserves long separate treatment, but I would note that the first steps for this volume were made in " . . . *qu'il y a le langage*: Heidegger, Derrida" (presented at the meeting of the Collegium Phaenomenologicum devoted to Derrida in Perugia, July 1987; the pages on Wittgenstein that follow are drawn from this text and mark the real starting point for this study). In the context of this introduction, I am reminded of words from Derrida's "Cogito and the History of Madness" (words with which Foucault certainly came to agree): "The fact of language is no doubt the only one that finally resists any placing between parentheses" (Derrida, *Writing and Difference*, trans. Alan Bass [Chicago: University of Chicago Press, 1978], 37).

. . . *that there is language*

1. This is Wittgenstein's word, as transcribed by Waismann: "In ethics, one constantly attempts to say something that does not, and can never, touch the essence of the matter. . . . But the tendency, the running up against, *points to something* [*deutet auf etwas hin*]." (See the complete English translation of this text in *Heidegger and Modern Philosophy*, ed. Michael Murray [New Haven, Conn.: Yale University Press, 1978], 80–83; an initial publication in the *Philosophical Review* elided the references to Heidegger, even the title: "Zu Heidegger.") The substance of Wittgenstein's remarks in this text, down to the phrase "running up against," clearly links it to the "Lecture on Ethics," delivered in the same year (1929) — the year of publication of Heidegger's widely circulated "What Is Metaphysics?"

Chapter 1

1. I want to emphasize that I will be attending to the allegory Heidegger constructs rather than to the texture of Trakl's poem. Véronique Fóti noted very appropriately after my initial presentation of this essay that Heidegger's reading of "A Winter Evening" should also be situated in the larger context of his reading of

Trakl (which includes Heidegger's essay "Language in the Poem," also in *On the Way to Language*, 157–98) and that Trakl's poem demands consideration in the context of his oeuvre. I am in full agreement with these points, but will pursue a specific focus that does not immediately require this broader perspective. Fóti's own helpful treatment of Heidegger's reading of Trakl appears in *Heidegger and the Poets: Poiēsis/Sophia/Technē* (Atlantic Highlands, N.J.: Humanities Press, 1992), 13–30.

2. "Relation of relations" is a phrase that recurs in the essays I will be reading in this volume. I use it here to recall that what the language of the poem traces or sets out is the relation or the measure governing what is finally a set of relations—the presence of the thing is defined by the way it bears in itself the relations between mortals, earth, sky, and the divine. When Heidegger speaks of a presence sheltered in absence, he is referring to the way the thing is given to us in and by these relations as they define a spatiotemporal disposition. What Heidegger calls the difference is the measure of these relations.

3. Heidegger never interprets this figure (at least not to my recollection), but it is clear that he would read it on the basis of Hölderlin's remarks to Böhlendorff regarding the "sureness" of the sign and in relation to his understanding of the notion of poetic founding. I take up this topic in *Heidegger: Thought and Historicity* (expanded edition [Ithaca, N.Y.: Cornell University Press, 1993], see esp. 215–16). My concluding remarks on Hölderlin's "In lovely blueness . . ." in the present discussion also draw from the context of this previous discussion.

4. Heidegger proposes, near the beginning of "The Origin of the Work of Art," a definition of allegory that is quite different from the more traditional one I am employing here: "The art work . . . says something other than the mere thing itself is, *allo agoreuei*. The work makes public something other than itself; it manifests something other; it is an allegory" (H 4/P 19). As his essay will demonstrate, this "something other" is difference. A more precise meaning of the term "allegory," as I want to use it here, would have to be developed in the light of Heidegger's notion of poetry that says the essence of poetry (as is preeminently the case with Hölderlin, in Heidegger's view) and in the light of what Heidegger says about the way a work shows its "createdness" (H 52/P 65).

5. In *Heidegger and the Essence of Man*, trans. William McNeil (Albany: SUNY Press, 1993), Michel Haar asks how Heidegger's attribution of terms such as pain, freedom, or desire to *difference* can escape anthropomorphism. Heidegger provides the beginning of an answer in "The Anaximander Fragment" when he argues that the charge of anthropomorphism presupposes a set of conceptual boundaries that such thinking calls into question (H 330–31/E 20–21). Nevertheless, Haar's question may alert us to the manner in which Heidegger systematically *displaces* such terms (from the human in the direction of the relation between Being and human being). He is thinking human experience from difference, but he finds it necessary to proceed with language traditionally anchored in that experience. What rhetorical/logical necessity is at work here?

6. In the later Heidegger no less than in the former, Being is thought in terms of conflict, and a certain violence is never eliminated. For the Mallarméan fold, see

Jacques Derrida's "The Double Session," in his *Dissemination*, trans. Barbara Johnson (Chicago: University of Chicago Press, 1981).

7. Martin Heidegger, "Hölderlin and the Essence of Poetry," trans. Paul de Man, *Quarterly Review of Literature*, 10, nos. 1–2 (1959): 82–83. I might note that Derrida's concept of "iterability" would be useful in this context. See, for example, his essay "Signature, Event, Context," in *Glyph 1*, trans. Samuel Weber and Jeffrey Mehlman (Baltimore: Johns Hopkins University Press, 1977), 179–80. See also Derrida's "Plato's Pharmacy," in his *Dissemination*, 61–172, in which Derrida demonstrates how the sign's "repeatability" haunts metaphysics from its inception.

8. For a discussion of this theme in "Mnemosyne," see Anselm Haverkamp, "Error in Mourning — A Crux in Hölderlin: 'Dem gleich fehlet die Trauer' ('Mnemosyne')," *Yale French Studies: The Lesson of Paul de Man*, no. 69 (1985): 238–53.

9. It is true that Heidegger describes the assumption of mortality as a passage and as a "going down" to a site in which there gathers the original essence of time; in this respect, one could draw the conclusion that there can be no more than a *crossing* of the threshold and no static dwelling within the difference that gathers. But when Heidegger hypostatizes death in "Language" ("Death has already overtaken every dying"), and when he evokes in "Language in the Poem" the possibility of a rebirth through the assumption of "accomplished pain" (US 67/OW 189), he effectively appropriates death as a possibility. Let us note that Heidegger describes the "rebirth" in question as the rebirth of one generation or race (*Geschlecht*) out of the decline (which is not a decomposition but a "going down") of the West as it assumes its historial destiny (US 73–75/OW 194–96). I cannot refrain from observing here that I find few texts by Heidegger — including his "Rectorial Address" — as unsettling as this one in a political perspective (which is to say also that it calls for careful and extended analysis). For the range of possible connotations of the word *Geschlecht*, see Jacques Derrida's essays "*Geschlecht*: Différence sexuelle, différence ontologique" and "La Main de Heidegger (*Geschlecht* II)," in his *Psyché: Inventions de l'autre* (Paris: Galilée, 1987), 395–452 and 415–51, respectively). David Farrell Krell has also devoted many rich pages to "Language in the Poem" over the years. For his latest remarks, see *Lunar Voices* (Chicago: University of Chicago Press, 1995); his note on p. 33 documents his past contributions.

10. Thomas Trezise's *Into the Breach: Samuel Beckett and the Ends of Literature* (Princeton, N.J.: Princeton University Press, 1990) offers a valuable reading of Beckett in this regard.

Chapter 2

1. We might compare here also Heidegger's remarks in *What Is Called Thinking?* on the manner in which the "precursory" character of thought shapes the unfolding of its "way": "In order to get under way, we do have to set out. This is meant in a double sense: for one thing, we have to open ourselves to the emerging prospect and direction of the way itself; and then, we must get on the way, that is, must take the steps by which alone the way becomes a way.... Only when we walk

it, and in no other fashion, only, that is, by thoughtful questioning, are we on the move on the way. This movement is what allows the way to come forward. That the way of thought is of this nature is part of the precursoriness of thinking" (WHD 164/169).

2. Intriguingly, Heidegger glosses his description of the occasion of which George's poem is presumably an instance ("However, when it is a matter of bringing to language what until this time has never been spoken . . ." [US 151/OW 59]) with a reference to his own experience of the "failing" of the word. In a marginal note, he writes, " 'Time and Being' — its nonemergence in 1923–1926 necessitated a meditation on language and the *non*publication of the portions that were initially sketched out." The counterplay of poetry and thought begins here with the implicit suggestion that Heidegger is now prepared to bring a thinking experience with language to language.

3. To these remarks on the possibility of a multiple speaking of the essence of language itself, I would add that perhaps only by multiplicity or ambiguity may the speaking of language be heard as such: one *Geheiss* making the other apprehensible in a kind of death knell. I explore this possibility in an essay on Derrida's "Le Dernier mot du racisme": "Apartheid: Word and History," *boundary 2*, 16, nos. 2–3 (Winter/Spring 1988): 1–12. In this essay I try to bring forth the historical/historial dimension of the engagement with language that Heidegger and Derrida attempt in their singular ways. The Derrida essay is in his *Psyché: Inventions de l'autre* (Paris: Galilée, 1987), 353–62.

4. The verse from Hölderlin comes from the couplet "Sophocles": "Many sought in vain to say joyfully the most joyful/Here finally, here in mourning, it pronounces itself to me" (Friedrich Hölderlin, *Poems and Fragments*, trans. Michael Hamburger [New York: Cambridge University Press, 1980], 71).

5. In a necessarily different mode, one might develop here an additional step to the ones made by de Man in his meditation on Benjamin's essay "Die Aufgabe des Übersetzers" (though other turns would certainly lie in store): Paul de Man, " 'Conclusions': Walter Benjamin's 'The Task of the Translator' " *Yale French Studies: The Lesson of Paul de Man*, no. 69 (1985): 25–46. The poetic ideology that de Man attacks in this essay would have to give way, but so would the evocation of "defeat" (which is actually foreign, I would argue, to the tonality of Benjamin's essay).

6. Hertz translates both *Zusage* and *Zuspruch* as "grant," and in the particular context, this is not entirely inappropriate (if we have some idea already of what is happening). But I would recall here that *Zuspruch* might also be translated as "encouragement" and *Zusage* as "promise." I would note also the play on *Anfragen* and *Nachfragen*. We put questions to a thing whose essence we inquire after. I would explicate this now only by suggesting that we approach something solely out of the approach (the way) that *has been offered* to that thing (in and by language). The essence of something *must have addressed us* for us to go toward it in questioning.

7. Writing these words (looking out over Quaker Lake, Pennsylvania), I was reminded of the "Boy of Winander" passage in Book Five of Wordsworth's "Pre-

lude." Very soon thereafter, I would also have to recall the succeeding episode from that book. Following Wordsworth's lead, we would want to remember here that the give and take with language that is at the origin of speech engages mortality.

8. It is no wonder that Hertz stumbles so severely in these passages; to translate this text, he would have had to renounce his very notion of translation. I hesitate to criticize a translation, knowing intimately how thankless and impossible the task is. But in this case, the English translation seriously impedes comprehension of the text.

9. The strength of Heidegger's statement about Hölderlin here is noteworthy: "In 1910, Norbert von Hellingrath, who was killed in action before Verdun in 1916, first published Hölderlin's Pindar translations from the manuscripts. In 1914, there followed the first publication of Hölderlin's late hymns. These two books hit us students like an earthquake" (US 172/OW 78). Without developing here the possible implications of the rhetorical link between the publication and the historical context (between an explosion and a tremor): is Heidegger saying something about an impetus, a *Stoss* from poetry that was essential for his way of thought (and here is one implication: as a German)?

10. In the essay that formed the germ of this volume (". . . *qu'il y a le langage*: Heidegger, Derrida," presented at the Collegium Phaenomenologicum in Perugia, July 1987), I argued that we can only begin to think the proximity of authors such as Heidegger and Derrida from the basis of their respective efforts to remark the fact that there is language, efforts that are characterized by a very similar daring. In attempting to write *à partir de la différance* and to draw out this movement manifestly, Derrida shows no less presumption than Heidegger; indeed, he is perfectly cognizant of the necessity of such daring (as we see in his essay "Le Retrait de la métaphore" [*Psyché*, 63–94], to which I will return below). Most commentators will allow that there is something "outrageous" about the texts of both Heidegger and Derrida — that they are excessive and presumptuous. My argument would be that they have grasped in their respective ways the necessity, for thought, of linguistic *provocation*.

11. The poet's relation to the word's holding back is one of astonishment, unfolding in a saying of this mystery (properly song) that is renunciation. The poet, as Heidegger illustrates with another poem saying the "same," sings of the manner in which language brings near its withheld essence (*vor-enthaltenes Wesen* — the prefix *vor-*, which I am separating, already marks the bringing forward of this self-containment; it remarks the withdrawal in a way that is not unrelated to the manner in which *ver-weigern* redoubles it: both work in the manner of *Entfernung*). The poet sings of the "far-tarrying power of the word."

12. I will return in my next chapter to *What Is Called Thinking?* and Heidegger's discussion of memory, thanks, and the heart. But I would note here an interesting (and fairly rare) mention of the "image" in this context: "Out of the memory, and within the memory, the soul pours forth its wealth of images — of visions envisioning the soul itself" (WHD 93/140).

13. Derrida has captured Heidegger's "linguistic" performance with this word in the most *answering* manner in "Le Retrait de la métaphore." That is to say, he

repeats this performance (though in a thoroughly singular act of translation and with an extraordinarily powerful reflection on the "destiny" of metaphor at the end of metaphysics) by rethinking the "contraction" of language and the writing of difference *from* the word *re-trait* (and the phrase *retrait de la métaphore*) and *as* such a *retrait*. *Retrait de la métaphore*, as Derrida mobilizes this phrase, *says* the *re-trait* of difference (or so he presumes) — it remarks what Heidegger calls the language of essence and thus opens a path to this opening of paths.

From the basis of this essay, we can begin to understand Derrida's strategy in texts such as "Ousia et grammé" and "La Différance" (both in his *Marges de la philosophie* [Paris: Minuit, 1972]), where he follows Heidegger in asserting that we must think the text of metaphysics as a trace of the effacement of the trace and then turns the argument on Heidegger's own earlier efforts to think the "meaning" or "truth" of Being and his determination of difference as "ontico-ontological difference." Such language must itself, Derrida insists, be submitted to reinscription by a thought of writing. The task of such a reinscription — thinking and writing these terms *from* the trace structure — necessarily calls for "another language." "Le Retrait de la métaphore" offers an instance of such a language and helps us understand what Heidegger is doing when he advances a term like *Aufriss*.

14. I recall the allusion to Dürer in "The Origin of the Work of Art": "Someone who was bound to know what he was talking about, Albrecht Dürer, did after all make the well-known remark: 'For in truth, art lies hidden within nature; he who can wrest it from her, has it.' 'Wrest' here means to draw out the rift and to draw the design with the drawing-pen on the drawing-board. But we at once raise the counterquestion: how can the rift-design be drawn out if it is not brought into the Open by the creative sketch as a rift, which is to say, brought out beforehand as a conflict of measure and unmeasure?" (H 58/P 70).

15. "But if the nearness of poetry and thinking is one of saying, then our thinking arrives at the assumption that the event of appropriation holds sway as that saying in which language commits to us its essence. Its promise does not cast about in the void. Rather, it has already struck. Whom else but man? For man is man only inasmuch as, accepting the exhortation of language, he is needed and used by language in order to speak it" (US 185/OW 90). I will take up the motif of "assent" as *Gelassenheit* in the next chapter. I would only underscore here that if language "uses" humankind, its assent to this usage is an "active" one. The human affirmation provokes language's speech; its own promise is an assenting vow.

16. To give some idea of the linguistic density of this passage, I will cite the last line of the German. Heidegger is drawing together (phonically) the notions of giving, clearing and concealing, country and way: *Das Freigebend-Bergende der Gegend ist jene Be-wëgung, in der sich die Wege ergeben, die der Gegend gehören.*

17. The Celtic and Germanic roots of the term *reichen* connote "leader" or "king" ("in the name of the king," once again). But the senses of the related, now obsolete English verb "rich," (linked to the verb *rücken*) are most suggestive for Heidegger's use of the term (beyond what we might do with *Reich* or *Reichtum*). As a transitive verb, it means "to draw" or "to pull"; as reflexive, "to address (oneself) to a place" or "to do something"; as intransitive, "to take one's way" or "to run."

18. Heidegger's work with *be-* here merits the same attention we should give to

ent- and *ge-*, though it is somewhat more resistant to conceptual articulation than the latter two. Could "be-" also express something of *zeigen* in the series of intensive verbs it constitutes (e.g., in English, "bedeck") or in a construction such as "bespeak"? I would add that Heidegger cannot be insensitive to what an English speaker hears in "be-."

19. This sentence justifies Gerald Bruns's undertaking in *Heidegger's Estrangements: Language, Truth, and Poetry in the Later Writings* (New Haven, Conn.: Yale University Press, 1989) — a study that is especially noteworthy for the extent to which it explicitly refuses the philosophical urge to seize a conceptual or propositional content in *On the Way to Language* and seeks to follow what Heidegger defines here as the "summons" of language's "hidden riches." Bruns's "literary" sensitivity leads him to important insights about the essays in question (largely the same essays I treat in this volume). As it happens, however, the deferral of a philosophical appropriation rests upon a methodological decision with its own philosophical presuppositions. The distinction between the hermetic and the orphic, while illustrative (particularly for its emphasis upon the "earthly" dimension of language), has limited pertinence for Heidegger's text *as a distinction*. When it is pursued so exclusively, moreover, it effectively forecloses any consequent attention to Heidegger's meditation on *technē* and ultimately everything we might term a *thought* of relation. Most gravely, perhaps, it lends Bruns's argumentation to the ideologically overdetermined effacement of the question of politics that characterized Heidegger studies until just recently. Bruns's book, in my opinion, remains a quite valuable and important corrective to various "conceptual" appropriations of Heidegger, but in giving itself up to Heidegger's "estrangements," it gives up a bit too easily the task (and play) of thought.

20. Here I refer back to the passage on US 240/OW 121 where Heidegger distinguishes the "proper meaning" of *Riss* from the "debased" one where it might refer to a crack in the wall. The example is curiously *speaking*. The bounding, delimiting rift, which provides passage or an opening to the other, is being carefully distinguished from a mere fissure in a wall. The rift, we might conclude, is not a mere break that might allow something of the one to escape or pass into the other, not a conduit of any kind. But if the latter sense of *Riss* is *debased*, is it because walls should be intact, even those that work in the manner of an *Aufriss*? Is Heidegger still warding off the danger of a contamination of essence with his notion of the *Riss*? The contrast of bright versus murky might also be examined in this perspective.

21. Let us imagine the scene. It is 1959, and Heidegger is presenting the second of his "Essence of Language" lectures. He has declared that he will bring us to hear what all of Western thought has failed to hear and think. And this is *Heidegger* — who else could do it? He has strained to bring his audience before the difference as such, to that "edge" where difference would be thought without reference to beings. The word, he announces, is *Aufriss*. Numerous auditors are not certain they caught it. "*Aufriss*?" they repeat to their neighbors. The next morning, Heidegger will read in the local *Zeitung* about what occurred in the preceding evening's lecture — "Professor Heidegger pronounced that the heretofore hidden essence ..." — and a little smile will be observed. Well, perhaps not a smile — but part

of the very point I have made about mimesis, language, and thought is that such levels of thought are indissociable from a form of play, and that such play is legible in the "staging" to which I have referred. This is where Heidegger is "Heidegger."

22. The ultimate trap in a post-Heideggerian philosophical framework, in my mind, is, as I described earlier, that of pretending to speak in the name of language without assuming at the same time the precariousness of such pretension, or what I have called the "singularity" of the language of thought — turning a gay science into a pretentious and solemn version of what Keats and Rudolph have named "onto-speak."

23. The entire development on *be-langen* (and thus Heidegger's "willful usage") has *also* been preparing what Heidegger does here with *bewëgen*. The prefix indicates a giving, yielding to, or providing, while *wëgen* creates a verb of *Weg* (in the manner of *die Sprache spricht*) while transforming the preposition *wegen* ("because of," "by reason of"). *Be-wëgen* means "to provide the country with ways." I might note here also that the *Grosse Duden Herkunftswörterbuch* indicates that the substantive *Weg* is originally the same word as the adjective form pronounced with a short *e* and meaning "away." Everything Heidegger says about *Entfernung* and nearness has its source in the movement of *be-wëgen*.

24. Here again a prefix plays a crucial role in the transition. The third lecture, Heidegger says, is to lead us into the possibility of undergoing an experience, but Heidegger's work with the prefix *er-* helps to transform "possibility" into what enables and experience into a setting under way: *Der dritte Vortrag möchte uns eigens vor eine Möglichkeit, d.h. in eine Er-möglichung bringen, mit der Sprache eine Erfahrung zu machen* (US 187). I note this point in order to suggest again how far Heidegger's work with language reaches.

25. Bringing forth a bit more the American idiom I want to sound here, I would translate *eine arge Zumutung* as "one mean demand." Heidegger's use of the term *arge* here (underscored in the succeeding sentence) is noteworthy. *Arg* means "bad," "evil," "hard." It derives from the Indo-Germanic root *ergh*, which means "to move violently," "to be stirred up," "to quake or tremble." The possible we are approaching, which *er-möglicht*, is anything but a gentle surge or swaying for thought. Thinking the source of all movement involves a violent shaking — an *Erschütterung*, as Hegel would say.

26. It would be worthwhile to pause here and compare Heidegger's use of "Germanien" vis-à-vis his reading of the poem in his lecture course of 1935 (see HH). Quite a lot is at stake in Heidegger's undeveloped reference to dialects and the implicit reference to a people. My emphasis here, however, is on the movement of the essay and the way in which Heidegger is rethinking the very meaning of the "proper" (thought here from *physis*) in view of a "free use of the proper" that is groundless. I am following Heidegger to find the means of deconstructing any national determinations.

Chapter 3

1. The last phrase, "and our relation . . . ," does not figure in the original version of *On the Way to Language* translated by Hertz. It is accompanied in the *Gesam-*

tausgabe by the following marginal note, which I will translate only partially at this time: *Ver-Hältnis: Ortschaft des Zu-einander von Brauch und Ereignis* ("*Ver-Hältnis:* Locality of the belonging to one another of *Brauch* and *Ereignis*"). The foregrounding of the human relation to language as *the* relation in the phrase from the second paragraph echoes another marginal note accompanying the title, of which I will cite the first part. "Why not '*a*' way to language among others?" Heidegger asks. "The essay is seeking: to let the peculiar property of language be re-marked and *named — to call* into the questionworthiness of the *inapparent* (the inapparent of something withheld, its domain of wealth)" (US 239). The essay concerns *the* way to language, it seems, because the way is via *das Eigentümliche* (which will be revealed as concerning the relation of language and humankind), and perhaps because the only way to *das Eigentümliche* is through a naming: but a naming of that which cannot be brought to appear and for which there is no proper word — a naming that re-marks with its calling. Undoubtedly, the naming might occur in any number of ways depending on the choice in *Sprachgebrauch*: what "soundings" are tried or invented by the researcher. But these soundings will all belong to *the* way to language in that they will always realize — in "principle" — the same contract of language and humankind.

2. Another way of evoking the displacement to which I have referred would be to observe the shift from the motif of hearing to that of seeing. The relation of humankind to language will be defined here principally, as in the prior discussions we have seen, in terms of a belonging (*Gehören*) that renders possible a hearing (*Hören*). But the appropriation of humankind by which it is assigned to language — admitted to it and given to belong to it — occurs through the event of *Ereignis* as an *Er-äugnen* ("beholding" [US 249/OW 129]) of humankind. As Heidegger moves through the motifs of *Sagen* and *Zeigen* in his account of the "essencing" of language in the second section of his essay, he will be leading us toward an "experience" of the *Ereignis* that is figured(?) eventually as a seeing.

3. Humboldt accounts for the nature of language by subsuming it under a set of general concepts such as energy and the activity of spirit rather than allowing it to be experienced *as language* and thus as it comes about (*west*) and is "gathered in what it properly grants to itself" (US 238/OW 119). Heidegger will attempt, on the contrary, to bring forward everything that belongs to language as language. In a certain sense, he will come close to referring it to something other than itself, for he will describe how language's self-relation entails a movement by which language exposes an otherness in itself or is exposed to an otherness — i.e., *Ereignis* and the relation between language and human being it contracts. But this "other," experienced as that which grants in the essence of language, can only be thought as occurring *in* language and by way of language, and never as its "ground." Heidegger remains strictly faithful to a logic of finitude.

I have referred here to Humboldt's place in the metaphysics of subjectivity (to which we must also refer Novalis, and which thus forms the backdrop for Heidegger's meditation on the manner in which language unfolds the "same"). I would add here that the latter determination of modern metaphysics must also be thought in terms of what Heidegger calls in the second volume of his Nietzsche lectures the metaphysics of representation (*Nietzsche* [Pfullingen: Neske, 1961]). From this perspective, we can grasp better the continuity between Humboldt's treatise and the modern notion of language as information to which Heidegger returns twice in his essay.

4. The same could not be said of Heidegger's own earlier meditations on language and world, but it is noteworthy that these remarks on Humboldt could well reflect back on Heidegger's more "mimetological" statements in "On the Essence of Ground": " 'Dasein transcends' means that in the essence of its being it is *world-forming*, and indeed 'forming' [*bildend*] in the manifold sense that it lets world happen and through the world provides itself with an original view (image [*Bild*]) which does not grasp explicitly, yet serves as a model [*Vor-bild*] for, all of manifest being, to which belongs each time Dasein itself" (Martin Heidegger, "Vom Wesen des Grundes," in *Wegmarken*, vol. 9 of *Gesamtausgabe* [(Frankfurt am Main: Klostermann, 1976], 158).

5. I have cited and discussed this passage in which Heidegger brings forward the name *Aufriss*, so I will merely recall that *Aufriss* is said to name the whole of the traits of the design or signature (*Zeichnung*: what orders the showing of all signs, *Zeichen*) that prevails and joins throughout the "opened freedom" of language. It is the design that composes the unity of the *Sprachwesen*: the structure (or jointure) of a showing (*Gefüge eines Zeigens*) that articulates "speakers and their speaking, the spoken and its unspoken from out of the addressed [*Zugesprochene*]" (US 240/OW 121).

6. It is noteworthy that Heidegger's first step in defining the term "speaking" is to repeat his earlier gesture (in "Language") of bracketing the question of *Verlautbarung* by insisting that a phonetic-acoustic-physiological explanation of language's sounding fails to think the provenance of this sounding in the "peal of stillness" (*das Geläut der Stille*) and the manner in which this latter determines (*bestimmt*) the *Lauten* that occurs in human speaking. "The Essence of Language" justified this move. But his elision of the motifs of *Lauten* and *Verlautbarung* is remarkable here for the fact that his aim in this essay is to foreground the relation between language and humankind. In describing the human response to language in the third section of the essay, he will assert that what is proper to humans as those who speak is *das Lauten des Wortes*, to which he adds in a marginal note, *Lauten und Leiben — Leib und Schrift* (a phrase to which I will be returning). Humankind, to repeat, responds to language out of what is *proper* to it (*aus dem ihm Eigenen*): "Sounding and bodying — body and writing" (US 249). Thus, when he leaves aside *Verlautbarung*, he leaves aside one of the essential components of the relation this text is devoted to bringing forth. Later, near the end of his essay, he will add that we dwell *as mortals* in the domain into which we are drawn inasmuch as we are used for the speaking of language (US 255/OW 134). Thus it could be that what Heidegger is touching but leaving undeveloped here (in order to circumscribe it thoroughly) is the point where the relation between language and humankind involves the relation between mortality and the body (not to mention that inexpungible corpse, writing).

7. In the new version of the account, only Heidegger's last statement is at all

surprising: "The addressed [*Zugesprochene*] speaks to us as dictum [*Spruch*] in the sense of something imparted [*Zugewiesen*], something whose speaking does not even require to be sounded." This assertion would seem to contradict both the statement in "Language" according to which what is addressed in language requires the sounding of human speech and a restatement of this notion in "The Way to Language" itself (US 254/OW 134).

I might add here that *zuweisen*, translated by Hertz with the term "impart," also suggests an assigning or allotment (the *Seinsgeschick*). It appears in this passage, it would seem, because *weisen* is related to *zeigen* as a pointing or showing. Etymologically, *weisen* connotes a "making knowing" (*wissend machen*). The Old German *wis[e]* from which it derives means "aspect" or "form of appearance," and the Indo-Germanic root is *ueid*: "glimpse, see" (cf. the Greek *idein*, "to see, to perceive or know," and *eidenai*, which would be translated by the German "*wissen*" and means properly "to have seen"). As Heidegger weaves the motif of "seeing" into his account of language's speaking, he prepares for the *Er-äugnen* of *Ereignen*.

8. We will see that the prefix Heidegger privileges for terms evoking *Brauch*, as a relation between humankind and *Ereignis* (or Being, or truth, as he sometimes says by abbreviation) is *ver-*: e.g., *vereignen*, *vergegnen*, *verwahren*, and finally *ver-hältnis*. The *ver-*, with its suspending hyphen, marks the articulation of *Brauch*.

9. Let me recall here again the concluding sentence of the second paragraph: *und unser Verhältnis zu ihr sich als das Ver-hältnis bekundet* — to which Heidegger adds in a marginal note: *Ver-Hältnis: Ortschaft des Zu-einander-Gehörens von Brauch und Ereignis* (US 229).

10. *Schätzenswert* would almost seem to condemn any Heideggerian use of these lines by reason of its invocation of "value," but a "redeeming" commentary linking the term to the problematic of *Brauch* is to be found in "The Anaximander Fragment" (H 358–59/E 45).

11. In defining the "use" of the earth in art (in contradistinction to its use in "handicraft"), Heidegger employs the term *brauchen* quite demonstratively (H 52/P 64). He also uses the verb to define the work's "need" for creators and preservers (H 54/P 66). *Brauchen*, as we see, is already a key term for thinking the finitude of truth.

12. This construction, "for itself," had already appeared in 1935 in a passage in *An Introduction to Metaphysics*, cited by Michel Haar in his *Heidegger and the Essence of Man*, trans. William McNeill (Albany: SUNY Press, 1993): "Yet if man is constrained to such a *Da-sein*, if he is thrown into the distress [*Not*] of such being, it is because the overwhelming as such *needs* [*braucht* — Heidegger's emphasis] the site of openness *for itself* [*für es*] in order to appear in prevailing. The essence of human being opens itself to us only when it is understood in terms of this distress necessitated by Being itself" (130). In stressing the motif of mortality (which figures importantly in the *Introduction*) and a necessary "caesura," I will try to disrupt the "reflexive" character of this originary fold. I might note here that Haar's is the only discussion of *Brauch*, to my knowledge, that approaches the importance of the motif in Heidegger's text (though its importance for practical

philosophy is fully recognized, in passing, by Reiner Schürmann in "The Ontological Difference and Political Philosophy," in *Philosophy and Phenomenological Research*, 40, no. 1 [Sept. 1979]: 99–122). However, I am attempting to engage the "reciprocal relation" it names far more than does Haar, who is inclined to read Heidegger as subverting his own claims for this reciprocity and assigning humankind to a fundamental receptivity. I am pursuing, I believe, a much more severe concept of finitude than Haar wants to allow (an inclination marked by the constant rhetorical questions in his essay).

13. Derrida has explored this motif in his usual groundbreaking way in "La Main de Heidegger (*Geschlecht* II)" (in his *Psyché*, 415–51). My analysis will depart from his only in that I am concerned with the precise character of Heidegger's delimitation of the hand's reach over against the *Brauch* that uses it.

14. I suggest reading the Parmenides lectures and *What Is Called Thinking?* together because the latter text raises a question about the relation of *Handwerk* and modern forms of work with machines (whose modern essence is determined by *Technik*) that the former text effectively answers. In *What Is Called Thinking?*, Heidegger insists upon the relation of the human hand to the materiality of that dimension of nature with which it works. His example is the cabinetmaker's relation to wood (hardly an example among others since the Greek concept of *hyle* itself is originally thought in relation to wood); the corresponding matter for the philosopher or the poet is clearly language thought from the basis of its *physis*, as Heidegger proposes we do in relation to the notion of *Natursprache* in "The Way to Language." In the transitional remarks following the second hour of his lecture course, Heidegger invites us to consider what happens to the hand in the realm determined by the modern relation to the machine (something that Marx, he says, was unable to do) but leaves the topic undeveloped. In the Parmenides lectures, however, he considers the example of the impact upon the meaning of writing created by the introduction of the typewriter and the modern printing press. The latter development, he suggests, effectively suspends, or rather *denatures* the essential relation between hand and word. For a discussion of this topic, see Derrida, "La Main de Heidegger."

I might note as well that in *What Is Called Thinking?* Heidegger evokes the possibility of a pure *Handwerk* that would be without writing. Socrates, he says, represents a unique case of a pure sign or "character" (pointing to what withdraws) that is pure precisely for the fact that it never writes itself (unlike the entire tradition of Western philosophy). Quite a few questions might be raised here — the first of them being whether it is even possible to conceive of a sign's showing itself as such without there being some kind of writing (Derrida, of course, has developed the logic of this question extensively). We might also wonder whether Heidegger does not bring into question this notion of purity himself in his later discussion of usage and through his citation of Hölderlin's lines "The crude, too, is useful,/That the pure may know itself" (WHD 117/194). I will return to this point.

15. I take part of the importance of Heidegger's meditation on *Brauch* to lie in the fact that his work with the term represents a sustained effort to think a notion of *praxis* beyond its metaphysical opposition to *poiēsis* and the traditional subor-

dination of the latter to the former through the notion of production. Robert Bernasconi, in a useful overview of Heidegger's treatment of the traditional opposition, is appropriately attentive to Heidegger's effort to think a more original meaning of praxis (and poiēsis) from his notion of dwelling and its relation to the notion of *pragma* developed in the lectures on Parmenides. (See his "The Fate of the Distinction Between *Praxis* and *Poiēsis*," *Heidegger Studies*, 2 (1986): 111–39; one might also consult Jacques Taminiaux's "The Nicomachean Ethics: *Poiēsis* and *Praxis* in the Articulation of Fundamental Ontology," in his *Heidegger and the Project of Fundamental Ontology*, trans. and ed. Michael Gendre [Albany: SUNY Press, 1991], 111–44.) But the present discussion will show how Heidegger thinks dwelling from *Brauch* and indicates, I believe, that *Brauch* is the term with which Heidegger attempts to think this more original meaning. As such, it is the term with which he renews his earlier effort to think the relation between *physis* and *technē* (perhaps his most fundamental task of the 1930s, as I have argued, and one whose urgency he recognized still in 1967 in the lecture in Athens). The significance of the term for the trajectory of Heidegger's path of thinking is clearly considerable, and its importance emerges even more fully when it is brought into play with the notions of use and praxis deployed by authors such as Marx, Nietzsche, Bataille, Nishida, and Wittgenstein. For what is at stake, as I will try to show with William Haver in another study, is a different thought of praxis and a new meaning of "pragmatics."

16. Heidegger insists in his essay on Hölderlin's "Remembrance" that this is not a dialectical relation, and it is worth emphasizing here that usage is to be thought from a notion of nearness, not one of negation: "The pure itself can be the pure only as it admits the crude close to its own essence [*in die Wesensnähe lässt*] and there holds it" (WHD 118/195).

17. Elsewhere, Heidegger will take up the same motif from the basis of another phrase from "Bread and Wine": *es fehlen heilige Namen*, "holy names are lacking." It is interesting to consider what Heidegger might have done with the phrase *es fehlen*, for as I will suggest in returning to "The Way to Language," an experience of language's "lack" would be the condition of a knowledge of the lack of holy names. Both "lacks" are grounded in what needs and uses language.

18. *Brauch*'s truest form, that is, within the order of *Ge-stell*. Avital Ronell has grasped this logic profoundly throughout her meditation on *Technik*. For the most recent installment on this specific topic, see Ronell's *Crack Wars* (Lincoln: University of Nebraska Press, 1993).

19. In my reading of Benjamin's "The Task of the Translator," I will argue that Benjamin is working with a similar logic of nearness and with a comparable "eschatological" horizon. For this use of the term "eschatology," see Heidegger's "The Anaximander Fragment" (H 327/E 18).

20. We see a reference to this allotment in the following citation from "The Question Concerning Technology," a citation whose first sentence is also marked by the kind of precariousness of formulation we have followed in "The Way to Language." Humankind is committed (destined) to its share in unconcealment and used in this belonging *via Ge-stell*, which is nevertheless itself destined — it "grants

as a destiny that is granted" (*Ereignis* does not subsist somewhere outside its destiny but is not reducible to a given destiny). "Every destiny of revealing comes to pass from out of a granting and as such a granting [*aus dem Gewähren und als ein solches*]. For it is granting that first conveys to man that share in revealing which the appropriating event [*Ereignis*] of revealing needs" (VA 36/32).

21. The motif of desire at the level we are considering it here appears explicitly in these lectures on Nietzsche. See, for example, Martin Heidegger, *Nietzsche* (Pfullingen: Neske, 1961), 1: 226 (cited by Haar, *Heidegger and the Essence of Man*, trans. William McNeil [Albany: SUNY Press, 1993], 119): "As soon as man, in looking at Being, lets himself be bound by Being, he becomes transported beyond himself, so that he stretches, as it were, between himself and Being and is outside himself. This being raised over beyond oneself and being attracted by Being itself is *eros*. Only insofar as Being is able to unfold 'erotic' power with respect to man is man able to think of Being itself and to overcome the forgottenness of Being." Haar defines the relation named here with an intriguing phrase: "Being and man share a desire that is fulfilled in language" (118). But, of course, I would argue that the term "fulfilled" is quite inappropriate.

22. "Memory, in the sense of the human thinking that recalls [*Andenken*], dwells in that which keeps everything that is given to be thought. We shall call it the keeping [*Verwahrnis*]. It harbors and conceals what gives us to think. The keeping alone *gives* freely what is to-be-thought, it frees it *as a gift*. But the keeping is not something that is apart from and outside of what is most thought-provoking. The keeping itself is this most thought-provoking; it is the way [*Weise*] out of which and in which [*aus der es und in der es gibt*] there is given — itself — which ever and always gives itself to be thought. Memory as the human recall of what is to be thought about rests in the keeping of the most thought-provoking" (WHD 97/150–51).

23. In the paragraph following the one I have just cited (WHD 97/151), Heidegger writes, "All thinking and all appearing of what is to be thought find the open in which they arrive and meet only where the keeping of what is most thought-provoking takes place. Humankind *in-habits* [*be-wohnt*] only the keeping of what gives it to think."

24. The play of abbreviation here, and more generally in Heidegger's work (I think of the usage of "Being" in particular), might merit consideration. In the present passage, the abbreviation works in an intermittent fashion and allows Heidegger to avoid entering too precisely into his definition of "that which regions" as "the hidden essence of truth" (G 64/83). One might also observe in this passage an interesting play of distinction between the human and its essence: "The independence of truth *from* humankind is clearly a relation *to* the human essence." Finally, we note another appearance of the *für es selbst*, this time as denied to humankind.

25. Though Heidegger seems to attribute to Hölderlin the most consequent thought of usage, it could be interesting to read Meister Eckhart on this topic. I think of what Reiner Schürmann has described as a thought of being as event, and of Eckhart's motifs of "detachment" and of the work to which God is obliged in a

soul that is a pure receptivity or openness: *sô muoz sich got des werkes under-winden unde muoz selber dâ werkmeister sîn und sich selber dâ gebern in die lîdende vernunft* (cited by Niklaus Largier in his *Zeit, Zeitlichkeit, Ewigkeit: Ein Aufriss des Zeitproblems bei Dietrich von Freiberg und Meister Eckhart* [New York: Peter Lang, 1989], 168).

26. Such an interruption is enigmatically named in the opening "conversation" of Blanchot's *The Infinite Conversation*, a conversation that turns around the problem of independence via what Blanchot calls "the non-concerning" and its exigency. From the basis of this connection, I am inclined to answer the question I posed earlier in this paragraph by saying that it is an *arrêt de mort* that releases to death.

27. Near the end of the transitional remarks preceding the fourth lecture, Heidegger brings forward an archaic sense of *verdanken* that turns the earlier, already noteworthy "reflexive" usage of *sich verdanken* in the direction of a "settling": "When the transaction of a matter is settled, or disposed of, we say in Alemannic dialect that it is 'thanked' [*verdankt*] (WHD 158–59/146).

28. I am alluding here to Heidegger's remarks in the "Addendum" to "The Origin of the Work of Art" concerning the "distressing difficulty" presented by the question of the relation between Being and human being, a difficulty, he writes, "which has been clear to me since *Being and Time* and has since been expressed in a variety of versions" (H 74/P 87).

29. The problematic of *Sprachgebrauch* (as engaging the problematic of *Brauch*) figures prominently in Heidegger's justification of his translations from the Greek. The "bound" character of these translations is marked strongly, for example, in the opening pages of "The Anaximander Fragment" (H 328/E 19), where thought is also named the originary mode of poetizing and as such the originary *dictare* wherein language first comes to language as the *Diktat* of the truth of Being. Near the end of the essay, Heidegger stresses the daring character of his translation (H 367/E 52), though he holds out for "the unique word" dictated to a thinking that meditates on an oblivion of Being never before thought as such. *What Is Called Thinking?*, concerned with "translating into language what we show as signs," also returns repeatedly to the problematic of translation and the problem of violence in translating in the concluding pages on Parmenides' maxim (where the trans-lation of thought must follow by a leap the passage or relation of Being to beings).

30. I use the term "cultural" in order to recall that the "bodily" is never engaged outside a practice where a cultural usage is involved. But to reverse things once more, "cultural" must name here what exceeds the *defined* categories of cultural politics and where the meaning of the "political" and of "sociality" are fundamentally in question.

Chapter 4

1. I refer here to Heidegger's discussion in "The Essence of Language" of the everyday occurrence of words failing us and of George's poem "The Word." Celan's experience of silence is incomparably more severe than anything described

by Heidegger in his essays on language, but the experience is essentially the same. Language gives itself (or gives a relation to itself in its nearness/withdrawal) in a suspension of speech that is indissociable from an experience of mortality.

2. In what hardly seems an accidental manner (though the echo does not seem conceptually active), *angereichert*, "enriched," echoes Celan's use of *erreichbar*, "reachable," in the first part of his speech (*Klang des Unerreichbaren*; *erreichbar*; *das zu Erreichende*; and again *erreichbar*). This linguistic echo, working by etymology, is then further developed at a semantic level with the term *hindurchgreifen*. James K. Lyon remarks in an essay that *angereichert* is a term drawn from mineralogy, as is *zutage treten* (translated above as "resurface"). See his "Paul Celan's Language of Stone: The Geology of the Poetic Landscape," *Colloquia Germanica*, 8, nos. 3–4 (1974): 298. Celan's quotation marks around *angereichert* might be signaling this technical reference — but this would not exclude the fact that he is using the term with some irony.

3. My reading of "The Meridian" will pass close at times to the one offered by Lacoue-Labarthe in *La Poésie comme expérience* (Paris: Bourgois, 1986) — a reading with which I fully concur. I arrive at an understanding of Celan's notion of dialogue similar to the one offered by Lacoue-Labarthe, though I follow a direction noted but not followed by him, namely, that of Heidegger's thought on language. This path was indicated to me by Celan's very Heideggerian notion of a *Gegenwort*. Lacoue-Labarthe is attentive to Celan's use of the preposition *gegen*, but he expresses concern regarding the possible dialectical or representational overdeterminations of the term. For my part, I am struck by the extent to which Celan pursues Heidegger's textual work with it in an effort to produce a nondialectical, nonrepresentational thought of relation. Werner Hamacher, I would note, offers a more formidable challenge to Heidegger's use of *gegen* in "Des contrées des temps" (in *Zeit-Zeichen: Aufschübe und Interferenzen zwischen Endzeit und Echtzeit*, ed. Georg Christoph Tholen and Michael O. Scholl [N.p.: VCH, 1990]). Following Celan and Benjamin, he obliges us to think the relationality implied in the *Gegend* more consequently *from the caesura* than Heidegger perhaps allows in an essay like *Discourse on Thinking*. I might add further that the reading I offer here is also essentially in agreement with the one proposed by Jacques Derrida in *Schibboleth pour Paul Celan* (Paris: Galilée, 1986). See in particular Derrida's suggestions concerning the notion of encounter (19–28). These essays by Derrida and Lacoue-Labarthe are collected in *Word Traces*, ed. Aris Fioretos (Baltimore: Johns Hopkins University Press, 1994).

4. GW 3: 197/48. The fact that the *Atempause* marks the time of a thought and hope is another indication that Celan associates breath (in accordance with an ancient, etymological tie) with spirit. Lucile, we remember, is one who has "perceived language as a physical shape and also . . . breath, that is, direction and destiny." From this line, however, we also see that if spirit is thought in its historicity, it is also embodied thought — thought that exists only as the "language become shape of a single person." If Celan confesses to a "u-topian" drive in speaking of the poem, he nevertheless makes it clear that the "non-site" of encounter toward which he seeks to move "exists" only in and by language. There is no

metaphysics of presence in "The Meridian," if such a metaphysics presupposes a notion of a transcendental signified and the presence to self of mind or spirit. Rather, presence is understood here as occurring in and by a relation to alterity, and spirit breathes only in the letter, conceived "bodily."

5. Indeed, Celan is describing the same event as does Heidegger in "The Origin of the Work of Art"; for when the singular human Dasein comes to itself in its finitude, it also stands before — more properly it traces out: when it remarks its own limits it *opens upon* and *draws out* — the difference that Heidegger thinks in this text as the relation between world and earth, and more originally, between concealment and unconcealment.

6. US 186/OW 91. Celan would appear to be thinking of essence along these lines — that is, as what "regards" us or concerns us (*angehen*) — when he speaks of the poem's other as "reachable [*erreichbar*], as able to be freed, as perhaps vacant and at the same time turned — like Lucile, let us say — toward it" (GW 3: 197/48). Later, in speaking of the *Atemwenden* that punctuate his address, Celan writes: "Twice, with Lucile's 'Long live the King' and when the sky opened as an abyss under Lenz, there seemed to occur an *Atemwende*, a turning of breath. Perhaps also while I was trying to head for that inhabitable distance which, finally, was visible only in the figure of Lucile" (GW 3: 200/52). Lucile thus not only provides an example of a *Gegenwort* with her "Long live the King" but is also taken as a figure of the other toward which the poem moves and which comes to its encounter.

7. Precisely because it might mean that no gathering or grounding measure might be found for existence, I cannot help but suspect that Heidegger's concern for the gathering character of relation (or difference) prohibited him from carrying far a radical thought of singularity. Such a thought is certainly present in his text — it is there to be read and developed, but it remains largely latent.

I might note here that the direction taken by Celan is anticipated in a remark made my Emmanuel Lévinas in an early essay on Blanchot. See the *Revue des Sciences Humaines*, 51–52 (1948): 117. In speaking of a possible "philosophical exegesis of art" that would fulfill the task of criticism, Lévinas writes, one "would have to introduce the perspective of the relation with the other [*autrui*] without which being could not be told in its reality, that is, in its time." This remark is cited by Paul Davies in his forthcoming *Experience and Distance: Heidegger, Blanchot, Lévinas* (Albany: SUNY Press).

8. Thus the *gegen* relation, the "over against," *gegeneinanderüber*, is asymmetrical: the relation of one Dasein to an other is not the same as the relation of the other to this Dasein, though each is only in relation to the other. Blanchot has developed a notion of such an asymmetrical relation in *L'Entretien infini*.

9. The one addressed in this couplet could also be the reader — in the succeeding paragraph, Celan refers to poetry as "paths from a voice to a listening you." Thus this quatrain could also be saying something about the countering character of the poem for a reader — a countering that must be answered in some other manner than "reading under a lamp." Inasmuch as Celan speaks of encountering himself in this quatrain, however, it is clear that the addressed subject — at least here, in "The Meridian," here in this recollection of dates — must be "Celan."

Chapter 5

NOTE: As with the other chapters in this volume, my relation to the material has been shaped significantly by exchanges with students at Binghamton University. I would also like to thank Judith Butler for a challenging reading of this chapter and acknowledge the important support of Joan Scott and Sandra Jamieson.

1. Let me be precise here. The mimetic character of this "feminine" reflexivity lends it the fluidity (in a wider sense of this term now) that Plato recognized and so feared, as Irigaray notes indirectly at the outset of her text (S 239/192; see also the long essay on Plato that concludes *Speculum*). But it is all too easy to stop here and fail to think in mimesis itself a relational structure that offers the possibility of "mimetic" engagement, an engagement that may be thought as a relationality that preserves difference (a relationality of singular beings). Of course, mimesis also lends itself more immediately to a kind of capture, and the difficulty of following this text is one of engaging its mimetic play without slipping into an identification of some kind. The worst trap, especially for a male reader, I believe, would be one of playing out this identification in a "sympathetic" pathos, replaying, in effect, a very traditional scene of desire (the scopic dimension of masculine desire makes it particularly susceptible to this trap). Irigaray refers to such a version of pathos, I believe, when she refers to the difficulty of constituting a "memory of the threshold" rather than a "nostalgia of the flesh" that is without such a memory, in *An Ethics of Sexual Difference*, trans. Carolyn Burke and Gillian C. Gill (Ithaca, N.Y.: [Cornell University Press, 1993], 141).

2. See, among several other references to this motif, Irigaray's *Ethics of Sexual Difference*, 18 and 129. The latter instance comes in the context of one of Irigaray's references to a thought of the divine whose possibility opens with Irigaray's reflection on a "transcendental sensible." She speaks here of "another epoch of history" and another advent of language: "The *il y a* giving again place or a site to a 'we are' or 'we become,' 'we dwell,' together." This creation, she continues, "would be our chance, from the most humble in daily life to the most 'grand,' through the opening of a *sensible transcendental* coming about through us, for which *we would be* the mediators and the bridges."

3. In the pages that follow, I hope it will become clear why the scene of desire constructed in this text is exemplary only in what it offers of the conditions of its own figuration. The possibility of the figuration of a "feminine" desire is what is staged in this text, not a representation of the truth of feminine sexuality (unless we understand "truth" from the (non)ground of finitude and historicity). As I will continue to emphasize, there is no essentialism here, biological or spiritual, though Irigaray is taking a path that is deeply laden in historical terms. The point that I am making about the form of staging (which exemplifies or "enacts" without being exemplary in an imposing sense) applies first to Irigaray's own text. I would not want to be understood as saying that this scene and what it conveys is *the* privileged site for understanding what Irigaray has to say about feminine sexuality (though it is certainly *a* privileged site, as Irigaray acknowledges in *An Ethics of Sexual Difference*, 114–15). This is not to take anything away from the *speculation* that is advanced here and that I consider vitally important to retain. But from

the grounds of this speculation (I use the term to avoid a language of thetic positing or a language of "claims"), we can well imagine other scenes. The speculation to which I am referring concerns, to begin with, the material ground(s) of hetero-affection (the possibility of a touch) that force us to rethink all our categories of matter and spirit, inside and outside, same and other, and our understanding of the construction of desire.

4. I echo Bataille here because Irigaray draws strongly from his text—though she takes her distance from any "economy"—even while drawing with great fidel-ity from a body of mystic literature. For another contemporary reference, see chapter 2 of Blanchot's *Thomas l'obscur* (Paris: Gallimard, 1950); *Thomas the Obscure*, trans. Robert Lamberton (Barrytown, N.Y.: Station Hill, 1988).

5. A compromise for this quarrel over translation is offered by a passage in Irigaray's *An Ethics of Sexual Difference* (110–11). There, in an absolutely un-compromising claim for the importance (ontological, ethical, religious) of thinking the mucous, Irigaray describes the latter as "the 'tissue' of the unfolding of *la durée*. The condition of the possibility of the extension of time." Her reflections on the mucous develop but do not depart from this reflection on the material ground of a feminine self-relation and "transcendence."

6. Margaret Whitford has pointed to the breadth and significance of this ques-tion in her important volume, *Luce Irigaray, Philosophy in the Feminine* (New York: Routledge, 1991). All her references in her remarks on the context of Iri-garay's own use of the term "imaginary" are pertinent, and her analysis of the psychoanalytic dimensions of a "female imaginary" bring out dimensions of the differences between the sexes that I only approach here in pushing back (some-what more than does Whitford on the topic of the imaginary) to Irigaray's thought of the "transcendental sensible."

7. One might ask here about the status of the "other" in this scene. To all observers, after all, the mystic is quite alone and her imaginary production, pre-sumably, a phantasm (which is to take nothing from the "reality" of the experi-ence). What must be stressed here is that her imagining (or exposure) takes the impression of difference. It is not necessary that a finite other offer her this experi-ence, here in this *repetition* of a touch that has necessarily always involved an other (human being). I return to this topic in my discussion of Blanchot.

8. For a related discussion of such a notion of mimesis, one might consult Philippe Lacoue-Labarthe's "Typography" (in *Typography: Philosophy, Mimesis, Politics*, ed. Christopher Fynsk [Cambridge, Mass.: Harvard University Press, 1990]), Jacques Derrida's "The Double Session" (in *Dissemination*, trans. Barbara Johnson [Chicago: University of Chicago Press, 1981], 172–286), and Jean-Luc Nancy's *Le partage des voix* (Paris: Galilée, 1982), which I have implicitly cited in the last line. Lacoue-Labarthe's treatment of this topic is invaluable and highly relevant, but his own reference to Irigaray's *Speculum* stresses only the instability of the feminine from a "Platonic" perspective; he does not recognize the answer Irigaray has proposed to the question with which he concludes concerning the relation between mimesis and language. Derrida's essay is perhaps particularly pertinent here (beyond its valuable pages on the topic of mimesis and truth) if we

pause to contrast the mimetic undertaking of the subject of "La Mystérique" with the play of the mime Derrida analyses from the basis of Mallarmé's "Mimique," where it is again a question of miming nothing in an "auto"-erotic experience. The contrast is challenging because of the profoundly divergent structure of the two texts; to begin with, the structure of the subject's *address* in the two cases is fundamentally different. But when Derrida generalizes the structure of the mimesis he is treating in relation to the question of writing, we have the terms for an intriguing juxtaposition of Mallarmé's mime, that "solitary captive of the threshold," and Irigaray's mystic, whose mimetic play involves no less of a suspension of representation but also the kind of passage (the passage of an *experience* of difference in this originary constitution of self) that Derrida is particularly attentive to in his later work.

9. Again, one might wonder how significant it is that the "other" here happens to be "God." Is such a partner the condition of a "pure" mimesis (this mimesis of "nothing") inasmuch as the sacred, the site of the divine exposure, can be no thing? I would suggest that the offering of *autrui*, as Lévinas and Blanchot describe it, is no less "pure" in its (quasi)transcendental character. If the reader is troubled by the place of religious experience in this scene, I would note that there is nothing here more "transcendental" than what we find in a consequent thought of Dasein and its encounter with *autrui* — if that is any consolation. This text remains faithful to a thought of finite transcendence (which, on the other hand, is not to *exclude* a thought of the divine). I would add that Blanchot's descriptions of the other's offering of the nothing of their being helps actually to move us beyond a thematics of negativity that may well linger in this term "nothing" (which, of course, Irigaray continues to use in this text but which may still bear a metaphysical imprint).

10. Friedrich Nietzsche, *Beyond Good and Evil*, trans. Walter Kaufmann (New York: Random House, 1966), 161. I draw these last remarks from work I have done on Nietzsche's *Genealogy of Morals* under the title "Cruelty and Sovereignty," forthcoming in *The Eight Technologies of Otherness*, ed. Sue Golding (London: Routledge).

11. Whitford, among a number of others, takes up this topic; see her *Luce Irigaray*, 70, where she cites the passage that names this strategy of mimesis explicitly in *This Sex Which Is Not One* (trans. Catherine Porter [Ithaca, N.Y.: Cornell University Press, 1985], 76). See also Naomi Schor, "This Essentialism Which Is Not One: Coming to Grips with Irigaray," *differences* (Summer 1989): 47–48.

12. "Closed up (again) over this mystery where the love placed within her is hidden. Revealing itself [herself?: *se révélant*] in this secret of desire" (S 249/200). Irigaray has given all of the terms I am using here (appropriation, origin, opening) a (post)Heideggerian turn, undoing in this manner the dialectical movements of phallogocentrism, including those economies by which the "feminine" figures as a play of presence and absence for a masculine desire mobilized by her "secret" (see *This Sex*, 210). She is thus thinking desire from the basis of difference and moving toward a corresponding erotics (which I will describe briefly as an erotics of *Entfernung*). One will recognize that her thought points to a "sexualization" of a

thought of the *Riss* (and all this might mean for the "truth" of desire) in a way that requires a rethinking of Heidegger's own latent "sexualization" of the difference. Heidegger did not go far in thinking the sexual *relation* from the ground of difference—and need I recall here (referring to my discussion of *On the Way to Language* in the second chapter) how troubling some of his latent sexual metaphorics can be. One might well reply that this scene of desire has its own troubling sides; but I would emphasize that Irigaray is working from (*miming*) a historical configuration, moving toward a new thought of the "transcendental sensible." This scene, as I want to show, opens upon the possibility of an open-ended play. For an important recollection of this history, one that also emphasizes its promise, see Irigaray's *An Ethics of Sexual Difference*, 115, particularly the paragraph preceding the conclusion where Irigaray remarks, "The same of women, between women, would always take place from and in the *open*."

13. Let me reiterate that the identificatory recognition of a form moves from the sight of the *suspended*, *offered* body, this visible manifestation of the passion, to the wounds of this body ("the unfathomable wound"). The abyssal, gaping wound figures on the ground of an abandon. Identification clearly requires some *limit*; but Irigaray is trying to conceive a (self)representation that preserves difference or that "opening" that is the "same" for women. "She must arrive at a love of the invisible and the memory of a touch that is never seen, that she experiences often only in pain for want of perceiving the site, its 'substance,' its qualities. A touching without instrument or object other than the trial, the experiencing, of interiority. From within, and from its potential passage from inside to outside, from outside to inside without it being a matter there of something that passes from one site to another, but rather of a site of passage, and of its movement" (*An Ethics of Sexual Difference*, 70). In the paragraphs that follow these lines, Irigaray develops a notion of the "icon" as the possible condition of a self-representation that preserves the invisible space and time of this passage, "a reality that *insists*, and not only as the reverse or inverse of the visible, but as its texture, its collection, here now." The figure of the suffering Christ in the scene we are reading is such an icon.

Chapter 6

1. Benjamin states in "The Task of the Translator": "The translatability of linguistic creations ought to be considered even if men should prove unable to translate them. Given a strict concept of translation, would they not really be untranslatable to some degree?" (GS 4.1 10/I 70). Where a translation begins to exceed the limit indicated here (no longer merely marking this limit and pointing "intensively" beyond itself), it risks tumbling "from abyss to abyss" (GS 4.1 21/I 82). But this limitation is anything but a reason to abandon the task.

2. I take this notion from Benjamin's statement concerning the possibility of deciding the question of translation "apodictically": "It should be pointed out that certain concepts of relation [*Relationsbegriffe*—Benjamin is speaking here of the relation between a work and its possible translation, of the fact that the work *offers* itself to translation] retain their correct, and even best meaning, when they are not from the outset referred exclusively to humankind" (GS 4.1 10/I 70). The

translator, Harry Zohn, inverts the meaning of this sentence by omitting the negation, as Paul de Man has pointed out (" 'Conclusions': On Walter Benjamin's 'The
Task of the Translator,' " *Yale French Studies: The Lesson of Paul de Man*, no. 69
[1985]: 38).

3. Carol Jacobs is nicely sensitive to this play in her own way in "The Monstros-
ity of Translation" (*MLN*, 90 [1975]: 755–66) and sensitive as well to the necessity of a "literal" attention to Benjamin's German. I depart from her reading
principally in relation to the notion of pure language, though I find her formulations precise. Where she writes that pure language is "nothing but language,"
however, I would read this notion in relation to the essay of 1916 and attempt to
give it all its "ontological" import, recognizing it, in fact, as a "materialization of
truth" (where "truth," however, is thought in its finitude — an argument I will
pursue throughout these three chapters). In the same spirit, one could perhaps read
differently her wonderful concluding literal translation of holy scripture ("without
the same is nothing made which made is").

I will not try to review here the other literature devoted to Benjamin's "The Task
of the Translator." I would note only that the "immanent" approach I am taking
should be complemented by the kind of approach Winnfried Menninghaus has
taken in reading Benjamin's philosophy of language in relation to figures such
as Wilhelm von Humboldt (see his *Walter Benjamins Theorie der Sprachmagie*
[Frankfurt am Main: Suhrkamp, 1980]). Such an approach (which must extend
quite far historically and through various mystical strains) would help to give the
"speculative" dimensions of Benjamin's reflections a firmer foundation and allow
his philosophy of language to occupy a more central place in readings of his text. It
would also help to break down some of the disciplinary, "school," and ideological
barriers that normally inhibit passage between this and some of the other texts I
have taken up in this volume.

4. In "The Task of the Translator," Benjamin does not, in fact, give us the means
for thinking the relation between "symbolizing" and "symbolized" (the latter remaining entirely unclear — Benjamin merely refers to the "analagons and symbols"
of nonlinguistic life earlier in the essay). Nor does he clarify the relation of both of
these to *Darstellung*, the *Darstellung* of pure language as well as that of translation. Later, in the "Epistemo-Critical Prologue," he will refer to philosophy's attention to the "symbolic" character of the word (that dimension of the word that is
founded in the name), though this does not help us with the distinctions in question. But one is not far off from Benjamin's intention, I believe, if one uses "symbolizing" to refer to that dimension of linguistic creations in which the drive to
self-presentation of pure language manifests itself, and I will do so in what follows.
I will leave for another occasion the question of the relation between the "symbolizing" character of human language and the "material" communication of
"natural" language described in the essay of 1916 or the mimetic play described in
"On the Mimetic Faculty."

5. The differential relation of "complementation" must be thought eventually
in relation to this manner in which languages differentiate themselves *against* one
another. Benjamin underscores repeatedly the conflictual character of their respec-

tive modes of intention: "all individual elements . . . exclude one another [*sich ausschliessen*]"; the words *Brot* and *pain* "strive to exclude each other [*streben sich . . . auszuschliessen*]"; "the modes of intention in these two words strive against one another [*einander widerstreben*]" (GS 4.1 14/I 74).

Chapter 7

1. In a letter to Gershom Scholem of February 19, 1925, Benjamin refers to his "Prologue" as an "enormous *Chuzpe*, nothing more or less than the prolegomenon to a theory of knowledge, a kind of second, I'm not sure if better, stage of the early language essay, this time tricked out as a doctrine of the ideas" (cited by Michael Jennings in *Dialectical Images: Walter Benjamin's Theory of Literary Criticism* [Ithaca, N.Y.: Cornell University Press, 1987], 195). In a letter to Theodor Adorno of May 31, 1935 (cited by Susan Buck-Morss in *The Dialectics of Seeing* [Cambridge, Mass.: MIT Press, 1989], 230), Benjamin refers to the fact that the "foundations of the theory of knowledge" were "put to the test" in relation to the study of Baroque allegory.

2. "Naming . . . is the innermost essence of language. Naming is that by which nothing beyond it is communicated, and *in* which language itself communicates itself absolutely. In naming, the mental essence that communicates itself is *language*. Where mental being in its communication is language itself in its absolute wholeness, only there is the name, and only the name is there. Name as the heritage of human language therefore vouches for the fact *that language as such* is the mental being of man. . . . Man is the namer, by this we recognize that through him pure language speaks" (GS 2.1 144/R 318).

3. The passage I will cite is from "Anmerkungen zum *Oedipus*," in Friedrich Hölderlin, *Sämtliche Werke*, vol. 5, ed. Friedrich Beissner (Stuttgart: Kohlhammer, 1952), 195–96; translated as "Remarks on *Oedipus*" in *Friedrich Hölderlin: Essays and Letters on Theory*, trans. Thomas Pfau (Albany: SUNY Press, 1988), 101–2.

4. Benjamin refers to other figures as well, of course, including Alois Riegl, as Michael Jennings's discussion in *Dialectical Images* would seem to suggest. It seems quite probable that Benjamin is drawing upon Riegl's attempt to provide a historical grounding of literary form. We should look also to Wilhelm von Humboldt's *The Diversity of Human Language-Structure and Its influence on the Mental Development of Mankind* (trans. Peter Heath [New York: Cambridge University Press, 1988]), where we will find suggestions concerning the possibility of reading literary form in relation to linguistic development.

5. "The enormous, anti-artistic subjectivity of the baroque converges here with the theological essence of the subjective. . . . There is no evil in the world. It arises in man himself, with the desire for knowledge, or rather for judgment. . . . This knowledge, the triumph of subjectivity and the onset of an arbitrary rule over things, is the origin of all allegorical contemplation. In the very fall of man the unity of guilt and signification emerges as an abstraction" (GS 1.1 327–28/O 233–34). In the 1916 essay on language, Benjamin writes the following concerning the recoil to which I have referred: "The knowledge of things resides in the name,

whereas that of good and evil is, in the profound sense in which Kierkegaard uses the word, 'prattle,' and knows only one purification and elevation, to which the prattling man, the sinner, was therefore submitted: judgment. Admittedly, the judging word has direct knowledge of good and evil. Its magic is different from that of the name, but equally magical. This judging word expels the first human beings from paradise; they themselves have aroused it in accordance with the immutable law by which this judging word punishes — and expects — its own awakening as the only, the deepest guilt" (GS 2.1 153/R 327–28).

6. In "On Language as Such," Benjamin describes the "silencing" of nature by the signifying human word (the interruption of the communication of nature's essence) as an "overnaming" — a term that marks the externality of relation when language becomes a means for the designation of something outside it. Again, nature mourns because it is mute; but it is mute because it mourns the muteness imposed by this interruption of a divinely grounded communication — an interruption experienced as an exposure without relation: "to be known comprehensively by the unknowable" (GS 2.1 155/R 330).

7. The entire discussion of the relation between the "profane dynamic" and "the direction of Messianic intensity" might be cited here by virtue of its relevance to Benjamin's thought of the relation between history and its redemption. But consider simply the following passage on the downfall of the earthly, from the "Theological-Political Fragment":

To the spiritual *restitutio in integrum*, which introduces immortality, corresponds a worldly restitution that leads to the eternity of downfall, and the rhythm of this eternally transient worldly existence, transient in its totality, in its spatial but also in its temporal totality, the rhythm of Messianic nature, is happiness. For nature is Messianic by reason of its eternal and total passing away.

To strive after such passing, even for those stages of man that are nature, is the task of world politics, whose method must be called nihilism. (GS 2.1 204/R 313)

8. Irving Wohlfarth has reminded me of Benjamin's remark to the effect that he would never end a text again as he did his *Trauerspiel* study.

It will be apparent that I cannot share Susan Buck-Morss's conclusion in *The Dialectics of Seeing* about a critical judgment on Benjamin's part regarding the Christian resolution. Buck-Morss reads the final movement as a triumph of subjectivity, missing the fact that when subjectivity is "left entirely on its own," it is *discovered* for the first time in its unreality, exposed as subjectivity. The conclusion, as I have tried to show, is devoted to tracing the *limit* of the baroque allegoresis in its abstraction. To support her argument, Buck-Morss places critical weight on Benjamin's reference to the allegorists' "betrayal" of nature and politics, their "faithlessness." But "faithfulness" would mean *pure abstraction*, as Benjamin's own earlier reference to the faithfulness of melancholic contemplation reveals — i.e., continuing subjection to the fascinating play of signification to which a "fallen" nature invites the allegorist. The baroque form of allegory has *always* betrayed nature. From within the baroque dialectic of allegory, there can be no meaningful political action (as the allegorists demonstrated in ceaseless repetition); only a betrayal of this subjective position could lead toward the political act that Buck-Morss rightfully sees Benjamin seeking in the later reflections on the dialectical image (though of course the leap must take a different form from the one envisioned by Hamlet). It could be that Benjamin glimpsed the possibility of another form of fidelity (via a nihilism), but this is clearly not what Buck-Morss has in mind.

9. I refer to Benjamin's reflections in "On the Mimetic Faculty," and specifically to the concept of "nonsensuous similarity" as Benjamin draws it from astrology and what he calls the "canon" of language in its "onomatopoeic" character. A "nonsensuous correspondence," Benjamin hypothesizes, governs the relation between words of different languages in relation to their common signified, between the written and this signified, and between the spoken and the written. Benjamin's remarks in his penultimate paragraph are of particular interest here in that they clearly anticipate the meditation on the dialectical image: "The mimetic element in language can, like a flame, manifest itself only through a kind of bearer. This bearer is the semiotic element. Thus the coherence of words or sentences is the bearer through which, like a flash, similarity appears. For its production by man — like its perception by him — is in many cases, and particularly the most important, limited to flashes. It flits past" (GS 2.1 213/R 336).

Hans-Jost Frey takes account of Benjamin's reflections on the mimetic element in language in "On Presentation in Benjamin" — an unpublished essay that discusses the presentation of allegory in Benjamin's later work. Frey places appropriate and important emphasis on the discontinuity of (linguistic) presentation and offers rich suggestions concerning the Baudelaire essays.

10. Max Pensky (to whom I am grateful for a generous response to my next chapter) has worked through the problem of the subjective component of the methodology Benjamin proposes in his "Prologue" and in his meditation on the dialectical image, in "The Trash of History" (in Max Pensky, *Melancholy Dialectics* [Amherst: University of Massachusetts Press, 1993], 211–39). While I find his argument strong, especially in that it respects the importance Benjamin attributes to the destructive character of allegoresis, I remain convinced that the question of subjectivity in Benjamin's text must be treated in relation to the philosophy of language, and I believe that the resolution to the problem Pensky raises lies in the notion of invention I will pursue in my next chapter.

11. On the question of sovereignty, see Samuel Weber's excellent discussion in "Taking Exception to Decision: Walter Benjamin and Carl Schmitt" (*Diacritics*, 22, nos. 3–4 [Fall–Winter 1992]: 5–18). Weber's argument helps bring forth what is at stake for Benjamin in the posture I am describing, if not the harsh theatrical light of its impossibility.

Chapter 8

1. In a rapid description of common traits shared by baroque literature and contemporary literary productions, Benjamin suggests that the history he is sketching in his study is in fact the fore-history of the present, and that only a critical approach like the one he outlines in his methodological preface can provide the means for turning repetition into self-understanding. In distinctly Nietzschean

tones, he attacks contemporary researchers for the passivity of their relation to history and to *this* history in particular. Their notion of an empathetic relation to a past work or period betrays, he says, a "pathological suggestibility" and a "lack of self-sufficiency" that cannot resist the force of baroque art. Only the force and sobriety of the methodological approach he has outlined can prevent a historical stance from being captured by the spectacle offered in the German baroque literature he is reading and the consequent dissolution of any historical stance: "Confronted with a literature which sought, in a sense, to reduce both its contemporaries and posterity to silence through the extravagance of its technique, the unfailing lavishness of its productions and the vehemence of its claims to value, one should emphasize the necessity of the sovereign attitude which the representation of the idea of a form demands. Even then the danger of allowing oneself to plunge from the heights of knowledge into the profoundest depths of the baroque state of mind is not a negligible one. . . . Only by considering the subject from some distance, and, initially, foregoing any view of the whole, can the mind be led, through a kind of ascetic apprenticeship, to the position of strength from which it is possible to take in the whole panorama and yet remain in control of oneself" (GS 1.1 237/O 56). I would note finally that this statement throws an intriguing light on Benjamin's earlier statements from the "Prologue" on the "sober style" of philosophical exposition, for it implies that sobriety is to be understood at least in part in relation to what Benjamin will later call "presence of mind" (GS 5.1 598/B 70) and that the halting character of this exposition serves (at least in part—for it also answers to the very structure of the idea) a prophylactic function with regard to the force of the object of philosophical contemplation.

2. Susan Buck-Morss's *The Dialectics of Seeing* (Cambridge, Mass.: MIT Press, 1989) conveys this context nicely. I would also point to Benjamin's note N 1.3 for the importance of considering the matter of his reflections and their differential complexity ("sobriety" is also a Nietzschean feel for intervals): "Say something about the method of composition itself: how everything that comes to mind has at all costs to be incorporated into the project one is working on at the time. Be it that its intensity is thereby disclosed, or that, from the very outset, the ideas bear this project within them as a telos. So it is with the present method, which should characterize and maintain the intervals of reflection, the distances between the most intensively exoteric, essential parts of the work" (GS 5.1 570/B 43).

3. Pursuing the allusion to Heidegger is all the more tempting in that this remark is frequently cited in such a way as to presume that it settles the issues it raises. To pursue it, we would have to assume that Benjamin's parentheses acknowledge in some manner the profound differences between the phenomenology whose "essences" lack the "historic index" proper to the dialectical image and the "existential phenomenology" within which Heidegger elaborated his notion of historicity (and if they do not, Benjamin's assertion requires simply too much qualification to bear interpretive development). We would then have to weigh his claim against Heidegger's argument in *Being and Time* that the experience of finitude includes a confrontation with a historically determined factual situation as well as the possibility of a choice vis-à-vis the tradition. The relevant discussion

here would be Heidegger's chapter 5, "Temporality and Historicity," a chapter that undoubtedly held Benjamin's attention inasmuch as it contains a latent reading of Nietzsche's *Untimely Meditations* and pursues a notion of historical action as repetition in an event that Heidegger terms "the moment of vision" (*Being and Time*, trans. John Macquarrie and Edward Robinson [New York: Harper and Row, 1962], 437). We would also want to consider Heidegger's notion of repetition as a *Widerruf*—the answer ("provocative," I would argue) to an address.

The proximity between the two thinkers on the topic of language and history is far more interesting than most of Benjamin's commentators have recognized. It passes via Nietzsche and their (singular) appropriations of Nietzsche's notion of the invention of history.

4. I write "im-mediate" because Benjamin introduces a difference between the "language" of things and the "Adamic" language of names in the course of his reading of Genesis. The human name, he says, involves a "translation" of the nameless language of things that is in part receptive, in part spontaneous. This point has been developed by Philippe Lacoue-Labarthe in unpublished material, and by Alexander Garcia-Düttman in *La Parole donnée* (Paris: Galilée, 1989], 79–90.

5. In "Konvolut K" (2.3), Benjamin writes: "It is said that the dialectical method is concerned with doing justice each time to the concrete historical situation of its object. But that does not suffice. For it is concerned equally as much with doing justice to the concrete historical situation of the *interest* in its object. And this latter situation is always determined by the fact that this interest preforms itself in that object, but above all by the fact that it concretizes that object in itself, that it feels it advanced from out of its previous being into the higher concretion of the Now-being (being awake!). How this Now-being (nothing less than the Now-being of the 'Now-time,' but which is intermittent, in the manner of a thrust [*Stoss*]) can mean in itself a higher concretion — this question cannot be grasped by the dialectical method within the perspective of the ideology of progress. It requires a vision of history that surpasses this ideology in all its parts" (GS 5.1 494–95).

6. This critical power is in-finite and abyssal — it is the a-historical condition of history. On this point, I am in deep agreement with Werner Hamacher's assessment of Benjamin's "anarchism" in "Afformative, Strike" (*Cardozo Law Review*, 13, no. 4 [Dec. 1991]: 1133–57; later published in Andrew Benjamin and Peter Osborne, *Walter Benjamin's Philosophy: Destruction and Experience* [Routledge: London, 1994], 110–38), an anarchism that has to do with an engagement with the ground of sociality that lies in pure "impartability" (an excellent translation of *Mitteilbarkeit*). Hamacher stresses quite rightly that the Benjaminian caesura has an apocalyptic character and marks an absolute interruption with regard to any representation (any posited relation of means and ends, etc.). It occurs, I want to argue, only by a kind of *legein* (the forms of reading or translation I have noted), but at the heart of the latter lies this abyssal caesura.

Chapter 9

1. Compare here *The Space of Literature*, where Blanchot describes Orpheus's quest for Eurydice as a movement "which does not want Eurydice in her daytime

truth and her everyday appeal, but wants her in her nocturnal obscurity, in her distance, with her closed body and sealed visage — wants to see her not when she is visible, but when she is invisible, and not as the intimacy of a familiar life, but as the foreignness of what excludes all intimacy, not to make her live, but to have living in her the plenitude of her death" (EL 228/173).

2. "Il y va de l'autre," Derrida writes, "qui ne peut s'approcher *comme autre*, dans son phénomène d'autre, qu'en s'en éloignant, et apparaître en son lointain d'altérité infini qu'à se rapprocher" (approximately and reductively, starting with the first words: "It is a matter of the other: which can only approach *as other*, in its phenomenon as other, by distancing itself, and *appear* in its distance of infinite alterity by drawing nearer" ["Pas," 130]). The engagement of/with/in that movement of *Ent-fernung, é-loignement*, is *pas*.

3. "Between (she) who 'is there' for (not only *in order to* but also *by the fact of*) responding to 'Viens' and (she) who *already* will have given all her force and called 'Viens,' there is no incompatibility, no contradiction, but also no synthesis or reconciliation, no dialectic. Hence the boundless affliction. And the impossibility of deciding between an eternal return of the affirmation in which the recited . . . is intact, good only once, the unique force of a 'Viens' that never reproduces itself (saving 'Viens') and, on the other hand, but at the same time, a repetition of what has already been reissued in quotation marks, writing and citation in the everyday sense. Contamination by the everyday sense is not an accident — it belongs to the structure of affirmation; it is always risked inasmuch as it demands the narrative. Writing is also this irreducible contamination, and narrative the boundless affliction of which he can say, 'I rejoice immeasurably' " (Derrida, "Pas," 117).

Chapter 10

1. The phrase I have cited is from the footnote with which Blanchot concludes "The Narrative Voice" (EI 567/462). It is appended to a statement concerning our tendency to confuse this voice with "the oblique voice of affliction or the oblique voice of madness," and reads as follows: "It is this voice — the narrative voice — that I hear, perhaps rashly, perhaps with reason, in the narrative by Marguerite Duras that I mentioned a while back. The night forever without dawn; the ballroom where the indescribable event occurred that cannot be recalled and cannot be forgotten, but is retained in forgetting; the nocturnal desire to turn around in order to see what belongs neither to the visible nor to the invisible, that is, to remain for a moment, through the gaze, as close as possible to strangeness, where the movement of revealing-concealing has lost its rectifying force; then the need (the eternal human wish) to place in another's charge, to live once again in another, in a third person, the dual relation, the fascinated, indifferent relation that is irreducible to any mediation, a neutral relation, even if it implies the infinite void of desire; finally, the imminent certainty that what has once taken place will always begin again, always give itself away and refuse itself. Such are, it seems to me, the 'coordinates' of the narrative space, that circle where, in entering, we enter incessantly into the outside." The pertinence of these words for *Death Sentence* should become clear as we proceed.

2. Two points should be noted here concerning the agonistic relations between J. and the narrator. We know, first, that the narrator — shall we call him "X"? (A 78/47) — J. will call him "death" (A 48/28) — has been waiting for her death; in fact, he consents, out of *ressentiment*, to the idea of suicide at one point, apparently offended by the success of her struggle against her sickness ("This consent was hardly excusable, was even perfidious; for, in thinking about it, as I have done since, I realize it came obscurely from the thought that the sickness would not overcome her. She struggled too much. Normally, she should have been dead long ago. But not only was she not dead, she had continued to live, to love, laugh, run around the city like someone whom illness could not touch" [A 13/5]). He cannot bear the "excess" of her survival, and in this respect his absence is a kind of death sentence. But second, we should note J.'s relation to the narrator's own dying (or "something worse than dying" [A 16/7]); what she most fears in the night, the narrator tells us, is something like this "other" dying (A 17/7). J. knows the narrator, in other words, as both one who would have her dead and one in relation to whom she knows the impossibility of dying.

3. Blanchot's narratives cannot resist becoming illustrations in their very intelligibility (hence the impossibility of not "rediscovering"), but they also always resist with the density of the image. Commentary, in the mode I will follow here and throughout this reading of *Death Sentence* in which I will appeal to a number of "theoretical" texts, is both illegitimate and unavoidable once we have "lost silence" in attempting to come to grips with a textual event that both tempts and refuses reading. Blanchot himself pursues such a movement throughout his highly self-reflective writing (significant portions of *The Infinite Conversation* itself may be read, in part, as such a movement vis-à-vis its opening dialogue and the latter's own repetition of other *entretiens*). My own approach here will be somewhat more flat-footed, for I have ceded to the temptation to figure out as much as possible what is going on; but I hope that even this crude approach to the narrative will reveal its own wholly provisional and limited character.

4. I have been referring here to the discussion surrounding Blanchot's presentation of a "narrative" he prefaces with the question (in parentheses) "A primal scene?" Let me cite here much of the paragraph preceding the narrative (a paragraph that follows the reference to a death that is "the collapse of a little heap of sand"). Blanchot has commented in the preceding paragraphs upon related notions in D. W. Winnicott and Serge Leclaire of an "infancy" prior to language that must in effect "die" as the subject accedes to language (relating these discussions to his prior treatment of what Hegel calls a murder). He proceeds here from Leclaire's notion (and the title of the book in which it is presented: *On tue un enfant* [Paris: Editions du Seuil, 1975]), underscoring that "the child is a child, but one who is indeterminate and without relation to anyone at all" (ED 116/71). He continues: "A child already dead is dying, of a murderous death — a child of whom we know nothing (even if we characterize him as marvelous, terrifying, tyrannical, or indestructible) except this: that the possibility of speaking and of life depend on the fictive establishment, through death and murder, of a relation of singularity with a mute past, with a prehistory, with a past, then, which is outside the past and of

which the eternal *infans* is the figure at the same time that he is concealed therein. 'A child is being killed.' Let us make no mistake about this present: it signifies that the deed cannot be done once and for all, that the operation is completed at no privileged moment in time — that it operates inoperably and thus tends to be nothing but the very time that destroys (effaces) time. This is the effacement or destruction, or gift, which has always already avowed itself in the precession of a Saying outside the said, a speech of writing whereby this effacement, far from effacing itself in its turn, perpetuates itself without end, even in the *interruption* that constitutes its mark." The pertinence of these words for *Death Sentence* should be clear, up to and including the "interruption" that marks the saying of the "dying into language" to which I referred in my reading of the "referent" of "this woman" in "Literature and the Right to Death." Blanchot's last words on the phrase "a child is being killed" are also worth citing inasmuch as they bring out the necessary "interruption" represented by such a phrase: "This silent passive, this dead eternity to which a temporal form of life must be given in order that we might separate ourselves from it by a murder — . . . there is nothing (neither knowledge nor unknowledge) that might warn us of it, even if the simplest of sentences seems, in four or five words, to divulge it (a child is being killed). But this sentence is immediately torn from any language, for it draws us outside consciousness and unconsciousness each time we are given — other than ourselves and in a relation of impossibility with the other — to pronounce this unpronounceable" (ED 116–17/72).

5. My understanding of the "extra-ordinary" (I divide the word in recollection of the description of the *jour ordinaire* that the child sees as he first looks at his play space in the "primal scene[?]" to which I referred in my previous note) is that the narrative effectively opens upon what "suicide" reveals, as Blanchot describes this event in *The Writing of the Disaster* just before presenting the "primal scene" (ED 114/70).

Let me add that there is no capturing (no reducing) the ambiguity marking the words *arrêt de mort*, no way of arresting the movement between the sentence the narrator (who becomes "death in person") passes on J., the arrest of death that he performs in calling her back, the "arrest" that he knows at the end of the first narrative, and the sentence under which he stands and that he comes to assume in the second section, beyond that line or edge (*arête*) that is passed in his encounter with N.

6. Blanchot continues as follows: "The Ancients had already sensed that *Lēthē* is not merely the other side of *Alētheia*, its shadow, the negative force from which the knowledge that remembers would deliver us. *Lēthē* is also the companion of Eros, the awakening proper to sleep, the distance from which one cannot take one's distance since it comes in all that moves away; a movement, therefore, without a trace, effacing itself in every trace, and nonetheless — the expression must be used, however faultily — still announcing itself and already designating itself in the lack of writing that writing — *this senseless game* — remembers outside memory as its *limit* or its always prior illegitimacy."

7. "It truly seemed that my acquiescence reverberated in her, that it had been in some way awaited, out of an immense waiting, by an invisible responsibility to which she lent only her voice, and that now a superb power, sure of itself, and

joyous—not for my consent, which was quite useless to it, but for its victory over life, and also because of my faithful comprehension, my unlimited abandon—took possession of this young being and gave her a clairvoyance and a mastery that dictated my thoughts to me as well as my few words" (A 124/78).

8. In this context, we would also have to ask about the relation between the time(s) of this narrative and its historical context: the events of Munich (the date, as the narrator is careful to specify in his first part, is July–August 1940 [A 8/1]). The narrator insists upon the unbridgeable difference between his experience and these events (see, for example, A 76/46 and A 117–18/73–74)—his experience, he tells us, is not of the world. But these events also suffuse the narrative, as Michael Naas has helped me recognize, in such a way that one must ask whether the interruption of the narrative also has something to do with the madness of the day. This topic would require an independent study.

9. "If the thought of the impossible were entertained, it would be a kind of reserve in thought itself, a thought not allowing itself to be thought in the mode of appropriative comprehension" (EI 62/43). Two lines later, Blanchot adds a statement that reflects immediately on the movement I am attempting to follow in *Death Sentence*: "The impossible is not there in order to make thought capitulate, but in order to allow it to announce itself according to a measure other than that of power . . . the measure of the *other*, of the other as other." The "in order to," *pour*, is a little odd here; but it points, I believe, to what we will see described in a moment as "another exigency."

10. "I have lost silence, and the regret I feel over that is immeasurable. I cannot describe the affliction that invades a man once he has begun to speak. It is a motionless affliction, itself committed to muteness; through it, the unbreathable is the element I breath. I shut myself up in a room, alone, with no one in the house, almost no one outside, but this solitude itself began to speak, and I must in turn speak about this solitude that is speaking, not in derision, but because a greater solitude hovers above it, and above that solitude, another still greater, and each, receiving the word in order to smother it and silence it, instead echoes it to infinity, and infinity becomes its echo" (A 57/33).

11. "I will go on with this story, but now I will take some precautions. . . . Perhaps these precautions will not be precautions. For some time I lived with a person obsessed by the idea of my death. I had said to her: 'I think that at certain moments, you would like to kill me. You shouldn't resist that desire. I am going to write down on a piece of paper that if you kill me you will be doing what is best.' But a thought is not exactly a person, even if it lives and acts like one. A thought demands a loyalty that makes any ruse difficult. Sometimes it is itself false, but behind this lie I still recognize something true that for my part I cannot betray" (A 54–55/31–32). This is a delightfully teasing passage if we pause to consider the status of this narrative in relation to the words on that piece of paper.

12. The status of such "scenes" in Blanchot's narratives is worthy of a separate study. See, for example, the scene that occurs near the center of *The Madness of the Day*. Or one might consider the structure of the "primal scene" in *The Writing of the Disaster* (ED 117/72).

13. "Choice" is perhaps not the right word, for as the narrator tells us, she cannot help going wherever her desire indicates, for fear that madness (or at least painful and miserable things) will reach out to seize her from that place. I rather suspect that it is in part the fear of such madness that silences her when the narrator interrogates her in a familiar manner (in the second person): "You are mad; why did you go out today?" (A 71/42; the second person will appear otherwise only in the *Viens* that he says to her/the thought). These are the words, I suspect, that she did not think she should have to hear. I might also note here how N.'s words are elided in this passage (note the interruptions of her words on A 70/42 and A 71/42, the latter producing an incomplete sentence): this is one of the first instances of her *absence* from this narrative.

14. There is a rare reference to the earth in *The Writing of the Disaster*: "'for terrible is the earth.' The disaster, always belated — the disaster, strangled sleep — could remind us of this, if there were memory of the immemorable" (ED 175/114).

15. "Still unable to sleep, I spent part of the night looking at the armchair, which was quite far from the bed but turned towards me. Neither light nor darkness have ever bothered me. A persevering thought is completely sheltered from its conditions. What has sometimes impressed me about this thought is a sort of hardness, the infinite distance between its respect for me and my respect for it; but hardness is not a fair word: the hardness came from me, from my own person" (A 87/53). The infinitely slight distance between his thought and himself (the nondistance of a quasi-transcendental) is staged here between the second and third sentences.

16. "My frankness was therefore a new right, a warning given in the name of a truth which did not require any ordinary proofs and that emerged of itself out of hidden things to assert itself proudly in my mouth" (A 83/51). With such loyalty and "responsibility," founded in the emergence of a "new right," the narrator would seem to be responding to the thought (recall his opening remarks of the second part: "A thought demands a loyalty that makes any ruse difficult" [A 55/32]).

17. It is entirely possible that the change that overcomes the narrator has to do with the phenomenon of glass — a phenomenon, he says, that pushes him toward the day (as we see after he takes up with N.) and away from what "interests" him. The syntax of the phrase that announces the change does not allow us to determine whether it follows the sickness or the subsequent events with N. ("When I think about it carefully, the change which appeared in Nathalie after this accident was not evident to me at first, because I myself was changing, and it was an affliction. I spoke about this above. An empty movement threw me into each instant; it was my blood that was playing this dirty trick on me" [A 90/55].) But could it be that the glass phenomenon also accompanies the act of writing, at least at its outset? (cf. EL 55/54).

18. I link the description of the room I have just cited (a description that follows the narrator's expression of his sense of imminent *malheur*: "a certainty of affliction so great" [A 107/66]) with the narrator's concluding words, where he declares, "I gave it [*la pensée*] all my force, and it gave me all its own, so that this

force too-great, incapable of being ruined by anything, commits us to an affliction without measure" (A 127/80). What the narrator approaches in the room (in writing), in other words, is the *shared* site of his existence: a sharing/division that he has already affirmed in order to approach this "literary space" and engage the (impossible) touch that is at its heart.

19. The reference to recognition in this passage would seem significant — it appears to name engagement. N.'s problem, as we learn at the outset of the second part, is recognition (cf. A 70/42); it is recognition that provokes the "tumble" of the narrative (A 63/37), and the jealous voice of the concluding declaration will be described, in the second edition, as *reconnaisante* ("thankful," but literally, "recognizing"). Interestingly enough, the first version gave *renaissante* for the last term; it is hard to imagine there was a typographical error.

20. It is interesting to note how far ahead of the narrator Nathalie is in assuming the truth of their relations — Nathalie who is always tempted "to go out ahead of her desires" (A 84/51). Not only does she sign their common fate as soon as it is decided (with her hands and face) and then call the narrator back to it after his worldly infidelities, but she precipitates it by stealing his key and violating his room. It is not clear that this is quite the indiscretion the narrator takes it for (wouldn't her answer to his question as to why she stole the key — if he dared pose it — be "aren't we married"?); but there is a certain violence in her manner of forcing a truth he himself cannot quite assume. The narrator, as we will see, will declare that she has perhaps finally done no more than answer his command; but she will have already done so long ago: her absence constitutes a "responsibility."

21. Cf. EI 102/71:

— The neutral, the neutral, how strangely this sounds for *me*.

— *Me*, myself: can one then still speak of a self? We have to do, perhaps, with an I without a self, a non-personal punctuality oscillating between no one and someone, a semblance that only the exigency of the exorbitant relation invests silently and momentarily with this role, or establishes in the position of the Self-subject with which it can then be identified in order to simulate the identical — so that, on this basis, through writing, the mark of the absolutely non-identical in the Other might announce itself.

In this index an "f" after a number indicates a separate reference on the next page, and an "ff" indicates separate references on the next two pages. A continuous discussion over two or more pages is indicated by a span of page numbers, e.g., "57–59." *Passim* is used for a cluster of references in close but not consecutive sequence.

Library of Congress Cataloging-in-Publication Data

Fynsk, Christopher, 1952–
Language and relation : . . . that there is language /
    Christopher Fynsk.
        p. cm.
    Includes bibliographical references and index.
    ISBN 0-8047-2713-9 (alk. paper). — ISBN 0-8047-2714-7
    (pbk. : alk. paper)
    1. Language and languages — Philosophy. I. Title.
    P106.F96 1996
    401 — dc20   96-19903
                                                        CIP

∞   This book is printed on acid-free, recycled paper.

Original printing 1996
Last figure below indicates year of this printing:
05   04   03   02   01   00   99   98   97   96